WHITMAN COLLEGE

D0204920

The Parties Respond

TRANSFORMING AMERICAN POLITICS
Lawrence C. Dodd, Series Editor

Dramatic changes in political institutions and behavior over the past three decades have underscored the dynamic nature of American politics, confronting political scientists with a new and pressing intellectual agenda. The pioneering work of early postwar scholars, while laying a firm empirical foundation for contemporary scholarship, failed to consider how American politics might change or to recognize the forces that would make fundamental change inevitable. In reassessing the static interpretations fostered by these classic studies, political scientists are now examining the underlying dynamics that generate transformational change.

Transforming American Politics brings together texts and monographs that address four closely related aspects of change. A first concern is documenting and explaining recent changes in American politics—in institutions, processes, behavior, and policymaking. A second is reinterpreting classic studies and theories to provide a more accurate perspective on postwar politics. The series looks at historical change to identify recurring patterns of political transformation within and across the distinctive eras of American politics. Last and perhaps most importantly, the series presents new theories and interpretations that explain the dynamic processes at work and thus clarify the direction of contemporary politics. All of the books focus on the central theme of transformation—transformation in both the conduct of American politics and in the way we study and understand its many aspects.

FORTHCOMING TITLES

Broken Contract? Changing Relationships Between Citizens and Their Government in the United States, edited by Stephen C. Craig

Congress and the Administrative State, Second Edition, Lawrence C. Dodd and Richard L. Schott

The New American Politics, edited by Bryan D. Jones

Young Versus Old: Generational Gaps in Political Participation and Policy Preferences, Susan MacManus and Suzanne L. Parker

Campaigns and Elections, edited by James A. Thurber and Candice J. Nelson

Cold War Politics, John Kenneth White

Bureaucratic Dynamics: The Role of the Bureaucracy in a Democracy, B. Dan Wood and Richard W. Waterman

WHITMAN COLLEGE LIBRARY

The Parties Respond

CHANGES IN AMERICAN PARTIES AND CAMPAIGNS

Second Edition

EDITED BY

L. Sandy Maisel

Colby College

Withdrawn by
Whitman College Library

Westview Press

BOULDER • SAN FRANCISCO • OXFORD

JK
2261
. P29
1994

FOR PATTY AND LIZ

PENROSE MEMORIAL LIBRARY
WHITMAN COLLEGE
WALLA WALLA, WASHINGTON 99362

Transforming American Politics

All rights reserved. No part of this publication may be reproduced or transmitted in any form or by any means, electronic or mechanical, including photocopy, recording, or any information storage and retrieval system, without permission in writing from the publisher.

Copyright © 1990, 1994 by Westview Press, Inc.

Published in 1994 in the United States of America by Westview Press, Inc., 5500 Central Avenue, Boulder, Colorado 80301-2877, and in the United Kingdom by Westview Press, 36 Lonsdale Road, Summertown, Oxford OX2 7EW

Library of Congress Cataloging-in-Publication Data
The parties respond : changes in American parties and campaigns /
   edited by L. Sandy Maisel. — 2nd ed.
      p.   cm. — (Transforming American politics)
   Includes bibliographical references and index.
   ISBN 0-8133-1722-3. — ISBN 0-8133-1723-1 (pbk.)
   1. Political parties—United States.   I. Maisel, Louis Sandy,
1945–   .   II. Series.
JK2261.P29   1994
324.273—dc20
                                                             93-39411
                                                             CIP

Printed and bound in the United States of America

The paper used in this publication meets the requirements
of the American National Standard for Permanence of Paper
for Printed Library Materials Z39.48-1984.

10   9   8   7   6   5   4   3   2   1

Whitman College
Library

Contents

NOV 1 0 '94
95- 4108
Acquisitions Dept.
APR 1 1 1995

PART SIX
TOWARD THE FUTURE

Acknowledgments

The second edition of a book, one would think, should not involve as much work or require as many thanks as did the first. In this case, I believe my debts have increased.

I again want to acknowledge the contribution of Larry Dodd, the editor of the marvelously conceived series of which this book is a part. Without ever being intrusive, Larry has provided leadership as a series editor that is a model I hope others will follow.

My greatest debt is to Jennifer Knerr. I have worked with many editors over many years. Jennifer's skill in seeing a project through from conceptualization to completion is unmatched. She is a careful and thoughtful critic, a gentle but persistent prodder. Other editors fill those roles; Jennifer is unique because of her knowledge of the field and uncanny instincts regarding what will work and what will not in a book of this type. And she is especially treasured because she is a helpful and understanding friend as well as a highly prized colleague, a combination that makes her a pleasure to work with. I think most highly of her colleagues at Westview who have played key roles in seeing this work through to completion: Ellen Kresky, Cindy Hirschfeld, and Diane Hess.

Any editor owes thanks to those who contributed to a book. And I do thank those whose work appears in the pages that follow. We sought to do something special with this book—to update a study of political parties and elections with data through the 1992 election and to do a thorough job of analyzing what that very interesting election meant in the long run instead of rushing to press with a quick turnaround job. All of the authors shared this goal; for some it was more difficult than for others, as needed data were slow in arriving. I want to express my continuing gratitude to my friends and colleagues whose hard work has made this volume as successful as its predecessor.

In the same vein I want to thank those who used the first volume of *The Parties Respond* and who shared their views of how that book worked in the classroom. Those of us who teach courses on parties and elections have long recognized the need for a collection of essays that brings together the work of scholars who study various aspects of partisan politics.

We worked hard to make the first edition a book that met those needs. We hope that our responses to the constructive comments of those who used the first edition have made this an even more useful tool for teachers and their students.

As I have done in the past, I want to thank those here at Colby who have worked with me in preparing this book for the publisher. Patricia Kick has been my secretary for more than twenty years; her organizational skills are legendary among those who have passed through our halls in Miller Library. My colleagues in the Government Department make this a terrific place to work and also constantly inform my own research. What is unique about Colby, of course, is our students. As I worked on this project I benefited from the help of Jay Hartshorn, Lisa Prenaveau, Chuck Thompson, and, especially, Stephanie Pennix, who served as my research assistant and, for many chapters, as co-editor of this book. I also want to thank Dana Maisel and Neil Sinclair for their help as my deadline approached.

Finally, my family is, as always, my most important source of support. It amazes me that Dana and Josh are now reading my books in their college classes, that they are the audience and the critics at whom my work is aimed, and that, whereas once I thanked them for staying quiet while I worked, now I thank them for editorial assistance and careful reading. My sisters, Patricia Cotsen and Elizabeth Schulman, to whom this book is dedicated, have been more important to me as my life has wound its complex way through the past decades than even they can know. I hope they know how much their love and support means to the one who will always be their little brother.

L. Sandy Maisel
Rome, Maine

Prologue

In 1992 Americans once again voiced their dislike of political parties. According to a survey conducted by the *Los Angeles Times* in March 1992, one in four American voters did not approve of the way we choose our national leaders. Four months later, a Gallup poll conducted for *USA Today* and CNN found that nearly one in three respondents felt that "political parties do not make democracy work better." And, on election day 1992, Ross Perot, the independent, antiestablishment, and anti–major party candidate for the presidency, polled a higher percentage of votes than has any non-Democrat or non-Republican since Teddy Roosevelt ran as the Bull Moose party candidate in 1912—and Roosevelt, of course, was a former Republican president.

But Americans have always loved to hate political parties. The persistence of American political parties through nearly two centuries of criticism stands as a testimony to their role in our system of government. Despite the fact that they are never mentioned in the Constitution, parties have had an impact on virtually every aspect of American political life.

The role of political parties has deserved particular attention in recent decades as the parties have responded to ongoing transformations in American politics. Think of the environment in which political parties operate. In broadest terms, parties seek to attract voters to support candidates for office, based on allegiance to the party label and on agreement with the policy positions supported by the party. They do so within a legal and political context that is constantly changing because of world events, a context that varies from state to state and even from community to community within states. Rarely in this nation's history have those changes been as marked as during the past forty years.

Four decades ago the civil rights movement was the major social and political force in the nation. In 1954 the Supreme Court had ruled, in *Brown v. Board of Education*, that separate was no longer legally equal; but government officials throughout the South were resisting integration as a matter of public policy, and northern society was nearly as segregated as southern. Politics reflected a society in which racial taboos still dominated. James Meredith had to be accompanied by federal marshals when he integrated the University of Mississippi over the objections of Governor Ross Barnett in 1962; Sidney Poitier broke another racial barrier when he starred in and won the Best Actor Oscar for *Lilies of the Field* in 1963, a feat matched in television by Bill Cosby's Emmy-winning starring role in "I Spy" two years later (see Weisbrot, 1990).

A variety of Jim Crow laws kept black Americans from voting throughout the South; in Mississippi, less than 10 percent of the black population was registered to vote when John Kennedy was elected president. Even in the supposedly liberal North, few black politicians successfully sought elective office, and virtually none were elected except in areas where blacks constituted a racial majority.

The civil rights movement began to change American society in important ways. In 1964 the Twenty-Fourth Amendment to the Constitution banned the Poll Tax, a lingering example of Jim Crowism. The Voting Rights Act of 1965 led directly to a dramatic increase in black participation in the political process; at the time of the passage of that act, fewer than 100 African Americans held elective office. According to the Joint Center for Political Studies in Washington, that number is now approaching 7,000, including 4,000 in the South. And the political parties have had to respond to those changes. The changes have been so profound that the chief beneficiary of a rule change to increase the influence of southern states in the Democratic party's nominating process in 1988 was Jesse Jackson, a black minister whose political roots were in the civil rights movement that brought about these changes.

But the civil rights movement has not been the only force influencing American politics in recent decades. Indeed, the Vietnam War dominated the political landscape for nearly ten years. Its political legacy included not only the Twenty-Sixth Amendment to the Constitution, which gave those old enough to fight in Vietnam the right to choose the governing officials who make foreign policy, but also a generation of young people who were uncertain if electoral politics and the traditional political parties could meet their needs. And, again, as the political landscape was transformed, parties had to respond.

The women's movement also had a profound impact. Forty years ago most of the women active in electoral politics were widows of prominent politicians. Even the legendary Margaret Chase Smith (R-ME), so prominent early in the 1950s for her defiance of Senator Joseph McCarthy (R-WI), first sought office to fill a seat vacated by the death of her husband. But the role of women in American society and American politics was fundamentally transformed in the 1970s and 1980s. Female politicians, many of them initially drawn to politics through their participation in the civil rights and anti-Vietnam movements, became more and more prominent. And just as the civil rights movement led to increased participation by

black voters, to increased concern for political issues of particular importance to racial minorities, and to an increase in the number of black office
holders, so too did the women's movement lead to the mobilization of
women as active political participants, to definable differences (the so-
called gender gap) between male and female voters, to a concern for issues of gender from the Equal Rights Amendment (ERA) to abortion to
improved day-care facilities, and to an increase in prominent female politicians. Once again the parties had to respond as the body politic underwent a transformation. In 1993 more women won major party nominations for the House and Senate than had ever been the case before. "The
year of the woman" ended with forty-seven female House members and
six women sitting in the Senate, both record numbers.

Other changes could be added to this list—the Supreme Court rulings
requiring appointment schemes that, to the extent possible, equalized the
value of votes, the increase in the numbers of Hispanic and Asian Americans, an increased public concern about ethics in government largely as a
result of the Watergate affair, the movement of the nation's population
from the Snowbelt states to the Sunbelt states with consequent shifts in the
size of congressional delegations—but the lessons remain the same. As
the nation has undergone dramatic changes, the political parties, as institutions that must function within this changing context, have had to respond.

And there is no doubt that the parties—as well as the politicians who
run under party labels and the institutions in which they serve—*have* responded. Some of their responses have been abrupt and some more subtle. Some have been successful, and some have failed. Some have been
welcomed and some criticized. By any account, however, the list of reforms, many of which were promulgated during the turbulent 1970s, is
impressive—major changes in the committee and seniority systems in the
Congress, Government in Sunshine laws and sunset legislation to close
the books on unneeded programs, imposition of more stringent ethical
standards in the Congress and the executive branch, redefinition of the relationship between the executive and the legislature as they work on the
federal budget and conduct foreign policy, public funding of presidential
campaigns and restrictions on the financing of congressional campaigns
and campaigns in nearly every state, restructuring of the delegate-selection process for national conventions (reflecting a move toward more
popular and less organization influence), and, finally, the reactions to
those reforms, such as affirmative action programs for women and minorities.

The Democrats and the Republicans have not always responded in the
same way to these changes in American politics; partisan differences on
some reforms have been pronounced. But the parties have been involved

in all of these matters, and neither party in the 1990s comes even close to what it was in the 1950s in terms of organization, membership, how it appeals to the electorate or serves its candidates, and its impact on governing. This book examines the parties' responses.

The essays written for this volume examine contemporary political parties. But the historical context of that examination is important as well. As Joel Silbey persuasively argues in the opening essay, the centrality of the party role has varied significantly over time. Not only the intensity of that role but also the locus of its impact has shifted.

The essays that follow Silbey's historical introduction do not examine political parties as a whole; rather, each chapter looks at one aspect of the role played by these resilient institutions as they have adapted to a changing political context. For instance, the second through fourth chapters look at party organization. The next two chapters focus on the role of the party in the electorate; the five after that examine the role of parties in the more broadly defined electoral arena. The three subsequent chapters on the role of party in government recognize the fact that party as an institution has more than an electoral role. And the final two essays speculate on how this role will change in the decades ahead.

The sixteen essays that make up this book represent the most recent thinking by leading scholars; yet they have been written with an undergraduate audience in mind. They not only cover the varying aspects of this topic from differing perspectives, but they also employ a range of research methods so that students can be exposed to the various modes of analysis used by contemporary researchers.

In Chapters 2 and 3, John Bibby and Paul Herrnson examine political parties as organizations in search of a role, at the state and national levels, respectively. In each case, the question is whether these organizations, once perceived as weak and ineffectual, have found a niche through which they can regain the influence they once had. And in each case, the answer is a qualified "yes." In Chapter 4, Walter Stone, Ronald Rapoport, and Alan Abramowitz refer to surveys of state convention delegates in their examination of the views of political activists who influence party decisions. When activists in the two parties, among them the party leaders, emphasize different issue positions and thus become further separated in ideological terms, their positions might well presage similar differences among their followers.

In Chapters 5 and 6, Warren Miller and Morris Fiorina analyze the relationship between parties and voters. Using national survey data from the presidential elections of the 1980s, Miller refutes the arguments of those who claim that the electorate has lost its allegiance to the major political parties. He maintains that the voters (as opposed to citizens who do not vote) retain party as an important referent group and that the evidence points to a realignment toward the Republicans that began during the Reagan administration and was cemented in the election of 1988. He also looks at the 1992 election in light of this finding. Fiorina, looking at how voters decide on the array of choices with which they are presented on each election day, and contrasting the elections of the 1980s and of 1992 with those a half-century earlier, concludes that elections, once party-centered, are now office-centered (i.e., voters view presidential elections and congressional elections in different ways) and person-centered (i.e., voters relate to those candidates they come to know). Now that ticket splitting and divided government are accepted parts of the electoral scene, the traditional concept of realignment caused by divisive issues is no longer meaningful.

The next five chapters concern the role of political parties in the conduct of elections. In Chapter 7, Sandy Maisel, Linda Fowler, Ruth Jones, and Walter Stone present a model to explain candidate decisionmaking and explore the limitations of the role that party can play in determining who will be candidates in state and local elections. The authors also speculate on how that role can be enhanced. In Chapter 8, Elaine Kamarck and Kenneth Goldstein demonstrate the effect of national party rules on the strategies and outcomes of recent presidential nominations. They conclude with a discussion of the party context in which future nominating contests will occur. Anthony Corrado reviews the 1992 election in Chapter 9 and examines the extent to which the most recent election signifies a major change for political parties as they compete for the nation's highest office. In Chapter 10, Frank Sorauf and Scott Wilson explore the means by which political parties have responded to the evolving cash economy of modern campaigns. As modern campaigns require more money and less manpower, parties have found a new niche; but Sorauf and Wilson reveal evidence that this new role may prove to be as transitory as previous ones. Then, in Chapter 11, Andrew Gelman and Gary King explore how media messages influence presidential elections; they derive a theory of media impacts on two-party competition from their examination of political scientists' and pollsters' election forecasts.

Decades ago, V. O. Key directed political scientists to look at the role of political parties in government as well as in the electoral arena. In Chapters 12 and 13, accordingly, Barbara Sinclair and David Brady and Kara Buckley analyze the complex impact of party on Congress. Drawing on her experiences as a participant observer, Sinclair shows evidence of re-emerging strength in party leadership in the process by which the legislature defines the policy agenda and structures the two chambers. But Brady and Buckley claim that, despite evidence of increased party voting in recent Congresses, structural factors and many of the same political factors on which Fiorina commented lead one to conclude that one must increasingly look at cross-party coalitions in order to understand legislative behavior. Cal Mackenzie, in Chapter 14, then argues that party is much less a resource on which presidents can draw to staff their administrations than it once was, largely because party leaders do not tend to be as concerned about issues as they are about the techniques of winning office. Thus, the party in government connection has been further weakened.

In Chapters 15 and 16, David Shribman and Sandy Maisel conclude with a look to the future. Shribman deconstructs President Clinton's winning coalition and raises questions about its implications for future partisanship. And Maisel speculates on the evolution of political parties—in their various roles—as the twenty-first century approaches.

Taken together, these sixteen essays paint a fascinating picture of American political parties. Parties in the role of institutions have adapted as the nation has changed over two centuries. But as parties are not monolithic, any analysis must take into account not only their complexity but also the various points at which they affect the American polity. The authors of these chapters come to the topic from different perspectives—not only as political scientists but also as historians, journalists, and activists, as students not only of political parties but also of organizations, of voting behavior, of elections, of the Congress, and of the presidency. Only by looking at the entire picture can one begin to understand the complexity of American political parties, the ways they have responded to a changing country, and the reasons they have persisted as they have.

L.S.M.

PART ONE

Parties in the American Context

1

The Rise and Fall of American Political Parties 1790–1993

JOEL H. SILBEY

Since the 1790s, few elections in America have occurred without the involvement of national political parties. From the Jeffersonian Republicans and Federalists in the first years of the new nation to the Democrats and Republicans of the present day, along with the range of third-party movements from the Anti-Masons in the 1820s to the supporters of Ross Perot in 1992, parties have dominated the American political scene, serving as the main organizers of social and economic conflict, mobilizers of voters, and critical cue-givers to legislators and other office holders. In their functions and appearance parties have seemed to enjoy great stability for over 200 years. Yet their role and importance have significantly varied over time, reflecting major changes in the way Americans live, think, and go about their politics.

Scholars have distinguished five distinct party systems in our history: (1) the original Federalist-Republican system, which lasted until about 1815; (2) a Democratic-Whig system, between 1828 and 1850s; (3) the first Republican-Democratic system, from 1860 to 1896; (4) a second such system, lasting between 1896 and 1932; and (5) the New Deal party system, after 1932. These analytic distinctions are based on the lineup of the particular interests and social groups supporting each party—not occasionally and haphazardly but in a sustained, repetitive fashion in election after election throughout the years of a particular party system. Each system has been bounded by an electoral realignment in which major shifts in voting choice occurred among these groups—shifts powerful enough, and long-lasting enough, to fundamentally change the shape of subsequent party warfare (Chambers and Burnham, 1975; Kleppner et al., 1981).

In addition to these electoral shifts, sharp variations and significant changes have occurred in the reach and importance of political parties throughout our history. Given contemporary attitudes toward parties, their role, power, and, most critically, the centrality of their place in the American political system, we might consider a somewhat different delineation of the changing shape of the partisan dimension in the American political universe. According to this view, the chronology consists of (1) a pre-party era from the 1790s to the late 1830s; (2) a party era from the 1830s to the 1890s; (3) a post-party era from the 1890s to the 1950s; and (4) a nonparty era ever since (Silbey, 1991).

The justification for arranging American party history in this way grows out of the different kinds of political institutions, norms, and behavior that have *predominated* in each era. Thus, although two parties have always been on the scene, only once—from 1838 to 1893—did parties totally dominate the American political landscape. Before 1838 they were incompletely developed and seen as foreign, unwelcome, and, one hoped, temporary intrusions into public affairs. Since the 1890s, they have been in sharp decline throughout the nation's political system, plummeting to their present position of limited relevance to most people in a nonparty, candidate-centered age (Formisano, 1974; Wallace, 1968, 1973; Wattenberg, 1986).

FACTIONS ORGANIZED AROUND TEMPORARY ISSUES

The 1790s were contentious years in American politics. The recently ratified Constitution had established a new national political arena with a central government of great potential, power, and authority. The efforts of Treasury Secretary Alexander Hamilton to invigorate the federal government were not universally supported, however. Given all that was at stake and the geographic extent of the political battlefield, those opposing the Hamiltonian initiatives as detrimental to their own interests came together under the banner of Jeffersonian Republicanism in time to contest the congressional elections of 1794. Two years later they bitterly fought to wrest the presidency away from their still-dominant enemies (Chambers, 1963). These dramatic contests, occurring early in our history as a nation, were only the forerunners of ever-recurring conflict in American life and the constant need to mobilize in the battle for political power.

But these original attempts to establish political parties were incomplete. The Jeffersonian Republicans and the Federalists were only partially accepted by politically involved people, and they ultimately foundered, not just as electoral coalitions but as institutions having any role at all to play in American politics. They were neither deeply rooted in the political soil nor all-encompassing in their influence and importance. To be sure, some coordinated efforts were made to select candidates, manage campaigns, attract voters, and bring legislators and other office holders under the discipline of party. From Washington to the state capitals, party labeling and party coordination of political activities took place, as did the polarized articulation of contrasting policies. All of these practices were repeated in successive election campaigns and in meetings of Congress and the state legislatures. Federalists and Republicans seemed to be everywhere (Banner, 1970; Fischer, 1965; Banning, 1978; Goodman, 1964).

Nevertheless, there was always an intermittent, ad hoc quality to all of these efforts and a casual attitude toward the partisan forms. Although these early combatants had much ideological vigor, they were quite deficient organizationally. There was little coordination of party warfare between the national level and the political battles in the states. The network of institutions needed to mobilize voters and to present each party's policy stances was only partially developed and erratic in its activities and relevance. In some places, such as New York and North Carolina, these institutions were built quite early and were used extensively. Elsewhere, party organization was not even rudimentary (Formisano, 1974, 1981, 1983). Early political development remained elite focused rather than popular. The voting behavior of the relatively small electorate remained quite volatile and was only occasionally party oriented throughout the years of Federalist-Republican battles. It was not until later years that election days were characterized by sustained partisan alignments and behavior (Benson, Silbey, and Field, 1978; Bohmer, 1978; McCormick, 1982).

The full development of political parties in the United States was hampered in this early period by a powerful mindset against them, combined with little appreciation of their potential usefulness in an expansive, pluralist society. There was a profound distrust of any institution that organized and sustained domestic political conflict. Such distrust originated in the still-potent eighteenth-century fear that recurrent internal conflict endangered all republics. Parties, by organizing such conflict, made matters worse and jeopardized a nation's very survival (Shalope, 1972; Watts, 1987).

According to some scholars of this early period, therefore, even to label the institutions of the 1790s as parties distorts the record, given the strong evidence of their weakness, incompleteness, and irrelevance as well as the hostility toward them. Indeed, as one such scholar has written, "until the idea exists that parties are legitimate, that there are necessary divisions within a complex society, that there are continuous, enduring group conflicts that can and should be organized in a sustained, partisan political fashion, [it is] anachronistic" to call what existed in the decade and more after the Constitution "anything but factions organized around temporary issues" (Benson, 1981:24). In a pre-party era, Federalists and Republicans could be little else.

ESSENTIAL TO THE EXISTENCE OF OUR INSTITUTIONS

The failure to establish political parties as a normal part of American politics lasted for about a half-century after the ratification of the Constitution. The era ended because political activities had increased in scope and vigor, thus demanding a more extensive, powerful, and permanent system to deal with the problems of American politics. As the nation continued to grow after 1815, as incipient sectional tensions and regional rivalries became more vocal, as social antagonisms grew along religious and nationality lines, and as different economic interests renewed their battles to control government and its policies, it soon became clear that the pressing political needs of a pluralist nation of great size and many conflicts required political institutions beyond the Constitution and the limited forms of organization that had occasionally been present (Formisano, 1971; McCormick, 1967; Shade, 1981; Silbey, 1991).

The push for parties came out of three streams: the need to manage and guide a rapidly growing electorate; the need to bring together likeminded interests and factions into coalitions in order to win elections; and the need to enact specific policies in an arena where real differences over public policy existed alongside perceptions of serious public danger if the wrong policies, people, or groups dominated. For ten years after 1815, political excitement increased in intensity in America—initially at the state and local levels, stimulated by battles over economic development and social cohesion, and then in renewed contests over national problems and the presidency. As these conflicts developed, they involved more people than ever before, inasmuch as suffrage requirements for adult white males had eased up dramatically. Political leaders had to give sustained attention to dealing with a larger electorate that had spread much further geographically than ever before and had been aroused by the renewal of a wide range of bitter policy and group conflicts (Nichols, 1967; McCormick, 1967; Benson, 1961; Williamson, 1960; Watson, 1981).

These political leaders were successful in finding a way to deal with their political problem. At first, the impulse toward both mass politics and collective political organization originated with outsider movements such as the Anti-Masons, which took the lead, ahead of the conventional political leadership, in their willingness to mobilize the masses. Their example was not lost for very long on many astute political observers, who were searching for ways to structure the changing political landscape. New York's Martin Van Buren and his well-organized associates—the Albany Regency—learned from what was happening around them, made the case for parties, and acted collectively, accepting the direction and discipline that such action entailed. As Michael Wallace (1973:138) has argued, "for the individualism so dear to Whig and Republican theory [they] ... substituted an almost servile worship of organization." A Van Buren lieutenant, Churchill Chambreleng, set forth the new tone clearly and forcefully in a speech before Congress in 1826: Political parties, he argued, are "indispensable to every Administration [and] ... essential to the existence of our institutions; and if ... an evil, [they are ones] we must endure, for the preservation of our civil liberty." But parties "never yet injured any free country. ... The conflict of parties is a noble conflict—of mind to mind, genius to genius" (*Register of Debates*, 1826:1546; Remini, 1951; Benson, 1961).

The original organizational impulse and the assault on ideological antipartyism culminated in the election of Andrew Jackson in 1828. But that victory, far from being an end to party development, was in fact the beginning. In the subsequent decade, the intellectual defense of parties and the building up of partisan institutions utterly transformed the political scene into something quite different from anything that had preceded it. The excitement of the process by which the Jackson administration defined itself, and the persistent battles over the presidential succession and economic policy that followed, completed the movement toward a partisan-dominated nation (Benson, 1961; Formisano, 1971; Watson, 1981).

Whatever hesitancies some politically involved Americans continued to have about these organizations, and however intense the demands of these organizations for the subordination of the individual in the collective, more and more political leaders played by the new political rules in order to achieve their specific policy goals. The party impulse spread into the camp of Jackson's opponents. Still deeply imbued with the old-style antiparty attitudes of an earlier era, the Whigs (reluctantly at first) adopted the style of, and argument for, political parties. Ultimately, many of them became powerful articulators of the necessity for party. They built up their organization as well and even celebrated the political parties (Silbey, 1991).

This development meant more than rhetorical acceptance and behavioral exhortation. What occurred moved from intermittence, individualism, and voluntarism to persistence, structure, and organized professionalism. Parties sank very deep roots into the system, among leaders and followers alike, and came to shape all but a small part of the American political world. Organizationally, their arrival meant the building of patterned, systematic institutions to do the necessary work. Elections were frequent in nineteenth-century America. Parties were always nominating, running, or preparing to nominate or run some candidate for one or another of the great array of elected offices. As they emerged, parties designated candidates at every level, replacing individual and group free-wheeling with disciplined processes of choice. They collectively shaped what they would say and controlled all other aspects of the mobilization of the electorate. Party organizations grew into a regular array of committees, legislative caucuses, and conventions, designed to hammer out decisions about candidates, priorities, and programs, to run the actual campaigns, and to bring the voters to the polling booth on the day appointed. These institutions had a symmetrical shape across time and place. Their organization was decentralized, but they looked, and generally acted, the same everywhere. Wherever parties were present, their constituent elements and responsibilities remained constant from state to state across the country (McCormick, 1967; Gienapp, 1982; Silbey, 1991).

The heart and soul of nineteenth-century party organization were the conventions that were held at every political level from the local to the national. Conventions had occasionally met earlier in American history, but it was only from the late 1830s onward that they became a widespread and normal part of the political scene. Each level of activity replicated the pattern whereby people were called together to hammer out policy initiatives, choose candidates, and select delegates to the next highest level convention. Topping all such activities was the national convention held every four years. All of these meetings, at every level, were cloaked with tremendous power. Their authority in party affairs was considered to be total, as they represented the place where major decisions were made about all things (Thornton, 1978; Silbey, 1991).

Once the conventions were over and the party's candidates had been chosen, with their arguments clarified and formalized, the Whigs and Democrats proceeded to disseminate each campaign's political discourse through a growing network of partisan newspapers, pamphleteering, and organized mass rallies. The parties' platforms originally codified each party's stance. In the debates that followed, Whigs and Democrats presented quite polarized images to the voters. They remained forever nose to nose. Party leaders drew on a rich pool of ideas about policies to sharpen differences among the voters overall and to draw together their own tribes. In their platforms, newspaper editorials, and campaign speeches, they enshrined the religious, nationality, sectional, and cultural animosities between groups, reflected the most up-to-date differences over the economic direction of the newly liberated, rapidly developing society, and provided a way for politically involved Americans to understand the world and its problems. The party leaders also became adept at mobilizing the tensions that were present and at bringing them together into large policy frameworks. In sorting out the political world, they defined what was at stake and linked the different outlooks and perspectives into a whole (Benson, 1961; Howe, 1979; Silbey, 1991).

Each political party in this dialogue aggregated society's many interests and social groups in a selective way, reaching out not to everyone but only to a portion of the electorate. What resulted, in the 1840s, was a party of social homogeneity and governmental vigor in all things, economic and social—the Whigs. Another party, the Democrats, espoused social and ethnic pluralism and was suspicious of too much government activity in human affairs. Both parties clearly and repeatedly articulated the differences between them. They hammered home, once again, how "utterly irreconcilable" they were—"as opposite to each other as light and darkness, as knowledge and ignorance" (*Louisville Journal*, 1852; Benson, 1961; Holt, 1978).

The extent of party organization varied across the country and was never as complete or as tight as party leaders desired. But despite all of their reservations and the incompleteness of the structure, the ideal of comprehensiveness was always sought. The many elements constituting an efficient model were present, if not quite as developed as they would yet become. More the point, I suggest, was the trajectory of party development and the similarity of party operations across the nation. There was a more widespread commitment than ever before, a movement in a particular direction, and a shift in values toward collectivities as the means to promote and achieve political goals. The atmosphere and mechanics of each campaign became the same everywhere (Shade, 1981; Silbey, 1991).

More critical still, popular voting behavior became extremely party driven from the end of the 1830s, as the battles over policies penetrated popular consciousness and the parties' mobilization machinery matured. Turnout at the polls dramatically increased over earlier levels in response to each party's extensive mobilization activities. When voters cast their ballots, their sustained commitment to a party in election after election became the norm in a way that was never the case before. Each succeeding election was viewed not as a separate contest involving new issues or new personalities but as yet another opportunity to vote for, and reaffirm, an individual's support for his or her party and what it represented. As the editor of the Albany *Argus* put it in the 1840s, "the first duty of a Democrat is to vote; the next to vote the regular ticket." Each voter did both much more often than not (Albany *Argus*, 1846; Kleppner, 1979; Formisano, 1971; Benson, 1961).

By the beginning of the 1840s the American people were worshipping more and more at the "shrine of party." Their commitment to the parties moved beyond instrumentalist calculation of the rewards of specific policies or the benefits to be gained from particular candidates. Each party's popular support was rooted in the intense, deep, persistent loyalty of individual voters to their party home. The electoral pattern furthered such commitment. Party warfare split Americans decisively and evenly. The battles between Whigs and Democrats, and later between the Republicans and Democrats, were highly competitive. Close electoral contests were the rule. Indeed, their closeness reinforced the drive to organize and turn out the vote and to expand, even further, the commitment to individual parties and to the party system as a preferred mode of organizing the nation's political affairs and settling its major problems (Silbey, 1967, 1977, 1985; Gienapp, 1982).

As a result, parties had great vitality in the 1840s and thereafter. They were everywhere. For the first time, they were considered both natural and necessary. They came to control all but a small part of American politics, and they staffed the government through their patronage operations. Once in office, the party leaders were expected to carry out the policies their party stood for—as, indeed, they attempted to do. Although elaborate policymaking was unknown in the middle of the nineteenth century, whatever efforts were made occurred in response to party promises and arguments. Finally, both the appeals of the two major parties and the loyalty of voters and leaders to them occurred at a national level. Whatever sectional tensions existed in the United States, as the parties developed, both the Whigs and the Democrats were able to attract support and make their influence felt, regardless of the pressures to divide along other gradients (Silbey, 1967; McCormick, 1986; Formisano, 1981; Shade, 1981).

Two major disruptions of the political system—first the electoral realignment of the 1850s and then the Civil War—demonstrated that the passionate commitment to one's party had limits. The increase in ideological intensity along sectional lines in the 1850s and 1860s shook the political nation severely. It was a destructive, chastening experience for those in command of the traditional political channels. Nevertheless, when the smoke cleared after a series of intense voter shifts after the death of one party and the rise of another, the essential structure of American politics remained largely as before. Electoral coalitions were reshaped, sectional tensions became the norm, and one party—the Republican party—was no longer national in its reach. But the central reality of partisan-defined and -shaped political activities stood firm. The nation's agenda and institutions, as well as the reactions of both leaders and voters to the events of the day, continued to reflect the dominance of existing patterns of two-party politics and the intense loyalties that had been such a crucial aspect of them since the late 1830s (Gienapp, 1987; Silbey, 1977, 1991).

After the Civil War, the reach of political parties expanded further than ever before as the party era continued to make its way in American life. New partisan forms, such as the urban political machine, developed to meet new needs. But, in general, the structures, appeal, and meaning of parties remained much as they had been for the preceding thirty years. Much emphasis was put on reinforcing party loyalty and eliciting automatic partisan responses to new issues and conflicts, whatever their nature. Even as society began to change dramatically from an agricultural to an industrial-urban one, Democrats and Republicans continued to confront each other in the well-disciplined, predictable phalanxes of people deeply committed to powerful, closely competitive institutions designed to fulfill group and individual needs (Kleppner, 1979; Jensen, 1971; Mc-Seveney, 1971; McCormick, 1981).

The extent of the partisan imperative in nineteenth-century American politics was demonstrated, finally, by the behavior of the many challenges to the Democratic-Whig-Republican hegemony. From the beginning of this partisan political era, there were regular protests against the central tenets of the political nation from people ever impatient with or continually frustrated by the national parties, their advocacy, and their command of the system. Yet, the way in which these challenges interacted with politics suggests their adherence to many of the central political values of their era, despite their persistent outsider questioning, stance, and self-image. Between 1838 and the early 1890s, minor parties organized and campaigned much as the major political parties did; they also nominated candidates, thought about whom they wished to appeal to, and sought to mobilize particular voters behind their policies. Most held national conventions and issued national platforms. Somewhat more sporadically, they called state, district, and local conventions as well. They staged campaign rallies and organized to get out the vote. They issued pamphlets and published party newspapers. In emulating their enemies to the extent that they did, they underscored the power of the partisan impulse on this particular political landscape (Holt, 1973; Kleppner, 1979).

TOO IMPORTANT TO BE LEFT TO POLITICIANS

This party era lasted into the 1890s. With the electoral realignment of that decade, the role of the parties began to shift dramatically. Launched against them was a full-scale assault that included shrewd (and ultimately successful) legislative efforts to weaken their organizations, their command of the landscape, and the powerful partisanship that had made the system what it was. Parties found themselves less able than before to resist the reformist onslaught. As a result, the equilibrium between them and their challengers was upset. The churning and destabilization of the electoral landscape led to profound systemic disintegration. From the 1890s on, the nation's politics started to become nonpartisan. The vigor of American electoral politics, rooted in the passionate confrontations between two well-developed and dominant parties, gave way to an antiparty, and ultimately nonparty, way of carrying on political activities. America's political ways went from focusing specifically on the ceremonies and rituals of partisan polarization to appealing, organizing, and working beyond parties. As that happened, Americans went from strong commitment to one party and angry dissatisfaction with the other to vituperative dissatisfaction with all parties (McCormick, 1981; Burnham, 1965, 1970; McGerr, 1986).

There was no sudden upheaval or coup d'etat. The new era opened with an extended period of transition during which many of the institutions, values, and approaches of the past continued to be important. At the national level, after 1896, the Democrats vigorously contested the new Republican electoral hegemony in the traditional manner. The two parties' internal processes of defining themselves, resolving their divisions, and choosing their candidates also remained largely as they had been. The same was true of their external behavior during campaigns as well as their approach to government staffing, responsibilities, and policymaking. But with the loss of electoral competitiveness in many parts of the country in the 1890s, the fires of political confrontation cooled. Organizing elements became flabby as the losers in one-sided electoral situations lost workers, coverage, heart, and vigor. As a result, politics shifted into new channels. At the same time, as a major element of the nation's transformation, an alternate vision of political propriety developed and then took firm hold. The basic ambivalence this vision manifested toward the political world evolved into a powerful negativism stimulated by what was seen as excessive political expediency and increasingly sordid partisan manipulation of democratic politics. Coupled with the rise of new, very powerful external forces that were reshaping the society, this negativism eventually imposed its view of prosperity on the American system (Benson, 1955; Hays, 1957, 1959; McCormick, 1981).

As Richard Jensen has succinctly noted, the Progressives sought, early in the new era, "to banish all forms of traditionalism—boss control, corrupt practices, big business intervention in politics, 'ignorant' voting and excessive power in the hands of hack politicians" (Jensen, 1978:27). For the Progressives, political reform, especially the concerted attack on the parties, was a prerequisite to all else they wished to accomplish. Party politics was corrupt, irrational, and unprincipled. And so they redefined politics as a detached search for objective, and therefore correct, policies—a search unrelated to the passions, rituals, self-interest, and deception connected with political parties (Hays, 1957; Wiebe, 1967; Ranney, 1975).

In the first decade and a half of the twentieth century, the Progressives and their allies were able to take a series of legislative actions that attacked and ultimately uncoupled several of the links between parties and voters. They energized the efforts under way since the 1880s to reform election laws—especially to institute voter registration and government-controlled official ballots. Their successful passage of a large number of such legislative initiatives had a major impact on the political system. Nonpartisan electoral reforms weakened the partisan imperative by challenging, first, the politicians' control of nominations and the election process and, then, the party-dominated, unrestrained wheeling and dealing over policy priorities (Kousser, 1974; McCormick, 1981).

At the same time, in the economic realm the Progressives successfully promoted the growth of government power and a shift in focus from generalized, distributive policies to new regulative channels, which demanded technical expertise, well-developed budgeting and financial skills, and an ability to deal with sophisticated control mechanisms—rather than the more generalist negotiating talents of party leaders, which had previously dominated a simpler, more limited government apparatus and its activities. As a result, there was a steady increase in the number of, and activities by, specialized nonpartisan interest groups, each of which sought to shape specific government policies without the mediation of political parties. In addition, government eventually took over responsibility for matters the parties had traditionally controlled, social welfare being one prime example. The nonpartisan civil service continued to expand—challenging, and ultimately weakening, the partisan patronage resources that had been so important to party operations (Benson, 1955; McCormick, 1981; Wiebe, 1967).

All of this indicated the success, over several decades, of what Daniel T. Rodgers calls "the explosion of scores of aggressive, politically active pressure groups into the space left by the recession of traditionally political loyalties" (1982:114). This nonpartisan occupation had significant long-range effects on the political nation. The emerging organizational society of technicians, bureaucrats, and impersonal decisionmakers had no faith in, or commitment to, mass politics—especially as expressed through the parties. Although no one group was solely responsible for the changes that occurred, all reforming groups, whatever their interests, aims, and nature, shared a commitment to move in the same direction. As their numbers and reach increased, their vision grew to be quite popular. The Progressives' political agenda was antipartisan in direction and vigorously pushed (McCormick, 1981; Hays, 1957, 1959).

The range of changes under way worked its way through the political nation slowly. The impact of each of the pressures was cumulative. From the first, the reform challenge meant that parties had competition at the center of the political world for the first time since the 1830s. For decades well into the 1940s, however, there were different balances between old and new. In some areas, parties retained vestiges of influence and a capacity to shape events, as evidenced by the electoral vigor of the urban political machines and the success of their policy initiatives. For a time, during the New Deal years, there was evidence that political parties still had a strong kick, reminiscent of an earlier time and perhaps suggestive of a return to dominance by them. An electoral realignment in the 1930s not only restored the Democrats to power with a new agenda but also invigorated voter loyalties, fired by the Depression and the Rooseveltian response. These loyalties took deep hold and shaped much about electoral politics and something about policy, as well, for a generation thereafter. The era from the 1890s into the 1950s, therefore, was a mixed, post-party one in which, amid the signs of party decay in government affairs, policymaking, and the structure of electoral involvement, partisanship still anchored much voter choice as it had in the past (Campbell et al., 1960; Burnham, 1970; Andersen, 1979; Silbey, 1991).

ANARCHY TEMPERED BY DISTRUST

But the partisan honeymoon of the 1930s and 1940s, however powerful and dramatic, was only a deviation from the long-range pattern of party collapse. The decline of political parties resumed and quickened as the New Deal began to fade from popular memory after World War II. Other, extraparty elements became even more firmly entrenched on the landscape. Over time, parties as organizers and as symbols of the battles over public policies lost more and more of their relevance. Party control of the electoral process continued to weaken. Shifts in the way political information was presented—moving from partisan to nonpartisan sources—had been under way throughout the twentieth century. Party newspapers, with their relentless, clear, direct, and unambiguous message, gave way to a different journalistic style serving a broader clientele. Cheap, sensationalist, nonpartisan, and often cynical about politics, newspapers came into their own at the turn of the century. But they failed to provide quick and easily absorbed partisan guides, as their predecessors had done—an oversight that had a long-term effect (McGerr, 1986; Burnham, 1970, 1982).

This transformation accelerated greatly with television's rise in the 1950s. In its style of presentation and dominance of the scene, television even more sharply cut off much of the partisan shaping of what was at stake—a central factor in mobilizing voters into loyal party channels in the nineteenth century. Parties had once been able to argue that all political legitimacy lay with them. Independent newspapers and television challenged that assumption in both direct and indirect ways. Television, to the parties' detriment, emphasized imagery and personality against the allegedly artificial styles and deceptive auras of the political parties; it also ignored or downplayed the distinguishing features of parties that made them important to the political process (Ranney, 1983).

In the post–World War II years, as well, the size, reach, and influence of the federal government became the central fact of the political nation. With this growth of state power, a partisan-directed model of activities and behavior lost its last vestiges of importance among many Americans. Instead, the interest group pattern, unmediated by partisan priority-setting and influence, finally replaced it. The well-entrenched, nonpartisan, economic interest groups began to forge and make permanent the kinds of links with the legislative and administrative branches that they had been groping toward since the end of the partisan political nation in the 1890s. Their earlier belief that parties were a barrier to their best interests was succeeded by a growing sense of the irrelevance of parties to their activities at any level. From the 1930s on, the expansion of nonpartisan interest groups accelerated, reaching well beyond their original economic base among the new industrial forces to encompass any segment of the society that sought government assistance. By the 1960s, every policy impulse had its own organization that moved readily into the legislative and administrative arenas, largely as if parties did not exist. Many different groups, with many different agendas and enthusiasms, articulated issues, mobilized voters, financed campaigns, and organized legislative and administrative support for their limited goals. These in turn became vested interests in their areas of concern and dominant as articulators of specific demands. The result was a cacophony of voices, continuous discordant battling, and, often, policy fragmentation (Lowi, 1979).

At the same time, in the 1960s, the legitimacy of parties was subjected to a renewed assault, echoing a theme once dominant and now reborn with a virulence and power long forgotten. All of the earlier deficiencies of parties, from corruption to elite manipulation and the denial of democracy, were once again widely rehearsed. Much media commentary took up the assault and gave it a repetitive reality, especially during such unpleasant episodes as the Democratic National Convention of 1968. This unrelenting negative commentary took a toll. Its intellectual offensive against parties, coupled with the massive shifts in communications—and both resting on the Progressives' changing of the playing field and the rules of the game—added up in such a way as to impel the creation of a new nonparty political nation (Ranney, 1975; Burnham, 1982).

All of the antiparty tendencies at play, which had become quite clear by the end of the 1950s, determined the course of the next decade. A *New York Times* reporter later argued that John F. Kennedy, at the outset of the 1960s, was "the last great representative of the politics of loyalty, human intermediation, compromise and tradition" (1980:E19). With his death, the parties' last bastion—the electoral arena—gave way. Throughout the 1960s, there was certainly a profound shift in the ways in which mass politics was organized, its rituals were displayed, and its supporters were mobilized. Party-dominated mass meetings, conventions, and campaign rallies continued, but they were in a prolonged state of decay and became increasingly irrelevant to the country's political business. The parties' ability to coalesce a range of interests was gone. Although national party conventions still nominated and labeled candidates, they had less and less influence over the actual process of choosing who the party would put forward. Delegates were no longer the key players they once had been. They had lost their bargaining, reviewing, and reflecting power. In Richard Jensen's apt summing up, more and more "candidates for office selected themselves" (1981:219) by mobilizing the nonpartisan resources on the political scene. This situation affected the subsequent runs for office as well. In many campaigns, party labels became less prevalent than they once had been. Increasingly, candidates preferred to run as individuals, emphasizing their personal qualities rather than their adherence to party norms.

The impact of the successful century-long assault against parties on the way the American voter engaged in politics was enormous and emblematic of the whole thrust of the post–1893 American political nation. First, individual involvement in the electoral system changed dramatically over the years. American voters in 1990 no longer behaved as their ancestors did in 1890. The size of the electorate expanded throughout the twentieth century as various legal and social constraints on the participation of particular social groups fell away. But while that was happening, popular interest in politics waned. It could be reinvigorated from time to time, as in the New Deal years, but once again the trend line was clear: downward, toward popular nonparticipation. All of the destabilizing elements at work against political parties were coterminous with a massive fall-off in voter involvement, demonstrated most starkly by the steep decline in turnout at the polls over the course of the twentieth century. By the 1980s, in fact, a sizable "party of nonvoters" existed on the American scene. This group was, at best, sporadically mobilized; it consisted of people eligible to vote but who usually did not do so (Burnham, 1965, 1970, 1982).

Added to popular deinvolvement was popular partisan dealignment. When they did come to the polls, the voters demonstrated that they had become increasingly unstuck from party moorings and caught up, instead, in what Burnham (1973:39) refers to as a "volcanic instability." The all but automatic identification with parties became the minor key in voter behavior. Whatever the power of certain economic or other issues to reawaken such party identification for a while, such issues became less and less influential as time passed. Whatever their differences, whatever distinct ideological and policy stances they fostered, parties could no longer draw voters to them as they had once routinely done. The electorate, in Everett Ladd's terms, less and less considered "voting for 'my party' a sociological or psychological imperative" (1985:2). Each election, at every level of political activity, became a new throw of the dice; and the electorate behaved differently each time, with the ordering of choice among many voters between the parties increasingly unpredictable from contest to contest. "The politics of the 1930s and 1940s resembled a nineteenth century battlefield," one scholar wrote, "with two opposing armies arrayed against each other in more or less close formation; politics today is an altogether messier affair, with large numbers of small detachments engaged over a vast territory, and with individuals and groups frequently changing sides" (King, 1978:372).

Given all this volatility and the absence of strong, widespread partisan influences across the voting universe, electoral strategy had to shift. Candidates, already themselves free from many party constraints, no longer ran for office primarily by mobilizing the party faithful, if they did so at all. There were no longer enough of them to do so. Rather, their efforts centered on appealing to uncommitted, or partially committed, voters. Campaign advertising almost never identified candidates with their party, emphasizing their personal attributes instead. Who or what an individual was, rather than a party's policy stance or deeply rooted partisan loyalties, became the centerpiece of political affairs. In those offices where incumbents seemed all but immune from overturn, such as the House of Representatives, such campaigning turned more and more on the emphasis of extreme personal deficiencies (King, 1978; Brady, 1988; Wattenberg, 1991).

All of this was of a piece. By the early 1990s, there could be no uncertainty about current differences from America's political past. The contrast is marked, indeed. The nineteenth-century political nation reflected a culture that sought first to bring people into the system and then to tame them and their desires through disciplined collectivities. America's powerful individualism, it was felt, needed such discipline. Toward the end of the twentieth century, the political process powerfully highlighted that individualism, becoming a system in which a premium was placed on the seeking of individual rather than party-defined objectives. The reputation of political parties continued to plummet—irreversibly, it seemed.

The success of Ross Perot in the presidential election of 1992 in drawing almost 20 percent of the popular vote from two candidates perceived as particularly flawed leaders—and on a platform that emphasized highly individualistic, self-centered claims to personal virtue and denounced the normal ways of parties and politicians and their inability to pursue effective policies or discipline themselves to behave responsibly—only underscored, once again, how far the party system had fallen (Pomper, 1993; Nelson, 1993). Parties were increasingly considered to be "at best interlopers between the sovereign people and their elected officials and, at worst, rapacious enemies of honest and responsible government," irrelevant to, or destructive of, our ability to solve the critical problems facing the nation (Ranney, 1978a:24). Few people seemed to disagree or care whether they would ever return to their former position in national affairs. All of this cynical negativism, was a very far cry from the celebration of political parties and their role that had once filled the American scene so forcefully.

PART TWO

The Evolving State of
Party Organization

2

State Party Organizations: Coping and Adapting

JOHN F. BIBBY

In the face of a changing and often unfriendly environment, political parties in the American states have demonstrated adaptability and resiliency. This capacity to cope with the forces of political change has meant, of course, that the parties have undergone substantial alteration. Indeed, today's state party bears little resemblance to either the old-style organization of the late nineteenth century or the weak and nonprofessional organizations that existed in the 1950s and 1960s.

The state party organization at the turn of the century was often a hierarchically run operation that was closely tied to local machines, fed by federal, state, and local patronage, and frequently supported and influenced by corporate interests. In many of the states, these old-style party organizations were capable of controlling nominations and providing the resources needed to conduct general election campaigns. They placed great emphasis on mobilizing their supporters on election day. In this activity, they were greatly assisted by an absence of popular cultural support for independent voters who evaluated candidates on their merits. Independents were often called "mugwumps" and scorned as "traitors" and "corrupt sellers of their votes." Walter Dean Burnham has characterized turn-of-the-century organizations as "militarist" in the sense that they drilled their supporters to turn out and vote a straight party ticket (Burnham, 1970:72–73).

Progressive reformers early in this century sought to undermine the organizations' bases of power by instituting the direct primary system of nomination to diminish their control over nominations, the civil service system of public employment to severely limit their patronage, and corrupt-practices legislation to cut off some of their sources of financing (Mayhew, 1986:212–237). These reforms, particularly the direct primary, had the desired effect. The hierarchically organized state party organization had largely passed from the scene by the 1920s. The Republican and Democratic state party organizations that replaced them had vastly reduced influence over nominations and gradually lost the ability to direct state-level campaigns. By the early 1960s state party organizations were in a weakened condition in all but a few states (Key, 1956:271; Epstein, 1986: 144–153).

Since the 1960s state parties have demonstrated their adaptive capacity when faced with new challenges and competitors for influence. These potentially party-weakening influences have included (1) a weakening of partisan ties among the voters—that is, a dealignment of the electorate; (2) the emergence of candidate-centered campaigns run by candidates' personal organizations, instead of by party organizations (Wattenberg, 1991); (3) changes in campaign finance including an increasingly prominent role for political action committees (PACs); and (4) a strengthening of national party organizations.

After exploring the legal and electoral environment in which state party organizations must operate, this essay describes the processes of adaptation and change that have occurred within these organizations since the 1970s. The development of more professionalized state party organizations capable of providing campaign assistance to their candidates is analyzed to demonstrate the remarkable durability of the organizations. The changing national-state party relationship and the implications of the heightened levels of intraparty integration are also explored.

THE CHANGING LEGAL ENVIRONMENT OF STATE PARTIES

In most Western democracies, political parties are considered to be private associations much like the Rotarians, Elks, or Sons of Norway and, as such, have been permitted to conduct their business largely unregulated by government. American political parties, however, can be likened to public utilities in the sense that they perform essential public functions (e.g., making nominations, contesting elections, organizing the government) that have sufficient impact upon the public to justify governmental regulation (Epstein, 1986:Ch. 6).

State governments' most significant regulatory device has been the requirement that the parties nominate their candidates via the direct primary. Before the direct primary was instituted, party leaders could exert substantial influence over party nominating caucuses and conventions. By involving ordinary voters in the selection of party nominees, the direct primary has reduced the capacity of party leaders to control nominations. It has also encouraged candidates to form personal campaign organizations in order to win primary elections.

But the state regulatory process goes well beyond party nominating procedures. State laws determine the eligibility criteria a party must meet in order to be listed on the general election ballot, regulate who can vote in partisan primaries, and govern campaign finances. State regulations frequently extend to matters of internal organization such as procedures for selecting officers, composition of party committees, dates and locations of meetings, and powers of party committees. Only five states (Alaska, Delaware, Hawaii, Kentucky, and North Carolina) do not specify in state law some aspect of the parties' internal organizational operations (Advisory Commission of Intergovernmental Relations, 1986:128). Although the content of statutory regulation varies from state to state, the net effect of state laws has been to mold state parties into quasi-public agencies and to limit party leaders' flexibility in devising strategies to achieve organizational goals.

The legal status of political parties as quasi-public entities that are subject to extensive governmental regulation is, however, in the process of modification as a result of a series of Supreme Court decisions (Epstein, 1986:189–199; 1989:239–274). These decisions have extended to parties the rights of free political association protected by the First and Fourteenth Amendments. By according constitutional protection to parties, the Court has struck down a series of state-imposed restrictions upon political parties.

In the case of *Tashjian v. Connecticut* (479 U.S. 20 [1986]), the Court ruled that Connecticut could not prevent voters registered as independents from voting in a Republican primary if the state Republican party wanted to allow independents as well as registered Republicans to vote in partisan primaries. Although the Connecticut case has potential long-term implications for state regulatory policy, its immediate consequences appear to be quite limited. Only a few state parties have sought to open their primaries to independents, as they are clearly authorized to do under the *Tashjian* decision. Nor is there any realistic likelihood that state parties will use the power seemingly granted them in *Tashjian* to abolish state-mandated direct primaries. The direct primary is simply too popular and well ingrained in the political culture (Epstein, 1989:260–274).

In 1989 the Supreme Court followed its *Tashjian* decision by further limiting state regulatory authority over parties in a case arising under California laws (*Eu v. San Francisco County Democratic Central Committee*, 109 S. Ct. 1013 [1989]). Asserting that California statutes violated the political parties' rights of free association, the Court struck down state laws that banned party organizations from endorsing candidates in primary elections (pre-primary endorsements), limited the length of state party chairmen's terms to two years, and required that the state party chairmanship be rotated every two years between residents of northern and southern regions of the state.

In these cases, the Supreme Court has clearly indicated that there are limits on the extent of regulation that may be imposed by the states. However, in spite of the Court's willingness to free state parties from excessively burdensome regulation, the Connecticut and California cases do not appear to have created a significant movement toward deregulation or the "privatization" of parties. Most state parties, long ago adapted to living with state regulation, have not moved to challenge existing regulations. Also working against the "privatization" of parties is a willingness on the part of federal courts to accept the notion that there are legitimate state interests in regulating parties. For example, the U.S. Court of Appeals for the Seventh Circuit upheld a Wisconsin law, which resembles the laws of most states, banning candidates from cross-filing—seeking the nomination of more than one party (*Swamp v. Kennedy*, Nos. 90-2781 and 90-2884, 1991). In this case, the state's Labor-Farm party argued that its rights of free association should permit it to nominate on its primary ballot a candidate who was also on the Democratic party's primary ballot. The three-judge panel, however, ruled that Wisconsin's law served a compelling state interest in avoiding voter confusion; preserving the integrity of the election process; and ensuring that the winner of an election was the choice of a majority, or at least a plurality, of the voters. Although the Wisconsin case shows that there are limits on parties' First Amendment rights, it also indicates that the doctrine of parties' rights of free association is likely to be a continuing source of litigation concerning the legal status of parties.

THE STATE ELECTORAL ENVIRONMENT

There is great diversity among the states in terms of the election laws, the strength of their political parties, political traditions, and citizens' partisan, ideological, and policy orientations. This diversity should not, however, obscure the common features of the electoral environment within which every state party must operate. Common to all the states are candidate-centered campaigns, growing use of sophisticated campaign techniques and professional managers, an increasing role for PACs in funding campaigns, heightened interparty competition for statewide offices, and high rates of reelection for incumbent members of Congress and state legislators.

Candidate-Centered Campaigns

Candidates run under party labels that help them attract votes from among the party adherents in the electorate, but there is nothing that forces them to let the party organizations run or participate in their campaigns (Beck and Sorauf, 1992:316). Indeed, there are substantial obstacles to party control of campaigns.

Candidates are encouraged to rely on their own personal campaign organizations by the direct primary system of nominations. Party organizations can rarely guarantee victory in the primaries for favored candidates. The direct primary, therefore, imposes a personal responsibility upon each candidate to create a campaign organization capable of winning the primary. This candidate organization is carried over to the general election because the resources of the party organization are seldom sufficient to ensure victory. The large numbers of offices that are contested as well as the frequency of elections in America strain and dilute the effectiveness of even the most dedicated and sophisticated party organizations.

Candidate independence from party organizations is also encouraged by the reduced role played by party affiliation in voter choices on election day. Voters commonly split their tickets—for example, on average 28 percent of voters in the 1980s cast ballots for candidates of different parties in presidential and House races (Wattenberg, 1991:38); and in ten of the thirty-five states with senatorial elections in 1992, voters elected a senator of a different party than carried their state in the presidential contest. In the American political culture, it is frequently advantageous not to be perceived as closely tied to a political party. Many voters glorify the candidate who stands above party.

New Campaign Technologies and Professional Management

Campaigns for major statewide offices, competitive congressional seats, and even some state legislative seats increasingly utilize the latest and most sophisticated campaign techniques and technologies. To a limited degree, as noted further on, state party organizations can provide candidates with essential campaign services. But state party organizations seldom have sufficient resources to provide all the services a candidate needs, and parties must assist a variety of candidates. As a result, candidates find it necessary to hire their own professional campaign consultants. With adequate financing, candidates now can create personal organizations that employ professionals capable of conducting polls, exploiting the persuasive qualities of the electronic media, targeting direct-mail advertising, and getting out the vote.

The candidates' need for surrogates for old-style machines and face-to-face campaigning thus has spawned a major industry—the professional campaign consulting firm (Sabato, 1981). These consultants are loosely affiliated with the parties in the sense that they work almost exclusively for only one party's candidates. But they work primarily for candidates, not parties, and hence tend to reduce the party role in modern campaigns and reinforce the tendency toward candidate-centered campaigns.

The Growth of PACs

Most commentary on the role of PACs in campaigns has focused on their role in congressional elections and their tendency to support incumbents. The expanding role of PACs is not, however, transforming campaigns only for the Senate and House; it is affecting races of state politics as well. All states permit corporations and unions to create PACs that solicit voluntary contributions from employees, stockholders, and members. As is true at the national level, industry and trade association PACs, in particular, have proliferated dramatically in the states. In New Jersey, for example, there was a 118 percent increase in the number of state-level PACs between 1983 and 1987 (Alexander, 1992:20). There are an estimated 12,000 PACs nationwide (Alexander, 1992:138). The level of PAC financing varies from state to state, but there is ample evidence that PACs are becoming an increasingly important source of campaign funds. For example, PACs constituted 62 percent of Colorado House candidate funds in 1986, 69 percent of Michigan legislative candidate funds in 1988, and 75 percent of Oregon legislative candidate funds in 1986 (Alexander, 1992:19).

State-level PACs contribute primarily to incumbents in an attempt to gain access and, unlike party organizations, do not focus their contributions on marginal legislative races. Thus, although they clearly compete with the parties for a role in legislative campaigns, PACs tend not to be involved in the struggle to effect changes in the composition of state legislatures (Jones, 1984).

State-Level Competitiveness and Incumbent Reelection
in Congressional and Legislative Races

Interparty Competition in Statewide Races. Across the country it is now possible for either party to win statewide elections. This is particularly true in presidential contests. For example, in 1988 the winning margin in twenty-one states was 54 percent or less of the popular vote, and in an additional fourteen states it was between 55 and 59 percent. With a national swing toward the Democrats in 1992, this level of competitiveness enabled Governor Bill Clinton to carry twenty-two states that had supported George Bush in 1988. Both the Republicans and the Democrats also have the capacity to win U.S. Senate and gubernatorial elections in virtually every state. This is true even of former one-party bastions such as the states of the Confederacy, where since 1966 only Georgia has failed to elect at least one Republican governor, and only Arkansas and Louisiana have failed to elect a Republican U.S. senator. Similarly, in traditional citadels of Republicanism such as Kansas, Maine, Nebraska, and North Dakota, the Democrats have won the governorship more frequently since the 1970s than the GOP. There is even evidence that, in the once solidly Democratic South, electoral competitiveness is seeping into lower-level state constitutional offices. Since 1988 the GOP has won statewide elections for Supreme Court judge, secretary of state, lieutenant governor, state treasurer, or railroad commissioner in Florida, North Carolina, and Texas.

Incumbent Advantage in Congressional and State Legislative Races. The results of most congressional and state legislative contests can be summarized in two words—"incumbents win!" Accordingly, only a limited proportion of House and state legislative seats normally change party control from election to election. Incumbent advantages make it difficult for both parties to recruit strong challengers to take on incumbents. This difficulty diminishes meaningful electoral competition and means that intense campaigns tend to be waged either in the small number of constituencies in which an incumbent may be considered vulnerable or in open seats, where no incumbent is seeking reelection (Jewell and Breaux, 1988).

Parties that for decades were the traditional minority parties within a state have had their greatest difficulty in achieving a competitive status in congressional and state legislative elections. For example, in spite of strong showings in gubernatorial elections, Democrats since 1968 have never controlled the Kansas Senate or the South Dakota House, and Republicans after the 1992 elections did not control a legislative chamber in the entire South. Indeed, GOP legislators remain a rare commodity in Alabama, Arkansas, Louisiana, and Mississippi.

The pattern of meaningful competition in statewide elections and incumbent reelection in congressional and state legislative contests is related to the increasingly candidate-centered nature of American politics. Inasmuch as statewide races tend to emphasize individual candidates instead of party affiliations, it is possible for either Democrats or Republicans to win gubernatorial and Senate contests in each of the fifty states. At the same time, incumbent members of the House and state legislatures have been able to use their offices to build both personal followings among the voters and personal campaign organizations (often heavily funded by PAC funds) to gain a high level of electoral security. It is within this two-tiered electoral system that state party organizations must operate.

THE INSTITUTIONALIZATION OF THE STATE PARTY AS A SERVICE AGENCY

In the late 1960s and early 1970s the conventional wisdom among political observers was that parties were in a state of decline. The likely future of parties seemed to be captured by the *Washington Post*'s ranking political reporter, David Broder, who entitled his 1971 book *The Party's Over* (Broder, 1971). The prophets of party demise, however, have been proven wrong. Since the 1960s American state party organizations have become more professionalized and organizationally stronger in the sense that they can provide campaign services to their candidates. They still do not control nominations because of the direct primary, but many are playing an important role in campaigns. The state parties have also become more closely integrated with the national party organizations and are being utilized by those organizations in presidential, senatorial, and congressional elections.

Striking parallels exist between party development within the states and the resurgence of party organizations that has occurred at the national level (see Chapter 3 of this volume). Like the Republican and Democratic National Committees, state central committees have strengthened their fund-raising capacities and developed the ability to provide services to candidates. There are also parallels between the major campaign role now played nationally by the congressional and senatorial campaign committees and the emergence of the state legislative campaign committees as the principal party campaign resource in legislative races.

The Demise of the Old-Style Organization

Powerful state party organizations capable of controlling nominations and based upon patronage continued to operate, particularly in the middle Atlantic states, New England, and lower Great Lakes states into the 1960s (Mayhew, 1986:205). However, a survey conducted by A. James Reichley (1992:383–384) in the mid-1980s revealed that this type of organization had almost ceased to exist. Civil service laws, the spread and strengthening of public employee unions, and adverse public opinion had severely weakened patronage systems. To these antipatronage forces was added the legal might of the Supreme Court. In a series of decisions, the Court made old-fashioned patronage operations that controlled thousands of nonpolicymaking jobs virtually illegal. In 1976, the Court ruled that the Cook County (Illinois) Democratic organization could not fire people on the basis of party affiliation (*Elrod v. Burns,* 427 U.S. 347). Then in 1990 the doctrine was extended in a case involving the Illinois GOP by a ruling that "party affiliation and support" could not be used as a basis for filling state jobs unless party affiliation was an "appropriate requirement" for the position (*Rutan v. Republican Party,* 488 U.S. 1872).

The comments of party leaders in once patronage-rich states confirm the demise of patronage as a basis for building an organization. An aide to Pennsylvania Governor Robert Casey lamented that "the unions and the civil service have just about put an end to patronage. We still have a personnel office that checks with county chairmen to fill what jobs we have. But the jobs just aren't there anymore" (quoted by Reichley, 1992:384). And the Illinois Democratic chair observed that "the party no longer functions as an employment agency. More and more, we must rely on the spirit of volunteerism that moves so many other organizations in American society" (quoted by Reichley, 1992:385).

Although state parties can no longer rely upon patronage jobs for party workers and funds, other types of patronage do remain important. Gubernatorial appointments to state boards and commissions with jurisdiction over professional licensing, gambling, highways, recreational facilities, environmental policy, universities, hospitals, and historical/cultural activities are much sought after by people seeking policy influence, recognition, public service, and material gain. Politics also often intrudes on state decisions regarding state contracts, bank deposits, economic development, and purchase of professional services. As Reichley observes, these types of preferments are useful primarily as a means of raising money for the party and candidates. However, these types of patronage do not provide campaign workers the way doling out patronage-type jobs did for the old-style organizations (Reichley, 1992:385).

To survive and perform a meaningful role in state politics, the parties have had to adapt to a changed environment characterized by (1) an absence of significant numbers of patronage-based workers, (2) candidate-centered campaigns often staffed by professional consultants and funded in significant degree by PACs, (3) heightened interparty competition for major statewide offices, and (4) strengthened national party organizations. In adapting to these late twentieth-century conditions, state party organizations have become service agencies for their candidates and local affiliates.

The Modern Service-Oriented Organization

Indicators of the evolution of most state parties into organizations capable of providing significant services to candidates and local parties include (1) permanent party headquarters, (2) professional leadership and staffing, and (3) adequate budgets and programs to maintain the organization, support candidates and office holders, and assist local party units (Cotter et al., 1984:13–40; Advisory Commission on Intergovernmental Relations, 1986; Reichley, 1992:386–391).

Permanent Headquarters. Even into the early 1970s state party headquarters often had an ad hoc quality and led a transitory existence. State chairmen frequently ran the party from their offices or homes and the headquarters moved from city to city depending upon the residence of the leader (Huckshorn, 1976:254–255). Today virtually every state party has a permanent headquarters increasingly housed in a modern office building equipped with high-tech equipment. The Florida GOP head-quarters, for example, operates with a budget of $6 million and is packed with computer hardware, telephone banks, and printing facilities (Barnes, 1989:70; Sabato, 1988:91).

Professional Staffing. In the 1960s it was common for a state headquarters to operate with minimal staff—often just a secretary or an executive director plus volunteers. Modern campaigning and party building, however, require more extensive and professional staffing. Virtually all state parties now have full-time professional leadership. Over 30 percent of state chairmen work full time in their positions, and almost all state parties have either a full-time chairman or an executive director (Cotter et al., 1984:16–19; Reichley, 1992:389).

The level of headquarters staffing fluctuates between election and non-election years, and depends upon the financial condition of the party. The basic trend since the 1960s, however, has been growth in the size of staffs and greater division of labor and specialization within the headquarters. In addition to the chairman and executive director, a reasonably well-staffed headquarters is likely to include the positions of finance director, political director, comptroller, communication director, field operatives, and clerical personnel. Although the state parties have made substantial progress in developing more professional staffs, they constantly face the problem of high turnover in leadership and staff positions. For example, state chairmen serve an average of only two to three years. Staff members normally stay in their positions for less than two years (Cotter et al. 1984:18). As professional political operatives, they move about the country from job to job with party organizations and candidates following leads frequently provided by either the Republican or Democratic national committees (Reichley, 1992:391–392).

Budgets. If state parties are to operate as service agencies to candidates and local organizations, they require augmented financial resources. This has been accomplished in most states by adopting sophisticated fund-raising techniques, including direct-mail (sustaining membership) programs to supplement more traditional methods such as dinners and large contributor solicitations. As a result, state party budgets have increased since the 1960s, with election year budgets in the mid-1980s averaging in excess of $1 million. In several states, party expenditures were well above the national average, for example, California Republicans, $10.7 million in 1984; New Jersey Republicans, $4.2 million in 1985; and Ohio Democrats, $2.3 million in 1984 (Reichley, 1992:388).

This pattern of significant fund raising by most Republican and Democratic state parties stands in contrast to that reported by Alexander Heard in his 1960 classic study of campaign finance. Heard reported that two-thirds of the Republican state committees had centralized fund-raising programs and that the Democrats had generally failed to develop regularized fund-raising operations (Heard, 1960:218–222, 228–229). Although the fund-raising capabilities of both parties have expanded substantially since Heard's study, Republican state committees do continue to lead their Democratic counterparts. The gap, however, appears to be narrowing.

Party Activities: Party Building and Candidate Support. Since the 1960s state parties have expanded their activities in both party building and candidate support. In the sphere of party building, a larger share of Republican and Democratic parties now have regularized fund-raising operations, conduct voter identification/list maintenance/get-out-the-vote programs, publish newsletters, assist local party units, engage in issue development, and utilize public opinion polling.

The active role of state parties in providing assistance to their candidates is shown in Table 2.1, which reports the results of a survey conducted by the Advisory Commission on Intergovernmental Relations (ACIR). The survey also reveals a pattern similar to that in party fund raising: The Republican state committees tend to be more active in supporting candidates than the Democrats (see also Reichley, 1992:389–390). One of the advantages of state party services to candidates is economy of scale. It is, therefore, often possible to provide services at a lower cost than would be the case if individual candidates were purchasing the services from consultants.

Although the state parties are organizationally stronger and provide a broader array of campaign services than in the past, their role in campaigns is supplementary to that of the candidates' own personal campaign organizations. The job of the party is normally to provide technical services—training, advertising, polling, and get-out-the-vote services—as well as funds and volunteers. For example, Republican state organizations frequently have major programs to make certain that their supporters cast absentee ballots when they will be out of town on election day. In 1988 the Florida GOP state organization spent $200,000 to send instructions on how to get an absentee ballot to 1 million voters (Babcock, 1988:A35).

Although state parties have been invigorated by adopting the service agency role, the adoption of this role also reveals the limits of their influence over nominations and campaigns in a candidate-centered age. With nominations in most constituencies in the hands of voters who select nominees in direct primaries, candidates must build personal organizations. And even the most party-oriented candidates view party services as supplementary to those developed within their own organizations. Witness the observations of U.S. Representative David Price (D-NC), a former

TABLE 2.1
Assistance Provided by State Parties to Candidates for State Office (in percent)

Assistance/Service Provided	Republican	Democratic
Financial contributions	90	70
Fund-raising assistance	95	63
Polling	78	50
Media consulting	75	46
Campaign seminars	100	76
Coordinating PAC contributions	52	31

Source: Advisory Commission on Intergovernmental Relations (1986:115).

state Democratic party chair and political scientist, who actively involved the party organization in his campaigns.

> Neither my recognition among party activists nor my wider exposure as a party spokesman gave me anything approaching a decisive edge in the Democratic primary. ... [The] nomination was not within the power of local, state, or national party organizations to deliver. I and my fledgling campaign team, including many active local Democrats, were largely on our own pursuing it. ... While my campaign thus evidenced relatively strong participation by ... party organizations, it could not ... be judged a party-centered campaign. (Price, 1992:140–141)

Republican-Democratic Differences. On the various indicators of party organizational strength considered in this section, Republican state committees generally score higher than do the Democrats. This is true in all sections of the country and normally the case even where the Republicans are a traditional minority party (Cotter et al., 1984:26–30; Jewell and Olson, 1988:63–70; Reichley, 1992:386–390).

This Republican organizational strength advantage is also present at the national level (Herrnson, 1990). It reflects not only a basic difference between the parties but also the fact that the party organization tends to be a more important campaign resource for Republican candidates than for Democrats. Democratic candidates and state organizations are more apt than their Republican counterparts to rely on the assistance of allied organizations such as labor unions, teachers, and social action groups (Cotter et al., 1984:137–141). These differences between the parties in their reliance upon allied organizations point up the need to view parties from a broadened perspective as encompassing more than the formal and legally constituted organization (see Schwartz, 1990). Because certain nonparty groups that are major players in campaign politics support almost exclusively the candidates of one party, the resources and activities of these groups should be factored into an assessment of state party organizational strength. Even the frequently maligned private campaign consultants should be considered part of a party's resource base because they are normally strong partisans who sell their services to either the Republicans or the Democrats, but not to both.

Party Organizational Strength and Election Outcomes. The organizational strength of state parties affects their ability to mobilize votes on election day and is a factor in determining the extent of interparty electoral competition within the states (Patterson and Caldeira, 1984). An analysis of gubernatorial elections has shown that the party with an organizational strength advantage over the opposition gains an incrementally higher percentage of the vote (Cotter et al., 1984:100–101). But improved party organizational strength does not necessarily lead to electoral victories. The relationship between party organizational strength and votes is complex and often indirect. In some cases, strong party structures—such as those of the Indiana Republicans, the Minnesota Democrats, and the Republicans and Democrats of Pennsylvania—have clearly contributed to their parties' electoral victories. In these instances, electoral success and the presence of meaningful competition have provided incentives to maintain the viability of party organizations. However, in other states in which one party has enjoyed a long history of electoral success, the dominant party may have little incentive to develop or maintain its organization. This was true of the Democratic party in the South until it was recently challenged by the Republican party. It is frequently the electorally weaker of the two parties that has the greater incentive to build an effective party organization as a first step toward gaining electoral victories. This has been the pattern of the Republican party in the South, where, after a period of organization building in the early 1960s, it now competes with the once-dominant Democratic party in statewide and a substantial proportion of congressional and legislative elections. Party organizational strength, therefore, can have long-term consequences. A strong party structure can provide the infrastructure for candidates and activists to continue competing until political conditions become more favorable. The Republicans of Florida, a long-time minority party in the state, provide an example. The party's organizational strength helped it take advantage of favorable circumstances to elect a governor in 1986 and U.S. senators in 1980 and 1988; gain a majority in the state's congressional delegation in 1988, 1990, and 1992; and achieve parity with the Democrats in the state Senate in 1992.

The Expanding Role of the State Legislative
Campaign Committees and Leadership PACs

The expanding role of state legislative campaign committees parallels the greatly increased involvement of the senatorial and congressional campaign committees at the national level (see Chapter 3). State legislative campaign committees, composed of incumbent legislators, operate in both the upper and lower chambers of most state legislatures. The emergence of legislative campaign committees in the 1970s as major participants in the state's electoral process came in response to legislators' need for additional campaign assistance in the face of rapidly increasing campaign costs, intensifying competition for control of legislative chambers, and rising uncertainty about election outcomes. The strongest legislative campaign committees are found in states with high levels of interparty competition, high campaign costs, or weak state central committees. Legislative campaign committees are least likely to operate in the South, where the Democrats continue to dominate legislative elections and many seats are still uncontested by the GOP. Some of the best-developed legislative campaign committees tend to be those of the Democrats, for example, in Indiana, Maine, Minnesota, and Wisconsin—all states in which the Democrats have weaker regular state organizations than the Republicans (Gierzynski, 1992:11–14).

Legislative campaign committees have become the principal party support organizations for legislative campaigns. Indeed, they are so active that in a number of instances they have become the party's strongest organization in the state, for example, in New York for both parties, and for the Democrats in Illinois. The committees tend to be led and dominated by party leaders in the legislative chambers and to operate independently of the state central committees, although there is some cooperation and coordination of campaign activities (Gierzynski, 1992:48–49). However, as Frank J. Sorauf has pointed out, legislative campaign committees are party organizations built by incumbents that serve primarily the agendas and priorities of legislative partisans and "insulate them from the pressures of other parts of their party. Collective action has helped to bring legislative parties freedom from the agendas of the presidential or gubernatorial parties" (Sorauf, 1992:120).

To raise money, legislative campaign committees often take advantage of the access of incumbent legislators and party leaders to PACs, lobbyists, and large contributors. Accordingly, the levels of expenditure by these committees can be substantial. For example, the Ohio Republican State Senate Caucus spent $3.6 million in 1988 on a "highly structured package of in-house polling, campaign managers, phone banks, media planning, issues research, and other campaign services."[1]

Legislative campaign committees are much more than incumbent-protection institutions. They tend to follow a strategy designed to achieve or maintain majority status in the legislative chambers. Resources are concentrated upon challengers to opposition party incumbents, open seat races, and incumbents in electoral trouble (Gierzynski, 1992:71–91; Stone-cash, 1988:477–494; Jones and Borris, 1985:89–106). The ability of these committees to help cause a change in party control of legislative chambers is, however, limited by the incumbents' substantial electoral advantages.

Unlike the situation with state central committees, in which the Republicans tend to be organizationally stronger, the Democratic legislative campaign committees do not seem to operate at a disadvantage. The explanation for the strength of these legislative campaign committees appears to stem from the Democrats' control of significantly more legislative chambers than the GOP. They have been able, therefore, to use incumbency and the power that goes with chamber control to raise more money for legislative campaigns than have the Republicans. In several states, the Democrats' effectiveness has been substantially enhanced by their alliance with activist teachers' unions (Gierzynski, 1992:56).

Although they started out as organizations that simply distributed money to candidates, the legislative campaign committees, like the state central committees, are increasingly campaign service agencies. In the words of the Ohio Senate Republican Caucus chief of staff, "We are a full service operation for individual campaigns."[2] That is, most of the campaign services are geared to the needs of individual candidates. The role of the legislative campaign committee was captured by the Speaker of the Wisconsin Assembly, Thomas Loftus. "We raised [money] to help Democrats running in marginal seats. In most cases we recruited the candidate. We provide training through campaign schools. We provide personnel and logistical support, issue papers, press releases, speakers for fund raisers, fund raisers themselves, and phone banks; we pay for the recount if it's a close race; we pay for the lawyer if it goes to court; if they have kids, we pay for the baby-sitter. ... We do everything a political party is supposed to do" (Loftus, 1985:100).

As Loftus has noted, campaign committees are not only affecting the types of campaigns candidates run through their control of resources but are affecting the pool of candidates through their recruitment efforts. These recruitment activities in turn affect the quality of candidates and the competitiveness of legislative races (Gierzynski, 1992:57).

A further basis for the enhanced role of the state legislative party has been the emergence of PACs controlled by legislative leaders who are in a position to raise more money than required for their own reelection. Leadership PACs tend to contribute primarily to marginal races and thus augment the role of legislative campaign committees. However, there are also states in which leaders have used their personal PACs to promote their own careers within the legislature rather than party electoral goals (Gierzynski, 1992:68).

Adapting to the PACs

PACs have customarily been considered a threat to political parties. However, simultaneous with their rise, state central committees have gained organizational strength and legislative campaign committees have become increasingly important. As has been true at the national level, state parties have learned to adapt to a political environment in which PACs are major players. Both the state central committees and the legislative campaign committees have worked closely with the PACs to channel PAC funds to candidates. In these efforts, the state committees have been aided by the fact that many state-level PACs are run by persons who are not specialists in electoral politics or by lobbyists who are specialists in the legislative process but not in statewide electoral strategies. The party is, therefore, in a position to provide PAC leaders with political intelligence.

In legislative races, the state legislative campaign committees have become increasingly adept at channeling PAC money. The executive assistant to the Speaker of the Indiana House, for example, observed that "for every one dollar we [the caucus committee] raise, we direct two dollars of interest group money"; and the president of the Maine Senate says that his committee performs a "matchmaking service" by "identifying a candidate's philosophy with PACs and connecting them" (quoted by Gierzynski, 1992:55). The legislative campaign committees are also in a position to give candidates legitimacy in the eyes of PAC leaders by committing their own resources in support of a candidate. As the Illinois House Republican Campaign Committee's executive director remarked, "If you're not targeted by the HRCC, most givers will not be willing to contribute (Gierzynski, 1992:55).

Ruth Jones, the leading expert on state campaign finance, has observed that by channeling PAC money to candidates, the parties have gotten "new funds into legislative campaigns that carried the imprimatur of the party at no direct expense to the party coffers" (Jones, 1984:197). State parties have also achieved coordination with PACs in providing in-kind services to candidates.

THE CHANGING RELATIONSHIP BETWEEN THE NATIONAL AND STATE PARTY ORGANIZATIONS

Until the late 1970s, most political scientists stressed fragmentation and dispersion of power as prominent characteristics of American parties. For example, V. O. Key (1964:334), the leading scholar of political parties in the postwar period, described the relationship between national and state parties as independent and confederative. The Republican and Democratic National Committees were dependent on state parties for financing and so lacking in power that a landmark study characterized them as "politics without power" (Cotter and Hennessy, 1964). During the 1970s and 1980s, however, the national committees were transformed into substantially more powerful institutions capable of exerting considerable influence over their state affiliates. This increased national party influence has resulted in greater integration and interdependence between the national and state party structures. It has also led to a strengthening of state parties as the national parties have poured resources into their state affiliates, utilizing them to achieve national party objectives.

Enforcement of National Party Rules

Since 1968 the Democratic party has intensified its efforts to ensure the loyalty of state parties toward the national ticket. Through a series of party reform commissions, the national party has developed detailed rules governing the method by which the state parties must select their national convention delegates. It has also implemented a National Democratic Charter, which contains prescriptions concerning the organization and operation of state parties. These national party rules have been vigorously enforced upon state parties, even against prominent party officials. For example, in 1972 an Illinois national convention delegation that had been handpicked by the leader of the Chicago Democratic organization, Mayor Richard J. Daley, was not seated at the convention because of failures to follow national party rules of delegation selection. Similarly, when Wisconsin Democrats failed in 1984 to comply with national party rules that banned the use of the state's traditional open presidential primary system to select national convention delegates, they were forced by the Democratic National Committee (DNC) to select their delegates via a party caucus system. The national committee's power to require compliance with its rules has been upheld in a series of Supreme Court decisions (e.g., *Cousins v. Wigoda*, 419 U.S. 477 [1975]; *Democratic Party of the United States v. Wisconsin ex rel La Follette*, 450 U.S. 107 [1981]).

In contrast to the Democrats, the GOP has not sought to gain influence over its state affiliates through rules enforcement. Instead, it has maintained the confederate legal structure of the party, and the Republican National Committee (RNC) has assumed a relatively permissive posture toward its state parties with regard to delegate-selection procedures and internal organization. Party centralization and integration have moved forward within the GOP by different means, however. The national party has gained power through providing assistance to its state organizations and their candidates (Bibby, 1981:102–155).

Providing Financial and Technical Assistance
to State Parties

The RNC's efforts to provide assistance to state parties started in a modest way while Ray C. Bliss was serving as national chairman (1965–1969).

They were greatly expanded by Chairman Bill Brock (1977–1981) and further augmented by his successors. The RNC has developed multimillion-dollar programs to provide cash grants, professional staff, data-processing services, and consulting services for organizational development, fund raising, campaigning, media, and redistricting. Major investments of money and personnel have been made to assist state parties in voter-list development and get-out-the vote efforts.

Beginning in 1978 the RNC entered the arena of state legislative elections (Bibby, 1979). In its initial effort, it spent $1.7 million to support legislative candidates and has continued the program in successive election cycles. The RNC has supplemented its legislative election activity with programs designed to persuade Democratic legislators to switch parties and join the GOP, mass mailings in key states urging Democratic voters to switch their party registrations, and cash grants to key county organizations. However, twelve years of Republican control of the White House between 1980 and 1992 tended to stunt the growth of state party assistance programs because the RNC focused upon maintaining control of the presidency.

The RNC's fund-raising advantage over the DNC enabled it to begin its program of assisting state parties well before the DNC followed suit. Its continuing financial advantage also has meant that the RNC's efforts have been much more extensive than those of the DNC. Under DNC chairmen Paul Kirk (1985–1989) and Ronald H. Brown (1989–1993), however, significant strides were made to narrow the RNC's fund-raising advantage and broaden the services provided to state parties. Kirk created and funded a Democratic Party Election Force of trained professionals in sixteen key states for the 1986 elections. In those states, the DNC paid for a full-time political operative and fund raiser. In exchange for these services, recipient state parties were required to sign agreements committing them to continue DNC-sponsored party-building programs and to cooperate with the DNC in matters relating to presidential nominating politics and national campaigns (Broder, 1986:A23).

Under Chairman Brown, the DNC strongly encouraged and supported the creation within the state parties of "Coordinated Campaign" structures to serve a broad range of candidates. The Coordinated Campaign organization is geared to provide basic campaign services such as voter registration, voter-list development, get-out-the-vote drives, polling, targeting, press relations, media purchasing, and scheduling to a wide range of Democratic candidates within a state. Coordinated Campaign organizations were funded with contributions from the DNC, state parties, candidates, in some instances legislative campaign committees, and key Democratic constituency groups like organized labor. In the 1990s, the

DNC supported Coordinated Campaign organizations in thirty-six states and continued and intensified the strategy in 1992 (Longley, 1992:8–9).

Instituting a Coordinated Campaign program within a state involves extensive negotiation among the cooperating state party units, candidates, and the DNC. DNC support and funding is always contingent upon its acceptance of the negotiated campaign plan. The level of national party involvement in the actual implementation of the Coordinated Campaign varies from state to state depending upon the institutional readiness of the state party organization. Thus in 1992 in Wisconsin (a state targeted by the Clinton-Gore organization and the Democratic Senatorial Campaign Committee), the state party was authorized by the DNC and Clinton-Gore organization to run the Coordinated Campaign because the state party was able to raise a large share of the costs and had staff experienced in running Coordinated Campaigns. However, in other states where the state organization was deemed incapable of running an effective Coordinated Campaign, the DNC brought in staff on a temporary basis to run the operation.

The Republicans have operated programs similar to the Democrats' Coordinated Campaign structures in recent elections. The GOP's Victory '92 organizations, operating under the legal aegis of state parties, drew funds from the RNC, Bush-Quayle organization, senatorial and congressional campaign committees, candidates, and state sources to operate voter identification and get-out-the-vote programs. In some instances, the RNC (which was controlled by Bush supporters from 1988 to 1992) took steps to place personnel capable of running Victory '92–type operations in state party headquarters. As one state chairman noted, the RNC "parachuted people into state headquarters around the country and they did this over a year in advance of the election to be sure that the operation was ready to go."[3]

State party assistance programs of in-kind services, financing, and campaign organizations like the DNC-sponsored Coordinated Campaign and the RNC's Victory '92 structures have in many instances strengthened the state parties by providing extremely valuable campaign assets; for example, state parties as a result of national party assistance have been able to develop and refine voter lists for get-out-the-vote drives. In addition, intraparty cohesion among party units and candidates' organizations has been fostered in some states through coordinated campaign efforts.

It should be clear, however, that national party assistance tends to flow to those state parties that are considered critical to achieving national party objectives in a given election cycle. Therefore, continuity of support from election cycle to election cycle is not ensured. A state party can be the favored beneficiary of national party largesse in one election cycle and be largely ignored in the next.

State parties, especially those with weak organizational structures, can be quite literally taken over by national party operatives in a presidential election year as staff are brought in to run the campaign efforts. These campaign operatives and their supporting resources are normally pulled out as soon as the election is over; the state organization may not, therefore, be strengthened in any significant way by the national party's involvement.

National-to-State Party Fund Transfers and the FECA

During the 1980s and 1990s large-scale transfers of funds have been made from national party organizations to state and local organizations. In addition, the national party organizations have channeled direct contributions from large givers to party organizations in states considered critical to winning presidential, senatorial, and House elections. It is estimated that in 1988, $55 million was solicited for state parties to spend in support of the candidacies of George Bush and Michael Dukakis. Table 2.2, derived from Federal Election Commission (FEC) data, demonstrates that national party funds flowed profusely to state parties again in 1992 in the form of direct transfers of dollars, contributions to state and local candidates, and, most important, to support joint activities being run under the legal sponsorship of the state parties (i.e., the Republicans' Victory '92 and the Democrats' Coordinated Campaigns supporting federal and state candidates). Money the national parties use for these purposes is normally referred to as "soft money"—money raised outside of the restrictions of federal law but nonetheless intended to influence federal elections (Sorauf, 1992:147). Soft money is held in nonfederal accounts, which are separate from the federal accounts ("hard money") used for direct contributions to or expenditures on behalf of federal candidates.

The transfers of funds from the national to state levels documented in Table 2.2 have been encouraged by the Federal Election Campaign Act (FECA), which imposes strict limits on the amount of money national party organizations can spend on behalf of candidates for federal office. However, 1979 amendments to the FECA permitted state and local parties to spend without limit on "party-building activities" such as voter registration, phone banks, facilities, and get-out-the-vote drives. Since national party organizations are now capable of raising more money than they can legally spend on federal elections, they have used their "surplus" funds to support state level "party-building" activities.

As was noted previously, in some instances these party-building activities are actually operated by the state parties with national party assistance. But in states where the state party is deemed by the national party to lack the capacity to run an effective party-building operation, the state

TABLE 2.2
Disbursements from Nonfederal Accounts, 1991–1992 (in $)

	Transfers to State Parties	Contributions to State/Local Candidates	Share of Joint Activity[a]
Republicans			
RNC	5,371,110	1,247,000	17,853,015
NRSC	1,674,603	0	4,055,306
NRCC	1,732,150	n/a	600,602
Total	8,777,863	1,247,000	22,508,923
Democrats			
DNC	9,458,112	212,091	16,318,348
DSCC	0	0	0
DCCC	34,550	565,781	1,641,614
Total	9,492,662	777,872	17,959,962

[a]Joint activity includes such party-building activities as voter-registration drives, voter-list development, and get-out-the-vote drives.
Source: Federal Election Commission.

party is merely the legal entity (often a check-writing vehicle to pay campaign vendors) through which the national party operates in pursuit of its electoral goals.

With the FECA encouraging the national party organizations to channel funds to state parties in an effort to influence the outcome of federal elections, the state parties are being integrated into the national campaign structure to play a significant role in presidential, Senate, and House elections. Accordingly, the distinction that is commonly made between state and national party organizations and between the candidate's personal organization and the party organization has been blurred at the state level. As Sorauf has noted, the use of nonfederal accounts—soft money— as a strategy for funding elections reflects several "very American institutions or conditions." First, soft money is a creature of American federalism in that both the national government and the states regulate campaign finance, but the states choose to regulate less vigorously. Second, the soft money strategy "reflects the indivisibility of national and local politics" and the fact that money spent by state parties on such activities as voter registration in some measure helps party candidates for national office as well as state candidates. And third, the soft money strategy reflects intentional congressional concessions to American grass-roots politics (Sorauf, 1992:148).

Party Integration and Nationalizing Campaign Efforts

As earlier noted, the national party committees have used their resources and legal authority to nationalize the parties' campaign efforts. Leon

Epstein has characterized this process as being analogous to the categorical grant-in-aid programs that the federal government has used to enlist state governments in achieving national policy objectives. Like the federal government, which requires state and local governments to comply with federal guidelines in order to receive grants-in-aid, the RNC and DNC attach conditions—albeit quite flexible ones—to the assistance they give to state parties and candidates (Epstein, 1986:223). In the process, the national parties have achieved greatly increased influence over their state parties.

Through their programs of financial and technical assistance to state parties and their support of party-building activities, the RNC and DNC have reversed the direction of resource flow from what it was prior to the 1970s. In the past, funds flowed from the state parties to the national committees, and with those funds went substantial state party influence over the activities of the national committees. As Alexander Heard accurately observed, however, "any changes that freed the national party committees of financial dependence on state organizations could importantly affect the loci of party power" and enable the parties to develop "a more cohesive operational structure" (Heard, 1960:294). The power shift that Heard foresaw in 1960 has occurred. Now that the national committees are able to raise unprecedented amounts of money and then allocate some of those funds to their state affiliates, the RNC and DNC have gained substantial autonomy as well as leverage over the state parties. In the process, of course, state parties have lost a significant amount of their traditional autonomy.

National-to-state transfers of funds, joint campaign activities, and technical assistance have also meant that substantially heightened levels of integration have been achieved between the two strata of party organizations. This heightened level of intraparty integration as well as the nationalizing of party campaign efforts that has occurred since the 1970s constitute changes of major proportions in the American party system. No serious observer of American political parties can any longer assert, as did the author of the leading 1960s text on the subject, that "no nationwide party organization exists. ... Rather, each party consists of a working coalition of state and local parties" (Key, 1964:315). Thanks in part to the assistance provided by the national party committees, state parties have undergone a process of strengthening. At the same time, however, they have grown increasingly dependent on the national party organizations and have lost some of their traditional autonomy.

STATE ELECTIONS AND NATIONAL POLITICS

Although state parties are organizationally stronger now than they were in the 1960s, their electoral fortunes are affected by factors over which they have little control, including national-level influences such as economic conditions, presidential popularity, and public perceptions of the national parties. And as partisan loyalties are normally kindled in the fires of presidential campaigns, it is extremely difficult for a state party to sustain a public image in state politics that is at odds with its national image. An example can be found in the Democratic parties in the South, which traditionally sought to project a policy posture to the right of the national party and its presidential nominees. This disparity between the national party and state parties, along with the changing population and economy of the region, allowed Republican presidential candidates—Eisenhower, Nixon, and Goldwater—to win key southern states in the 1950s and 1960s. These Republican inroads were followed by significant Republican victories in gubernatorial, senatorial, and congressional elections after the mid-1960s. Although the Republicans have made only limited gains in state constitutional offices and state legislatures, the electoral alignment of southern voters is becoming increasingly congruent with that of the rest of the nation.

Analyses of the relationship between presidential and state legislative election outcomes have shown that state legislative elections are affected by the drawing power of the parties' presidential candidates (Campbell, 1986:45–65). In an effort to insulate state elections from such national influences, almost three-quarters of the states have scheduled elections for governor and state constitutional offices, as well as for the state legislature in nonpresidential election years. Despite the reformers' best intentions, national economic and political conditions continue to intrude and to play a significant role even during these off-year elections (Chubb, 1988:113–154). In every off-year election since World War II (with the exception of 1986), the president's party has lost governors, just as it has also lost seats in the House of Representatives. The magnitude of gubernatorial losses, however, has often been much greater than in the House. The vulnerability of governors in midterm elections reflects both the competitive nature of statewide races in most states and the high visibility of governors within their states. As the most visible figures on midterm election ballots, they are likely to be held accountable for the state of their states and to be convenient targets for discontented voters (Bibby, 1983:111–132).

THE ADAPTABLE AND ENDURING STATE PARTY

State parties entered the 1990s substantially changed and stronger than they had been three decades earlier. They adapted to the challenges posed by candidate-centered campaigning and the development of PACs as major candidate-support mechanisms. They also became more closely integrated into the national parties' campaign structures. A series of judicial decisions hold the potential for freeing them from the most onerous of state regulations so that they will have greater flexibility in achieving their objectives.

Although this record of adaptability and durability of state parties is impressive, the American political environment is not conducive to strong European-style parties capable of controlling nominations and running political campaigns. From a cross-national perspective, therefore, American state parties appear to be rather modest political organizations that supplement the personal campaign organizations of candidates.

Probably the most significant question concerning the future of the state parties relates to the evolution of their relations with increasingly strong national party organizations. The national parties now give extensive assistance to and exert unprecedented influence over their state affiliates. Their priorities, however, are not necessarily identical to those of the state organizations—a situation that is apt to be a source of continuing tension. Furthermore, national party finances may not continue to grow as they did in the 1970s, 1980s, and into the 1990s. As a result, the national committees may not be able to provide assistance to the states at the level or with the regularity that the state parties have come to expect. Such a development would slow the process of party integration and perhaps cause some weakening of the state parties. The national-state party relationship could also be dramatically affected by changes in federal campaign finance legislation that restricted the use of soft money. Given their demonstrated resiliency and adaptability, however, state parties doubtless will continue to be significant participants in the electoral process.

NOTES

1. "Guru in Ohio," *Congressional Quarterly Weekly Report*, November 4, 1989.
2. Ibid.
3. Interview with author.

3

The Revitalization of National Party Organizations

PAUL S. HERRNSON

Once characterized as poor, unstable, and powerless, national party organizations in the United States are now financially secure, institutionally stable, and highly influential in election campaigns and in their relations with state and local party committees. The national party organizations— the Democratic and Republican national, congressional, and senatorial campaign committees—have adapted to the candidate-centered, money-driven, "high-tech" style of modern campaign politics. This essay examines the development of the national party organizations, their evolving relations with other party committees, and their role in contemporary elections.

PARTY ORGANIZATIONAL DEVELOPMENT

Origins of the National Parties

The birth and subsequent development of the national party organizations were the outgrowth of forces impinging on the parties from the broader political environment and of pressures emanating from within the parties themselves. The Democratic National Committee (DNC) was formed during the Democratic national convention of 1848 for the purpose of organizing and directing the presidential campaign, promulgating the call for the next convention, and tending to the details associated with setting up future conventions (see Cotter and Hennessy, 1964). The Republican National Committee (RNC) was created in 1856 at an ad hoc meeting of future Republicans for the purposes of bringing the Republican party into existence and conducting election-related activities similar to those performed by its Democratic counterpart. The creation of the national committees was an important step in a process that transformed the

45

parties' organizational apparatuses from loosely confederative structures to more centralized, federal organizations.

The congressional campaign committees were created in response to electoral insecurities that were heightened as a result of factional conflicts that developed within the two parties following the Civil War. The National Republican Congressional Committee (NRCC) was formed in 1866 by Radical Republican members of the House who were feuding with President Andrew Johnson. The House members believed they could not rely on either the president or the RNC for assistance, so they created their own campaign committee to assist with their elections and to distance themselves from the president. As is often the case in politics, organization begot counterorganization. Following the Republican example, pro-Johnson Democrats formed their own election committee—the Democratic Congressional Campaign Committee (DCCC).

Senate leaders created the senatorial campaign committees in 1916 after the Seventeenth Amendment transformed the upper chamber into a popularly elected body. The Democratic Senatorial Campaign Committee (DSCC) and the National Republican Senatorial Committee (NRSC) were founded to assist incumbent senators with their reelection campaigns. Like their counterparts in the House, the Senate campaign committees were established during a period of political upheaval—the Progressive Movement—to assuage members' electoral insecurities during an era of exceptionally high partisan disunity and political instability.

The six national party organizations have not possessed abundant power during most of their existence. Flowcharts of the party organizations are generally pyramid-like, with the national conventions at the apex, the national committees directly below them, the congressional and senatorial campaign committees (also known as the Hill committees) branching off the national committees, and the state and local party apparatus placed below the national party apparatus (see, e.g., Frantzich, 1989). However, power is not, and has never been, distributed hierarchically. Throughout most of the parties' history, and during the height of their strength (circa the late nineteenth and early twentieth centuries), power was concentrated at the local level, usually in countywide political machines. Power mainly flowed up from county organizations to state party committees and conventions, and then to the national convention. The national, congressional, and senatorial campaign committees had little, if any, power over state and local party leaders (Cotter and Hennessy, 1964).

Local party organizations are reputed to have possessed tremendous influence during the golden age of political parties. Old-fashioned political machines had the ability to unify the legislative and executive branches of local and state governments. The machines also had a great deal of influence in national politics and with the courts. The machines' power was principally rooted in their virtual monopoly over the tools needed to run a successful campaign. Party bosses had the power to award the party nominations to potential candidates. Local party committees also possessed the resources needed to communicate with the electorate and mobilize voters (Bruce, 1927; Merriam, 1923; Sait, 1927; Sorauf, 1980).

Nevertheless, party campaigning was a cooperative endeavor during the golden age, especially during presidential election years. Although individual branches of the party organization were primarily concerned with electing candidates within their immediate jurisdictions, party leaders at different levels of the organization had a number of reasons to work together (Ostrogorski, 1964; Schattschneider, 1942). They recognized that ballot structures and voter partisanship linked the electoral prospects of their candidates. Party leaders further understood that electing candidates to federal, state, and local governments would enable them to maximize the patronage and preferments they could exact for themselves and their supporters. Party leaders were also conscious of the different resources and capabilities possessed by different branches of the party organization. The national party organizations, and especially the national committees, had the financial, administrative, and communications resources needed to coordinate and set the tone of a nationwide campaign (Merriam, 1923; Sait, 1927; Bruce, 1927; Kent, 1923). Local party committees had the proximity to voters needed to collect electoral information, conduct voter registration and get-out-the-vote drives, and perform other grass-roots campaign activities (Merriam, 1923). State party committees had relatively modest resources, but they occupied an important intermediate position between the other two strata of the party organization. State party leaders channeled electoral information up to the national party organizations and arranged for candidates and other prominent party leaders to speak at local rallies and events (Sait, 1927). Relations between the national party organizations and other branches of the party apparatus were characterized by negotiation and compromise rather than by command. Party organizations in Washington, D.C., did not dominate party politics during the golden age. They did, however, play an important role in what were essentially party-centered election campaigns.

Party Decline

The transition from a party-dominated system of campaign politics to a candidate-centered system was brought about by legal, demographic, and technological changes in American society as well as by reforms instituted by the parties themselves. The direct primary and civil service regulations instituted during the Progressive era deprived party bosses of their ability to handpick nominees and reward party workers with government jobs and contracts (see, e.g., Key, 1958; Roseboom, 1970). The reforms weakened the bosses' hold over candidates and political activists, and encouraged candidates to build their own campaign organizations.

Demographic and cultural changes reinforced this pattern. Increased education and social mobility, declining immigration, and a growing national identity contributed to the erosion of the close-knit, traditional ethnic neighborhoods that formed the core of the old-fashioned political machine's constituency. Voters began to turn toward nationally focused mass media and away from local party committees for their political information (Ranney, 1975; Kayden and Mahe, 1985; McWilliams, 1981). Growing preferences for movies, radio, and televised entertainment underscored this phenomenon by reducing the popularity of rallies, barbecues, and other types of interpersonal communication at which old-fashioned political machines excelled.[1] These changes combined to deprive the machines of their political bases and to render many of their communications and mobilization techniques obsolete.

The adaptation of technological innovations developed in the public relations field to the electoral arena further eroded candidates' dependence on party organizations. Advancements in survey research, computerized data processing, and mass media advertising provided candidates with new tools for gathering information about voters and communicating messages to them. The emergence of a new corps of campaigners—the political consultants—enabled candidates to hire nonparty professionals to run their campaigns (Agranoff, 1972; Sabato, 1981). Direct-mail fundraising techniques helped candidates raise the money needed to pay their campaign staffs and outside consultants. These developments helped to transform election campaigns from party-focused, party-conducted affairs into events that revolved around individual candidates and their campaign organizations.

Two recent developments that initially appeared to weaken party organizations and reinforce the candidate-centeredness of American elections were party reforms introduced by the Democrats' McGovern-Fraser Commission and the Federal Election Campaign Act of 1971 (FECA) and its amendments. The McGovern-Fraser reforms and reforms instituted by later Democratic reform commissions were designed to make the presidential nominating process more open and more representative. One side effect of the reforms was that it was more difficult for long-time "party regulars" to attend national party conventions or play a significant role in other party activities. They also made it easier for issue and candidate activists who had little history of party service (frequently labeled "purists" or "amateurs") to play a larger role in party politics. The rise of the "purists" led to tensions over fundamental issues such as whether winning elections or advancing particular policies should have priority (Wilson, 1962; Polsby and Wildavsky, 1984). Heightened tensions made coalition building among party activists and supporters more difficult. Intraparty conflicts between purists and professionals, and the purists' heavy focus on the agendas of specific candidates and special interests, also resulted in the organizational needs of the parties being neglected. The reforms were debilitating to both parties, but they were more harmful to the Democratic party, which had introduced them (Ranney, 1975; Polsby, 1983; Polsby and Wildavsky, 1984).

The FECA also had some negative effects on the parties. The FECA's contribution and expenditure limits increased disclosure provisions, and other regulatory requirements forced party committees to keep separate bank accounts for state and federal election activity. The reforms had the immediate effect of discouraging state and local party organizations from fully participating in federal elections (Price, 1984; Kayen and Mahe, 1985). The FECA also set the stage for the tremendous proliferation of political action committees (PACs) that began in the late 1970s. The Federal Election Commission's SunPAC Advisory in 1976 provided a gateway for PACs to become the major organized financiers of congressional elections (Alexander, 1984).

Progressive reforms, demographic and cultural transformations, new campaign technology, recent party reforms, and campaign finance legislation combined to reduce the roles that party organizations played in elections and to foster the evolution of a candidate-centered election system. Under this system, candidates typically assembled their own campaign organizations, first to compete for their party's nomination and then to contest the general election. In the case of presidential elections, a candidate who succeeded in securing the party's nomination also won control of the national committee. The candidate's campaign organization directed most national committee election activity. In congressional elections, most campaign activities were carried out by the candidate's own organization both before and after the primary. The parties' seeming inability to adapt to the new "high-tech," money-driven style of campaign politics resulted in their being pushed to the periphery of the election process. These trends were accompanied by a general decline in the parties' ability to structure political choice (Carmines, Renten, and Stimson, 1984; Beck, 1984), to furnish symbolic referents and decisionmaking cues for voters (Burnham, 1970; Ladd and Hadley, 1975; Nie, Verba, and Petrocik, 1976 [1979]; Wattenberg, 1984), and to foster party unity among elected officials (Deckard, 1976; Keefe, 1976; Clubb, Flanigan, and Zingale, 1980).

National Party Reemergence

Although the party decline was a gradual process that took its greatest toll on party organizations at the local level, party renewal occurred over a relatively short period and was focused primarily in Washington, D.C. The dynamics of recent national party organizational development bear parallels to changes that occurred in earlier periods. The content of recent national party organizational renewal was shaped by the changing needs of candidates. The new-style campaigning that became prevalent during the 1960s placed a premium on campaign activities requiring technical expertise and in-depth research. Some candidates were able to run a viable campaign using their own funds or talent. Others turned to political consultants, PACs, and special interests for help. However, many candidates found it difficult to assemble the money and expertise needed to compete in a modern election. The increased needs of candidates for greater access to technical expertise, political information, and money created an opportunity for national and some state party organizations to become the repositories of these electoral resources (Schlesinger, 1985).

Nevertheless, national party organizations did not respond to changes in the political environment until electoral crises forced party leaders to recognize the institutional and electoral weaknesses of the national party organizations. As was the case during earlier eras of party transformation, crises that heightened office holders' electoral anxieties furnished party leaders with the opportunities and incentives to augment the parties' organizational apparatuses. Entrepreneurial party leaders recognized that they might receive payoffs for restructuring the national party organizations so that they could better assist candidates and state and local party committees with their election efforts.[2]

The Watergate scandal and the trouncing that Republican candidates experienced in the 1974 and 1976 elections created a crisis of competition that was the catalyst for change at the Republican national party organizations. The Republicans lost 49 seats in the House in 1974, had an incumbent president defeated two years later, and controlled only twelve governorships and four state legislatures by 1977. Moreover, voter identification with the Republican party (which had previously been climbing) dropped precipitously, especially among voters under 35 (Malbin, 1975).

The crisis of competition drew party leaders' attention to the weaknesses of the Republican national, congressional, and senatorial campaign committees. After a struggle that became entwined with the politics surrounding the race for the RNC chair, William Brock, an advocate of party organizational development, was selected to head the RNC. Other party-building entrepreneurs were selected to chair the party's other two national organizations: Representative Guy Vander Jagt of

Michigan took the helm of the NRCC in 1974, and Senator Robert Packwood of Oregon became chair of the NRSC in 1976.[3] The three party leaders initiated a variety of programs aimed at promoting the institutional development of their committees, increasing the committees' electoral presence, and providing candidates with campaign money and services. All three leaders played a major role in reshaping the missions of the national parties and in placing them on a path that would result in their organizational transformation.

The transformation of the Democratic national party organizations has been more complicated than that of their Republican counterparts because DNC institutionalization occurred in two distinct phases. The first phase of DNC development, which is often referred to as *party reform* and associated with party decline, was concerned with enhancing the representativeness and openness of the national committee and the presidential nominating convention. The second phase, which resembles the institutionalization of the Republican party organizations and is frequently referred to as *party renewal,* focused on the committee's institutional and electoral capabilities.

Democratic party reform followed the tumultuous 1968 Democratic National Convention. Protests on the floor of the convention and in the streets of Chicago constituted a factional crisis that underscored the deep rift between liberal, reform-minded "purists" and "party regulars." The crisis and the party's defeat in November created an opportunity for major party organizational change. The McGovern-Fraser Commission and later reform commissions introduced rules that made the delegate-selection process more participatory and led to the unexpected proliferation of presidential primaries; increased the size and demographic representativeness of the DNC and the national convention; instituted midterm issue conferences (which were discontinued by Paul Kirk after his selection as DNC chair in 1984); and resulted in the party adoption of a written charter. Some of these changes are believed to have been a major cause of party decline (see, e.g., Crotty, 1983).

Other changes may have been more positive. Upon adopting the decisions of the McGovern-Fraser Commission, the DNC took on a new set of responsibilities that concerned state party compliance with national party rules governing participation in the delegate-selection process. The expansion of DNC rule-making and enforcement authority has resulted in the committee usurping the power to overrule state party activities connected with the process that are not in compliance with national party rules.[4] This represents a fundamental shift in the distribution of power between the national committee and state party organizations. Democratic party reform transformed the DNC into an important agency of intraparty regulation and increased committee influence in both party and presidential politics.

The second phase of Democratic national party institutionalization followed the party's massive defeat in the 1980 election. The defeat of incumbent President Jimmy Carter, the loss of 34 House seats (half of the party's margin), and the loss of control of the Senate constituted a crisis of competition that was the catalyst for change within the Democratic national party organizations. Unlike the previous phase of national party development, Democratic party renewal was preceded by widespread agreement among DNC members, Democrats in Congress, and party activists that the party needed to increase its competitiveness by imitating the GOP's party-building and campaign service programs (Cook, 1981).

The issue of party renewal was an important factor in the selection of Charles Manatt as DNC chair and Representative Tony Coelho as DCCC chair in 1980. It also influenced Democratic senators' choice of Lloyd Bentsen of Texas to chair the DSCC in 1982. All three party leaders were committed to building the national party organizations' fund-raising capabilities, improving their professional staffs and organizational structures, and augmenting the Republican party-building model to suit the specific needs of Democratic candidates and of state and local Democratic committees. Like their Republican counterparts, all three Democratic leaders played a critical role in promoting the institutionalization of the Democratic national party organizations.

INSTITUTIONALIZED NATIONAL PARTIES

The institutionalization of the national party organizations refers to their becoming fiscally solvent, organizationally stable, and larger and more diversified in their staffing and to their adopting professional-bureaucratic decisionmaking procedures. These changes were necessary for the national parties to develop election-related and party-building functions.

Finances

National party fund raising improved greatly in the late 1970s and 1980s. During this period the national parties raised more money from more sources and using more varied approaches than ever before. The information presented in Table 3.1 indicates that the Republican committees raised more money than did their Democratic rivals in all seven election cycles (but also that, following the 1980 election, the Democrats began to narrow the gap in fund raising). The GOP's financial advantage reflects a number of factors. The Republican committees began developing their direct-mail solicitation programs earlier and have had a more businesslike approach to fund raising. The greater wealth and homogeneity of their

TABLE 3.1
National Party Receipts, 1976–1992 (in million $)

Party	1976	1978	1980	1982	1984	1986	1988	1990	1992
Democrats									
DNC	13.1	11.3	15.4	16.5	46.6	17.2	52.3	14.5	65.8
DCCC	.9	2.8	2.9	6.5	10.4	12.3	12.5	9.1	12.8
DSCC	1.0	.3	1.7	5.6	8.9	13.4	16.3	17.5	25.5
Total	15.0	14.4	20.0	28.6	65.9	42.9	81.1	41.1	104.1
Republicans									
RNC	29.1	34.2	77.8	84.1	105.9	83.8	91.0	68.7	85.4
NRCC	12.1	14.1	20.3	58.0	58.3	39.8	34.5	33.8	34.4
NRSC	1.8	10.9	22.3	48.9	81.7	86.1	65.9	65.1	72.3
Total	43.1	59.2	120.4	191.0	245.9	209.7	191.4	167.6	192.1

Source: Federal Election Commission.

supporters also makes it easier for the Republican committees to raise money. Finally, the Republicans' minority status also provides them with a powerful fund raising weapon. Negative appeals, featuring attacks on those in power, are generally more successful in fund raising than are appeals advocating the maintenance of the status quo (Godwin, 1988). Although Republican fund raising appears to have reached a plateau and the Democrats have made strides in improving their fund-raising programs, whether the Democratic national party organizations will be able to catch up to the GOP committees remains questionable.

Most national party money is raised in the form of direct-mail contributions of under $100. Telephone solicitations also are used to raise both small and large contributions. Traditional fund-raising dinners, parties, and other events experienced a revival as important vehicles for collecting large contributions from individual donors during the 1988 election. Sometimes individuals will contribute to a party organization's building fund or some other nonfederal, "soft money" account such as the Republicans' Victory '92 or the Democratic Victory Fund.[5] These accounts enable wealthy individuals to make contributions in excess of the FECA's contribution limits (Drew, 1983; Sorauf, 1988; Jackson, 1988). In August 1992, for example, Seagram's liquor company executive Edgar Bronfman gave the RNC a check for $150,000; philanthropist Swanee Hunt, software developers Peter and Eileen Norton, and Axem Resources executive Merle Chambers gave the DNC over $200,000 (Babcock, 1992).

PACs also give substantial sums of money to the national party organizations. Many PACs pay dues of up to $5,000 per year to belong to one of the national committees' labor or business councils, the DCCC's Speaker's Club, the DSCC's Leadership Council, the NRCC's Congressional Leadership Council, the NRSC's Senate Trust Club, or some other "club" created by one of the national party organizations for the purpose of raising large contributions. In return for their donations, club members get the opportunity to meet with members of Congress and other prominent party officials. Club members also receive electoral briefings from the committees and other useful "perks." The existence of these clubs is indicative of the symbiotic nature of the relationships that exist between the national parties and many PACs (Sabato, 1984; Herrnson, 1988).

Infrastructure

Success in fund raising has enabled the national parties to invest in the development of their organizational infrastructures. Prior to their institutionalization, the national party organizations had no permanent headquarters. For a while, the four Hill committees were quartered in small offices in congressional office buildings. Upon leaving congressional office space they became transient, following the national committees' example of moving at the end of each election cycle in search of cheap office space. The national parties' lack of permanent office space created security problems, made it difficult for them to conduct routine business, and did little to bolster their standing in Washington (Cotter and Hennessy, 1964).

All six national party organizations are now housed in party-owned headquarters buildings located only a few blocks from the Capitol. The headquarters buildings furnish the committees with convenient locations for carrying out fund-raising events and holding meetings with candidates, PACs, journalists, and campaign consultants. They also provide a secure environment for the committees' computers, records, and radio and television studios. The multimillion-dollar studios, each of which is owned by one of the congressional campaign committees, allow the parties to produce professional-quality campaign commercials for their candidates (see, e.g., Herrnson, 1988).

Staff

Each national party organization has a two-tiered structure consisting of members and professional staff. The members of the Republican and Democratic national committees are selected by their state parties, and the members of the Hill committees are selected by their colleagues in Congress. The national parties' staffs have grown tremendously in recent years. Republican committee staff development accelerated following the party's Watergate scandal, whereas the Democratic party experienced most of its staff growth after the 1980 election. In 1992 the DNC, DCCC, and DSCC employed 270, 64, and 35 full-time staff, respectively, whereas their Republican counterparts had 300, 89, and 135 full-time employees.[6] Committee staffs are divided along functional lines; different divisions are responsible for administration, fund raising, research, communications, and campaign activities. The staffs have a great deal of autonomy in running the committees and are extremely influential in formulating their campaign strategies. In the case of the NRCC, for example, committee members have adopted a "hands-off" attitude toward committee operations similar to that of a board of directors (Herrnson, 1989).

Relationships with PACs and Political Consultants

Although it was first believed that the rise of political consultants and the proliferation of PACs would hasten the decline of parties (Sabato, 1981; Crotty, 1984; Adamany, 1984), recent evidence suggests that political consultants and PACs are seeking to cooperate with the political parties rather than to destroy them (Herrnson, 1988; Sabato, 1988). National party organizations, consultants, and PACs frequently work together in pursuit of their common goals. Fund raising constitutes one area of party-PAC cooperation; the dissemination of information and the backing of particular candidates constitute others. National party organizations handicap races for PACs and arrange "meet and greet" sessions for PACs and candidates. The national parties also mail, telephone, and "fax" large quantities of information to PACs in order to keep them abreast of developments in competitive elections. PAC managers use party information when formulating their contributions strategies.

Relations between the national party organizations and political consultants have also become more cooperative. During election years, the national parties facilitate contacts and agreements between their candidates and political consultants. The parties also hire outside consultants to assist with polling and advertising, and to furnish candidates with campaign services. During nonelection years, the parties hire private consultants to assist with long-range planning. These arrangements enable the parties to draw upon the expertise of the industry's premier consulting firms and provide the consultants with steady employment, which is especially important between election cycles.

The symbiotic relationships that have developed among the national parties, political consultants, and PACs can be further appreciated by looking at the career paths of people working in electoral politics. Employment at one of the national party organizations can now serve as a stepping stone or a high point in the career of a political operative. It is common for the parties to hire past employees and their firms to conduct research, give strategic or legal advice, or provide campaign services to candidates. The "revolving door" of national party employment provides political professionals with opportunities to gain experience, make connections, establish credentials that can help them move up the hierarchy of political consultants, and maintain profitable relationships with the national parties after they have gained employment elsewhere.

Party Building

The institutionalization of the national party organizations has provided them with the resources to develop a variety of party-building programs. The vast majority of these are conducted by the two national committees. Many current RNC party-building efforts were initiated in 1976 under the leadership of Chairman Brock. Brock's program for revitalizing state party committees consisted of (1) appointing regional political directors to assist state party leaders in strengthening their organizations and utilizing RNC services; (2) hiring organizational directors to help rebuild state party organizations; (3) appointing regional finance directors to assist state parties with developing fund-raising programs; (4) making computer services available to state parties for accounting, fund raising, and analyzing survey data; and (5) organizing a task force to assist parties with developing realistic election goals and strategies. Brock also established a Local Elections Campaign Division to assist state parties with creating district profiles and recruiting candidates, to provide candidate training and campaign management seminars, and to furnish candidates for state or local office with on-site campaign assistance (Bibby, 1981; Conway, 1983).

Frank Fahrenkopf, RNC chair from 1981 to 1988, expanded many of Brock's party-building programs and introduced some new ones. The national committee continues to give Republican state parties financial assistance and to help them with fund raising.[7] An RNC computerized information network created during the 1984 election cycle furnishes Republican state and local party organizations and candidates with issue and opposition research, newspaper clippings, and other sorts of electoral information. RNC publications, such as "First Monday" and "County Line," provided Republican candidates, party leaders, and activists with survey results, issue research, and instructions on how to conduct campaign activities ranging from fund raising to grass-roots organizing. Moreover, NRCC and NRSC agency agreements with Republican state party organizations enable the two Washington-based committees to make the state parties' share of campaign contributions and coordinated expenditures in House and Senate elections. Agency agreements enable the state parties to spend their money on party-building functions and party-focused campaign activities (Federal Election Commission, 1984; Jacobson, 1985).

The DNC's party-building activities lagged behind those of its Republican counterpart and did not become significant until the 1986 election. During that election Chairman Paul Kirk created a task force of thirty-two professional consultants who were sent to sixteen states to assist Democratic state committees with fund raising, computerizing voter lists, and other organizational activities. In 1988, the task force went to another sixteen states to help organize and strengthen their Democratic state committees. The task forces are credited with improving Democratic state party fund raising, computer capacities, and voter-mobilization programs and with helping Democratic state and local committees reach the stage of organizational development achieved by their Republican rivals in earlier years.

National committee party-building programs have succeeded in strengthening, modernizing, and professionalizing many state and local party organizations. Agency agreements between the Hill committees and state party organizations further contribute to these efforts by encouraging state parties to spend their money on organizational development, state and local elections, and generic party campaigning rather than on House and Senate elections. These programs have altered the balance of power within the parties' organizational apparatuses. The national parties' ability to distribute or withhold party-building or campaign assistance gives them influence over the operations of state and local party committees. The DNC's influence is enhanced by its rule-making and -enforcement authority.[8] As a result of these developments, the traditional flow of power upward from state and local party organizations to the national committees has been complemented by a new flow of power downward from the national parties to state and local parties. The institutionalization of the national party organizations has enabled them to become more influential in party politics and has led to a greater federalization of the American party system (Wekkin, 1985).

NATIONAL PARTY CAMPAIGNING

The institutionalization of the national parties has provided them the wherewithal to play a larger role in elections, and national party campaign activity has increased tremendously since the 1970s. Yet the electoral activities of the national parties, and of party organizations in general, remain constricted by the electoral law, established custom, and the level of resources in the parties' possession.

Candidate Recruitment and Nominations

Most candidates for elective office in the United States are self-recruited and conduct their own nominating campaigns (see Chapter 7). The DNC and the RNC have a hand in establishing the basic guidelines under which presidential nominations are contested, but their role is defined by the national conventions and their recommendations are subject to convention approval. The rules governing Democratic presidential nominations are more extensive than are those governing GOP contests, but state committees of both parties have substantial leeway in supplying the details of their delegate-selection processes.

Neither the DNC nor the RNC expresses a preference for candidates during its party's presidential nomination. Such activity would be disastrous should a candidate who was backed by a national committee be defeated, because the successful, unsupported candidate would become the head of the party's ticket and its titular leader. As a result, candidates for the nomination assemble their own campaign staffs and compete independently of the party apparatus in state-run primaries and caucuses. Successful candidates arrive at the national conventions with seasoned campaign organizations composed of experienced political operatives.

The national party organizations, however, may get involved in selected nominating contests for House, Senate, and state-level offices. They actively recruit some candidates to enter primary contests and just as actively discourage others from doing likewise.[9] Most candidate-recruitment efforts are concentrated in competitive districts, but sometimes party officials will encourage a candidate to enter a primary in a district that is safe for the opposite party so that the general election will not be uncontested. National party staff in Washington, D.C., and regional coordinators in the field meet with state and local party leaders to identify potential candidates and encourage them to enter primaries. Party leaders and staff use polls, the promise of party campaign money and services, and the persuasive talents of party leaders, members of Congress, and even presidents to influence the decisions of potential candidates.[10]

In 1992, the parties encountered a somewhat unique set of challenges. Redistricting resulted in the creation of a large number of new and vastly redrawn House seats, and it encouraged an abundance of the highly qualified candidates to run. Final district boundaries in many states were not completed until late in the election cycle, however, making it virtually impossible for the parties to encourage some of their best candidates to avoid running against one another in the primaries. In some cases, highly experienced nonincumbents paired off against each other or an incumbent in one district while a less able candidate ran unchallenged in a primary in a neighboring district. In other cases, such as Louisiana's Sixth or Illinois's Third districts, sitting House members were unable to relocate to new districts, resulting in two incumbents facing each other in a primary.[11]

National party candidacies recruitment and primary activities are not intended to do away with the dominant pattern of self-selected candidates assembling their own campaign organizations to compete for their party's nomination. Nor are these activities designed to restore the turn-of-the-century pattern of local party leaders selecting the party's nominees.

Rather, most national party activity is geared toward encouraging or discouraging the candidacies of a small group of politicians who are considering running in competitive districts. Less focused recruitment efforts attempt to arouse the interests of a broader group of party activists by informing them of the campaign assistance available to candidates who make it in a general election.

National Conventions

The national conventions are technically a part of the nominating process. After the 1968 reforms were instituted, however, the conventions lost control of their nominating function and became more of a public relations event than a decisionmaking one. Conventions still have platform-writing and rule-making responsibilities, but these are overshadowed by speeches and other events designed to attract the support of voters.

The public relations component of the national conventions reached new heights during the 1980s. Contemporary conventions are known for their technically sophisticated video presentations and choreographed pageantry. Convention activities are designed so that they can be easily dissected into sound bites suited for television news programs. National committee staff formulate strategies to ensure that television newscasters put a desirable "spin" on television news coverage. Party public relations activity at national conventions reached a new plateau in 1988, when the DNC's Harriman Communications Center set up its Convention Satellite News Service, which featured satellite uplink capabilities, and former CBS News anchor Ike Pappas reported activity from the convention floor. Television correspondents from around the nation were invited to use the Harriman Center's facilities to interview delegates and members of Congress, or to report to their local stations. In 1992, both parties gave television stations across the country the opportunity to use live feed from the conventions in their nightly news shows. One innovation, introduced by the Republicans, used satellite technology to enable party dignitaries including Jack Kemp, Lynn Martin, and Newt Gingrich to speak from the convention floor to partisans attending GOP fund-raising events across the country.

The national parties also conduct less visible convention activities to help nonpresidential candidates with their bids for office. Congressional and senatorial candidates are given access to television and radio taping facilities. The Hill committees also sponsor "meet and greet" sessions to introduce their most competitive challengers and open-seat candidates to PACs, individual big contributors, party leaders, and the press (Thompson, 1988; Ward, 1989; Rintye, 1989). The atrophy of the national conventions' nominating function has been partially offset by an increase in its general election–related activities.

The General Election

Presidential Elections. Party activity in presidential elections is restricted by the public-funding provisions of the FECA. Major party candidates who accept public funding are prohibited from accepting contributions from any other sources, including the political parties. The amount that the national parties can spend directly on behalf of their presidential candidates is also limited. In 1992, George Bush and Bill Clinton each received $55.2 million in general election subsidies, and the national committees were each allowed to spend approximately $10.3 million directly on behalf of their candidates.

The legal environment reinforces the candidate-centeredness of presidential elections in other ways. Rules requiring candidates for the nomination to compete in primaries and caucuses guarantee that successful candidates will enter the general election with their own sources of technical expertise, in-depth research, and connections with journalists and other Washington elites. These reforms combine with the FECA to create a regulatory framework that limits national party activity and influence in presidential elections.

Nevertheless, the national parties do play an important role in presidential elections. The national committees furnish presidential campaigns with legal and strategic advice and public relations assistance. National committee opposition research and archives serve as important sources of political information. The money that the national committees spend directly on behalf of their candidates can boost the total resources under the candidates' control by more than 15 percent. The national committees also assist their candidates' campaigns by distributing "soft money" to state parties so they can finance voter-mobilization drives and party-building activities. In 1992, the Republican party's three national organizations raised over $51 million in "soft money," roughly $15 million more than their Democratic counterparts raised. Most of these funds were distributed in accordance with the strategies of their presidential candidates. "Soft money" enabled the national parties to wage a coordinated campaign that supplemented, and in some cases replaced, the voter-mobilization efforts of presidential and other candidates.

Congressional Elections. The national party organizations play a larger role in congressional elections than in presidential campaigns. The national parties contribute money and campaign services directly to congressional candidates. The parties provide candidates with transactional assistance that helps them obtain campaign resources from political consultants and PACs. Most national party assistance is distributed by the Hill committees to candidates competing in close elections, especially those who are nonincumbents. This arrangement reflects the committees' goal of maximizing the number of congressional seats under their control (Jacobson, 1985–1986; Herrnson, 1989).

As is the case with presidential elections, the FECA limits party activity in congressional races. National, congressional, and state party organizations are each allowed to contribute $5,000 to House candidates. The parties' national and senatorial campaign committees are allowed to give a combined total of $17,500 to Senate candidates; state party organizations can give $5,000. National party organizations and state party committees also are allowed to make coordinated expenditures on behalf of their candidates. Unlike the independent expenditures of PACs, party-coordinated expenditures are made in cooperation with candidate campaign committees, giving both the party and the candidate a measure of control over them. Originally set at $10,000 per committee, the limits for coordinated expenditures on behalf of House candidates are adjusted for inflation and reached $27,620 in 1992. The limits for coordinated expenditures in Senate elections vary according to the size of a state's population and are also indexed to inflation. They ranged from $55,240 in the smallest states to $1,227,322 in the most populous state—California—during the 1992 election cycle (Federal Election Commission, 1993). The national parties give virtually every competitive House or Senate candidate the maximum contribution, and most also benefit from a large coordinated expenditure. The Hill committees routinely enter into agency agreements that allow them to make some of their national and state party committees' coordinated expenditures.[12]

The figures in Table 3.2 indicate that most party money, especially in Senate elections, is distributed as coordinated expenditures, reflecting the higher legal limits imposed by the FECA. Republican party organizations spent more than Democratic party organizations in 1992, but the gap between the parties is narrower than it was in previous elections. The bulk of national party spending is done by the four Hill committees. Both national committees spent only small amounts in House elections and made no direct expenditures in Senate contests.

The figures for the NRCC and NRSC call attention to a relatively new phenomenon known as "crossover spending," which occurs when a senatorial campaign committee spends money in House elections or a congressional campaign committee spends money in Senate races. It is generally the result of shared polling or some other coordinated campaign activity that is conducted by one of the campaign committees in cooperation with the other campaign committee, a Senate candidate, or one or more House candidates who typically reside in the same state.

Table 3.3 provides further insights into the parties' role in campaign finance. The figures demonstrate that Republican candidates generally receive more assistance from party committees than do Democratic candidates. Both parties spend substantial sums in open-seat races. They spend the next largest amount in races waged by challengers. Substantially less

TABLE 3.2
Party Contributions and
Coordinated Expenditures in the 1992 Congressional Elections ($)

	House		Senate	
	Contributions	Coordinated Expenditures	Contributions	Coordinated Expenditures
Democratic				
DNC	0	913,935	0	195,351
DCCC	818,846	4,132,292	18,682	2,606
DSCC	10,000	2,600	618,450	11,233,120
State and local	366,477	750,451	72,699	487,415
Total	1,195,323	5,799,278	709,831	11,918,492
Republican				
RNC	778,503	832,347	9,000	0
NRCC	686,916	5,166,647	3,500	0
NRSC	78,500	0	614,814	16,485,039
State and local	626,057	868,908	127,960	3,617,303
Total	2,169,976	6,867,902	755,274	20,102,342

Note: Includes only general election activity. Figures are calculated from a preliminary version of campaign finance data, which may be subject to minor revision or amendment.
Source: Federal Election Commission.

is spent in connection with incumbent campaigns. The figures for the parties' share of congressional spending indicate that the importance of party money varies with candidate status. Party money accounts for over 11 percent of the general election funds spent by or on behalf of House challengers and over 14 percent of the money spent on Senate challengers. An impressive 17 percent of the funds spent by or on behalf of Republican Senate challengers was furnished by party committees.

The national parties target most of their money to candidates in close races. Challengers who show little promise and incumbents in safe seats usually are given only token sums. In 1992, for example, the parties spent over $40,000 in connection with each of 153 House candidacies and spent under $200 in connection with each of 142 others. The discrepancies in party spending in Senate elections were even greater, reflecting party strategy and the FECA's contribution and spending limits. At one extreme, the Republican party spent a mere $3,326 in the Florida contest between Republican challenger Bill Grant and Democratic incumbent Bob Graham. At the other, the GOP spent over $2.47 million and the Democrats $1.76 million in the open-seat race in California between Bruce Herschensohn and Barbara Boxer, accounting for roughly 24 percent and 15 percent, respectively, of all of the money spent in the campaign over which the candidates had some control.[13]

Even though individuals and PACs still furnish candidates with most of their campaign funds, political parties are currently the largest single

TABLE 3.3
Average Party Spending in the 1992 Congressional Elections ($)

	House			Senate		
	Incumbent	*Challenger*	*Open Seat*	*Incumbent*	*Challenger*	*Open Seat*
Democratic						
Party contributions	2,133	2,272	4,016	16,131	19,971	19,880
Party coordinated expenditures	11,833	16,219	12,849	174,794	433,969	396,546
Candidate expenditures	616,461	131,206	467,308	2,947,608	2,545,108	3,204,695
Total spending[a]	628,294	147,425	480,157	3,122,402	2,979,077	3,601,241
Party share (%)[b]	2.2	12.5	3.5	5.4	14.5	11.2
(N)	(204)	(124)	(88)	(14)	(12)	(8)
Republican						
Party contributions	4,627	4,622	5,832	21,049	21,892	19,648
Party coordinated expenditures	11,593	15,938	23,945	612,222	255,045	567,222
Candidate expenditures	564,883	166,087	393,854	4,795,594	1,207,395	2,803,777
Total spending[a]	576,476	182,025	417,779	5,407,816	1,462,440	3,370,992
Party share (%)[b]	2.8	11.3	7.1	9.7	17.2	5.6
(N)	(131)	(196)	(85)	(12)	(14)	(8)

Note: Includes all general election candidates in contested races except for Louisiana's Sixth District race, which pitted two Republican incumbents against each other. Figures are calculated from a preliminary version of campaign finance data, which may be subject to minor revision or amendment.
[a]Equals candidate expenditures plus party coordinated expenditures.
[b]Denotes percentage of candidate-controlled money (candidate expenditures and party coordinated expenditures) composed of party money.
Source: Federal Election Commission.

source of campaign money for most candidates. Party money comes from one, or at most a few, organizations that are concerned with one goal—the election of their candidates. Individual and PAC contributions, however, come from a multitude of sources that are motivated by a variety of concerns. In addition, it is important to recognize that, dollar for dollar, national party money has greater value than the contributions of other groups. National party contributions are often given early and function as "seed money" that candidates use to generate more funds. National party contributions and coordinated expenditures often take the form of in-kind campaign services that are worth many times more than their reported value. Moreover, national party money and transactional assistance help candidates attract additional money from PACs.

The national parties also furnish many congressional candidates with campaign services ranging from legal advice to assistance with campaign advertising.[14] The national parties distribute most of their services to competitive contestants, especially those who are nonincumbents. National party help is more likely to have an impact on the outcomes of these candidates' elections than on those incumbents holding safe seats or of nonincumbents challenging them.

The national parties provide a variety of management-related campaign services. They hold training colleges for candidates and campaign managers, introduce candidates and political consultants to each other, and frequently provide candidates with in-kind contributions or coordinated expenditures consisting of campaign services. The national parties also help congressional campaigns file reports with the Federal Election Commission and perform other administrative, clerical, and legal tasks. Most importantly, the national parties furnish candidates with strategic assistance. In 1992, the DCCC and the NRCC had field workers who visited campaign headquarters to help their candidates develop campaign plans, plan and respond to attacks, and perform other crucial campaign activities.

The national party organizations assist congressional candidates with gauging public opinion in three ways. They distribute newsletters that analyze voter attitudes toward party positions and report the mood of the national electorate. The Hill committees, too, conduct district-level analyses of voting patterns exhibited in previous elections to help congressional candidates locate where their supporters reside. They also conduct surveys for their most competitive candidates. These surveys help the candidates ascertain their levels of name recognition, electoral support, and the impact that their campaign communications are having on voters.

National party assistance in campaign communications takes many forms. All six national party organizations conduct issue and opposition research. DNC and RNC research revolves around traditional party positions and the issue stands of incumbent presidents or presidential candidates. Congressional and senatorial campaign committee research is more individualized. The Hill committees send competitive candidates issue packets hundreds of pages long that detail the issues that are likely to attract press coverage and win the support of specific voting blocs. The packets also include suggestions for exploiting an opponent's weaknesses.

In addition, the national party organizations furnish candidates with assistance in mass media advertising. In 1992, the NRCC's media center produced 188 television commercials for 23 incumbents and 22 challenger and open-seat candidates. The DCCC's Harriman Communications Center produced television advertisements for 171 incumbents and 70 challenger and open-seat contestants, but it did not record the actual number of ads produced.[15] The Republican committee also arranged for many other House candidates to receive media assistance from professional consultants at its expense. Moreover, the NRCC provided House candidates with more comprehensive media packages than did its Democratic counterpart. The NRCC helped develop advertising themes, wrote scripts, and arranged for its candidates' advertisements to be aired on local stations. Democratic candidates, in contrast, were given use of the Harriman Center's recording facilities and technical staff but had to supply their own creative talent (Kontnik, 1989). The DSCC and NRSC generally do not get as deeply involved in their candidates' campaign communications. They offer advice and criticisms and occasionally pretest their candidates' television and radio advertisements. The senatorial campaign committees play more of an advisory role because Senate campaigns have enough money and experience to hire premier consultants on their own.

The national parties help their congressional candidates raise money from individuals and PACs both in Washington, D.C., and in their election districts. The Hill committees help congressional candidates organize fund-raising events and develop direct-mail lists. The Hill committees' PAC directors help design the PAC-kits many candidates use to introduce themselves to the PAC community, mail campaign progress reports, "fax" messages, and spend countless hours on the telephone with PAC managers. The goals of this activity are to get PAC money flowing to the party's most competitive candidates and away from their candidates' opponents. National party endorsements, communications, contributions, and coordinated expenditures serve as decisionmaking cues that help PACs decide where to invest their money. National party services and transactional assistance are especially important to nonincumbents running for the House because nonincumbents typically do not possess fund-raising lists from previous campaigns, are less skilled at fund raising than incumbents, have none of the clout with PACs that comes with incumbency, and begin the election cycle virtually unknown to the members of the PAC community.

State and Local Elections. The national parties' state and local election programs bear similarities to those for congressional elections. The DNC and RNC work with state party leaders to recruit candidates, formulate strategy, and distribute campaign money and services. The national committees hold workshops to help state and local candidates learn the ins and outs of modern campaigning. The committees also recommend professional consultants and disseminate strategic and technical information through party magazines and briefing papers.

Important differences also exist between national party activity in state and local contests and in congressional elections. First, the parties give less campaign money and fewer services to state and local candidates, reflecting the smaller size of state legislative districts. Second, national committee strategy for distributing campaign money and services to state and local candidates incorporates considerations related to presidential elections and reapportionment. The Hill committees, by contrast, focus almost exclusively on factors related to individual candidates' prospects for success. Last, the national committee staffs go to great lengths to locate state and local candidates worthy of assistance, whereas the Hill committee staffs are inundated with requests for campaign assistance by candidates for Congress (Victor, 1989; Messick, 1989; Chalmers, 1989).

Party-focused Campaigning. In addition to the candidate-focused campaign programs discussed earlier, the national parties conduct generic, or party-focused, election activities designed to benefit all candidates on the party ticket. The most visible of these activities are the party-focused television commercials first aired by the RNC in 1980. Television commercials such as the Republicans' "Going to Work" or the Democrats' "Children" advertisements are designed to convey a message about an entire political party and to activate voters nationwide.

More traditional forms of party-focused campaigning include rallies and other grass-roots events. Party-sponsored voter registration and get-out-the-vote drives reached unprecedented levels during the 1992 election. Most of these activities are spearheaded by the national committees and conducted in cooperation with the congressional, senatorial, state, and local party committees and candidates. The RNC and the Reagan-Bush campaign dwarfed Democratic voter-mobilization efforts in 1984 by investing over $10 million to register more than 4 million previously unregistered Republican identifiers and to contact almost 30 million households (Herrnson, 1988). Following that election, the Democrats made tremendous efforts to catch up to the GOP. Democratic party officials claim that they reached parity with the Republican party in 1992, citing record figures for Democratic registration and voter turnout as evidence.

CONCLUSION

American political parties are principally electoral institutions. They focus more on elections and less on initiating policy change than do parties in other Western democracies (Epstein, 1986). American national party organizations were created to perform electoral functions. They developed in response to changes in their environment and the changing needs of their candidates. National party organizational change occurs sporadically. Electoral instability and political unrest have occasionally given party leaders opportunities to restructure the national parties. The most recent waves of party organizational development followed the turbulent 1968 Democratic convention, the Republicans' post-Watergate landslide losses, and the Democrats' traumatic defeat in 1980. These crises provided both opportunities and incentives for party entrepreneurs to restructure the roles and missions of the national, congressional, and senatorial campaign committees.

The result of this restructuring is that the national parties are now stronger, more stable, and more influential in their relations with state and local party committees and candidates than ever before. National party programs have led to the modernization of many state and local party committees. The national parties also play an important role in contemporary elections. They assist presidential candidates with their campaigns. They give congressional candidates campaign contributions, make coordinated expenditures on their behalf, and provide services in areas of campaigning that require technical expertise, in-depth research, or connections with political consultants, PACs, or other organizations possessing the resources needed to conduct a modern campaign. The national parties provide similar types of assistance to candidates for state and local offices. Although most national party activity is concentrated in competitive districts, candidates of varying degrees of competitiveness benefit from party mass media advertisements and voter-mobilization drives. The 1980s witnessed the reemergence of national party organizations as important players in party politics and elections.

NOTES

I thank Robert Biersack for his assistance in compiling Tables 3.2 and 3.3.

1. The development of radio and especially television was particularly influential in bringing about an increased focus on candidate-centered election activities. These media are extremely well suited to conveying information about tangible political phenomena, such as candidate images, and less useful in providing information about more abstract electoral actors such as political parties (Ranney, 1983; Graber, 1984; Robinson, 1981; Sorauf, 1980).

2. For further information about the roles that political entrepreneurs played in restructuring the national party organizations during the 1970s and 1980s, see Herrnson and Menefee-Libey (1988).

3. Senator Ted Stevens (R-AK), who chaired the committee during the 1976 election cycle, was not very committed to building up the committee (Herrnson and Menefee-Libey, 1988).

4. This power has been upheld by a number of court decisions, including the U.S. Supreme Court's decisions in *Cousins v. Wigoda* and *Democratic Party of the U.S. v. Wisconsin ex rel LaFollette*. The DNC, however, has retreated from strict enforcement of some party rules. For example, it decided to allow Wisconsin to return to the use of its open primary to select delegates to the national convention following the 1984 election (Epstein, 1986).

5. "Soft money" cannot be spent directly on behalf of federal candidates. The national parties use it to purchase equipment and other organizational resources, to strengthen local party organizations, and to finance voter registration and get-

out-the-vote drives. It should be noted that some of the Republicans' Victory '88 accounts were "hard money" accounts, which were subject to FECA regulations, rather than "soft money" accounts. The term *soft money* was coined by Elizabeth Drew (1983).

6. Estimates were provided by party committee staff members.

7. The NRSC and NRCC also provide selected state party organizations with financial assistance.

8. As explained in Note 4, the DNC has not been inclined to fully exercise this power.

9. For further information on the candidate-recruitment activities of the national party organizations, see Herrnson (1988).

10. The national parties have given money and campaign assistance to few candidates competing for contested primary contests since the 1984 election cycle. Prior to the 1984 election, the Republican national party organizations backed a number of candidates in contested primaries. Protests registered by state and local party activists in 1984 led RNC members to pass a rule prohibiting committee involvement in House and Senate nominating contests and led the NRCC to institute a policy requiring primary candidates to have the support of their state delegation in the House and of local party leaders before they are given support. The NRSC continues to get involved in a small number of primaries. The DCCC's bylaws bar it from becoming involved in contested primaries, and the DNC and DSCC rarely get involved in them.

11. The Louisiana Sixth District primary matched up GOP Representatives Richard Baker and Clyde Holloway, and the primary in Illinois's Third District pitted Democratic Representatives Marty Russo and William Lipinski against each other.

12. The coordinated expenditure limit for states with only one House member is $55,240 (Federal Election Commission, 1992a).

13. These figures exclude independent expenditures by PACs, which are made without the candidates' knowledge or consent, as well as party spending on party-focused television commercials, voter-mobilization drives, and other forms of party-focused campaigning. The figures are calculated on the basis of those reported in Federal Election Commission (1989).

14. For further information on national party campaign services, see Herrnson (1988), especially Chapters 3 and 4.

15. The Harriman Center recorded the amount of time that candidates used its facilities rather than the number of advertisements produced.

4

Party Polarization:
The Reagan Revolution and Beyond

WALTER J. STONE
RONALD B. RAPOPORT
ALAN I. ABRAMOWITZ

The process of party change has long been of interest to scholars and other close observers of American politics. The immediate prospect of a partisan realignment, with its far-reaching consequences for the coalitional makeup of the parties, the leadership of the nation, and the policy agenda of national institutions, has excited interest since the mid-1960s (Burnham, 1970). Realignment, however, is only the most extreme form of partisan change. Changes of a less dramatic nature such as leadership turnover, increased partisan identification with the minority party, and major party reform may have substantial short-term effects on American politics and may even contribute to an eventual realignment. Since the election of 1980, questions about the effects of the Reagan presidency on partisan change have divided scholars. Some see a realignment as having occurred, others see a realignment at the presidential level only, and still others see the Reagan years as only a temporary aberration. (See Chapter 5.) Understanding the change that occurred during that decade is crucial to putting the 1992 presidential results in perspective and to understanding the future direction of partisan change in America. In this essay we describe the changes that occurred during that period and speculate about the lasting effects of the Reagan presidency on partisan prospects in the American political system.

In 1980 Ronald Reagan and the Republican party won the presidency from an incumbent Democratic president. The fact that the Republicans also won control of the U.S. Senate for the first time since 1952 suggests that the 1980 election had broader repercussions than those implied by a mere changing of the guard at the White House. Ronald Reagan, moreover, was not just another Republican candidate. He identified himself with the Republican party's conservative wing on economic, social, and foreign policy issues in order to present a clear set of policy alternatives to the traditional Democratic (and Republican) programs.

After winning the presidency, Reagan quickly set to work enacting his agenda, particularly in the areas of economic and foreign policy. He was successful in getting Congress to reduce domestic welfare expenditures by significant amounts, in cutting taxes, and in increasing the nation's budgetary commitment to defense. In doing so, Reagan polarized the parties in Congress. Congressional Republicans were solidly in support of his programs and congressional Democrats were in opposition. Indeed, under Reagan, the indices of partisan polarization in congressional roll-call voting computed by *Congressional Quarterly* reached their highest levels in years (Stanley and Niemi, 1988).

When Reagan won reelection over Walter Mondale in 1984 by land-slide proportions, it was clear that he had changed the course of his party and of electoral politics at the national level. The presidential election of 1988 confirmed his success. Who would have guessed that a liberal nominee of the Democratic party, only eight years after Reagan's defeat of Carter, would have to devote so much attention to the question of how to balance the national budget? In addition, much of George Bush's success in sweeping to victory in a spirited nomination battle, and then easily besting Michael Dukakis in November, was attributable to the record popularity of Ronald Reagan.

Whether a true realignment accompanied the Reagan revolution remains unclear at this juncture. Reagan's personal victories did not penetrate the party system to the degree that Franklin Roosevelt's triumph in 1932 transformed the American parties. Reagan actually left office with eight fewer Republican senators than had accompanied him to victory in 1980. Republicans could not win control in the House of Representatives, nor did they make substantial gains in the number of seats they held. The Republican party gained ground in the electorate but failed to capture the loyalty of most party identifiers in the public, and its hold on state and local offices is still substantially the same as it has been throughout the post–World War II period. The Republican party remains a minority party in American politics, except at the presidential level.

However, those quick to dismiss the Reagan years as a passing phenomenon tied solely to the presidential career of its leader would do well to look more closely. Presidential politics, especially as practiced by Ronald Reagan, can have an enormous effect on the attitudes and perceptions of the public and the party system generally, particularly when the president has a unified set of policy initiatives to sell. Presidents occupy a position of extraordinary public visibility and legitimacy, and recent chief executives have not been reluctant about using their office to influence public opinion (Edwards, 1983). Indeed, as Samuel Kernell argues, Ronald Reagan was particularly willing to "go public" by appealing to his popular constituency in order to influence members of Congress and other decisionmakers (Kernell, 1986).

Our primary concern in this essay is with the effects of the Reagan years on the party system, particularly the activist strata of the political parties during the years of his presidency. We will then look for evidence of continuity and change in these strata in the succeeding four years of the Bush administration and at Bush's losing the election in 1992. Those individuals who are intensively involved in presidential nomination campaigns are of interest to us because they form important links between presidential politics and the party system as a whole. They help initiate and promote significant change in the issues they favor and the candidates they support. They are also particularly sensitive to, and likely to take positions on, policy initiatives promulgated by political leaders such as the president. In times of political change, it is these activists who are likely to help define and differentiate policy alternatives (Carmines, 1986). Thus, when these individuals change, the implications for the political system can be wide ranging. For example, were it not for the dramatic changes that took place among the activists participating in the Democratic presidential nomination campaigns between 1968 and 1972, George McGovern never could have captured the nomination. McGovern's candidacy, though doomed to failure, not only helped extend legitimacy to the opposition to the Vietnam war but also changed the direction of the Democratic party's foreign policy. And were it not for similar changes after 1976, the Republican party would have been unable to make the transition from the Nixon and Ford wings of the party to the Reagan ascendancy in 1980 (Miller and Jennings, 1986). Thus, an immediate consequence of change among nomination activists is that parties can shift directions rather dramatically in their choice of a presidential nominee and in the platform issues they endorse.

Changes in the activist core of a party reflect outward to the electorate by altering the bases of policy debate both between and within the parties. Party activists are well placed to influence opinion in the electorate and in the halls of government. Activists are more interested and conversant in political debate than most of the public, particularly during times of change. They also interact with the people in government and in party decisionmaking positions. For less involved voters, contact with activists may be as close as they come to contact with the parties. As a result, changes among those active in party affairs can be expected to change party behavior in government as well as to change party images in the electorate (Carmines and Stimson, 1989).

There is every reason to expect substantial change in the form of polarization between the parties in response to the Reagan years. Democrats were faced with a formidable opponent who could not only claim record personal popularity but who sought to use that popularity to promote a policy "revolution." The brand of liberalism promoted by Democrats since their New Deal heyday was clearly in jeopardy. And the Reagan reforms in domestic and foreign policy appeared to be working: Prosperity seemed at hand throughout most of the Reagan presidency, and the drift in American foreign policy during the Carter years appeared to be arrested.

Democrats had to confront the problem of how to recapture the public philosophy. How much of the Reagan agenda should they accept? How could they best protect their domestic constituencies and priorities against what many activists saw as an all-out assault from the right? The answers were not obvious. Unless it was clear that the shift to the right had been accepted by rank-and-file voters, there was little incentive for Democratic activists or candidates to accept Reagan's policies. And, although Reagan maintained record personal popularity, his policies did not. Popular support for the Contra rebels fighting against the Sandinista government in Nicaragua was low; there was a growing consensus as early as 1984 for cutting the military budget and for increasing at least certain categories of domestic social spending. Sensing these developments, congressional Democrats had hardened their opposition (and Republicans their support) during Reagan's last term, thereby producing the highest level of party polarization in the House throughout Reagan's entire term. In addition, as 1988 got under way there was a clear feeling of uncertainty about the future among the public. How could the Democrats best confront these problems and opportunities so as to become competitive once again at the presidential level?

Republicans also had a problem, albeit a less unpleasant one. Conservative activists had succeeded in nominating one of their own in 1980, and had seen him achieve enormous successes. They had realized gains in Republican partisanship over the previous eight years and, in Ronald Reagan, had a remarkably popular spokesman (Wattenberg, 1990). However, the downward reach of Republican gains to states and localities was limited, and Reagan's popularity masked substantial disagreement over his issue positions. Could the Republican party make its bid for realignment and dominance when much of its policy agenda was rejected by a majority of the American public?

There were also potential intraparty ideological difficulties for the Republicans coming into 1988. The moderate wing of the party had resisted much of the original Reagan agenda. Would this faction, which had supported a relatively moderate George Bush in 1980, be able to forget its commitment to the Equal Rights Amendment and its opposition to a constitutional amendment banning abortion, particularly when Bush shifted his positions on these issues in 1988?

Thus, as 1988 began, partisan prospects for both parties were unclear. Although the Democrats were confronting serious electoral problems, particularly at the presidential level, the lack of policy consensus in the mass public meant that there was little pressure on Democratic activists to shift to the right in issue position or candidate choice. For the Republican activists who had labored so hard for the Reagan victories, there was no incentive to compromise in the wake of an eight-year success story. Thus, we postulate that a pattern of increasing polarization between the parties occurred throughout the Reagan years, rather than a pattern of relative moderation.

To examine this possibility, we must probe for evidence about the response of the parties to the Reagan years. We shall do so by examining the activist stratum of the parties for evidence of change between 1980 and 1988 and then by extending the analysis into 1992.

THE 1980–1988 PARTY ACTIVIST SURVEY

In order to look at change over the Reagan presidency, we must be able to compare samples of Democratic and Republican activists from 1980 and 1988. Because of turnover in the activist ranks, activists participating in 1988 are not the same people who were activists in 1980. Therefore, to address the sources of change in the parties, we must be able to identify those who have circulated into the activist stratum as well as those who have dropped out. In addition, we must be able to follow activists from 1980 into 1988 to see how these individuals changed (or remained constant) in their attitudes throughout the Reagan years. Our research design allows us to trace the attitudes and behaviors of individual activists throughout the eight-year period, as well as to identify newcomers to the parties in 1988 and those who dropped out after 1980.

In 1980 and 1988 we surveyed Democratic and Republican state convention delegates during the presidential nomination campaign in Iowa and Virginia. These cross-section samples of the state conventions are the centerpiece of our analysis of party change. In both states, delegates to the state conventions were selected as the result of a process that began with local assemblies of the party faithful. Delegates to the state convention represent the culmination of the presidential selection process in their state, and they select from their midst delegates to attend the national presidential nominating conventions. By comparing our cross-sectional survey of 1980 delegates with the 1988 cross-sectional survey of the same stratum in the parties, we can observe the net pattern of change over the eight-year period.[1]

The second component of our design involves a panel of individuals whom we followed from the original 1980 survey and then resurveyed in 1988. The panel feature of the design allows us to monitor how activists responded to the Reagan years. It also permits us to compare those who dropped out of the activist stratum with those who remained active.[2]

Of course, a study of two states cannot capture the full measure of party change at the national level, and national samples would be preferable to our samples of activists in Iowa and Virginia. However, American parties are based on state organizations, and conducting a set of similar surveys in all fifty states would be prohibitively expensive. In addition, we purposely selected two states that exhibit important differences in the areas of political culture and history. By studying these two states, we hope both to capture a healthy portion of response in the parties to the Reagan presidency and to speculate in a reasonable way beyond the limits of our particular data.

ISSUE CHANGE BETWEEN 1980 AND 1988

Political parties are institutions devoted to winning control of public office and affecting the course of government policy. Ultimately, therefore, one of the most important dimensions of change one can examine is change in the policy preferences of those intensely active in the parties. These individuals play a major role in selecting the party's standard-bearer, are often involved in committing the party to certain positions both through candidate selection and through platform resolutions, and represent the party to other, less involved citizens (Carmines and Stimson, 1990). Our analysis of issue change depends on five common items from our 1980 and 1988 questionnaires. We asked respondents to place themselves on a liberal-conservative scale, and we requested their opinions on four specific issues: a constitutional amendment to prohibit abortions, defense spending, affirmative action, and a constitutional amendment to require a balanced budget. The liberal-conservative scale is designed to capture change in the broad philosophical orientations of the parties, whereas the issue items track narrow-gauge patterns of change. The issues are linked primarily to domestic problems because foreign policy problems have tended to be more episodic. The defense spending question taps respondents' attitudes toward increasing defense expenditures relative to domestic spending, an issue that has endured throughout the Reagan years.

In general, our analysis reveals that the parties became more polarized throughout the Reagan years. Many studies have found that Democratic and Republican party activists tend to adopt issue stands substantially more different from each other than is the case among Democrats and Republicans in the electorate (McClosky, Hoffman, and O'Hara, 1960; Miller and Jennings, 1986; Baer and Bositis, 1988). Not only did we find differences between activists in 1980, but these issue differences between the parties grew during the Reagan years. This increased polarization has important consequences for the nature of presidential campaigns, for the ability of the parties to reconcile their differences in Congress, and for the clarity of choice offered to the electorate. Partisan polarization may also be a sign of impending realignment as the parties sharpen their differences on a range of issues and carry those differences to the electorate in presidential campaigns (Pomper, 1972; Beck, 1979).

In Table 4.1 we present a profile of the parties' stands on the issues in 1980 and 1988 based on our cross-sectional surveys of the two states' nominating conventions. We have indicated the percentage of each party taking the liberal position on the item (scored −1) and the percentage adopting the conservative position (scored +1). We have also indicated the difference between the percentage within the party adopting a liberal position on an issue and the percentage adopting the conservative view. We label this percentage difference the "index of opinion," as it captures the dominant opinion in the party. A negative index score indicates a predominantly liberal opinion. An index score of −100 would mean that 100 percent of the party membership adopted the liberal view. A positive score (up to a maximum of +100) indicates that conservatives dominate the party.

One can immediately see that the parties tend to have very distinct centers of gravity, such that most Democrats adopt the liberal position on the issues and most Republicans prefer the conservative position. Take the parties' positions on the general liberal-conservative scale as an example. Sixty percent of Democrats in 1980 adopted the liberal position, whereas only 18 percent said they were conservative in their overall political philosophy. The preponderance of liberals among the 1980 Democrats is reflected in an index of opinion score of −42. Republicans were even more homogeneous: Fully 80 percent of their number adopted a conservative philosophy, and only 6 percent said they were liberal. The absolute value of the Republican index of opinion is larger than among Democrats because of the greater unity in the GOP, and it is positive rather than negative, of course, because Republicans overwhelmingly take the conservative view.

There are important differences among the issues that bear comment. For example, given the 1980 Republican national party platform stance in favor of a constitutional amendment to limit abortions (and the continued strong support for this position since), it may come as a surprise that a ma-

TABLE 4.1
Issue Opinions Among Democratic and Republican State Convention Delegates,
1980 and 1988 (in percent)

	1980		1988	
	Democrats (N=3181)	Republicans (N=2737)	Democrats (N=1379)	Republicans (N=1366)
Political philosophy				
−Liberal	60	6	68	3
+Conservative	18	80	13	92
Index of opinion:	(−42)	(+74)	(−55)	(+89)
Abortion amendment				
−Oppose	65	52	70	31
+Favor	25	37	24	64
Index of opinion:	(−40)	(−15)	(−46)	(+33)
Increase defense spending				
−Oppose	48	10	78	18
+Favor	36	83	17	75
Index of opinion:	(−12)	(+73)	(−61)	(+57)
Affirmative action				
−Favor	64	20	75	32
+Oppose	19	58	16	56
Index of opinion:	(−45)	(+38)	(−59)	(+24)
Balanced budget amendment				
−Oppose	56	28	41	9
+Favor	23	56	46	86
Index of opinion:	(−33)	(+28)	(+5)	(+77)

Note: On all issue items in this table, the "liberal" position is scored negatively.
Source: Authors' Party Activist Survey, 1980 and 1988.

jority of Iowa and Virginia Republican activists in 1980 actually took the liberal side and opposed the idea. Compare the abortion results in 1980 with those on defense spending in the same year. Republicans were overwhelmingly in favor of increasing defense spending relative to domestic spending, whereas Democrats were more closely divided on the question. Democrats opposed increases in defense spending, but just barely.

Of course, the major purpose to which we direct our analysis is uncovering and explaining patterns of change. The items in Table 4.1 enable us to sketch the nature of party change among state convention delegates through the Reagan years. From the data in that table we have calculated measures of party polarization and party change on the issues between 1980 and 1988 (see Table 4.2).

The data in Table 4.2 show that the parties became more polarized

TABLE 4.2
Partisan Polarization and Issue Opinion Change, 1980 and 1988

	Party Polarization			Direction of Issue Change[a]	
	1980	1988	Change[b]	Democrats	Republicans
Political philosophy	116	144	+28	−13	+15
Abortion	25	79	+54	−6	+48
Defense spending	85	118	+33	−49	−16
Affirmative action	83	93	+10	−14	−4
Balanced budget	61	72	+11	+38	+49

[a]A negative score indicates change in the liberal direction; a positive score indicates change in the conservative direction.
[b]Positive changes indicate increasing polarization.
Source: Authors' Party Activist Survey, 1980 and 1988.

throughout the Reagan years. We calculated from Table 4.1 the differences between the parties' indexes of opinion to provide a simple measure of party polarization in each year. Consider political philosophy in 1980 as an example. The Democrats scored −42 whereas the Republican score was +74. The polarization, or difference between the parties, in 1980 was thus 116, which reflects the substantial philosophical gap between activists in the two parties. This gap on the liberal-conservative scale increased substantially over the next eight years to 144. If every Democrat were a liberal (for a score of −100) and every Republican were a conservative (for a score of +100), the polarization score would reach the maximum of 200. The differences between the parties by 1988 were approaching the theoretical maximum on general political philosophy.

There was also an increase in party polarization on each of the specific issues included in our study. The greatest increases in polarization between the parties occurred on the abortion and defense spending issues. On affirmative action and the balanced budget amendment items, the parties differed more from one another in 1988 than they had in 1980, but the increase in polarization was much less than on the other issues.

The data on party change shown in Table 4.2 indicate how the polarization occurred. The indicators of party change are merely the signed or algebraic differences between the indexes of opinion for each party reported in Table 4.1. The most obvious examples of polarization result when the Republicans become more conservative and the Democrats, more liberal. Thus, for example, the 1980 index of opinion on abortion for Republicans was −15. By 1988, Republican delegates had moved to the right dramatically such that the index of opinion had changed to +33. The change in Republican opinion on abortion, therefore, was +48, which reflected the fact that delegates in 1988 were as a whole much more conservative than their colleagues had been in 1980. The change to a positive score indicates movement in the conservative direction; negative scores indicate movement toward a more liberal position. The Democratic index on abortion moved 6 points. The polarization, therefore, increased by 54 points. The increase in polarization on ideology was caused by a shift to the right by Republicans coupled with a leftward drift among Democrats.

This pattern of increased polarization is not the only one, however. On the remaining issues the parties moved in the *same* direction, although polarization nonetheless increased. Thus our finding that the differences between the parties increased through the 1980s does *not* imply that the parties always moved in opposite directions. Indeed, there was a substantial increase in polarization on defense, even though both parties moved in a liberal direction. However, the Democratic party, which consistently represents the liberal view, moved more strongly in the liberal direction than did the Republican party. On the balanced budget amendment, the Republicans increased their support to a greater degree than did the Democrats, even though both parties showed more support than they had in 1980. Reagan's committed ideological style enhanced the tendency of Democrats to enthusiastically embrace trends opposing the Reagan agenda, and to only grudgingly accept trends favoring his platform; not surprisingly, this Democratic stance elicited diametrically opposed reactions from Republicans. Whether the parties moved in opposite directions (as on abortion) or in the same direction, and whether that direction was in keeping with the Reagan agenda (as on the balanced budget amendment) or in opposition to the Reagan agenda (as on affirmative action), party polarization is the story of the parties' responses to the Reagan years. Reagan was a president who sought to make a difference. One important effect of his efforts was that he drove the parties further apart during his tenure in Washington.

ACCOUNTING FOR PARTY CHANGE ON THE ISSUES

We now consider two sources of change in attempting to account for the broad pattern of increased polarization between the parties on the issues. First, the polarization we have observed could have resulted from circulation effects among activists in both parties. That is, relatively moderate activists might have dropped out of the delegate stratum, perhaps because of the heightened ideological climate of political debate. If dropouts in each party were replaced by newcomers further apart on the issues, the net effect on the parties would be increased polarization. A second possibility is that the change in polarization was due to conversion effects. In this event, those who dropped out as delegates would have been very similar to delegates who were newcomers. The increased partisan polarization would have resulted from conversion among individuals who remained active as delegates. In the case of conversion, we would have observed delegates in each party who remained active throughout the period moving apart either because they moved in opposite directions or

TABLE 4.3
1988 Opinions of Circulating Cohorts of Delegates Compared with
Activists Who Continued as Delegates

	Continuing Delegates	Dropouts	Newcomers	Net Circulation Effect
Democrats				
Philosophy	−50	−45	−40	+5
Abortion	−68	−51	−40	+11
Defense spending	−74	−60	−59	+1
Affirmative action	−68	−36	−59	−23
Balanced budget	−50	+1	+31	+30
N=	(231)	(377)	(676)	
Republicans				
Philosophy	+86	+72	+96	+24
Abortion	+15	−5	+53	+58
Defense spending	+46	+13	+62	+49
Affirmative action	+29	+14	+20	+6
Balanced budget	+75	+56	+86	+30
N=	(158)	(274)	(678)	

Source: Authors' Party Activist Survey, 1980 and 1988.

because one party's cohort moved more than the other's. The implication is that the Reagan presidency had its greatest effects on those who remained active as delegates in their party.

The reality is doubtless a mix of both circulation and conversion effects. By examining the data with these two patterns in mind, we can ascertain the nature of that mix and come to a better understanding of the effects of the Reagan years on the parties.

Circulation Effects

Table 4.3 permits us to describe circulation effects by comparing those who remained active as state convention delegates in 1984 and 1988 ("continuing delegates") with the two circulating cohorts: "Dropouts" are those who dropped out of the delegate stratum of their party following the 1980 election, and "newcomers" are those new to the delegate stratum since 1980. Our 1980–1988 panel allows us to compare the 1988 opinions of those who continued to be active as delegates with those who dropped out as state convention delegates. We employ the 1988 cross-section surveys to identify "newcomers" since, by definition, they are not available to our 1980–1988 panel. Note that the entries in Table 4.3 are based entirely upon 1988 opinions. Thus we analyze the dropouts' 1988 opinions in order to ascertain which direction the state conventions would have taken had the dropouts remained as delegates.

In the case of both Democrats and Republicans, the comparisons of activists who continued as delegates with their 1980 colleagues who dropped out show a clear pattern. On the liberal-conservative scale, and on each of the four issue items, activists who remained as delegates were more extreme in their 1988 opinions than those who had dropped out—a finding that is true, without exception, for both parties. The regularity with which relatively moderate Democrats and Republicans tended to drop out of the delegate stratum in their respective parties is striking. It may be that the dropouts generally felt less strongly committed on the issue than those who continued. And as a result of their lower commitment on the issues, they may have been less willing to endure the continuing costs of prolonged party activity and accordingly reduced their commitment to partisan activity.

In order to determine how the parties were affected by dropouts and replacements, we must compare the positions of newcomers with those of dropouts in each party. Newcomers provide an infusion of new activists into a party. Because they are newly recruited, they might be expected to be particularly susceptible to the political environment of the moment, both candidate and issue. Given the dominance of Reagan over the years of the study, we should expect new Republican activists to reflect the Reagan agenda. Sources of Democratic recruitment over the eight-year period are far more varied and less likely to show consistency. We should find, then, much stronger replacement effects for the Republicans than for the Democrats.

As Table 4.3 shows, these expectations are supported. Compared with Republicans, Democrats show a much less consistent replacement effect because newcomers were more similar to the dropouts they replaced. We ascertained the net effect of circulation into and out of the delegate stratum by calculating the difference between dropouts and newcomers in each party (see the "Net Circulation Effect" column in Table 4.3). Take abortion as an example. Among Democrats, the net effect of circulation on this issue was to move the party in a conservative direction (+11) because newcomers were less liberal (–40) than the dropouts they replaced (–51). On defense spending, the net effect of circulation was almost zero because the dropouts and newcomers had virtually the same opinions on the issue. On the balanced budget issue, circulation moved the Democrats noticeably to the right. Newcomers on that issue were much more conservative than dropouts (+31 and +1, respectively), whereas on affirmative action, the party was moved in a liberal direction by circulation because the newcomers were considerably more liberal than those who dropped out. As Table 4.3 shows, the circulation effect on philosophy, abortion, and defense spending was much greater among Republicans than among Democrats. The result for Republicans, then, was a cumulative pattern rather than the offsetting pattern we observed for Democrats. Relatively moderate Republican dropouts, had they remained active in 1988, would have kept the party in a less conservative position than that favored by continuing activists. When the dropouts were replaced by newcomers even more extreme than the continuing group of delegates, the party was pushed markedly to the right.

Circulation of activists out of and into the parties, therefore, contributed to the increase in polarization that we have seen between Democrats and Republicans. Whereas the Democrats shifted only slightly to the right as the net result of circulation, the Republican shift to the right was far greater. The result was an increase in polarization because the Republican move to the right was much more dramatic than the relatively slight moderating effect among Democrats.

Conversion Effects

Circulation is not the whole of the party-change story. But it does contribute substantially to party change given the permeability of the party system. Over the eight-year period under discussion, a considerable amount of turnover occurred among state convention delegates in Iowa and Virginia. In both parties, only 30 percent of our 1980 panel respondents indicated that they continued to participate as delegates in both 1984 and 1988. Thus, the circulation effects described in Table 4.3 may seem to account for the lion's share of party change over the period.

Conversion effects are important because they help account for the pattern of party change, but they are also of interest in their own right. The conversion effects that result when the same individuals change their positions on the issues may seem unlikely among activists since they are much more interested in politics than the average citizens. They also tend to be much more committed to the ideological and issue opinions they hold, to follow campaigns and party affairs more closely, and to care much more deeply about political outcomes (Rapoport, Abramowitz, and McGlennon, 1986; Stone, Abramowitz, and Rapoport, 1989). Activists are likely to have given considerable thought to the opinions they hold and may change them reluctantly, even in the face of powerful political forces. At the same time, they may alter their opinions precisely because they are closer to politics and are in a position to respond to changing events and personalities. However, although both Democrats and Republicans experience the same "objective" political reality (implying the possibility for a lessening of polarization), they experience these from a strongly partisan perspective. Because of this difference in perspective, Reagan's perceived successes as president may have converted many Republicans who were initially suspicious of his policy goals or personal abilities; those same "successes" may have pushed Democratic activists further away from the president in their opinions. Such a pattern of individual change would have contributed to the polarization we observed throughout the Reagan years.

Table 4.4 presents the indexes of opinion in 1980 and 1988 for Demo-

TABLE 4.4
Conversion Effects Among Continuing Delegates, 1980 and 1988

	Democrats (N=231)			Republicans (N=158)		
	1980	1988	Net Change	1980	1988	Net Change
Philosophy	−54	−50	+4	+78	+86	+12
Abortion	−43	−68	−25	−10	+15	+25
Defense spending	−25	−74	−49	+74	+46	−28
Affirmative action	−48	−68	−20	+45	+29	−16
Balanced budget	−59	−50	+9	+44	+75	+31

Source: Authors' Party Activist Survey, 1980 and 1988.

cratic and Republican activists who continued as state convention delegates throughout the period. It is clear that there is significant conversion in both parties across all five items. It is interesting that on only one item in the set—abortion—did continuing delegates move in opposite directions: Democrats became more liberal as a whole, and Republicans became more conservative. On all other items the parties moved in the same direction, but in all cases this consistent directional movement produced higher levels of polarization. When the shift was to the left, it was the Democrats who moved more strongly; when the shift was to the right, it was the Republicans who showed the largest change. For example, Democrats executed a modest shift to the right on the balanced budget amendment, which was outrun by a more dramatic change in the conservative direction on that issue by Republicans; on defense spending, the dramatic Democratic move to the left outstripped a moderate Republican shift to a more liberal aggregate position in 1988.

Summarizing Issue Change

We can summarize our analysis of issue change in the 1980s, first, by combining our estimates of the net circulation and conversion effects in each party to provide an estimate of total change and, then, by assessing the effects of both sources of change on party polarization (see Table 4.5).[3] The net circulation and conversion effects are merely brought forward from Tables 4.3 and 4.4, respectively. The "total change" estimate in each party is based on the proportion of delegates circulating into the party conventions in 1988 and the proportions remaining active throughout the period. In both parties, 70 percent of the delegates from our 1980 sample dropped out, whereas 30 percent were "continuing." Therefore, we calculate the total change in Table 4.5A as the effect of circulation discounted by the proportion of the delegates circulating in and out (.7), plus the effect of conversion discounted by the proportion of our sample continuing as delegates throughout the period (.3).

Notice that circulation and conversion effects do not always work in tandem. On abortion for the Democrats and on defense spending for Re-

TABLE 4.5
Sources of Change and Party Polarization Among Delegates Between 1980 and 1988

| | *(A) Summary of Change* | | |
	Total Change =	*.7(Circulation Net)* +	*.3(Conversion Net)*
Democrats			
Philosophy	+5	+5	+4
Abortion	0	+11	−25
Defense spending	−14	+1	−49
Affirmative action	−22	−23	−20
Balanced budget	+24	+30	+9
Republicans			
Philosophy	+20	+24	+12
Abortion	+48	+58	+25
Defense spending	+26	+49	−28
Affirmative action	−1	+6	−16
Balanced budget	+30	+30	+31

| | *(B) Sources of Partisan Polarization* | | |
	Total Polarization =	*.7(Polarization from Circulation)* +	*.3(Polarization from Conversion)*
Philosophy	+15	+19	+8
Abortion	+48	+47	+50
Defense spending	+40	+48	+21
Affirmative action	+21	+29	+4
Balanced budget	+7	0	+22

Source: Authors' Party Activist Survey, 1980 and 1988.

publicans, circulation had the effect of making the party more conservative. The liberalizing effect of conversion on abortion among Democrats completely offset the circulation effect to yield an estimated change of zero. Among Republicans on defense spending, the conservative effects of circulation outweighed the liberalizing effects of conversion, leaving the party noticeably more conservative than it would have been had the full 1980 cohort of delegates remained active through 1988.

The estimates of the sources of partisan polarization (see Table 4.5B) are simply cross-party comparisons of the net circulation effects and the net conversion effects on party differences. Once again, these net effects are discounted by the proportions of activists in our sample who circulated and/or continued as delegates through the period. A positive score indicates that polarization increased on the item, whereas the zero on the balanced budget item indicates no change in polarization due to circulation. The total polarization effect is calculated by taking the differences between the total effects of circulation and conversion in the Democratic party and the total effects of both sources of change in the Republican party.

Our estimates of the effects of change on party polarization support the claim that the Reagan years saw the parties move apart. On every issue save the balanced budget amendment, both circulation and conversion had the effect of increasing the differences between the parties. And even on the balanced budget item, the net polarizing effect of conversion left the parties further apart in 1988 than in 1980, despite the failure of circulation to contribute to that trend. Thus, even when the effect of change was to move the parties in the same direction (as on the philosophy, affirmative action, and balanced budget items), the parties nonetheless moved further apart than they had been in 1980 (see Table 4.2) or would have been had all 1980 activists continued as delegates through 1988.

In short, the Reagan years drove a deeper wedge between the parties on the issues we have studied. A full explanation of this increase in polarization would take us beyond the purpose of this essay. However, we would be remiss not to consider the links between the issue changes we have observed and the changes in party leadership. Hence we turn next to an analysis of change in candidate coalitions to unravel further the nature and sources of party change in the 1980s.

CANDIDATE CHANGE IN THE 1980s

In one sense, candidate-centered analysis of change is trivial. Jimmy Carter was the Democratic party's incumbent nominee for the presidency in 1980; he was not a candidate in 1988. Because there was a completely different cast of characters vying for the Democratic presidential nomination, change took place. Such change is common in American presidential politics, especially within the losing party. If parties are permeable among the activist ranks, they are in constant turmoil in the candidate ranks as individual fortunes rise and fall with electoral outcomes and public opinion polls.

More interesting than the changing of the guard brought on by the American electoral calendar is the response of the activist core of each party to candidate change. Thus we are drawn back to our concern with issues and with the effects of circulation and conversion, for candidate change is a primary mechanism for promoting party change. For example, it remains an open question as to whether the Republican party after Reagan will be the same party as it was during the Reagan years. Certainly the candidacy of Pat Robertson was designed to reshape the party by capitalizing on the new right's political agenda. On the Democratic side, Jesse Jackson has made no bones about his desire to recruit new participants into the party and thereby work significant change. Therefore, we can look to candidate factions for important clues about sources of internal conflict within the parties, as well as for a fuller understanding of the forces at work creating party change.

TABLE 4.6
Candidate Preference Among Delegates, 1980 and 1988 (in percent)

| | 1980 | | | 1988 | |
	Democrats (N=3111)	Republicans (N=2702)		Democrats (N=1102)	Republicans (N=1331)
Carter	71	–	Dukakis	45	–
Kennedy	23	–	Gephardt	11	–
Other Democrats	6	–	Gore	10	–
			Jackson	11	–
			Simon	16	–
			Other Democrats	8	–
Reagan	–	59	Bush	–	33
Bush	–	24	Dole	–	20
Other Republicans	–	17	Kemp	–	9
			Robertson	–	33
			Other Republicans	–	5
	100	100		100	100

Source: Authors' Party Activist Survey, 1980 and 1988.

We begin by noting the distribution of candidate preferences among respondents to our 1980 and 1988 cross-sections (Table 4.6). Preferences among state convention delegates in the two states do not necessarily reflect the preferences of lower-level activists in the party, nor do they reflect the preferences of the nation as a whole. Because our surveys were conducted in Iowa and Virginia, two states with strong Robertson support, it is not surprising that Bush was the preferred candidate of only a minority of Republican activists in our sample and that Pat Robertson had a following equally as large. Because our major interest is not to explain the candidate preferences of the parties in 1988 per se but to note the continuities and discontinuities between candidate factions at the beginning and end of the Reagan years, of greater importance is the fact that substantial proportions of our samples preferred candidates other than the eventual nominee in each party. By tracing patterns of candidate support, we can observe some of the effects of party factionalism that attend candidate-based conflict within the parties.

The two major candidate factions within the Democratic party in 1980 were tied to Jimmy Carter and Senator Edward Kennedy. Carter had been elected president in 1976 as a moderate southerner with a strong commitment to civil rights. He was challenged for his party's nomination in 1980 by Senator Kennedy on several grounds linked both to his personal style of leadership and to his policy agenda. Carter was perceived by many Democrats to be an ineffective president who had failed to manage the economy and whose policies abroad were contributing to drift and confusion. Edward Kennedy in particular accused Carter of abandoning the liberal agenda of Franklin Roosevelt and Lyndon Johnson. Kennedy's challenge fell considerably short of winning the nomination, but it did succeed in drawing ideological and issue-based battle lines within the party.

The Republican fight for the nomination in 1980 was also waged between ideological factions within the party. Ronald Reagan stood for staunch conservatism in domestic and foreign affairs, whereas George Bush appealed to a more moderate brand of Republicanism. In the 1980 nomination campaign especially, Bush supported the Equal Rights Amendment and made clear his severe reservations about Reagan's economic policy. Ideology does not offer anything like a complete explanation of candidate support among activists in nomination campaigns (Stone and Abramowitz, 1983), but when candidates make appeals to ideological constituencies within their party, it is important to trace those factions in order to monitor party change. Table 4.7 begins that tracing by showing the 1988 candidate preferences of the principal 1980 candidate factions within each party in our 1980–1988 panel.

The remarkable thing about the 1980 Democratic factions is how similar they were in the areas of candidate preferences to those in 1988. There are vestiges of the ideological split between Kennedy and Carter in the greater proportions of Kennedy partisans who preferred the liberal Jesse Jackson in 1988, and in the relatively large number who favored the centrist southerner Albert Gore among Carter supporters. Nonetheless, the slight edge for Richard Gephardt in the 1980 Kennedy faction is not easily explained on ideological grounds, nor are there sharp differences in the proportions of Kennedy and Carter supporters favoring the liberal Paul Simon. Likewise, the proportions favoring Michael Dukakis were equal among both the Carter and Kennedy factions.

Factional continuity is much clearer in the Republican party, in part because George Bush was a candidate in both 1980 and 1988. In our panel, Bush retained almost three-quarters of his supporters from his first run for the GOP nomination. It is of particular interest that less than half of Reagan's faction preferred that the vice-president run on his own eight years later. Both of the 1980 camps contributed equally to the Robert Dole effort, but a far larger proportion of 1980 Reagan supporters than Bush partisans from that year preferred the conservative Jack Kemp. Likewise, although Pat Robertson did not attract much support from any of the 1980 delegates, he fared better among those who had preferred Reagan than among Bush supporters. Thus there is some evidence of ideological continuity on the Republican side as well, inasmuch as Reagan supporters were much more likely to be attracted to the conservative candidacies of Kemp and Robertson than were those who had preferred George Bush in 1980. But the continuity among Bush supporters from 1980 onward is particularly striking since, by all appearances, the George Bush who ran a campaign designed to capture the moderate wing of the Republican party

TABLE 4.7
Factional Continuity Among Continuing Delegates, 1980 and 1988 (in percent)

	Democrats	
	1980 Preference for Carter (N=552)	*1980 Preference for Kennedy (N=170)*
1988 Candidate preference		
Dukakis	27	26
Gephardt	13	18
Gore	22	4
Jackson	8	19
Simon	17	19
Other Democrats	12	14
	100	100

	Republicans	
	1980 Preference for Reagan (N=343)	*1980 Preference for Bush (N=129)*
1988 Candidate preference		
Bush	47	73
Dole	22	21
Kemp	21	2
Robertson	6	1
Other Republicans	3	3
	100	100

Source: Authors' Party Activist Survey, 1980 and 1988.

in 1980 was not the same candidate who captured the nomination of a more conservative GOP eight years later.

A second way of identifying factional patterns associated with the candidates is to examine the issue preferences of each candidate's supporters. Table 4.8 presents the index of opinion for each candidate's supporters on the political philosophy and issue items in 1980 and 1988. The results in this table were taken from our cross-section surveys of the state conventions in each year. The factional structure in 1980 was very clear in both parties. Reagan supporters were substantially to the right of Bush partisans on every item in the set, and Kennedy Democrats were plainly to the left of their co-partisans, who preferred to renominate Jimmy Carter. In 1988 the scenario was somewhat murkier, if only because there were more candidates with substantial support for the nomination in each party. The pattern among Republicans was that Bush attracted partisans who, on average, were to the right of Dole supporters but were less conservative than the Kemp and Robertson camps. On most of the issues, the differences among the factions were not terribly large (abortion among the Republicans was the glaring exception). The Bush faction in 1988 adopted a posi-

TABLE 4.8
Index of Opinion Scores for Major Candidate Factions, 1980 and 1988

	Republicans					
	1980		1988			
N =	Reagan (1647)	Bush (565)	Bush (509)	Dole (294)	Kemp (130)	Robertson (407)
Philosophy	+92	+49	+87	+75	+96	+99
Abortion	+11	−58	−10	−3	+68	+94
Defense spending	+86	+62	+58	+26	+74	+76
Affirmative action	+50	+23	+32	+8	+52	+17
Balanced budget	+62	+1	+72	+71	+82	+89

	Democrats						
	1980		1988				
N =	Carter (2102)	Kennedy (675)	Dukakis (479)	Gephart (118)	Gore (97)	Jackson (115)	Simon (169)
Philosophy	−29	−79	−53	−31	00	−66	−77
Abortion	−36	−50	−54	−21	−38	−55	−59
Defense spending	+4	−52	−62	−58	−28	−60	−77
Affirmative action	−37	−65	−55	−35	−21	−62	−68
Balanced budget	−26	−42	−1	+28	+12	−12	−12

Source: Authors' Party Activist Survey, 1980 and 1988.

tion that, on balance, was just a shade on the liberal side in opposition to a constitutional amendment prohibiting abortion. Indeed, the potential for conflict over the abortion issue within the GOP was reflected in the huge disparity between Bush and Robertson supporters.

The Democratic party's nominee, Governor Michael Dukakis, like his counterpart in the Republican party, attracted supporters who, on average, were between the extremes of the factional structure in his party. On most issues, the index of opinion among Dukakis supporters reveals them to be firmly situated in the liberal camp. But both Jesse Jackson and Paul Simon attracted Democratic activists who were more liberal on average than those who supported the Massachusetts governor. At the same time, Richard Gephardt and Senator Albert Gore attracted followers who were generally more moderate than the Dukakis faction.

Perhaps the most important findings in Table 4.8 for understanding party change are the differences between the 1980 Bush supporters and his backers in 1988. On every issue except defense spending, the Bush faction in 1988 was markedly more conservative then its counterpart in 1980. And on defense spending, the liberal drift in the Bush faction (−4) was not as great as the change in the Republican party as a whole (−16). Thus, although we can say that Bush was more moderate than two of his competitors in 1988, he was certainly attracting a more conservative following than he did in 1980. Of course, he lost the nomination to Ronald Reagan in

1980, and in the eight years since that loss his party drifted markedly to the right. It was nearly inevitable, then, that Bush's supporters in 1988 would be more conservative.

But knowing that the average Bush supporter in 1988 was much more conservative than his average supporter in 1980 tells us only part of the story. How did the candidate himself change over the period, and what forces created his 1988 supporting coalition? In an attempt to answer these questions, we asked our respondents in 1980 and 1988 to place Ronald Reagan and George Bush on the same liberal-conservative scale used to classify the activists' own political philosophy. We then coded their placements of Reagan and Bush in the same manner as we had done the issue coding earlier: −1 for a liberal placement, +1 for a conservative placement, and 0 for a placement in the middle of the scale. Table 4.9 presents the indexes of opinion calculated for the placements of Ronald Reagan and George Bush in 1980 and 1988.

Both Democratic and Republican activists in 1980 understood the difference between Ronald Reagan's brand of conservatism and that of George Bush. The dominant opinion in both parties was that Reagan was conservative, whereas Bush's placement was much more moderate. Particularly among Republicans, Bush was seen as moderately conservative and Reagan as very conservative (remember, the most conservative index of opinion is +100). In 1988 Republicans placed Reagan at exactly the same place they had in 1980, and Democrats were almost perfectly consistent with their 1980 placement of Reagan. But the change in Bush's placement was dramatic. Among Democrats the index of opinion on the ideological placement of Bush had changed by +30 points, and among Republicans it had changed +41. Democrats actually perceived Bush and Reagan as being at the same point on the liberal-conservative scale in 1988, whereas Republicans still saw Bush as more moderate than his mentor. Nevertheless, the gap between them was much less than it had been in 1980.

Very clearly, Bush's years in the vice-presidency under Ronald Reagan altered the activists' perception of his political philosophy. Although he had vigorously challenged some of Reagan's positions in 1980, the 1988 Bush brand of conservatism was seen as indistinguishable from Reagan's by Democrats and as only slightly more moderate by Republicans. In the 1988 campaign, Bush stood four-square against further taxation, having changed his position on the Reagan economic program from scoffing about "voodoo economics" to pugnacious attacks on the "tax and spend" Democrats and invitations to "read my lips." And although Bush had supported the ERA and had been cautiously in favor of abortion on demand, he took a strong anti-abortion stand in 1988. Bush's shift to the right during Reagan's terms seems to have been genuine, and our activist respondents probably perceived the magnitude of that shift correctly.

TABLE 4.9
Perceptions of Reagan and Bush Ideological Positions Among Delegates, 1980 and 1988

	1980		1988	
	Democrats (N=2810)	Republicans (N=2688)	Democrats (N=1152)	Republicans (N=1297)
Reagan	+88	+96	+89	+96
Bush	+59	+38	+89	+79

Source: Authors' Party Activist Survey, 1980 and 1988.

Can candidate change in the Republican party help explain the issue change we have observed? Table 4.10 shows the index of opinion scores for 1980 and 1988 in terms of candidate faction in the two elections. Although activists understood that George Bush had moved sharply to the right between 1980 and 1988, it cannot be said that he persuaded his 1980 supporters to move with him on the issues. On political philosophy, abortion, and the balanced budget, continuing Bush supporters moved to the right, but to a degree that was roughly consistent with the general conservative movement among continuing Republican activists. Notice also that the Bush supporters who continued from 1980 were considerably more liberal than the Reagan partisans who turned to Bush as their candidate in 1988. The continuing Bush supporters were also more liberal than Bush supporters generally (see Table 4.8).

These results suggest that Bush shifted between 1980 and 1988 to a position more compatible with his party. In doing so, he may have lost part of his 1980 coalition to the slightly more moderate Robert Dole. Notice that the 1980 Bush supporters who switched to Dole were more liberal on every item than those who stayed with the vice-president in 1988. At the same time, although Bush picked up a healthy proportion of conservative Reagan supporters, the more conservative of Reagan's 1980 supporters tended to prefer Jack Kemp in 1988. This makes perfect sense inasmuch as the one candidate remaining from 1980 changed his position in the eyes of activists far more than did the average Republican delegate. In moving to the right, Bush became more acceptable to the conservative wing of his party. But most true-blue conservatives opted for Kemp (or Robertson) as a standard-bearer in keeping with their ideology and issue opinions. Had the vice-president retained the relatively moderate stance he adopted in 1980, he might have had a much more difficult time securing the nomination. As matters stood in 1988, the Republican party was represented by a candidate who had artfully shifted his positions (or, depending on the perspective, had cynically manipulated his image) in order to be in step with his party. He did so without any apparent ill effects on his general election chances against the Democratic nominee. However, even though Bush did show a large shift away from even those who had supported him in both years, the conservative faction was still closer to him ideologi-

TABLE 4.10
Index of Opinions by Candidate Coalitions Among Republican Delegates, 1980 and 1988

Candidate Preference:	Bush '80–Bush '88 (N=105)		Reagan '80–Bush '88 (N=158)	
	1980 Opinion	1988 Opinion	1980 Opinion	1988 Opinion
Philosophy	+51	+69	+93	+92
Abortion	−65	−42	−7	+9
Defense spending	+61	+19	+91	+68
Affirmative action	+23	+12	+56	+30
Balanced budget	−2	+51	+43	+79

Candidate preference:	Bush '80–Dole '88 (N=28)		Reagan '80–Dole '88 (N=77)	
	1980 Opinion	1988 Opinion	1980 Opinion	1988 Opinion
Philosophy	+55	+59	+94	+90
Abortion	−45	−44	+18	+14
Defense spending	+50	+6	+74	+22
Affirmative action	+34	−26	+30	+16
Balanced budget	−11	+12	+74	+79

Candidate preference:	Reagan '80–Kemp '88 (N=73)	
	1980 Opinion	1988 Opinion
Philosophy	+96	+98
Abortion	+33	+54
Defense spending	+89	+68
Affirmative action	+62	+53
Balanced budget	+85	+72

Source: Authors' Party Activist Survey, 1980 and 1988.

cally than was any other in the party. Remarkably, Bush was able to execute his move to the right while holding on to the bulk of his moderate 1980 supporting coalition. And this hold on his coalition continued into the general election campaign, where this faction was more active both in support of the Bush-Quayle ticket and of Republican candidates for lower-level offices (U.S. House and state and local offices) than any other faction.

REPUBLICAN FACTIONALISM IN 1992

It should not be surprising that the faction supporting a candidate over an eight-year period of time shows high levels of support for that candidate and relative ideological closeness to him. However, the 1992 campaign was a difficult one in which Republican cohesiveness, long based on the Soviet threat and Democratic incompetence, was itself threatened in the nomination contests and ultimately shattered in the general election campaign. It was, ironically, the long-term Bush supporters—constituting a large and relatively moderate faction within the Republican party—who were under the greatest cross-pressure during the 1992 campaign. How did this faction and others within the Republican party respond to the Bush presidency? How did they perceive Bush? How did they themselves change on issues? And how did this translate into their activity in the 1992 election?

In 1992, immediately after the election, we resurveyed our 1980–1988 panel of state convention delegates. Of the 1,522 respondents from 1988, we were able to locate addresses for 1,263 respondents, and of these 930 responded, for a return rate of 73.2 percent (60.7 percent including those we could not locate or who were deceased). The return rates for Republicans (72.2 percent) and Democrats (73.9 percent) were almost identical. By using this twelve-year panel of activists, we can chart the different factions within the Republican party dating from the 1980 conventions to examine their perceptions and behavior in 1992.

As we saw, ideological perceptions of Bush shifted dramatically in 1988. Republicans viewed him as significantly more conservative than he had been in 1980. Not surprisingly, the perceptions of Bush's shift to the right were consistent regardless of candidate faction. By becoming a loyal part of the Reagan administration and changing his views on abortion, Bush sent unambiguous signals. Bush's presidency, however, sent less clear signals. In particular, Bush's renunciation of his "Read my lips. No new taxes" statement through the budget agreement of 1990 constituted for many Republicans a break with the Reagan platform. In addition, Bush confidants such as James Baker, Richard Darman, and Nicholas Brady never sat well with the true believers from the Reagan wing of the party. However, any hopes by Republican moderates that Bush would moderate his views on abortion and other social issues were thwarted by Bush's veto of fetal tissue research and his staunch support of the "gag rule" on birth control clinics' discussions of abortion as an alternative. The 1992 Republican convention, with its family values emphasis, added to the consternation of moderates within the party.

As a result of these mixed signals, the perceptions of Bush changed little between 1988 and 1992. In fact, overall Republican perceptions of Bush shifted by only one point over the four-year period. But this impression of aggregate stability masks significant changes at the factional level (as Table 4.11 shows). Although those individuals supporting Bush in both 1980 and 1988 actually saw Bush shifting by 16 points to the right, all the other factions actually saw Bush as less conservative than they had four years

TABLE 4.11
Change in Perceptions of Bush's Ideology, 1988–1992, by Party Faction

Faction	Change in Perception of Bush's Ideological Position[a]	Number of Cases
Bush-Bush	+16	53
Reagan-Bush	−4	97
Reagan-Dole	−5	41
Reagan-Kemp	−23	49
Total sample	−1	356[b]

[a]The reported number is the result of subtracting the "index of opinion" of opinion for Bush in 1988 from that index in 1992. A positive number indicates a perception that Bush has become more conservative; a negative number indicates a perception that Bush has become more liberal.

[b]The total includes not only the factions specified, but scattered votes for other combinations of candidates from 1980 and 1988. No other faction has more than fifteen respondents in it.

earlier, and the Reagan-Kemp group saw a significant movement to the center.[4] These countervailing perceptions of ideological movement were evident for neither Reagan nor Quayle nor the Republican party. For none of the three is there a mean perception of movement of more than 8 points for any faction. Neither is there evidence that those disliking Bush simply engaged in selective perception, pushing him away from themselves. In fact, there was only a very weak tendency for those liking Bush the least to see him as moving away from themselves.

Bush was therefore in the unenviable position of convincing those in the moderate wing of his party that he was becoming more extreme while at the same time convincing those in the conservative wing of the party that he was moving to the center. In effect, he moved away from both those who had supported him for the presidency since 1980 and those supporting him in 1992 for the first time. For every faction save Reagan-Dole, the result was that the difference between the mean faction activist and George Bush increased by a statistically significant amount between 1988 and 1992, regardless of the ideological position of the faction. And the largest increase was for those who had been for Bush since 1980, his natural constituency. With the Democrats nominating a more moderate candidate and Perot running as a fiscal conservative, Bush confronted a potentially serious problem, particularly with his most loyal supporters.

In spite of these problems, Bush's opposition for both the nomination and the general election appeared weak. Pat Buchanan was viewed as a mild irritant at best when he announced, and the Democrats seemed to be engaging in their quadrennial blood ritual of participatory nomination politics. Even if disappointed with some of Bush's policies, we might have suspected that the Republican activists, particularly those who had been with him for more than a decade, would rally to his support.

At the level of support for the nomination, such an expectation was fulfilled. Less than 2 percent of long-time Bush supporters went for Buchanan, and 87 percent chose Bush outright. This level of loyalty was surpassed by only the Reagan-Bush faction, and only to a slight degree. However, barely 70 percent of the Reagan-Kemp faction supported Bush and almost one in six supported Buchanan.[5] Our results for Bush nomination support in 1992 mirror activity levels from the 1988 general election campaign, where it was the Bush-Bush and Reagan-Bush factions showing by far the highest level of campaign support. This might have led us to expect these same factions to be most active on Bush's behalf in 1992. If so, we were disappointed.

But preference for the nomination is not the same as active support for the nomination, let alone for the general election. In order to assess levels of activity, we asked respondents in both 1988 and 1992 how many activities they performed on behalf of each candidate for the nomination, and then again how many activities they performed for the presidential ticket and state and local nominees in the general election campaign.[6]

Table 4.12 presents the mean number of activities performed in the nomination and general election campaigns for each faction. If we look at the general election results first, it is clear that there is an overall drop for the sample as a whole. And the drop is substantial. On average, activists performed almost 25 percent fewer activities (a decline from 1.89 to 1.45) on behalf of the presidential ticket in 1992 as compared with 1988.[7] And surprisingly, the largest drop by far came from the long-time Bush supporters. They performed about half the number of activities in the general election in 1992 that they had in 1988. In fact, their level of support went from being the highest of any faction in 1988 to being the lowest of any faction in 1992. Individuals who had opposed Bush in both 1988 and 1992 performed significantly more activities on Bush's behalf than did his long-term supporters, although even among these groups, only the Reagan-Kemp faction showed an increase in activity for Bush. These results do not control for other factors that might affect activity, specifically the degree to which an activist is ideologically closer to the Republican than the Democratic general election candidate. However, even when we do control for this factor, we find that the long-term Bush faction shows significantly greater activity levels than each of the other three factions in 1988. With similar controls, in 1992 we find that the Bush-Bush faction showed significantly *less* activity for the Bush-Quayle ticket than did the Reagan-Dole, Reagan-Kemp, or Reagan-Bush camp.

Alienation from Bush could be attributable to either Bush's term in office or the convention itself. We might suspect that the convention with its conservative social agenda would have had a particularly deleterious effect on the enthusiasm for campaign activity in the moderate Bush faction.

TABLE 4.12
Mean Number of Activities Performed for Republican Candidates,
1988 and 1992, by Faction

Faction	Activities for Bush-Quayle Ticket, 1988	Activities for Bush-Quayle Ticket, 1992	Nomination Activities, Bush, 1988	Nomination Activities, Bush, 1992
Bush-Bush	2.28	1.21	2.66	1.45
Reagan-Bush	2.19	1.61	2.32	1.92
Reagan-Dole	1.83	1.73	0.80	1.78
Reagan-Kemp	1.94	2.06	0.98	1.97
Total sample	1.89	1.45	1.56	1.63

To examine this possibility, we turn to the levels of nomination activity on behalf of Bush in both years (all of which occurs before conventions convene). What is most striking (see Table 4.12) is the extremely low relative level of nomination activity by the long-term Bush faction members in 1992 compared with 1988. This is to be expected given the far less competitive environment in 1992. Not surprisingly, Bush factional activists were by far the most active in Bush's 1988 nomination campaign. However, in 1992, even with a strong challenge coming from the right, they were the least active faction of the four, and substantially below the mean of the sample as a whole. Although the mean for the sample as a whole rose slightly over the four-year period, the Bush faction cut its activity almost in half. Clearly, alienation from Bush was at a high level among his natural constituency before the 1992 Republican convention even began.

Did this alienation from Bush among his long-term supporters indicate a general alienation from the party and its candidates? Table 4.13 presents the count of activities for Republican U.S. House candidates. It indicates that the rejection of the 1992 Bush campaign did carry over to Republicans running for lower-level offices. For example, in 1988, long-time Bush supporters performed 25 percent more activities for these U.S. House candidates than did the sample as a whole. In 1992, however, this same Bush-Bush factional group actually performed *fewer* activities on average than did the sample as a whole. And in 1988, they surpassed all factions except the Reagan-Dole group in activity level by at least .30 activities; in 1992, they surpassed no faction by more than .12 activities.

Ironically, then, it was the one faction that both had opposed him in his two previous tries and continued to show the strongest support for his opponent in 1992 (the Reagan-Kemp group) that provided George Bush with his highest level of active support in the general election. This same group showed the highest level of congressional candidate support as well. But it was his 1980–1988 supporters who showed not only the largest drop in support from 1988 but the lowest level of support in absolute terms, and by a substantial amount.

TABLE 4.13
Mean Number of Activities Performed for Republican U.S. House Candidates,
1988 and 1992, by Faction

Faction	Activities, 1988	Activities, 1992
Bush-Bush	1.64	0.85
Reagan-Bush	1.32	0.73
Reagan-Dole	1.68	0.80
Reagan-Kemp	1.31	1.41
Total sample	1.31	0.90

CONCLUSION

The eight years of the Reagan presidency saw the parties grapple with a number of potential sources of internal conflict. Between 1980 and 1988 the Democrats continued in vain their search for national leadership and an agenda that would allow them to recapture the White House. Republicans benefited from an extraordinarily popular leader whose policy agenda was clear, if not the source of the president's popularity. Change in the Republican party appeared, for the most part, to be occurring in the direction of Ronald Reagan's ideological inclinations. The Republican party was more conservative in 1988 than it had been in 1980 in its general political philosophy, on the abortion issue, and on the question of a balanced budget amendment. On affirmative action and defense spending, it moderated its position between 1980 and 1988. By 1988, the Democrats appeared to be reacting to Reagan on defense spending, abortion, affirmative action, and political philosophy. Only on the balanced budget amendment did Democratic activists change in a direction favored by the outgoing president.

It was no surprise to find that the parties moved apart as a result of the Reagan years. A president with a strong ideological commitment coupled with a widespread feeling that his program was working and great personal popularity is likely to move his party toward his own views. An important consequence of Ronald Reagan's presidency was that the stakes in political conflict were raised. The Democratic failure to win the White House in any of the three elections in the decade meant not merely losing the symbolic and material accoutrements of office but losing on a wide range of policy goals to which the Democrats had long-standing commitments.

Factionalism provided some semblance of continuity in both parties. Among Democrats, ideological and issue distinctions among the candidates were evident, but in the absence of the sort of continuity provided by the same individual remaining as a candidate, a fair amount of reshuffling of activist loyalties appeared to take place. For example, Democratic supporters of the centrist Jimmy Carter in 1980 supported Michael Dukakis for the nomination in 1988 at the same rate as did the liberal Kennedy faction. Gore, however, drew five times as heavily from Carter's support as from Kennedy's, and Jackson drew more than twice the support from Kennedy supporters as from Carter's.

On the Republican side factionalism was linked to the continued presence of Ronald Reagan and George Bush. In both 1980 and 1988 our panel respondents viewed Ronald Reagan as staunchly conservative. George Bush, however, migrated quite dramatically to the right between his first run at his party's nomination in 1980 and his successful campaign in 1988. Surprisingly, despite Bush's rightward shift, he retained a large majority of his more moderate supporters from 1980. To be sure, there was evidence of ideological factionalism in both parties tied to candidate support, but ideological conflict within the parties did not appear to rigidly categorize activists in 1988.

Unfortunately for George Bush, this flexibility from his moderate 1980 supporters did not last. In 1992 the Republican party had a far more serious problem. Although Bush supporters from 1980 who stayed with Bush in 1988 continued to prefer him to the alternatives in the party (in this case the right-wing Pat Buchanan), their displeasure with him was obvious. They saw Bush as moving further and further to the right (and away from themselves). Their affection toward him dropped to a greater degree than for any other Republican faction, and their activity on his behalf declined precipitously. In fact, activity on behalf of Bush from his 1980 and 1988 supporters was lower than that of any other faction for both the nomination contest and the general election.

The activist stratum we have studied is highly permeable, and we found considerable coming and going among our delegates in the 1980s. Circulation has the potential to work substantial change in an American political party simply because there is so much of it: Recall that fully 70 percent of delegates in our two states dropped out between 1980 and 1988. This leaves an incredibly potent source of change available to those who would attempt to influence national politics through the presidential selection process. Ronald Reagan's own career attests to the efficacy of this avenue of change. As the Reagan years continue to recede and the parties respond to new issues and new leadership, change is likely to continue. But new candidates do not have to win the nomination in order to effect change. Recruiting new activists may be sufficient. For example, we found that the overwhelming majority of supporters of Pat Robertson in 1988 were newcomers not only to activity as state convention delegates but to party activity of any sort. As Robertson faded from the presidential arena, many of these activists also dropped out, but many others continued. It is clear: The parties are available for the taking.

The shift of the Republican party to the right, which showed up among all factions in 1988, was reinforced in 1992 as the most conservative faction showed the greatest level of activity at both presidential and congressional levels, and the most moderate faction showed strong signs of alienation from Bush and the party. A third of long-term Bush supporters served as local party chairs at some point in time, compared to less than a quarter of Reagan-Kemp faction members, but in 1992 Reagan-Kemp supporters were twice as likely to hold chairs as those from the long-term Bush faction. Put another way, although almost 60 percent of the Reagan-Kemp faction supporters who had ever held local party chairs continued to do so in 1992, the same was true of less than 20 percent of Bush-Bush faction supporters. Just as newcomers can infuse a new perspective into a party, so selective exit can confirm an ideological shift. The nomination of a candidate from the right wing of the party in 1996 could lead to further disengagement by the moderates and the increased dominance of the right in Republican party matters. Whether the agenda for change is a liberal one associated with a George McGovern or a Jesse Jackson, or a conservative one associated with a Ronald Reagan or a Pat Robertson, the mobilization of new activists into the presidential nomination campaign, particularly with selective demobilization of the declining factions, is a viable strategy for influencing the direction of a party.

Of course, the Robertson, Kemp, and Buchanan phenomena, however episodic, must themselves be considered part of the Reagan legacy. Reagan prepared the way for a new-right candidate whose appeal was primarily to "amateurs" strongly motivated by moral and religious values. That legacy may well continue to influence politics within the Republican party for years to come. By the same token, the Democratic party has continued its struggle to find a coherent response to the Reagan challenge. The election of Bill Clinton may signal success in this venture. But the next four years may also present opportunities for the Republican party to reassert its strength. In either case, an important part of the resulting clash between the parties is very likely to be continued polarization with visible differences between the Democratic and Republican camps. In times of partisan change up to and including realigning change, the parties differentiate themselves clearly as they search for new bases of support, and new ways of confronting the opposition. There are tantalizing hints of such a pattern of change in our data, which conform with polarizing change in the Congress. The Reagan years doubtless had continuing effects on the American party system, which may result in long-term party polarization and realignment. If the result in the long run is a clearer sense of where the parties differ coupled with a revitalized debate over national priorities, the parties will emerge as stronger arbiters of the nation's political life.

NOTES

An earlier version of this chapter was presented at the Annual Meeting of the American Political Science Association, Atlanta, Georgia, August 31–September 3, 1989. We are grateful to the National Science Foundation for support of the party activist surveys and to Lonna Atkeson and Jay McCann for valuable research assistance.

1. We distributed questionnaires at the Democratic and Republican state conventions in Iowa and Virginia in both 1980 and 1988. The response rate in 1980 was 62.9 percent, with 2,780 Democrats and 3,385 Republicans responding. In 1988 we received 1,438 questionnaires from Democrats and 1,393 from Republicans, for a 60.6 percent response rate. The n's are smaller in 1988 than in 1980 because we sampled delegates in the latter year, whereas in 1980 we distributed questionnaires to all in attendance.

2. The panel component of the design required that we trace respondents from the 1980 cross section eight years after the original survey. Of the 3,645 1980 respondents for whom we had names and addresses, we were able to trace 2,842, or 78 percent, successfully. Of these, we received responses from 1,522, or 53.6 percent. For an extraordinarily long panel of eight years, this is a very satisfying response, but it was inevitably a small subset of the full 1980 cross section. In examining the distributions of all variables in the file of the full 1980 cross section compared with our panel subset, we found remarkably few significant differences. The panel was almost perfectly representative on the 1980 issue items of the larger cross section.

3. The estimates of net change and polarization in Table 4.5 do not match the estimates in Table 4.3 because the latter are based on direct comparisons of the 1980 cross section with the 1988 cross section. In Table 4.5, our estimates of circulation effects take into account the change in opinion among dropouts by basing the calculations on their 1988 opinion. Because the dropouts changed their opinions between 1980 and 1988, our analysis does not merely disaggregate the cross-sectional change reported in Table 4.3.

4. One likely reason for this change might be found in the increased significance attached to the abortion issue by the Bush-Bush faction. In 1988, only 8 percent named this as the most important issue. By 1992, this figure had more than doubled to 18 percent, making abortion the second most important issue of the eleven asked about.

5. The alternatives offered respondents were Bush, Buchanan, and "None of the Above." We combine Buchanan and "None of the Above" as non-Bush supporters.

6. The activities asked about were contributing money, fund raising, canvasing, attending meetings or rallies, and trying to convince others to support the candidate.

7. It is of course possible that this is a function of the aging of the sample or some other general effect in the political system. However, among Democratic activists, the number of activities actually increased (from 1.99 to 2.09) over the four-year period.

PART THREE

*The Changing Relationship
Between Parties and Voters*

5

Party Identification and the Electorate of the 1990s

WARREN E. MILLER

In 1952, at the same time the University of Michigan's Survey Research Center was conducting its first major study of electoral behavior in an American presidential election, V. O. Key, Jr., was bringing out the third edition of his classic text, *Politics, Parties, and Pressure Groups* (Key, 1952). In the opening paragraphs of Chapter 20, "Electoral Behavior: Inertia and Reaction," Key drew two broad conclusions about the American electorate: "In substantial degree the electorate remains persistent in its partisan attachments. The time of casting a ballot is not a time of decision for many voters; it is merely an occasion for the reaffirmation of a partisan faith of long standing. ... A second main characteristic evident in electoral behavior is that under some conditions voters do alter their habitual partisan affiliations. To what condition is their shift in attitude a response?" Latter-day political scientists have spent the better part of four decades testing these two conclusions and trying to answer Key's single question. Under the impetus of the Michigan research, "party identification" replaced "habitual partisan affiliation," but the basic terms of the query into the nature of the citizens' enduring partisan attachments have remained very much as Key identified them.

The results of the first four major Michigan studies of the national electorate were entirely in line with Key's first assertion as well as with his preoccupation with persistence and inertia as attributes of mass electoral behavior. From 1952 to 1964 national survey data, bolstered by a study that plotted individual change over time, documented a great persistence in citizens' identifications with the Democratic and Republican parties. There was a brief upturn in Democratic support in 1964, but it disappeared four years later, drawing perhaps too little attention to a condition under which partisan attitudes had shifted. Other than that temporary perturbation, Democrats enjoyed a consistent 15- to 18-point edge over

Republicans. During the same period, the measures of the strength or intensity of partisan attachments seemed to confirm the thesis of partisan stability; in election after election, strong identifiers outnumbered nonpartisans by virtually identical margins of about 25 percentage points.

Without destroying the suspense or giving away the story line (as the latter is not without its complexities), I think it fair to note that the period from 1952 to 1964 is now often referred to as the "steady state" era (Converse, 1976). A series of inquiries into this era established party identification as distinctly different from the partisan character of the single vote, both in concept and in operational measure. The role of party identification as a predisposition that powerfully influences citizens' perceptions and judgments was spelled out (Campbell, Converse, Miller, and Stokes, 1960). And in some reifications or glorifications of more sober analysis, party identification was sometimes referred to as the "unmoved mover," or the "first cause" of electoral behavior. Certainly, the evidence was all that V. O. Key could have hoped for as documentation of his hypothesis that partisan attachments had great stability at the level of the individual as well as that of the aggregate.

At the same time, the theme of party realignment continued to attract attention among political analysts. This was particularly so among Republican enthusiasts who saw in the Eisenhower victories (and the initial Republican congressional successes that accompanied them) the possibility of a resurgence for the Republican party. The narrow Kennedy victory in 1960, in the face of a presumably daunting Democratic plurality in the eligible electorate, added fuel to the Republican fire and, at least in part, aided the Republican nomination of Goldwater in 1964 on the premise that he would mobilize latent conservative Republican sympathies and bring an end to the Democratic hegemony (Converse, Clausen, and Miller, 1965).

Although the Goldwater candidacy was something less than a triumph of Republican expectations, another four years later the Republican Nixon *was* elected and, for the first time since systematic modern measurement had dominated social scientific analysis of electoral behavior, the bedrock of party identification cracked. The partisan balance was not disturbed and the Democratic dominance was unchanged, but the strength and intensity of partisanship declined. First in 1968, then in 1972, and finally again in 1976, each successive reading taken at election time revealed fewer strong partisans and more citizens devoid of any partisan preference.

PARTY ALIGNMENT, 1952–1980

Fortunately for the stability of the country, it was largely political scientists and not national leaders who reacted to the decline in the fortunes of party in the electorate. Political scientists, however, made the most of it, and many made far too much of it (Burnham, 1975). Even though persuasive evidence of a national party realignment was not to appear for another twenty years,[1] the literature on parties, elections, and electoral behavior from 1968 on was replete with analysis and discourse on party dealignment and realignment. When such analysis rested on a proper disaggregation of national totals and the examinations of subsets of citizens experiencing real change under local political conditions, the facts are not in dispute. Change *was* occurring in the South (Beck, 1977). Hindsight makes it particularly clear that change in party identification had begun among white southerners as early as 1956. A massive realignment was simply accentuated and accelerated in the late 1960s under the combined impetus of Goldwater's "southern strategy" and Johnson's promotion of civil rights. Legislation such as the Voting Rights Acts of 1964 and 1965 and the Great Society, and the economic as well as foreign policies of the Democratic party leaders in the 1970s and 1980s, did not enthrall southern Democrats and instead persuaded them to turn to the Republican party (Black and Black, 1987).

The most vivid contrast between the changes occurring in the South and the virtually total absence of change outside the South is provided in the comparison of white males in Table 5.1. In 1952 the one-party nature of the post–Civil War South was reflected in the fact that self-declared Democrats outnumbered Republicans among southern white males by 70 to 11.[2] The McGovern candidacy in 1972 saw that margin reduced to 42 to 21; and 1988 witnessed a virtual dead heat, 29 to 30. Apparently the Democratic candidacies of Johnson and Carter had slowed the tides of change without completely stemming them. Outside the South, there is no evidence among men or women of a trend either away from the Democrats or toward the Republicans until 1984. The year of Johnson's election, 1964, saw a brief surge of Democratic sympathies that was immediately followed by a decline, or return to "normalcy," among white citizens. Even so, the two regional patterns stand in stark contrast to each other.

The changing distributions of the party identifications of black citizens is, of course, a story unto itself. The figures in Table 5.1 understate the spectacular changes in the contributions of blacks to recent political history because they do not reflect the changes in the politicization and mobilization of blacks during the 1950s and 1960s.

The aggregation of the various patterns created by differences in gender, race, and region appears in the first columns of Table 5.1. The net result, nationally, does reflect meaningful year-by-year differences, but it also supports the overall conclusion that prior to 1984 there was little manifestation of a realignment that would end Democratic dominance of popular partisan loyalties.

TABLE 5.1
Partisan Balance of Party Identifications, 1952–1992, by Gender, Region, and Race

	National Electorate[a]			White Males		White Females		Blacks
Year	D	I	R	B	South	Non-South	South	Non-South	
1952	47	26	27	20	59	8	54	5	39
1956	44	27	28	14	55	5	39	−3	31
1960	45	25	29	16	40	3	39	2	27
1964	52	24	25	27	43	15	46	14	65
1968	45	31	24	21	29	4	36	8	83
1972	40	36	24	17	21	5	24	8	60
1976	40	37	23	16	25	6	22	3	66
1980	41	37	22	18	15	4	20	12	67
1984	37	36	27	10	13	−4	16	0	60
1988	35	37	28	8	0	−6	18	−5	56
1992	35	39	26	10	−1	−6	11	8	60
80–92	−6	+2	+4	−8	−16	−10	−9	−4	−7

Note: Entries are proportions of Republican identifiers, strong and weak, subtracted from proportions of Democratic identifiers, strong and weak. Data are for the entire eligible electorate.

[a]D: Democrat; I: Independent; R: Republican; B: Balance.

Source: Michigan Survey Research Center of the Center for Political Studies, National Election Studies series.

Despite occasional election-day evidence of some resurgence of Republican affinities, and despite reports of increased Republican organizational strength, the dominance of Democrats over Republicans in the eligible electorate across the nation did not waver throughout the 1960s or 1970s. Even despite the election and reelection of Richard Nixon in the 1968 and 1972 presidential elections, the data on the underlying partisan balance of party identification did not change. Not even in 1980—when Ronald Reagan's victory gave the Republicans five out of eight wins for the presidency, and with another Republican landslide making history with the defeat of an incumbent (Democratic) president—was there a suggestion of basic changes in partisan sentiments outside the South.

In order to reconcile all the evidence of stability and change in party identification and in the vote between 1952 and 1980, it is necessary to separate the analyses of the *directional balance* of partisanship between Democrats and Republicans from the study of changes in the *strength* of party identification (i.e., the ratio of strong partisans to nonpartisans).

CHANGES IN THE STRENGTH OF PARTISANSHIP

The story of the apparent decay and rebirth of partisanship is fascinating and complex, and it rests on evidence surrounding the elections of the 1980s. The first *national* decline in the strength of party identification after

1952 occurred in 1968, coincident with a retreat among white citizens outside the South from the partisan Democratic high of 1964. The drop in strength of party identifications was apparent in national estimates and was widely interpreted as an indication that strong partisans were rejecting old loyalties and taking on the role of nonpartisans. A relatively simple analysis of changes in the relationship between the partisanship and the age of citizens might have forestalled—or at least modified—such interpretations. It is true that the decline in the strength of partisanship was reflected in a temporary diminution of partisan intensity among *older* citizens, but the portent for the future, as well as the reason for the apparent decline in party fortunes, was contained in the contrast between the partisanship of the youngest and the oldest cohorts.

In keeping with established regularities that had found strength or intensity of party identification very much a function of increasing age, by 1968 the oldest cohorts, who were literally dying off (like those who had preceded them and like those who were to follow), were the strongest carriers of partisan attachment. Their "replacements," the young cohorts newly eligible to vote, not only followed the pattern of having the weakest of partisan attachments but, in 1968, far exceeded their counterparts from previous years in the extent to which they were nonpartisans, and were not strong partisans when they had any partisan inclinations at all.

Throughout the 1950s and early 1960s the youngest members of the eligible electorate had been less partisan than their elders, but, as Table 5.2 indicates, they had always counted many more strong partisans than nonpartisans in their ranks, usually by a margin of 10 to 20 percentage points (compared to margins of 45 to 55 points among the oldest cohorts). In 1968, however, the entering cohort of those eligible to vote for president for the first time actually contained more nonpartisans than strong party identifiers.

To the extent that 1968 ushered in an antiparty era of weak party control and weak party loyalties, the consequence was immediately and massively evident among the young; but it was scarcely reflected at all in the partisanship of the middle-aged and older cadres (see Jennings and Markus, 1984). Indeed, by 1972 the strength of party sentiments among citizens more than sixty years old had pretty much returned to the levels of 1960–1964. Among the very large number of citizens in their late teens and twenties, however, nonpartisans clearly outnumbered strong partisans. By 1972 these youngest cohorts made up a full 33 percent of the total electorate. The contribution of the young to national estimates of the strength of partisan sentiments was the primary source of the apparent nationwide decline in strength of party identification that continued until sometime after the election of 1976 (Miller and Shanks, 1982).

TABLE 5.2
Strength of Partisanship, by Four-Year Age Cohorts, 1952–1992

Age in 1952	Year of First Vote for President	1952	1956	1960	1964	1968	1972	1976	1980	1984	1988	1992	Age in 1992
	1992											−1	18–21
	1988										5	1	22–25
	1984									0	6	4	26–29
	1980								−5	6	16	3	30–32
	1976							−9	−8	10	14	18	33–36
	1972						−10	−3	0	11	14	22	37–40
	1968					−4	−1	−8	2	9	17	11	41–44
	1964				16	−3	−4	−1	10	10	16	20	45–48
	1960			14	20	17	0	0	4	10	32	18	49–52
	1956		15	23	23	19	1	6	18	23	18	27	53–56
21–24	1952	23	13	17	25	27	3	11	23	25	31	35	57–60
25–28	1948	24	23	28	29	11	12	25	18	36	35	21	61–64
29–32	1944	23	23	24*	24	12	20	21	20	23	28	27	65–68
33–36	1940	16	22	27	30	13	20	24	27	31	31	38	69–72
37–40	1936	30	24	29	27	27	19	20	25	35	35	33	73–76
41–44	1932	26	31	32*	37	30	28	11	42	31	41	37	77–80
45–48	1928	25	32	24	52	32	23	40	33	40	26	43	81+
49–52	1924	36	36*	38	37	36	24	25	40	34	38		
53–56	1920	38	35	+40	30	34	34	36	30	40			
57–60	1916	44	40*	32	53	43	37	32					
61–64	1912	37	40*	23	50	43	31						
65–68	1908	36	38	53	42	35	37						
69–72	1904	45	51	54	20								
73–76	1900	32	47	53									
77–80	1896	38	56										
81+	1892	53											
National totals		29	27	26	30	19	12	9	13	18	21	17	

Note: Entries are differences between the proportion of strong party identifiers and the proportion of Independent-Independents. The entries of 5 cells (out of 176), marked by *, have been "smoothed" by replacing those entries with the average of those in adjoining years and cohorts. The assigned values for these cells, reading by column, are as follows: 36 was 24, 40 was 30, 40 was 53, 24 was 11, and 32 was 19. This smoothing attempts to remove the most obvious instances of sampling error by substituting innocuous entries for those that are otherwise anomalous.

Source: All of the data are based on the Michigan Survey Research Center of the Center for Political Studies, National Election Studies series.

In examining the full set of four-year cohort data, following each new entering class across the forty years and eleven presidential elections covered by the Michigan data and presented in Table 5.2, we may reasonably conclude that the traumas of the late 1960s and early 1970s—failed presidencies, international frustrations, domestic turmoil, and the disruptive effects of civil rights protests, anti-Vietnam demonstrations, and counterculture happenings—did create a period effect felt throughout the electorate. The strength of partisan sentiments among the older cohorts rebounded in 1972 and 1976, but in 1992 these sentiments did not continue to advance to the high mark set by the oldest cohorts forty years earlier. At the same time, the larger impact of the antipolitics decade seems to have been a generational effect: The young reacted to the events of the period more sharply and possibly even more permanently than did the older cohorts. It was the refusal and delay of the young in accepting partisan ties, not the lasting rejection of loyalties once held by their elders, that produced the indicators of dealignment in the mid-1970s.

It now seems clear that too many of the scholarly discussions of dealignment and realignment—given the aggregate figures, which showed fewer strong partisans and more nonpartisans—inaccurately attributed the cause of this change. They simply *assumed* that dealignment had occurred because old partisans actively rejected former party loyalties in favor of dealignment, professing no support for either party in preparation for switching party loyalties. The absence of party loyalty among the large numbers of young people, with no implications of rejection, conveys a quite different sense. This is an important distinction because the post-1976 evidence points to an increase in the incidence of party attachments among the young and the strengthening of their partisan sentiments.

Indeed, particularly where the strength of partisan sentiments is concerned, a pervasive upturn since the 1970s has been led by the same young cohorts whose original entry into the electorate was dominated by nonpartisans. Each of the younger cohorts who contributed so much to the apparent national dealignment has experienced a dramatic increase in both the incidence and the intensity of partisan sentiments in each of the elections of the 1980s as the political climate normalized. Their level of attachment in 1988 remained much below the norm that we associate with their generational counterparts in the 1950s, but primarily because they started from such an abnormally low point when they first entered the electorate. They have in fact made a large contribution to the national indications of renewed partisanship.

In 1988 the ratio of strong partisans to nonpartisans in the younger cohorts had shifted by 10–20 points from a quarter of a century earlier. And by 1992 the post-1976 cohorts numbered more than 25 percent of the total electorate. Between 1976 and 1992 the eight youngest cohorts from 1976 increased their strength of partisanship by an average of 22 points; the remaining eight oldest cohorts in 1992 had gone up only 10 points in the same twelve years. At the same time, the composition of the electorate does continue to change over time inasmuch as old cohorts, whose normally quite intense feeling of party loyalty strengthened as they aged, continue to leave the electorate. Their departure has slowed the overall rate of recovery in national strength of partisanship, which otherwise would have reflected more clearly the increase in partisanship being contributed by the younger cohorts since 1976.

In sum, many arguments that took indicators of the declining strength of party identification in 1972 or 1976 as indicators of impending party realignment erred in the interpretation of these indicators. The actual *reduction* of intensity of individual partisan commitments was real, but it was very limited in magnitude and constituted a very brief episode for older members of the electorate. For the younger members, the turmoil of the late 1960s and early 1970s delayed but did not forestall their development of party loyalties. The magnitude of the delaying effect on them was so great, and they have been such a large and growing part of the electorate, that their simple lack of partisanship has been the largely unrecognized primary source of the indications of what was called dealignment but what was, in reality, nonalignment. To be sure, a nonalignment of the young may be followed by a first-time alignment that will differ from that of the old, and that might ultimately reshape the party alignment of the entire electorate. But the dynamics of partisan change that follow from such a beginning will probably be quite different from those anticipated or imagined when it was thought that an experienced electorate was rejecting its old loyalties in preparation for a *re*alignment involving switching parties by the individual citizen.

SOME IMPLICATIONS OF NEW ALIGNMENTS

Before considering further the topic of the realignment of national partisan sympathies, we may find it useful to reflect on some of the implications of the period effects and generational differences that have just been suggested. The very introduction of the idea of cohort analysis emphasizes the consequences of compositional change of the electorate during a period of political turbulence. Notwithstanding the rapid but ultimately incomplete rejuvenation of partisanship among older voters between 1972 and 1976, the concern with the changing composition of the electorate begs the direct question of Key's basic interest in individual-level stability and change in partisanship.

In approaching that question, we should first note that the observed generational differences that appeared rather suddenly in 1968 suggest that we modify some of the traditional as well as revisionist notions of the origins of party identification. Historically, party identification was thought to have been shaped by national traumas and watershed events such as the Civil War of the nineteenth century or the Great Depression of the 1930s. The lasting effects of such realigning epochs were thought to be carried by the influence of parents on the social and political attitudes of the successor generations. Early evidence for this view was provided by the recall of parental predisposition and supplemented by insightful arguments that described a waning transmission of the first causes through successive generations that are more and more remote from the shaping cataclysms (Beck, 1977). This latter theme was, of course, intended to account for the diminution of partisanship—the dealignment that logically might precede realignment.

The evidence of cohort differences in partisanship that we have reviewed would, of course, be consonant with the thesis that new disruptions of the party system simply accentuate the decay of family traditions and familial transmission of party loyalties. But it is more than this. The very abruptness of the cohort differences that appeared in 1968 suggests an active intrusion of new events into the process whereby partisanship is acquired among the young. This disruption of familial lines of inheritance may or may not have lasting effects that produce real discontinuities in the partisanship of the electorate. But it certainly produces short-term change, which was not anticipated in the early theories of political socialization. And the rapid recovery of partisanship among the older cohorts, with a much slower rate of development and growth in the younger (filial) generations, creates a generational gap that belies a pervasive influence of the older over the younger (Jennings and Niemi, 1981). In short, whatever the role of the family in shaping and preserving party traditions, the events of the late 1960s and early 1970s had an impact of their own on the partisan predispositions of the younger cohorts entering the electorate. Those most affected were not *re*aligned, and not even *de*aligned. They simply entered the electorate more often *un*aligned, with no partisan preference.

Moreover, the immediacy of that impact of events in young people did not allow for the habituation to behavioral patterns that has become a choice explanation of the origins of party identification (Fiorina, 1981). The notion that acts of crossing partisanship—Democrats voting for Eisenhower in 1952 and 1956, for Nixon in 1968 and 1972, or for Reagan and Bush in 1980, 1984, and 1988—have an impact on one's sense of party identification is not at issue (Converse and Markus, 1975). Rather, as with generational differences and family tradition, the sharp break with the partisanship of entering cohorts prior to 1968 makes the absence of partisanship in the new cohorts of 1968 more of a comment on the immediate impact of historical context than an extension of either family influence or rational-choice theory as the explanation for new partisan identities.

The amassing of new data that captures variations in historical context has enriched our understanding of the origins of party identification and partisanship. As an aside, we should note that the growing evidence of a multiplicity of origins may upset some old orthodoxies, but it does not necessarily address the question of whether the significance, meaning, and consequence of party identification are similarly enriched or altered. The meaning of "I generally think of myself as a strong Democrat/Republican" *may* vary with the origin of the sentiment, but that possibility must be the subject of much future research. In the meantime, we simply note the proliferation of evidence that party identification, in its origins, is a fascinating and many-splendored thing.

POLITICAL ENGAGEMENT AND PARTISAN STABILITY

The extent to which the incidence, strength, and direction of party identification vary with the context experienced by the identifiers is further illuminated if we define *context* in terms of the political depth of the partisan engagement of the individual citizen. We have already noted some of the correlates of the political context at one's time of coming of political age. We have also noted how aging, or experience, inoculates one against change in later years of life. An even more dramatic insight into the durability of partisanship is provided when we subdivide citizens into voters and nonvoters.

Let us turn first to national assessments of the strength of partisanship. In the "steady-state" elections of 1952–1964, strong partisans among voters outnumbered those with no partisan preference by a ratio of 39 to 7; among nonvoters the comparable averages were 26 percent (strong partisans) and 8 percent (no partisan preference). At the height of the excitement about dealignment (1968–1976), the ratio of strong partisans to nonpartisans was still 30 to 10 among voters; however, it had reversed to 16 (strong) to 19 (no preference) among nonvoters. In the elections of the 1980s, the ratio for voters was back to 35 (strong preference) to 8 (no preference); for nonvoters it was still 18 to 17. Thus there *was* some weakening of the aggregate indicators of the strength of partisanship among voters; indeed, the role of the young nonpartisan cohorts in changing the partisan composition of the entire electorate has already been noted. However, the dramatic change in the intensity of partisan sentiments that began in 1968 and persisted through the 1980s occurred primarily among nonvoters— that is, nonparticipants in the presidential elections of the period. The high point of contrast occurred in 1976, when strong partisans still outnumbered nonpartisans among *voters* by a ratio of 28 to 11; among nonvoters, however, the ratio was reversed, 12 to 22. Of course, the contrast was occasioned in part by the disproportionate incidence of young people among the nonvoters of that year, as in every election year.

In other words, the cry of alarm that the partisan sky was falling, with all of the strong implications for the future of the electoral process, was occasioned by indicators emanating primarily from the nonparticipants in presidential politics. A "dealignment" of these apathetic nonparticipants might also have deserved comment and even some analytic thought, but unfortunately it was the mistaken belief that future elections would no longer be shaped by a continuation of the party identifications of the past that commanded the attention of most analysts and commentators. Both the diagnosis (alienation of the voters) and the prognosis (realignment of partisanship at the polls) were flawed because it was largely the nonvoters who constituted the source of the alarming (or promising) indicators of impending change.

Now that we have separated voters and nonvoters in order to reexamine the aggregate indicators of partisan dealignment, it is a natural extension to turn directly to the theme of party realignment. This, in turn, results in still more evidence of the persistence of party identification, even as we introduce the first description of a significant shift in the numerical balance of the two parties. Table 5.3 indicates that prior to 1984 there was little hint in the national party identification distributions among voters of an impending realignment that would see the Republican party in the ascendancy. Indeed, the only visible departure from a thirty-year span of Democratic pluralities of some 14 percentage points occurred during and after the election of 1964. In that year, still an underanalyzed episode, party loyalties shifted and enhanced the "steady-state" Democratic margin by a full 10 points. Despite the chaos of the Democratic nominating convention in Chicago in 1968, and perhaps as a partial explanation of Hubert Humphrey's near victory in the fall election with strong black support, the preelection Democratic plurality of party identifications in that year remained visibly above the norms of the 1950s and 1970s. By 1972, however, and again despite the limited national appeal of the Democratic candidate, George McGovern, a kind of normalcy had returned to the two-party competition for party loyalties. The proportion of voters with no party identification had increased by a third over that of the late 1950s, but those numbers drew almost equally from Democrats and Republicans. The Democratic margin of party loyalties in 1972 and 1976 was virtually identical to that in 1956 and 1960. And that margin persisted through Reagan's first candidacy and his defeat of Jimmy Carter in 1980.

TABLE 5.3
Party Identification of Voters, 1952–1988

Year	Democrat	Independent	Republican	Partisan Balance
1952	46	24	31	+15
1956	44	24	32	+12
1960	45	22	33	+12
1964	52	20	28	+24
1968	45	28	27	+18
1972	40	31	28	+12
1976	39	34	27	+12
1980	41	32	27	+14
1984	38	31	30	+8
1988	36	30	33	+3
1992	37	35	28	+9

Note: In 1980, 1984, and 1988 the distinction between voters and nonvoters was validated by the National Elections Studies staff. For all other years the distinction relies on the self-reports of individuals.

Source: All of the data are based on the Michigan Survey Research Center of the Center for Political Studies, National Election Studies series.

Between 1980 and 1988, however, at least a limited version of the long-heralded partisan realignment took place. After eight elections, bracketing a span of twenty-eight years, during which Democrats outnumbered Republicans by almost identical margins among those voting for president, the Democratic edge virtually disappeared in the election of 1988. The Democratic plurality dropped from a "normal" 14 points in 1980 to no more than 3 points in 1988. A tentative explanation—or at least a description—of that change will be offered shortly. In the meantime, it is worth noting that the 11-point decline among voters was accompanied by a bare 4-point shift among nonvoters. The disparity stemmed, in part, from the fact that the Democratic edge among nonvoters actually appeared to *increase* between 1984 and 1988 (from 14 to 17 points), whereas it continued to erode among voters. This difference and others between the politically engaged portion of the eligible electorate and those less involved provide direction to our next effort to account for the equalizing realignment in the 1980s.

Just as the disaggregation of the eligible electorate into voters and nonvoters casts a very different light on the historical ebb and flow of partisan sentiments, so a deeper probing into differences in the level of political engagement *among voters* amplifies our understanding of those sentiments. In general, there is a clear if not dramatic evidence that those voters who are the least engaged by, or sophisticated about, politics are the most volatile in their political attitudes, including their political identities. A simplified version of the measure of "levels of conceptualization" introduced in

The American Voter (Campbell, Converse, Miller, and Stokes, 1960) can be used to sort voters into two groups: the more politicized (at the higher two levels) and the less politicized (at the lower two levels). Doing so is a step toward further refining our sense of the conditions under which party identification is persistent and stable, and of the circumstances under which voters alter their habitual party affiliations.

On the average, interelection shifts in the partisan balance of party identification among the voters classified as reflecting the higher levels of conceptualization amounted to changes of only 2 or 3 percentage points between 1952 and 1988. Among the remaining less politicized voters, the same average shift across the nine pairs of elections approximated 5 or 6 points. On average, the changes are not great in either case; hence they reflect the relative stability of party identification among voters, if not always among nonvoters.

However, closer examination reveals that the apparent greater volatility among the less sophisticated, or less engaged, voters is almost entirely the product of two election eras: 1960 to 1964 and 1980 to 1984. Between 1960 and the 1964 Johnson landslide there was an astronomical 35-point shift in party identification favoring the Democrats within the ranks of the less sophisticated voters. This shift erased a 13-point Republican margin in 1960 and produced a 22-point Democratic lead four years later in 1964. The proportion of Democratic identifiers increased by 19 percentage points (from 37 to 56, with 406 and 450 cases in 1960 and 1974, respectively), whereas the proportion of Republicans dropped 16 points (from 50 to 34). It should be noted that this massive exchange took place among voters during such a brief period that turnover in the composition of the electorate cannot be held responsible. There is nothing in the literature on party identification that provides a theoretical basis for anticipating such a high incidence of change.

Moreover, while the less engaged 40 percent of the voters in 1964 were moving precipitously toward the Democrats and away from the Republicans, the more engaged 60 percent were moving in the opposite direction. Although the net figures for changes in party identification among the more sophisticated voters (6 points between 1960 and 1964) did not depart from *their* average change of 5 points across nine pairs of elections, the direction of change favored Barry Goldwater and the Republicans rather than Lyndon Johnson, the Great Society, and the Democrats.

There was clearly something about the period from 1960 to 1964 that evoked very different responses from the more politicized and less politicized voters. This anomaly clearly merits greater attention than it has received because the election of Lyndon Johnson in 1964 marked the one and only significant net shift in the balance of party loyalties among voters between the first Eisenhower election of 1952 and the second Reagan election thirty-two years later in 1984. It is true that the overall Democratic gain of 11 points among voters in 1964 was not a lasting gain; by 1974 things were back to the three-decade norm. Nevertheless, the 1964 Democratic landslide was both a political event of significance and an occasion to learn more about the conditions under which party identifications change.

A similar pair of changes took place, though to a lesser degree and somewhat different in kind, between 1980 and 1984. Among the more sophisticated voters the proportion of self-declared Democrats dropped 2 points as the proportion of Republicans went up 3 points between the two Reagan elections. Among the less sophisticated voters the Democratic loss was 6 and the Republican gain was 7. An even greater contrast occurred on election day. Despite the pro-Republican shift in party identification, the more sophisticated voters increased their 1984 Democratic vote over their 1980 record, from 53 percent Republican and 47 percent Democrat to 48 percent Republican and 52 percent Democrat (a majority voted for Walter Mondale). In contrast the less sophisticated voters turned their 1980 vote, which favored Reagan by a margin of 63 percent Republican to 37 percent Democrat into an 80 to 20 percent rout on his behalf in 1984. By these calculations, Reagan was reelected by the less sophisticated voters. It is, however, of at least equal interest to the student of political change to note that, once again, the more politicized and less politicized voters moved in opposite directions in response to changing events in the world of national politics. Nevertheless, the contrasts in these responses should not be overdrawn. Apart from the two election periods just discussed, the parallelism between the two sets of voters has been notable in election after election over a period of thirty years.

THE REALIGNMENT OF 1980–1988 ... AND 1992

The 1980–1988 realignment among voters apparently took place in two phases, each phase affecting one of the two somewhat different groups of voters we have just noted. Between 1980 and 1984 at least some changes in party loyalties took place pretty much across the board, but the shifting loyalties were concentrated in two familiar sectors. First, young voters shifted more to the Republican side than did the old, again suggesting greater malleability or susceptibility to the winds of change among the less experienced voters. At the same time, among young and old alike, the voters with fewer resources for coping with complex matters of politics swung more heavily to the Republicans. Thus it was the less well educated young people who changed the most: A Democratic margin of 23 points dwindled to 9 points, resulting in a 14-point shift between 1980 and

1984. Among the better-educated older voters, a small 3-point plurality of Republicans grew to an 8-point margin, a shift of only 5 points.

During the second phase of the realignment, there was a further shift to the Republicans in only one sector of the voting population. In Table 5.3 we noted that, across the entire voting population, the Republicans gained only 5 points between 1984 and 1988. Apparently, all of that gain was concentrated in the ranks of the older, better-educated voters. These voters—precisely the group that had been most resistant to the national move into the Republican camp between 1980 and 1984—went from a modest 40 to 32 Republican margin in 1984 to a solid 46 to 28 plurality in 1988. If the first phase of the realignment was a tribute to the charismatic attraction that Ronald Reagan held for the less involved, less political of the voters, the second phase seems to have engaged the more ideologically predisposed voters who had come to appreciate that Reagan really was a conservative Republican president (Miller, 1986).

It is possible, of course, that the realignment of the Reagan years may vanish as swiftly as did the increment that Lyndon Johnson's election gave to the Democrats in 1964. Certainly every national leader is well aware of the speed with which short-run disaster can overtake long-term expectations. Prior to the election of 1992, it seemed more likely that the realignment of the late 1980s was a relatively durable part of the Reagan legacy to American politics. The rationale for such a forecast derives from a basic perspective on the nature of democratic political processes. That perspective, in turn, brings this essay full circle as we move on to another insight expressed by V. O. Key, Jr.—in this case, his metaphor of the electoral process as an echo chamber in which voters echo the message of political leaders. The more elaborate version of Key's perspective is presented as the conclusion to *Public Opinion and American Democracy* (Key, 1961). Key posits political leadership as the wellspring of mass politics and argues that it is the political elite, the subculture of activists, that articulates the alternatives that shape public opinion.

The political elite, including political leaders such as presidents, also gives definition to the political party. (Recall Chapter 4.) There are many reasons for the half-century dominance of American politics by the Democratic party, but not the least of these is the sense of habitual party affiliation that came to many citizens from voting four times for Franklin Delano Roosevelt as the leader of the Democratic party, three times to reaffirm a preference for having him continue as president. At this remove it is difficult to reconstruct the public opinion of fifty years ago, but the incomparable longevity of Roosevelt's presidential leadership must have contributed much to the contemporary meaning of being a "New Deal Democrat."

As we search for the roots of party identification, we may easily forget that following Truman, FDR's vice-president, Eisenhower's hallmark in the public presentation of self was his emphasis on bipartisanship. And although his signal contribution to postwar domestic politics may well have been his conversion of the Republican party from the party of isolationism and America First to the party of internationalism and the United Nations, his legacy was not the redress of the partisan balance in the electorate. It was Eisenhower, not Stevenson, who warned in 1960 of the future dangers of the military-industrial complex. And only rare commentators foresaw a party realignment at the end of Eisenhower's term.

I have already commented on the Kennedy-Johnson era, but it is worth noting again that in the aftermath of New Frontier, Camelot, and Great Society euphoria there were the hot summers and burning riot-torn cities of the late 1960s, Woodstock and the counterculture, and protests against Vietnam and for civil rights. As an antidote to the repressions of the 1950s, American foreign policy, and the heritage of racial discrimination, the decade of protest was undoubtedly overdue; but it was not calculated to endear the Democratic establishment to Main Street America any more than to the hearts of the protesters. In hindsight it is remarkable that the Democratic party did not suffer more as a consequence of the rejection of its leadership in 1968 and 1972, but in fact there was little subsequent evidence of realignment.

The Nixon era, like the Eisenhower years, constituted another opportunity foregone throughout eight years of presidential leadership for the Republican party. Nixon's personal triumph was almost unequalled in his reelection in 1972, but that outcome, Watergate, and the Committee to Reelect the President were all well separated from the Republican party—thus possibly preventing a "failed presidency" from actually disadvantaging Nixon's party.

Carter presided over yet another failed presidency, in large part because he was not the party's leader. He campaigned as an outsider from Plains, Georgia, and he presided as an outsider. Like Johnson, he benefited from his regional identification, and he momentarily slowed the southern white flight from his party with his 1976 campaign when he ran against the Washington establishment. He did not appear to hurt his party—at least not at the grass-roots level, where party identification flourishes—but he scarcely took honors as the revitalizing leader of the party in the electorate.

Ronald Reagan was the only president of the postwar era who took office as an avowed partisan and an unvarnished ideologue; held office for eight years, during which he championed his conservatism *and* his Republicanism; and retired at the end of two full terms with a legacy of goodwill sufficient to elect his successor. The textbooks say that the president is the titular head and leader of the party. Reagan may not have satisfied all the factions within the Republican party, but not because he wasn't an articulate Republican spokesman and an active campaigner openly partisan on the election trail as well as in Washington. And despite trials and tribulations that would have ended some careers, he remained popular to the end and retired from office with the country relatively at peace with itself and others.

In a more detailed account of the changes in party identification between 1980 and 1984, I attribute much of the 1980–1984 change to Reagan's personal popularity among the less experienced and less sophisticated sectors of the electorate (Miller, 1986). That analysis explicitly examined and rejected the hypothesis that it was the Reagan administration's conservatism rather than its Republicanism that provided the foundation for changing partisanship. Four years later, in 1988, it appeared that his sustained personal popularity as president prevented any visible backsliding on the part of the recent converts to Republicanism.

Another relatively elaborate analysis of the 1988 election (Shanks and Miller, 1989) provides two sets of evidence that conform to our interpretation of the two-stage sequence of realignment. In the first place, there is pervasive and powerful evidence of Reagan's contribution to the Bush victory. The election was in some ways a retrospective triumph for Reagan—a triumph of popular satisfaction with his policies, with the general state of the world and of the nation as he left office, and with his performance (Shanks and Miller, 1989). In the absence of evidence to the contrary, there seems no reason not to attribute the carryover of the 1984 increases in Republican party identification to Reagan's carryover popularity.

The second pertinent finding from this election analysis is of a different order. Across the three elections preceding 1988, the distribution of ideological predispositions among voters had not changed from the 13-point margin of self-designated conservatives over self-designated liberals. In 1988 that margin increased by 8 points. In disaggregating voters by age and education, as we have done to locate those who changed their party identification, we find that the older, better-educated voters who had a 15-point increase in their Republican margin (from a slim 34 to 31 in 1980 to a solid 46 to 28 in 1988) between 1980 and 1988 experienced a very substantial 17-point increase in their conservatism during the same interval. Among the better-educated young voters, a comparable increase in conservatism was associated with a full 7-point increase in Republicanism. By contrast, among the less well-educated voters, whose pro-Republican shift occurred entirely between 1980 and 1984 (in response to Reagan's popularity), there was no 1980–1988 increase in conservative predispositions at all. In 1988 the less well-educated voters were more Republican than they had been in 1980, but they were not more conservative; the better-educated voters were both more Republican *and* more conservative.

My analysis of the 1988 elections thus supports the thesis that a significant first phase of the 1980–1988 realignment occurred between 1980 and 1984 among the less experienced and less sophisticated voters who responded to Reagan's personal leadership with an increase in Republicanism. A smaller but perhaps more meaningful second phase then occurred between 1984 and 1988, particularly among the older and better-educated voters who ultimately responded favorably to the Reagan administration's emphasis on conservatism. Thus ideology and personality, articulated and presented by the same presidential party leader, may have reshaped the sense of party loyalty among different sections of the voting public. I am persuaded by this two-pronged explanation of the 1980–1988 realignment because it seems to fit a relatively broad view of the origins of party identification and yet makes explicit the importance of presidential leadership for party as well as for country.

More recently, the importance of political leadership in the shaping of party identifications was reflected in the shifts in party identification that occurred between 1988 and 1992. As Table 5.3 reveals, the ill-fated one-term administration of George Bush was not only another failure of an elected president to win reelection (following the Carter precedent of 1980), it destroyed most of the Republican gains in party identification realized under Bush's predecessor, Ronald Reagan.

The failure of the Bush presidency was, of course, highlighted by the candidacy of Ross Perot. The Perot candidacy, despite its on-again off-again nature, apparently provided an acceptable alternative to disaffected Republicans while mobilizing a sizable increase in the number of political independents who voted. The net result was a decrease in the proportion of Republicans in the national electorate in general and among voters in particular. Among older citizens there was an increase in the number of independents that matched the decrease in the proportion of Republicans. Among younger citizens the decrease in the number of Republicans was matched by an increase in the proportion of Democrats.

At the same time there was an interaction of the changes in party identification with the small increase in voter turnout. Between 1988 and 1992 there was an increase in turnout among Democrats, both young and old, of about 8 points. Among the diminished number of Republicans, there was less of an increase in turnout, and no increase among older Republicans. However, there was a 16-point increase in the turnout of young independents. The decrease in the sheer numbers of Republicans in the electorate can be attributed to the failure of Bush's party leadership because the decrease occurred between 1988 and 1990, well before Perot surfaced as a serious presidential contender and before Clinton was identified as the Democratic challenger. The Republican loss was then compounded by the Perot candidacy as disproportionate numbers of nonidentifiers (former Republicans?) were mobilized to go to the polls on his behalf on election day. The surprising strength of the Perot candidacy and the weakness of Bush as a party leader thus combined to produce changes in party identification that nullified much of the Reagan legacy to the future of the Republican party.

My rendering of the recent history of the persistence of partisan attachments and my examination of the conditions under which voters alter their habitual partisan affiliations are somewhat incomplete. Except for my limited speculation about recent presidencies, I have virtually ignored party in government as a partner in the shaping of mass partisan sentiments. And my disaggregations of the mass did not reach up to either the political activists or the nongovernmental elites that are so much a part of our political processes. Nonetheless, my accumulated resources have permitted explorations and reconstructions that were not available to earlier generations of scholars. The old question "What is a political party?" is answered as before: It is people, the people's leaders, and the symbols they present for public approval. The old question "What causes stability and change in the people's attachment to party?" is now, more than ever, an important question with a very complex set of possible answers rooted in the successes and failures of political leadership.

NOTES

1. At least since the time of Key's seminal article, "A Theory of Critical Elections" (Key, 1955:3–18), analysts have used the concept of political alignment to describe the composition of the competing sides in electoral competition. Realignment occurs when changes take place in the competitive balance between the parties. Realignment may also be *geographic,* as regional alignments change; *group-based,* as social or economic groups shift their party support; or simply *numerical,* as one party grows in size relative to the other. The idea of individuals or groups not taking sides is inherent in the concept of nonalignment, just as moving from support for one side to a middle ground between the parties is described as dealignment. For a good summary discussion, see Sorauf and Beck (1988).

2. In 1952, 80 percent of southern white males identified with one or the other of the two major parties (68 percent Democratic, 12 percent Republican). The Democratic advantage, as shown in Table 5.1, was 56 percent.

6

The Electorate at the
Polls in the 1990s

MORRIS P. FIORINA

In the 1992 elections Bill Clinton put an end to twelve years of Republican presidential control. Running on a simple platform ("The economy, stupid!") Clinton and his surrogates charged that the United States was mired in its worst economic crisis since the Great Depression. Whether the charge reflected economic reality or partisan hyperbole, Republican presidential support collapsed as George Bush saw his popular support drop more than 15 points from his 1988 total.[1]

For some Democrats, long out of power, the 1992 voting brought back warm memories of another Democratic candidate who put an end to twelve years of Republican presidential control—Franklin Delano Roosevelt in 1932. But despite a surface similarity—economic hard times leading to a Democratic victory after a dozen lean years—these two elections half a century apart are noteworthy more for their differences than for their points of similarity.

Consider that while Clinton was carrying thirty-two states, Democratic fortunes in the House of Representatives were actually declining slightly, from 268 seats to 259, and Democratic fortunes in the Senate improved only marginally—a gain of 2 seats. By way of contrast, in 1932 Democrats increased their House majority by 90, from 220 to 310, and captured the Senate with a gain of 13. At the state level, the Democrats in 1932 almost doubled the proportion of states they controlled, whereas in 1992 they only held their own. And, above all else, in 1992 there was the "no-party" candidate, Ross Perot, with 19 percent of the popular vote. Although Clinton carried thirty-two states to record an impressive electoral college victory, Perot denied Clinton a majority of the vote in all but one state—his native Arkansas.

All in all, the Democratic victory in 1992 was narrower and shallower than the victory of 1932, in much the same way that the Republican landslide of 1984 was narrower and shallower than the Democratic landslide of 1936. In the former election Reagan carried every state but Minnesota, a performance comparable to FDR's 1936 sweep in all states but Maine and Vermont. But in 1984 the Republicans gained a disappointing 14 seats in the House, leaving them far short of a majority, and lost 2 seats in the Senate, a performance much inferior to that of the Democrats in 1936, who enlarged both their House and Senate majorities.[2] Similarly, at the state level the Republicans came out of the 1984 elections holding full control in only *four* states, whereas the Democrats captured full control in twenty-nine states in 1936.

This essay addresses the individual voting behavior that generates the narrower and shallower victories in contemporary elections that contrast with the broader and deeper sweeps of half a century ago. In the 1930s the electorate behaved much as it had behaved for the preceding century. It was a *party-oriented electorate*. The great majority of those citizens who supported FDR at the top of the ticket also supported Democratic candidates further down the ticket. Conversely, the preponderance of the minority who supported Herbert Hoover and Alf Landon also cast votes for other Republican candidates. In 1984 and 1992, however, voters continued to behave as they began behaving in the late 1960s. A significant proportion of the citizenry—at least one-quarter and probably more than one-third—picked and chose among the names on the ticket and ended up casting their votes for both Democrats and Republicans (and in 1992, Perot).[3] The electorate today is both more *office-oriented* and more *person-oriented* than the electorate of past generations.[4]

This essay contrasts the voting behavior of the contemporary electorate with its more partisan counterpart of a generation ago. Ideally, one would compare contemporary elections with those of the 1930s, but lack of data makes that impossible. So the partisan electorates used as a contrast to the contemporary electorate are those of 1952–1960. Given that signs of change already were apparent in the 1950s (Alford and Brady, 1989), the comparisons in this essay undoubtedly underestimate the differences between contemporary American voters and their more partisan counterparts of earlier historical periods.

THE AMERICAN VOTER, THEN AND NOW

In 1960 Campbell, Converse, Miller, and Stokes published their monumental treatise, *The American Voter*. Relying on data from the 1952 and 1956 elections, the four Michigan researchers advanced a tripartite explanatory scheme: Voting behavior was motivated by attitudes toward the candidates, the issues, and the parties, with the first providing most of the variation over time, the third accounting for most of the regularity of behavior, and the second apparently trailing the other two in importance.

The Michigan team did not provide any separate analyses of voting for offices other than president; rather, there was an implicit presumption that voting for lesser offices was a simpler, paler reflection of the presidential vote decision. After all, most voters could not recall even the names of the House candidates and had very little information about House races; moreover, as one descended from the presidential level, the importance of partisanship appeared to grow stronger (Stokes and Miller, 1962). Hence "the American voter" described the most general case, one that subsumed the simpler forms of voting behavior.

By the mid-1970s students of voting behavior had come to recognize the need for revision of the prevailing model. The importance of issue attitudes appeared to have grown, and party identification seemed to be somewhat less the unmoved mover than it had been two decades previously. Thus it was only natural that Nie, Verba, and Petrocik (1976) entitled their revisionist treatise *The Changing American Voter*. Nevertheless, the revisionists retained the implicit notion that voting was singular; there was no explicit questioning of the notion that presidential voting behavior was only the most developed form of a particular kind of behavior known as voting.

More than a decade has passed since the revisionist heyday, but no new general treatise on American voting has appeared.[5] Rather, in the past decade students of voting behavior dropped all pretense of a general, unified treatment of voting. Following an outpouring of research on congressional elections, researchers have implicitly come to accept the notion that voting behavior is simply *different* across different offices: One cannot usefully treat the congressional voting decision as a special case of the presidential voting decision. Of course, one can still speak generally of attitudes toward the candidates, the parties, and the issues, but the specific realizations of these concepts differ greatly across offices. Discussions of congressional voting behavior emphasize incumbency, campaign spending, and the (in)visibility of challengers, concepts that are far down the list in any discussion of presidential voting.[6]

Today, research on presidential and congressional elections proceeds largely along independent tracks.[7] Although points of contact exist, different researchers are prominent in each arena and different agendas structure research in each arena. That is the natural approach to the study of an electorate that has become more person and office oriented. Still, an instructive way to highlight the changes that have occurred in American voting behavior is to chronicle the decay in the association between presidential and House voting behavior across time.

The Loosening of the Ties That Bind

Table 6.1 presents the most graphic indicator of the increasing independence of the presidential and House vote. At the turn of the century only a

TABLE 6.1

Percentage of Congressional Districts Carried by House and
Presidential Candidates of Different Parties

Year	Percent	Year	Percent	Year	Percent
1900	3	1948	21	1972	44
1908	7	1952	19	1976	29
1916	11	1956	30	1980	34
1924	12	1960	26	1984	44
1932	14	1964	33	1988	34
1940	15	1968	32	1992	23

Source: Adapted from Stanley and Niemi (forthcoming: Table 4-8).

handful of congressional districts registered pluralities for the presidential candidate of one party and the congressional candidate of another. There was a slight upward trend in the frequency of split outcomes throughout the first half of the century, a noticeable jump at mid-century, and still another sharp increase in the most recent elections. On average, the elections that followed the social upheavals of the 1960s have seen more than a third of all congressional districts turn in a split decision for the presidency and the House—most commonly a verdict for a Republican president and a Democratic member of Congress.[8]

Our interest, of course, is in the individual behavior that underlies the aggregate trend. We do not have individual-level data for the first half of the century, but from 1952 on, the rise in individual ticket splitting has clearly been a major contributor to the increasing proportion of split outcomes. Ticket splitting in the 1950s hovered at the 15 percent level and then jumped sharply in the late 1960s to its current level of approximately 25 percent (see Figure 6.1). Ticket splitting seems to be especially productive of split outcomes when presidents are reelected.[9]

When we begin to delve beneath the individual ticket-splitting series, matters become more complicated. There is every reason to believe that individual ticket splitting has been a response to different factors at different times. For example, practically speaking, ticket splitting was very difficult before the adoption of the Australian ballot at the turn of the century. Prior to that time the parties printed their own ballots, listing only their own nominees. This meant that splitting one's ticket involved crossing out and writing in names, or turning in two (possibly more) ballots with votes marked on each. As party ballots were often color coded and ballots were not marked in secret, ticket splitting was evident to party poll watchers. Thus, splitting one's ticket was both physically and psychically difficult. Institutional and procedural barriers were not the only obstacle to ticket splitting, however. Even after the Australian ballot reforms, the estimated rate of ticket splitting rose only slightly (Rusk, 1970). And obviously, the sharp rise in ticket splitting in the late 1960s has no obvious procedural or institutional basis.

FIGURE 6.1

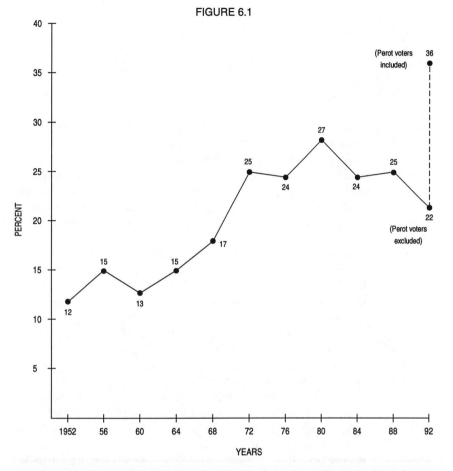

House/president ticket splitting. *Source:* Compiled by the author on the basis of data from Michigan Survey Research Center of the Center for Political Studies, National Election Studies series.

Political historians have argued that the political culture of the late nineteenth century was quite different from that of the early twentieth century, and especially from the contemporary political culture.[10] In the late nineteenth century *independent* was more a term of derogation than one of commendation. An independent was someone who lacked the courage of his ("hers" weren't permitted to vote) party convictions. Partisans, in contrast, were people of principle. Thus, even after ticket splitting became physically and psychologically easier, straight-ticket voting remained the prevailing norm. In contrast, the modern political culture exalts political independence: "Vote for the person, not the party" is a maxim inculcated in recent generations of American schoolchildren. But while political-cultural explanations are consistent with some of the broad pattern of differences between voting in the nineteenth and twentieth centuries, they too fail to account for much of the interesting detail.

For one thing, partisan voting has not steadily declined over the course of the twentieth century. On the contrary, partisanship undoubtedly increased during the 1930s. And far from parties losing their ability to organize the electorate, there was more unified government in the first half of the twentieth century than *either* before or since (Fiorina, 1990). As late as 1958, 85 percent of all American voters were loyally voting for the House candidate of their party. That is the contemporary high-water mark, however; the loyalty of partisans in House elections has dropped significantly since then (see Table 6.2). The exact numbers in these series are subject to some dispute, since they depend on whether one classifies those who say they are independent but lean toward a party as partisans or as independents.[11] But even strong partisans are less likely to support the House candidate of their party today than they were a generation ago.

What seems clear is that changes in the political culture or no, party identification in the population was a stronger correlate of voting in the 1930s and 1940s than it is today. Although the increased independence of the contemporary electorate clearly has been exaggerated, it is apparent that in the period covered by the American National Election Studies there has been a general weakening in the strength of partisanship (see Figure 6.2).[12] And in addition, there has been a decline in the capacity of partisanship to "structure" the vote. That is, even those who report that they are strong partisans today are less likely to support their party's candidates across the board than they were a generation ago. When we speak of the erosion of partisanship, we refer to the sum of both processes— more independents, fewer strong partisans, and a lessened partisan impact on voting for different offices.

Thus, with the abolition of procedural/institutional barriers to ticket splitting, only psychological barriers such as partisanship remained. When the latter began to erode, a space was opened in which other factors might affect the vote.

Filling the Space

A lesser reliance on partisanship does not logically entail a decline in straight-ticket voting. The diminished role of partisanship simply enhanced the opportunity for other factors to affect votes, especially the votes of independents and of those with weak partisan leanings. But those factors could just as easily have led to an *increase* in straight-ticket voting. For example, consider presidential coattails. Some congressional votes are the product of decisions to vote a particular way for president. A presidential nominee who raises his party's congressional vote total by a large amount is said to have long coattails.[13] If voters had come to focus more

TABLE 6.2
Party-Line Voting in Presidential and Congressional Elections
(as percentage of all voters), 1956–1988

	Presidential Elections			House Elections		
Year	Party-Line Voters	Defectors	Pure Independents	Party-Line Voters	Defectors	Pure Independents
1956	76	15	9	82	9	9
1958				84	11	5
1960	79	13	8	80	12	8
1962				83	12	6
1964	79	15	5	79	15	5
1966				76	16	8
1968	69	23	9	74	19	7
1970				76	16	8
1972	67	25	8	75	17	8
1974				74	18	8
1976	74	15	11	72	19	9
1978				69	22	9
1980	70	22	8	69	23	8
1982				76	17	6
1984	81	12	7	70	23	7
1986				72	22	6
1988	81	12	7	74	20	7
1992	68	24	9	71	21	7

Source: Adapted from Stanley and Niemi (forthcoming: Table 4-5).

FIGURE 6.2

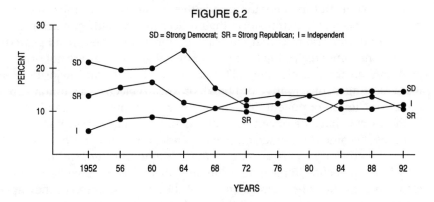

Declines in partisan identification. Source: Adapted from Stanley and Niemi (forthcoming: Table 5-1).

and more on their presidential vote decision as their partisanship weakened, then straight-ticket voting might have remained constant or might even have increased as voters associated their votes for lower offices with their votes for president. Coattails could have replaced partisanship.

In fact, the importance of presidential coattails has declined over time (Ferejohn and Calvert, 1984). The influence of presidential votes on congressional votes declined by more than 50 percent over the course of a generation (see Table 6.3). Rather than associate their House votes more closely with their presidential votes and the numerous national factors that determine the latter, voters increasingly seem to be casting their House votes on some different basis.

The most obvious other basis is incumbency. The importance of incumbency status has approximately quadrupled over the course of the past generation, with a particularly sharp upsurge in the late 1960s (see Table 6.3), precisely the time during which the split-ticket voting series showed its sharpest increase. Incumbents have always had some advantage—they are proven winners, after all. But during the 1960s the electoral value of being an incumbent increased sharply.[14] Too much has been written on this topic to summarize here (for comprehensive surveys, see Beth, 1981–1982, 1984). Suffice it to say that a number of reinforcing developments have rende ed careful incumbents all but invulnerable. They have permanent personal staffs, district offices, and travel and communications budgets that would cost challengers as much as a million dollars per year to duplicate; the growth of government has enabled them to provide impressive levels of nonpartisan constituency services; and they are able to raise hundreds of thousands of dollars in campaign contributions from PACs and other contributors.[15] For these and other lesser reasons, House incumbents have been able to transform their offices in 435 political machines.

The important point is that these 435 political machines are all geared toward one thing: reelecting the member of Congress. They are not principally geared toward electing a Democratic or Republican majority, toward electing a conservative or liberal, or toward electing a Clinton supporter or Clinton opponent. Individuation is the name of the game. And to the extent that voters can be induced to play that game, voting for Congress becomes that much more independent of voting for president.

So, the erosion of partisanship in the contemporary era did not logically imply a decline in partisan behavior. Citizens could have decided to focus on the office of the presidency, but they did not. Instead, they appear to have compartmentalized their decisions, relying on one set of considerations when deciding how to vote for president, another set of considerations when deciding how to vote for members of the House, and perhaps still a third set of considerations when deciding how to vote for senators. And this process of differentiation continues when attention turns to various state and local offices.

We summarize everything discussed thus far by comparing presidential-congressional voting in 1952 and 1960 with that in 1980 and 1988 (see Table 6.4). In 1952 and 1980 the electorate turned out unpopular Demo-

TABLE 6.3
The Effect of Presidential Votes and Incumbency on Votes for House Candidates,
1956–1980

	Seats with Incumbents	
Year	Presidential Votes	Incumbency
1956	.38	.09
1960	.47	.13
1964	.47	.15
1968	.50	.17
1972	.31	.24
1976	.24	.34
1980	.24	.34

Source: Ferejohn and Fiorina (1985).

TABLE 6.4
Comparison of Voting Models

	1952	1960	1980	1988
President				
Constant	$.33^b$	$.49^b$	$.38^b$	$.38^b$
Democratic ID	$.27^b$	$.17^b$	$.23^b$	$.32^b$
Republican ID	$-.05$	$-.18^b$	$-.10^b$	$-.11^b$
Party likes & dislikes	$.04^b$	$.03^b$	$.02^b$	$.02^b$
Candidate likes & dislikes	$.04^b$	$.05^b$	$.06^b$	$.04^b$
n	1181	885	845	1159
R^2	.59	.61	.58	.63
% Correctly predicted	89	89	87	89
House				
Constant	$.15^b$	$.25^b$	$.35^b$	$.46^b$
Democratic ID	$.26^b$	$.15^b$	.07	.00
Republican ID	$-.07^a$	$-.17^b$	$-.08^b$	$-.24^b$
Party likes & dislikes	.00	.00	.01	$.02^b$
Presidential vote	$.55^b$	$.49^b$	$.24^b$	$.22^b$
Dem. incumbent	–	$.08^a$	$.25^b$	$.28^b$
Rep. incumbent	–	.05	$-.13^a$	$-.17^b$
n	972	706	668	793
R^2	.63	.61	.39	.56
% Correctly predicted	87	88	78	85

$^a p < .05$
$^b p < .01$
Source: Compiled by author on the basis of data from Michigan Survey Research Center
of the Center for Political Studies, National Election Studies series.

cratic administrations and elected candidates of the minority Republican
party—along with a congressional majority in the first case, but not in the
second. In 1960 and 1988 incumbent vice-presidents attempted to succeed
popular presidents—unsuccessfully in the first case as the Democrats won
an across-the-board, if narrow, victory. In contrast, 1988 illustrates the

common late twentieth-century pattern—a Republican presidential victory coupled with a comfortable Democratic win in the House.

The major points of the preceding discussion are apparent in light of the following statistical results.[16]

1. The capacity of party identification to "structure" the vote across offices has declined: The difference between self-identified Democrats and Republicans in presidential voting has widened, if anything, but it has narrowed significantly in congressional voting.[17]
2. The importance of House incumbency has increased: In the 1960 House equation, incumbency is barely significant for Democrats and effectively zero for Republicans, whereas it is the single most important variable in the later equations.[18]
3. The impact of party evaluations (measured on a scale running from −10 to +10) declines over time in the presidential equations. Wattenberg (1990) has shown that fewer people offer party evaluations; this analysis reveals that those who do so are motivated less by them when casting their *presidential* votes. The importance of party evaluations in House voting, however, appears to have grown: The smaller proportion of people who advance party evaluations take more account of them when casting their House votes than did the larger proportion a generation ago.[19]
4. The impact of presidential vote choice (coattails) on the House vote in the 1980s was less than half what it was in 1952 and 1960.
5. As a consequence of the first four points, the presidential and congressional votes responded largely to the same factors in 1952 and 1960, but not in 1980 and 1984. Even without incumbency in the equation, the president and House equations predict virtually the same percent of voters correctly in 1960, whereas without incumbency the 1988 House prediction is almost 10 percent poorer than the presidential prediction, and the 1980 prediction is almost 10 percent poorer even with incumbency in the equation. In sum, the factors that produce an association between presidential votes and House votes operate less consistently today than a generation ago.

WHY THE CHANGES?

The preceding section describes the changes that have taken place in voting behavior in national elections over the past generation. But description is not explanation. The glue that unified the electoral behavior of previous generations—voter partisanship—has weakened, allowing voters to respond in a more differentiated way to the individual candidates and the offices they contest. Why has partisanship weakened? To discuss the possible answers, one must first understand the nature of partisanship.

In the original Michigan formulation, a voter's party identification was viewed as a psychological affiliation generally fixed early in life and highly resistant to change thereafter (Campbell et al., 1960, Ch. 7). Later research has given the concept a more instrumental interpretation. Party identification now is thought to reflect (at least in part) the similarity between a voter's opinions and the policy positions of the favored party (Jackson, 1975; Franklin and Jackson, 1983), and the voter's evaluation of the relative performance of the parties when they held office (Fiorina, 1981). Under these interpretations the partisanship of an electorate can be explained in fairly simple terms. Figure 6.3 depicts a simple two-dimensional policy space, where the horizontal dimension indexes left-right positions on economic policy issues and the vertical dimension indexes liberal-conservative positions on social issues. There is a large cluster of voters in the southwest corner of the space and another cluster in the northeast corner. If one party consistently locates near each cluster and implements policies favored by that cluster when in office, then over time we would expect to see the voters in each cluster develop an identification with the party nearer them. Socialist libertines would consistently oppose laissez-faire prudes, voters would believe that elections have major implications for the future course of their society and that their party would better handle the most important problems facing their society, and most voters would vote straight tickets.

Alternatively, for whatever reason (perhaps the influence of highly ideological but unrepresentative party activists), the parties might both locate far from the voter clusters (see Figure 6.4). Socialist libertine voters would be attracted by the economic positions of the socialist prude party but be repelled by its social issue positions; conversely, they might be attracted to the social issue positions of the free-market libertine party but be repelled by its economic policies. Free-market prude voters would be in an analogous situation of attraction-repulsion. In this system one would not expect to see voters develop strong party affiliations: Even though they would agree that there are important differences in what the parties stand for, most of them would be cross-pressured by the positions and performances of the contending parties.

Finally, Figure 6.5 depicts still a third situation. Now the voters are a heterogeneous lot, scattered evenly throughout the policy space. Wherever the parties locate, they will have no great appeal to most of the voters. Thus, here too, the electorate is unlikely to develop strong party affiliations: Whether the parties locate far apart or very near each other, most voters will not see them as terribly relevant for their own policy choices.

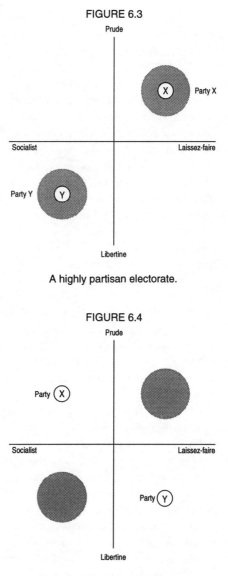

FIGURE 6.3

A highly partisan electorate.

FIGURE 6.4

Out-of-touch parties.

A highly partisan electorate, then, is likely to be one in which voters are polarized and, equally important, one in which each party makes clear, differentiated appeals to one or the other polarized sector of the electorate. Conversely, an electorate will not be highly partisan when either or both of two conditions hold: (1) voters are widely distributed over the cleavage space; (2) parties are out of touch with voters. Obviously, if vot-

FIGURE 6.5

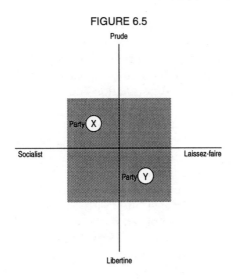

A heterogeneous electorate.

ers are sufficiently heterogeneous, then parties *must* be out of touch with many of them.

The explanation of the weakening of partisanship in the United States appears to be some combination of Figures 6.4 and 6.5.[20] In the New Deal party system, voters and parties were divided relatively clearly along economic lines with the Democrats taking a clear stand in favor of government intervention and the Republicans taking an equally clear position of general opposition to government intervention. After the outbreak of World War II foreign policy largely ceased to be a matter of partisan disagreement, and for many years the issue of race was kept off the agenda.

This simple equilibrium ended in the mid-1960s, however, as the Vietnam War divided the Democratic party's elite, and as race and social issues drove a wedge between working class whites, on the one hand, and blacks and cause groups, on the other. Changes in the nomination process that enabled the nationally unattractive George McGovern to win the nomination in 1972, and the disappointing economic performance of the Carter administration in 1976–1980, further eroded the accumulated political capital of the Democratic party. The cumulative impact of these developments can be seen in the erosion of Democratic partisanship from its 1964 high—in retrospect, the last hurrah of the New Deal Democrats (see Figure 6.2).[21] Apparently the Democratic losses came less from the outright desertion of older partisans than from the failure of their children to take on the expected Democratic coloration (see Miller, this volume).

Meanwhile, the Republican party was experiencing its own difficulties, though these were evidently less harmful to their electoral prospects than those of the Democrats. The Republican geographic base broadened and deepened under the impetus of social and economic change. The racial issue enabled them to become the preferred presidential party of the South and to capture a significant number of House and Senate seats. The growth of the sunbelt added population and wealth to areas already favorable to Republicans. At the same time, they were able to harness the energies of some of the cause groups that formed largely in reaction to Democratic policies—the complex of groups generally referred to as the "new right." These and other lesser developments made the party considerably more internally heterogeneous than in the past, but the splits did not emerge on the electoral level to anything like the degree that they did in the Democratic party (Mayer and Polsby, 1993). In fact, the mid-1980s saw a slight increase in Republican partisanship (see Figure 6.2), apparently reflecting the relative success of the Reagan administration in controlling inflation, promoting economic growth, and strengthening America's position in the international arena.

WHERE ARE WE NOW AND WHERE ARE WE GOING?

The late-century Republican presidential advantage was nowhere in sight in 1992. The question is whether its disappearance is temporary or permanent. Will the Republican advantage reappear once the wave of poor economic conditions recedes, or is the era of Republican presidential advantage over? We are too close to the election to have the benefit of detailed and relatively disinterested academic analyses, but two conflicting points of view have been articulated by those struggling to define the meaning of the election.

First, there is the orthodox Republican view, according to which the Clinton victory is an aberration attributable to adverse economic conditions, a poor candidate, a hostile press, or some combination of these. This view notes that Clinton won just 43 percent of the popular vote and expects him to overplay his hand with tax increases and proposals for new government programs. In the end, Clinton will be another Jimmy Carter, in fate if not in style.

Second, there is an orthodox Democratic view, according to which the Clinton victory is the dawn of a new Democratic era. The electorate finally realized the error of Reaganomics and expiated its guilt with a massive rejection of the incumbent administration. Though some frustrated citizens supported Perot, a vigorous Clinton presidency that deals effectively with the budget deficit and health care will consolidate the anti-Bush votes into a solid Democratic majority. In the terminology of this essay, such developments would move the electorate back in the direction of Figure 6.3.

At this time I would bet on the prototypical academic view: It is too early to tell exactly what happened, but eventually the truth will be found to lie somewhere between the sour grapes Republican view and the wishful-thinking Democratic view. I suspect that the main story line of 1992 will be a shift of the moderates from a generally pro-Republican stance to an anti-Bush, but not necessarily pro-Democratic, stance.

To elaborate, the issues on which the parties and candidates have contended during the past generation fall into four general categories: economic policy, foreign and defense policy, racial issues, and social issues. In each category most issues have liberal, moderate, and conservative positions. Briefly, the issues appear as follows:

Economic policy

> liberal: activist government—taxing, spending, and regulating are good things
>
> moderate: skeptical about efficacy of government programs; unwilling to pay higher taxes
>
> conservative: government is the problem

Foreign policy

> liberal: emphasis on human rights; America is often the problem
>
> moderate: avoid violence if possible but defend legitimate interests of the United States
>
> conservative: support anti-communist regimes—no questions asked; generous use of force

Racial issues

> liberal: affirmative action; culture of victimization
>
> moderate: equality of opportunity, not equality of result; individual responsibility
>
> conservative: Willie Horton

Social/lifestyle issues

> liberal: anything goes
>
> moderate: support traditional values but tolerate alternatives
>
> conservative: cultural warfare

My view is that within each general issue category the electorate is distributed in such a way that any two of the three positions outweigh the third. The story of the Republican presidential victories of the past generation is that the Democrats were reduced to their core base of support among the liberals in each issue category and that the Republican victories were fashioned by adding the majority of the moderates to their conservative base.[22] What happened in 1992 was that the moderates abandoned George Bush.

With the apparent demise of communism, foreign and defense policy simply ceased to be an issue. Foreign policy moderates had little reason to believe that Democratic pacifism would greatly endanger the nation. Racial and social issue moderates—including but not limited to "the Reagan Democrats"—voted their economic interests. Besides, Clinton took positions on some such issues (e.g., welfare) that would have sent liberal Democrats into orbit just a few years ago. And whatever their skepticism about government programs, economic moderates could understandably decide that taking a gamble was preferable to the drift that they observed.

At this time the data are not available to put such speculations on a firmer footing. Preliminary data indicate that more self-identified independents (who tend to be centrist in their views) supported the Democratic than the Republican candidate for the first time since 1964. Even with Perot in the race, Clinton received a higher proportion of the independent vote than did Mondale in 1984 (Table 6.5).

The Democratic fear and Republican hope, however, is that the moderates have only rejected George Bush and the Republican party he led, not embraced Bill Clinton and the Democratic party he leads. Consider the one-fifth of the electorate that supported Ross Perot, a group that could either solidify a Democratic majority or render it ephemeral if its members moved en masse toward either party. Numerous analysts have remarked that Perot voters differ from both Bush voters and Clinton voters in important respects (Table 6.6). On the one hand Perot supporters agree with Clinton supporters that the recession of 1990–1991 is not a normal cyclical downturn but part of a serious long-term decline. Bush supporters are much more optimistic. On the other hand Perot supporters agree with Bush supporters that government should be cheaper and leaner. Clinton supporters feel more positive toward government programs. On social issues Perot supporters are closer to Bush supporters than to Clinton supporters, though other data suggest that Perot supporters attach less importance to such issues. All in all, it does not appear that the hearts and minds of Perot supporters will be captured by liberal positions on economic and social issues.

Thus, the upset Democratic victory of 1992 does not alter the basic portrait of the electorate in the contemporary era. It continues to be an electorate not firmly committed to either party, reflecting both its own diversity (Figure 6.5) and the mismatch with both parties (Figure 6.4).[23] The conditions for a realignment that would restore a party-oriented elector-

TABLE 6.5
Presidential Vote of Independents (in percent)

Year	Democratic	Republican	Other
1976	48	52	–
1980	31	56	13
1984	36	64	–
1988	43	57	–
1992	38	32	30

Source: Data from *Public Perspective,* January-February 1993: 90–91.

TABLE 6.6
Political Views of Clinton, Bush, and Perot Voters (in percent)

Normal economic downturn or serious long-term decline?

Long-term decline	Clinton voters:	66
	Perot voters:	65
	Bush voters:	27

Rather have more government services and higher taxes, or fewer services and lower taxes?

More and higher	Clinton voters:	55
	Perot voters:	26
	Bush voters:	20

More important for government to encourage traditional family values or encourage tolerance of nontraditional families?

Nontraditional	Clinton voters:	42
	Perot voters:	19
	Bush voters:	9

Source: Public Perspective, January-February 1993:94–95.

ate are not present. Nevertheless, it is too early to sell Clinton short. The president controls the agenda. In health care and the budget deficit, Clinton faces daunting problems, but the greater the problems, the greater the opportunity. Our present problems are no worse than those confronted by Roosevelt in 1932. He seized the opportunity and forged the party-oriented electorate that persisted until the 1960s. Whether 1992 will eventually be considered similar to or a contrast with 1932 remains to be seen.

NOTES

1. According to some of the more traditional economic indicators, the condition of the economy was not all that bad, a fact that led some models of presidential voting to predict that Bush would be reelected.

2. The 12-seat House gain by itself may seem small, but it came on the heels of the only midterm election since the Civil War in which the party of the incumbent president gained seats (9) and followed a gain of 90 seats in 1932 and 53 in 1930.

3. One can make only rough estimates about levels of split-ticket voting across

time. In the 1980s somewhat more than a quarter of all voters in American National Election Study surveys report splitting their tickets between presidential and House candidates. When senatorial, gubernatorial, and state and local voting are considered, the total obviously must be higher. We do not have a reliable base of survey data for the 1930s, but as shown further on in the text, in 1956 president-House ticket splitting was only 15 percent. Given that a Republican president and a Democratic House were elected in 1956, it appears reasonable to presume that the 1932 and 1936 ticket-splitting figures must have been significantly lower.

4. Note that "person" does not mean "personality." One may support a particular candidate on the basis of his or her issue stands, past performance, and other reasons more substantial than "personality."

5. More than modesty leads me to subsume my own *Retrospective Voting in American National Elections* (1981) under this generalization. Following Ladd and Burnham, I argued in the final pages of that work that electoral behavior was becoming sufficiently disaggregated as to make a unified treatment problematic.

6. There is much less research on state and local elections, but it has a similar implication: The forces at work in such elections require attention to variables other than those required to describe presidential voting.

7. The principal exception to this generalization would be the study of economic voting, in which researchers move easily between voting for president and voting for Congress.

8. There has also been an increase noted in the number of states that are simultaneously represented by a senator from each party. This does not reflect ticket splitting in a single election, of course, but it does indicate some electoral instability from election to election. See Poole and Rosenthal (1984:Figure 1).

9. For statistical aficionados the regression equation that predicts split outcomes from ticket splitting (1952–1988) is

% split = 14.4 + .94(% ticket splitting),
adj R^2 = .37 (all coefficients p < .05).

When presidential reelection interacts with ticket splitting, the equation is a much superior

% split = 15 + .68(% ticket splitting) + .50(% ticket splitting) $\times$ reelection
adj R^2 = .83 (all coefficients p < .01).

10. For a thoughtful recent discussion, see McGerr (1986).

11. The figures in Table 6.2 are conservative, however, in that if independents who lean toward a party were classified as true independents, the figures for party-line voting would obviously be lower.

12. Wolfinger and his students provide a careful look at temporal changes in party identification, showing that the shifts have been much smaller than usually argued. See Keith et al. (1992).

13. In the popular press, a president's coattails are sometimes measured by the number of *seats* his party gains in Congress. Given the vagaries of the translation of votes into seats in single-member simple-plurality electoral systems, and strong evidence of change in that translation over time (Ansolabehere, Brady, and

Fiorina, 1992), seat totals do not yield accurate estimates of the strength of presidential coattails.

14. Jacobson (1987) has noted that, although incumbent vote totals went up sharply, incumbent reelection rates (already above 90 percent) increased only a little.

15. Note, however, that the sharp increase in the apparent advantage of incumbency preceded the PAC explosion by ten years or so.

16. Probit estimates are technically more appropriate, but their implications generally differ little from those of regression estimates when the dependent variable splits in the 60:40 range. The advantage of regression is that coefficients can be directly compared across equations. These regression results are fully compatible with probit results that are not reported. References to the percentage correctly predicted by the models denote the unreported probit results.

17. Democratic and Republican effects are measured relative to independents (the omitted category). Other things being equal, independents and Republicans were very close in 1952, whereas in 1960 independents were midway between Republicans and Democrats. In the 1980s independents were closer to Republicans in their presidential voting but closely resembled Democrats in their House voting.

18. In 1952 the Survey Research Center did not code the congressional district of the respondent, thus making it impossible to enter incumbency status into the equations for that year.

19. This is not the place to explore this finding at length. Possibly it reflects the increased distinctiveness of the congressional parties as southern Democrats have become more like other Democrats. See Rohde (1989).

20. There is another instrumental theory of partisanship proposed by Shively (1979) that has roots in Downs (1957). Party identification can serve as a means for economizing on decisionmaking costs: One need only ascertain the candidate's party label and vote accordingly. This theory can also account for the erosion of partisanship: As the electorate became better educated and as media coverage of politics increased, voters were presumably less in need of a simple means of making decisions. But the theory is also fully compatible with the performance-evaluation and policy-compatibility theories of partisanship discussed in the text. As voters become less enamored of the parties, for any of the reasons discussed in connection with Figures 6.4 and 6.5, party would become a less useful guide to voting.

21. At first glance this account might appear to be at odds with that of Wattenberg (1986), who discounts negative voter reaction to the parties as an explanation for the weakening of voter partisanship. Although he concedes that voter repulsion from the parties was evident in 1968 (p. 60), Wattenberg argues that the more general and important factor is that voters increasingly believe the parties are irrelevant. I think that there is a subtle but plausible way to reconcile Wattenberg's careful analysis with the more conflict-based account offered in the text and in much of the literature. Wattenberg focuses on leadership, arguing that "the link between issues and parties depends heavily on the candidate's actions, that is, his or her treatment of issues in partisan terms. ... It is thus crucial to note that for a variety of institutional reasons candidates now have substantially less incentive to foster the link between themselves and the parties, as well as between

political issues and the parties" (p. 74). Yes, but might there be something beyond "institutional reasons"? In 1960 John Kennedy wrapped himself in the Democratic party mantle because he expected to gain from it; Richard Nixon avoided the Republican tag because he expected to be hurt by it. Realizing that the party label carried too much harmful baggage, recent candidates of both parties have deemphasized it, thus contributing to the trend described by Wattenberg. Neutral feelings or no, the experience of the 1988 campaign strongly suggests that negative associations from the past can be reactivated very easily.

22. Jimmy Carter's 1976 victory is the exception. As a white southern evangelical, he appeared moderate on racial and social issues and, relative to other Democrats, appeared moderate on economic issues as well. As in 1992 he was also running after a recession on a Republican president's watch, not to mention Watergate.

23. One of the more intriguing bits of data to emerge from the 1992 campaign season was the following: According to NBC News/*USA Today* surveys of convention delegates, 46 percent of the Republican delegates reported that they were "born again Christians," and 45 percent of the Democratic delegates reported working for some level of government (Black and Black, 1992:5). Apparently, moderate voters have a choice between two contending political elites, one of which they suspect wants its nose in their bedrooms, the other of which they suspect wants its hand in their wallets.

PART FOUR

The Electoral Arena

7

Nomination Politics:
The Roles of Institutional, Contextual,
and Personal Variables

L. SANDY MAISEL
LINDA L. FOWLER
RUTH S. JONES
WALTER J. STONE

On the Tuesday after the first Monday in November, in even-numbered years, Americans go to the polls to elect tens of thousands of public officials. Although many office holders are elected on other days in other years, at no time is the vast expanse of our multitiered, federated system, which features separate legislative, executive, and judicial branches, so evident to even the most casual observer as it is on these election days.

Each state's entire delegation to the U.S. House of Representatives is elected every two years; Senate elections are held in approximately two-thirds of the states. Forty-five of the states elect representatives to the lower house of their state legislature every two years; thirteen states elect members of their upper house every two years; most of the other states elect state senators for four-year terms, with senatorial elections divided between presidential and nonpresidential election years; forty-seven of the fifty states elect governors for four-year terms, thirty-three of those in nonpresidential election, even-numbered years and five in odd-numbered years.[1] A common feature of all of these elections, save the elections to Nebraska's unicameral legislature, is that they are partisan elections; that is, candidates are listed on the ballot by political party.

Fewer commonalities exist for other elections held on the same day. Some states hold a series of statewide elections—for lieutenant governor, attorney general, treasurer, and like offices. In some states, county, municipal, and special district (e.g., school board and water district board) elections are held on the same day, while in others they are held on different days in the same year or in different years. In some states certain judicial posts are filled by election—on the same day or not—whereas in other states all judicial posts are filled by appointment. In some states all or some of the elections held are partisan, although roughly three-quarters of American towns and cities now conduct local elections on a nonpartisan basis (Sorauf and Beck, 1988:57; Welch and Bledsoe, 1986). The picture that emerges from this review is one of a vast array of elections, many of them held on the same day, many of them between candidates of political parties, to fill the offices that hold the executive, legislative, and at times judicial powers at the national, state, and local levels.

Representative democracy in the United States depends on competition for office (Dahl, 1956; Downs, 1957; and many others). If there is no competition for office, then the citizenry cannot replace those who are implementing policies with which they disagree. A healthy party system plays the role of guaranteeing this competition for office. According to V. O. Key (1964:10), "The electoral practices of democracies are associated with party systems which propose to the electorate a choice." Similarly, as Frank Sorauf (1964:10) has noted, "The parties facilitate the popular participation, the representation of interests, and the presentation of alternatives on which the processes of democracy depend." In the vast number of elections that are partisan, parties play this role by nominating candidates to contest for office.[2] That is, they create competition for office, and they structure choice for the voters.

However, all parties do not perform this task equally well in all contexts. In this essay, we shall explore the role that political parties, in differing political environments, play in selecting candidates for office. To anticipate the argument, we first examine the relative success of parties in providing electoral competition. We then explore the structural limitations on political parties and the ways in which contemporary parties have worked to increase their influence and thus their effectiveness in guaranteeing competition. Next we turn to the choices made by potential candidates for office. We present a model that helps define the role parties play in determining whether effective competition for office will exist. We conclude with some speculation about the emerging role of political parties in selecting candidates for office.

PARTY EFFECTIVENESS IN CANDIDATE RECRUITMENT

Parties vary significantly in their ability to recruit candidates to run for office. They may nominate strong contenders in some states but field only weak opposition in others. Or they may field tough competitors for some offices in a community but lack a full slate of qualified nominees across the entire ticket. The parties often battle each other intensely for certain offices and merely scuffle for many others. Consequently, voters frequently find themselves preferring one party's nominee for a particular office and selecting the opposing party's candidate for some other position. Uneven competition for many governmental positions and divided party control of the legislative and executive branches frequently result from such variation in party recruitment.

There are several reasons for so much diversity in the capacity of parties to recruit competitive candidates. First, American parties are extremely decentralized organizations. They lack mechanisms available to European parties for shifting money and talent from one community to another. If a local party organization is ineffective or badly outnumbered by the opposing party, it gets little help from the national or state party headquarters. Thus, a chronically weak party organization may suffer from uncompetitive or nonexistent candidates for a long period of time.

Second, because of numerous reforms, parties in the United States lost many of the resources and prerogatives for controlling nominations that they enjoyed in the nineteenth century. With the exception of a few remaining city and county political machines, parties have limited incentives to encourage prospective candidates to run. They have even fewer sanctions to protect their preferred nominees from a primary challenge. Parties thus are subject to the ambitions of individual politicians who initiate their candidacies and organize their own campaigns.

Given the prevalence of candidate-centered elections, parties may find themselves with either an embarrassment of ambitious politicians or a dearth of willing contenders. When the electoral climate looks good, parties experience hotly contested primaries. But when political conditions are unfavorable and no one wants to assume the costs and risks of campaigning, parties are left with two options: a blank ballot or a sacrificial lamb. It is not clear just what conditions prompt the emergence of competitive candidates, but scholars have concluded that it is some mix of local issues and party strength, national trends concerning the economy and presidential performance, and the presence or absence of a strong incumbent on the ballot.

The variation in the number and quality of party candidates shows up in several different patterns of competition. First is the incidence of elections in which one party fails to nominate a candidate. Second is the frequency of elections in which the outcome is lopsided because one of the party nominees ran an uncompetitive race. Throughout much of the twentieth century, the Republican party lacked any significant presence in the South and seldom fielded candidates in the region. Beginning in the 1960s, however, the GOP has gradually gained strength among southern voters and has increased its capacity to contest elections, particularly statewide offices such as governor and senator. At the same time, both the

Democrats and Republicans have developed weaknesses in other parts of the country that have inhibited their ability to place nominees on the ballot or to pick a strong contestant.

Uncontested Elections

The most extreme form of party failure in the nomination of candidates is the uncontested election. Clearly, if one or the other of the major parties does not run a candidate for office, no partisan competition can take place—and the party without a candidate has abdicated its most basic responsibility. In recent years, the parties have done a much better job of providing voters with a choice on the ballot for statewide offices than in fielding candidates for the U.S. House of Representatives or state legislatures. In Figure 7.1, for example, it is clear that after 1968, voters rarely encountered a statewide ballot that lacked either a gubernatorial or senatorial nominee. Since 1976, in fact, there have been no uncontested races for governor and only a handful of such races for senator in 1986 and again in 1990. Furthermore, in the past all of the party failures occurred in the South, where the Republicans lacked any sort of organization, but today the few cases of uncontested seats are as likely to arise outside the South and to involve either party.

Just the opposite pattern marks elections for the U.S. House and state legislatures. Although the frequency of uncontested races declined for the House because of the increased presence of Republicans in the South, just as it did for the Senate, it never fell as far, and by the 1980s it began to rise steadily. In Figure 7.2, the percentage of uncontested races peaked at 19.5 percent in 1990, nearly reaching the level of the 1950s. Equally striking about these data is the fact that both parties began to have difficulty nominating candidates, with Democrats accounting for about 40 percent of the party failures. Moreover, uncontested seats were no longer concentrated in the South but were appearing all over the country, particularly in large cities and in districts with popular incumbents.

The number of uncontested House races dropped sharply to 6.2 percent in 1992, however, because of an exceptional set of political events. The unprecedented number of fifty-two members retired from public life, two died in office, thirteen left to run for another office, and a record nineteen were defeated in primaries. Another ten incumbents ended up running against each other in newly drawn districts. Further opportunities were created by reapportionment, which established new districts and changed the partisan balance in many others. A final stimulus to competition was the anti-incumbent mood of the electorate, which led some political observers to predict, wrongly as it turned out, that fifty incumbents could be tossed out of office. Under these unique circumstances, both parties were able to field an unusual number of competitive candidates.

FIGURE 7.1

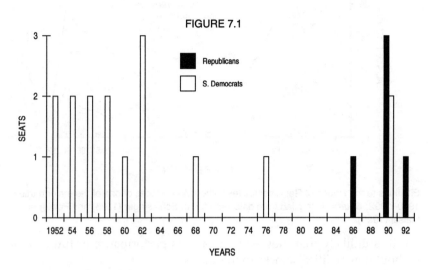

A: Uncontested senate seats.

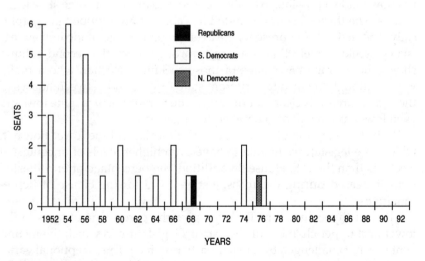

B: Uncontested gubernatorial seats.

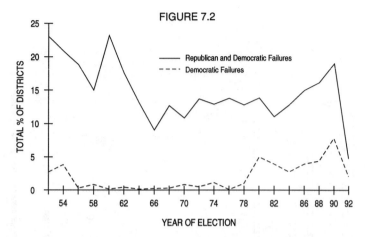

FIGURE 7.2

Elections to the House of Representatives without a candidate of one of the major parties, 1950–1992. *Source:* Compiled from data reported in Schlesinger (1985) and Fowler and Maisel (1990).

But it is unlikely that they will repeat this performance in future years without new political shocks to the status quo.

A similarly uncompetitive situation exists in many state legislatures, although it is more difficult to document. A comprehensive study by the Inter-University Consortium for Political and Social Research, however, has now made it possible to analyze electoral patterns for some state legislatures. The thirteen states included in Table 7.1 are grouped geographically. The first column presents the average percentage of incumbent legislators seeking reelection from 1978 through 1988; the second column shows the average percentage of those seeking reelection who actually won. Although the results vary from state to state and between houses of the legislatures, it is clear that turnover due to retirement is quite low, and even lower as a result of general election defeat.[3]

With the exception of Connecticut, California, and the lower house in Ohio, state legislatures tended to have even higher levels of uncontested elections than the U.S. House. In addition, the percentage of uncontested seats increased during the 1980s, just as it did for the House of Representatives.

The last five columns in Table 7.1 give the percentage of seats in the lower and upper chamber of each state's legislature in which the incumbent was not challenged by a major party nominee. The exceptional variation in uncontested races across these states indicates how widely local party organizations differ in their capacity to nominate candidates. The first three states in the table indicate this variability: In Connecticut, relatively few incumbents go unchallenged, in Rhode Island the proportion of uncontested seats is somewhat higher, and in Delaware it is higher still.

TABLE 7.1
Results of State Legislative Races in Selected States

State	1978–1988 Avg. Percent Incumbents Running	1978–1988 Avg. Percent Incumbents Winning	Percent Races with Uncontested Incumbents					
			1978	1980	1982	1984	1986	1988
Connecticut								
Senate	84	81	3	0	0	0	6	3
House	81	88	4	9	7	9	14	12
Rhode Island								
Senate	77	93	43	20	6[a]	8	20	48
House	79	96	32	27	38	26	27	56
Delaware								
Senate	85	92	30	18	33	50	45	40
House	85	90	20	22	22	37	39	51
Pennsylvania								
Senate	73	95	0	4	12	12	28	16
House	85	97	4	15	11	18	36	33
Michigan								
Senate[b]	64	99	8	–	13	–	3	–
House	81	95	12	17	15	4	3	9
Ohio								
Senate	83	85	6	6	0	0	11	0
House	85	97	6	17	3	6	14	24
Wisconsin								
Senate	76	93	12	25	12	18	6	25
House	83	93	18	23	9	12	19	28
Iowa								
Senate	71	90	8	8	10	52	40	20
House	81	93	20	12	13	27	31	21
Missouri								
Senate	77	99	12	29	35	41	41	41
House	82	97	25	42	39	58	47	45
Kentucky[c]								
Senate	76	94	37	47	42	–	42	58
House	83	96	49	47	–	41	50	66
Colorado								
Senate	56	97	24	22	28	32	29	16
House	71	90	20	23	17	31	25	26
Utah								
Senate	73	80	7	27	11	21	13	0
House	73	86	9	7	13	16	15	11
California								
Senate	82	94	0	0	10	0	5	5
House	83	96	7	5	11	11	2	2

[a]The Rhode Island Senate election was held on June 21, 1983.

[b]The Michigan Senate has nonstaggered four-year terms; all other senates have staggered four-year or two-year terms.

[c]Due to the fact that Kentucky scheduled legislative elections in odd years until 1984, the figures for 1978 to 1982 are in fact for elections from 1979 to 1983.

Source: The data were obtained from the state Legislative Election Returns in the United States, 1968–1989 data set compiled by the Inter-University Consortium for Political and Social Research, 5th ICPSR edition, January 1992, #8907.

The parties' lack of control over candidate recruitment is also indicated by the fact that in some states, such as Rhode Island and Wisconsin, the frequency of uncontested elections is higher for one house than for the other. Conventional wisdom would hold that Senate seats are "worth more" than House seats because senates tend to be smaller bodies and legislators in the upper house have bigger constituencies and more visibility. Nonetheless, the data show that higher proportions of uncontested races are not uncommon in the upper as compared to the lower chamber.

Taken as a whole, then, the parties' capacities to field a full slate of candidates is highly variable over time and across offices. But two patterns stand out: the greater incidence of uncontested races as the office becomes less visible and the gradual increase in uncontested seats, with the exception of 1992, for lower-level legislative positions.

Meaningful Election Contests

Ever since David Mayhew (1974a) first raised the question of the "vanishing marginals" in House elections, scholars have been concerned not simply with the presence or absence of competition, but with its magnitude. The size of the winning candidate's electoral margin provides an important indicator of how much competition actually took place. When the outcome is close, it is fair to assume that the opponents were well matched and that the voters had a genuine choice. But when the results are one-sided, it is usually because the party nominated someone who could not wage the kind of effective campaign that attracts voters from the opposition. There is considerable debate among scholars about the causes of weak party candidates, but what is important for our purposes is the fact that the pattern is highly variable across offices.

Again, the highest frequency of competitive party nominees is in statewide races for governor and senator. But despite the greater success enjoyed by parties in fielding strong nominees, there are considerable differences across states and over time. In Table 7.2, for example, the frequency of contests in which the winning candidate won with more than 60 percent of the vote is shown for governors, senators, and House members. From these results it is clear that the parties manage to nominate far more competitive candidates for governor than for any other office. Contests for senator are more closely fought than those for the House, but a good many senate races are not as hard-fought as we might expect. Small states, in particular, are less likely to have two well-matched opponents than larger states (Westlye, 1992).

Various measures have been used to indicate whether serious opposition in a race is present. For statewide offices we have presented data on lopsided races because the number of races contested was low and varied from election to election. For congressional and state legislative races, re-

TABLE 7.2
Races Won with 60 Percent or More of the Major Party Vote
for U.S. Senator, U.S. Representative, and Governor, 1966–1992

Year	Incumbent Senators	Incumbent Representatives	Governors[a]
1966	44.2[b] (86)	67.7 (401)	21.6 (37)
1968		72.2 (397)	16.7 (24)
1970		77.3 (389)	13.5 (37)
1972	44.6 (74)	77.8 (373)	23.8 (21)
1974		66.4 (383)	34.2 (38)
1976		71.9 (381)	31.3 (16)
1978	41.4 (70)	78.0 (377)	33.3 (39)
1980		72.9 (392)	26.7 (15)
1982		68.9 (383)	43.6 (39)
1984	54.1 (84)	74.6 (406)	33.3 (15)
1986		86.4 (391)	30.8 (39)
1988		88.5 (407)	42.9 (14)
1990	57.5 (87)	76.4 (406)	38.5 (39)
1992	34.6 (26)	65.0 (351)	41.7 (12)

[a]For governors the figures include both two-year and four-year election cycles. Figures for odd-numbered years are counted with the previous year.
[b]For the Senate the figures for 1966 also include races in 1962 and 1964.
Note: The number of candidates in the general elections is given in parentheses.
Source: Data for House and Senate incumbents taken from Ornstein et al. (1992:61–62). Data for governors are for all candidates and taken from *America Votes* (1990). Returns for the 1992 election taken from *CQ Weekly Report,* 1992:3600–3607.

gardless of the measure, a pattern emerges revealing that, over the past decade, incumbents' margins of victory have increased. Table 7.3 illustrates this point by using the mean percentage of incumbent votes for the U.S. House and for seats in selected state legislatures. Jewell and Breaux (1988:502) note that increases in the incumbents' margins of victory seem to occur more often in nonprofessional legislatures, a finding supported by the relatively modest increase in winning margins for Congress.

Two consequences flow from the striking variability in the parties' abilities to nominate competitive candidates. First, the abilities of voters to hold elective officials accountable are greatly limited. When voters find only one nominee on the ballot, they cannot exercise their franchise in any meaningful sense. Their choice is between abstention and support for a candidate whose philosophy or performance may be unsatisfactory. The same situation holds when one of the candidates is a well-financed incumbent and the other is an inexperienced unknown who cannot raise money. In such lopsided matchups, voters gain so little information about the challenger during the campaign that a high percentage end up preferring the incumbent by default.

The second consequence of the variation in party nominees is the phenomenon of divided government, which occurs when one party controls

TABLE 7.3
Percentage of Votes Received by Winning Incumbents in the
U.S. House and Selected State Legislative Elections

Legislature	1978	1980	1982	1984	1986	1988
U.S. House	71.8	70.8	71.0	72.8	74.1	73.9
Connecticut						
Senate	64.4	59.6	61.5	63.4	68.5	65.8
House	65.1	68.0	66.4	68.2	71.6	69.6
Rhode Island						
Senate	83.2	74.9	68.9[a]	72.8	72.8	85.1
House	79.4	79.7	83.5	76.2	77.4	88.9
Delaware						
Senate	73.8	74.0	75.2	80.2	85.6	83.2
House	72.9	75.7	78.3	80.7	81.4	84.1
Pennsylvania						
Senate	62.2	69.2	70.7	74.4	78.8	76.3
House	67.7	73.1	72.4	74.9	81.1	80.2
Michigan						
Senate[b]	75.3	–	72.6	–	70.3	–
House	75.0	74.8	75.8	70.0	73.1	72.2
Ohio						
Senate	71.7	65.2	63.9	63.0	72.6	64.8
House	68.3	72.9	66.6	69.0	71.6	76.6
Wisconsin						
Senate	72.0	73.8	68.5	70.0	68.3	77.7
House	72.8	74.6	70.1	71.0	74.2	77.3
Iowa						
Senate	66.9	63.0	65.9	76.7	85.2	68.1
House	73.7	65.8	70.2	72.9	77.0	70.7
Missouri						
Senate	70.2	80.6	81.2	85.5	80.4	86.2
House	78.9	84.3	84.4	89.6	84.8	85.3
Kentucky[c]						
Senate	83.4	84.3	85.2	–	90.4	91.5
House	86.4	85.2	–	83.8	88.4	91.1
Colorado						
Senate	86.2	73.0	91.0	83.8	81.2	74.8
House	75.7	75.5	74.7	81.0	78.1	76.4
Utah						
Senate	71.1	77.0	67.5	77.0	78.6	70.0
House	69.3	66.7	73.6	74.2	70.5	67.3
California						
Senate	67.4	68.4	70.6	70.4	69.2	70.6
House	68.8	68.6	71.9	72.0	70.7	69.2

[a]The Rhode Island Senate election was held on June 21, 1983.

[b]The Michigan Senate has nonstaggered four-year terms; all other senates have staggered four-year or two-year terms.

[c]Due to the fact that Kentucky scheduled legislative elections in odd years until 1984, the figures for 1978 to 1982 are in fact for elections held from 1979 to 1983.

Source: Jewell and Breaux (1988); Jacobson (1987b).

the executive branch and the other party controls one or both of the legis-lative chambers. Some argue that divided government leads to political stalemate; others conclude that it does not have much effect on govern-ment decisionmaking (Fiorina, 1992; Mayhew, 1991). Whatever its effect on policy outcomes, divided government nevertheless makes it difficult for voters to assign responsibility for failed policies. Each branch can blame the other, leaving the electorate confused about what went wrong and which party has the best plan for the future.

VARIATIONS AMONG THE INSTITUTIONAL CONTEXTS FOR PARTY ORGANIZATIONS

Endorsement Procedures

Most nominations at the state and local levels are determined by primary elections.[4] The original purpose of nominating by primary elections was to permit the voters, not party officials, to make decisions concerning who would run for office. As V. O. Key wrote thirty years ago, "Throughout the history of American nominating practices runs a persistent attempt to make feasible popular participation in nominations and thereby to limit or to destroy the power of party oligarchies" (Key, 1964:371; see also Maisel, 1993:Ch. 6; Sorauf and Beck, 1988:Ch. 9; Jewell and Olson, 1988:Ch. 4). But as party officials have a stake in the selection of those party nominees, they have attempted (either formally or informally) to maintain a role in the process.

In a few states, one or both parties retain the party convention as a means of nominating candidates for some offices. More common is the practice of states to permit party organizations to formally endorse candi-dates for office through local party caucuses or through conventions. Pre-primary endorsements carry with them varying advantages. In Utah and Connecticut, for example, the only way onto the primary ballot is through the acquisition of a certain percentage of the votes in conventions; in Rhode Island and Delaware, the convention endorsee is automatically on the primary ballot whereas other candidates must qualify by petition. Po-sition on the primary ballot, and whether the party endorsee is so desig-nated, also varies by state. Informal endorsement procedures are used in several states that do not have formal mechanisms for a party role. Again, experiences in different states vary significantly. It might be acceptable for a state party organization to endorse a candidate, but local party organi-zations might refrain from doing so in the same state. Endorsement proce-dures are a matter of party rules, not state law; thus they are more easily changed, and the role that party officials can and do play alters accord-ingly.

How effective are endorsement procedures? Again, there is significant variation from state to state, and from locality to locality within states. First, in some states and localities, competition for party nomination is rare. In such cases, the endorsement procedure is effectively determinative, because it is the end result of the party officials' quest to find a candidate to run for an office. In essence, the party officials can say to a potential nominee that they will "guarantee" the nomination (i.e., that no one else will run). In other cases, primary competition is rare because no one would challenge a party endorsee; these nominations might well be worth more than those discussed earlier, but the party role is the same. In still other states and localities, party endorsees are frequently challenged and, on occasion, beaten. In New York State, for example, receiving the party endorsement has been considered a negative factor by some politicians.[5]

Voter Eligibility for Primary Elections

In addition to maintaining a role in the endorsement of potential nominees, party officials have been concerned with determining who in the electorate is eligible to vote in partisan primary elections. In the past, conventional wisdom has held that party officials desire to restrict the primary electorate to those who have a close affiliation with the political party. Thus they favor "closed" primaries in which a voter must be registered in a particular party in order to vote in that party's primary election. Party officials argue that the voters with the greatest stake in a party (i.e., declared partisans) should be able to determine that party's nominees.

Those concerned with politics who are more opposed to the influence of political party—or, stated more positively, those who believe in the widest possible participation in all aspects of the political process—feel that "open" primaries, primary elections in which any registered voter can participate, are more appropriate. Some party officials worry about raiding in open primaries, a practice by which those who favor one political party vote for the weaker candidate in the other party's primary in order to improve the chances of their favored party's candidate in the general election. Although raiding seems an obvious strategy, implementing such a strategy is extremely difficult. Evidence of successful raiding has not been documented, but most party officials, especially leaders in a region's majority party, continue to advocate and to defend a primary system that is closed to all but the party faithful.

Eligibility for voting in primary elections has traditionally been viewed as a function of state law. Twenty-seven states have some form of closed primary, although the point at which one can change from one party to another, and the ability of nonparty enrollees to choose a party at the last minute, varies significantly. Twenty states have primaries generally categorized as open primaries, but, again, these vary as to whether a voter's participation in a party's primary is public information at the time of voting. The line between open and closed primaries is not a distinct one; rather, eligibility is on a continuum from the most closed primaries (those in which enrollment must be accomplished well in advance and cannot easily be changed, and in which independents cannot enroll at the last minute), through primaries that give voters more leeway in changing parties, to the most open primaries (those in which voters choose a party ballot in secret and their choice is never recorded) (see Carr and Scott, 1984). The final three states have unique and very open systems. Washington and Alaska use the "blanket" primary, so called because a single ballot is figuratively as big as a blanket and covers all ("blankets") candidate selection. A voter can vote in either party's primary for each individual office; thus, an individual could vote in the Democratic party primary for governor, the Republican primary for U.S. Senator, the Republican primary for member of Congress, the Democratic primary for state senator, and so on. Under this system, the voter has the most freedom—and can demonstrate the least commitment to one party or the other. Louisiana uses a "nonpartisan" primary, which sounds like a contradiction in terms. All candidates are listed on one ballot, and voters choose one candidate for each office. If any candidate achieves a majority, that candidate is automatically elected. If no candidate receives a majority, a runoff between the top two is held on the general election day. The two candidates for an office on the general election ballot can be of the same or different parties, depending on votes in the primary. Obviously, political party per se has little role in this system.

Until recently, state law determined the type of primary held in each state. If party officials wanted a different type of primary, they had to work through the state legislature to change the law. In 1984 the Republican party of Connecticut challenged that norm. Connecticut Republicans wanted an open primary, not for philosophical reasons but for political ones. In recent decades Connecticut has been a heavily Democratic state with a strong Democratic party organization. The Republicans wanted to attract unaffiliated voters, who constituted roughly one-third of the Connecticut electorate, to their side. They felt that they could do so by giving the unaffiliated voters a say in Republican nominations. The Republicans tried to achieve their goal by changing state law, but they were frustrated by a Democratically controlled legislature in 1984 and by a gubernatorial veto in the next legislative session. They subsequently challenged in court.

In *Tashjian v. Republican Party of Connecticut*, 479 U.S. 208 (1986), the Supreme Court ruled that the state of Connecticut had to allow the Republican party to define its own membership and thus to use an open primary if it so desired. This case is extremely important for defining the role of political parties (Epstein, 1989). Because of this ruling, state parties are now allowed to determine the eligible electorate for party primaries. In so ruling, the Court has given parties a greater say in who their nominees would be.

Epstein (1989:254–260) points out that political scientists who favor strong political parties in the American system of democracy have differed in their response to *Tashjian*. One group of Connecticut political scientists filed an *amicus* brief arguing in favor of closed primaries. They stated, in part, that the closed primary "tends to support the concept of the party as an association of like-minded people" and "that closed primary elections produce other benefits which are conducive to cohesive parties" (Brief of Cibes et al., 1986:23). That, in essence, is the pro-party conventional wisdom. In contrast, another group of political scientists, reflecting the views of the Committee for Party Renewal, a national association of politicians and political scientists searching for ways to revitalize parties as a vital element in American democracy, supported the view of the Republican party, arguing that "political parties can best contribute to American politics if permitted to steer their own courses" (Brief of Burns et al., 1986:4). These political scientists allowed that they might well differ on the merits of open versus closed primaries, but they agreed that the independence of political parties was the most important factor under consideration. Throughout *Tashjian,* that view has prevailed; but its impact on party efforts to control primary electorates—and thus on party efforts to influence who their nominees will be—has yet to be determined.

Legislative Term Limits

The term-limits movement is one very clear indication of massive popular dissatisfaction with incumbent safety in state legislatures and in the Congress. In the 1992 general election, voters were asked to consider referenda on various proposals to limit terms of legislators. All fourteen of these proposals passed overwhelmingly, bringing to seventeen the number of states with term limitations in place.

These proposals were not all identical. Some restricted the terms of state legislators only; others applied to U.S. representatives and senators as well. The number of terms legislators may serve is not uniform; twelve years in one house is the norm, but variations exist. Similarly, state laws vary as to whether office holders can go immediately from one legislative body to another and whether they can return to a legislative body after having "sat out" a term. In addition, some of these restrictions have been tested in the courts, and limitations of terms on state legislatures have been found constitutional. In one recent case, the California Supreme Court held that term limitations on state legislators were constitutional.[6] However, the constitutionality of laws that restrict terms in the U.S. Congress has yet to be determined.

Even with this caveat, we can speculate that the existence of a term limit for state legislators, or for holders of any office, affects the party organization in the nominating process (Maisel, Mackenzie, and Prenaveau, 1992). However, the direction of this impact is not totally clear, as the experience with term limits is just unfolding.

At one extreme is the argument put forth by David Brady and Douglas Rivers (1991). Brady and Rivers argue that the term-limits movement will make legislatures much more receptive to party domination. They contend that campaigns and, by implication, nominations will come to be more susceptible to party control. Their argument requires a leap of faith that candidate-centered campaigns and self-starting candidacies will give way inevitably to party domination if the party is held responsible for what occurs in the governing process.

We are not convinced that the change will be such a boon to the party organizations. It is true that party organizations will be responsible for nominating candidates for more open seats. If open seats are considered those most ripe for party change, the parties will attempt to field strong candidates in these races and will, of necessity, look to recruit candidates for seats they think might be won. If the term-limits movement does not entice more qualified individuals to run for office—and we see no logical reason why it should—then parties will have to find more nominees if some level of competition is to be maintained. We think it likely that term limits will reduce the influence of state legislatures by limiting expertise and experience, especially compared with the bureaucracy. If this occurs, parties may have greater difficulty attracting well-qualified candidates because serving in the legislature would be less desirable.

The lack of experience with term limitations means that we can only speculate on the consequences for future candidacies and the political parties (Mackenzie, Maisel, and Prenaveau, 1992); that is one of the problems with far-reaching political reform (Polsby, 1983:5). We do feel safe in concluding, however, that legislative term limitations are a factor that state party organizations increasingly will have to take into account as they undertake recruiting candidates for office (see also Benjamin and Malbin, 1992).

PARTY EFFORTS TO RECRUIT
MORE COMPETITIVE CANDIDATES

Political party leaders have long understood that one of their most important functions is to recruit candidates for office. Recruitment is often necessary because in the United States decisions on candidacy are ultimately personal decisions. V. O. Key (1956) argued that the rise of political primaries led to the demise of local organizations and that this decline, in turn, would decrease electoral competition and the voters' opportunity to express their preferences at the polls. In the 1970s many observers bemoaned the decline of party organization, and Key's conclusion seemed warranted.

More recently, however, evidence indicates that state and local political party organizations are not so weak as they were once thought to be (Cotter et al., 1984; Gibson et al., 1985). National party organizations, led by the Republican party, have begun to expend great resources in an effort to reinvigorate their local units (Sabato, 1988; Herrnson, 1988). Local political party organizations have continued to grow both in strength and in their ability to perform traditional campaign functions such as recruiting candidates to fill spots on the ballot (Gibson et al., 1989; Frendeis et al., 1990). (See Chapters 2 and 3.)

And these efforts have borne fruit. The probability that the minority party in an area will run a candidate for local offices is a function of the strength of local party organization. Even though minority party candidates might not win, their candidacies contribute to higher vote totals for other members of their party running for offices higher up on the ballot. The connection seems to be that local candidacies make higher-level candidates of a minority party appear more credible (Frendeis et al., 1990). The efforts to revitalize party organizations, including minority party organizations, have had the double impact of increasing the number of seats in which two-party competition is present and of raising the level of competition among candidates for higher offices—precisely the results that pro-party democratic theorists had predicted.

A second method used by parties to increase their ability to compete effectively has been their concentrated efforts to improve the quality of their nominees. The national parties—as well as their respective congressional and senatorial committees—have been actively involved in recruiting candidates for some time. These efforts do not signal a national dominance of local politics. Rather, as each election cycle begins, the staff of the national organizations and their regional political coordinators meet with state and local officials to determine which seats that they are holding might be vulnerable, which seats held by the opposition might be vulnerable, and which seats will be open and hotly contested.

National, state, and local party officials all have a vested interest in finding good candidates for those seats that appear likely to feature close competition. They identify potential candidates and attempt to convince them to run. In the late 1970s and early 1980s, the Republican party went so far as to contribute to primary campaigns for selected candidates. This practice caused some controversy, however, when designated candidates were unsuccessful in winning nominations.

In more recent years the effort has been to assure good potential candidates that the party is interested in their campaign and will help in any way it can. For example, the Democratic Senatorial Campaign Committee helped convince Connecticut Attorney General Joseph Lieberman to challenge incumbent Republican Senator Lowell Weicker, and its Republican counterpart worked to convince Congressman Connie Mack of Florida to seek the Senate seat left open by the retirement of Democrat Lawton Chiles. The most controversial part of party prenomination efforts has been "negative recruitment"—the effort to convince someone considering a race to drop the idea. When parties are successful in negative recruitment, they not only avoid intraparty competition but are also able to begin their assistance to unopposed candidates well in advance of the general election campaign. But when they are not successful, as when the Republicans failed to dissuade Congressman Hal Daub from challenging appointed incumbent David Karnes for the Republican Senate nomination in Nebraska, leftover resentment tends to spill over into the ensuing general election campaign.

Recruitment of candidates is one of the important functions of a campaign organization. It is a critical function at the stage of filling the ballot. But it is also important to ensure, to the extent possible, that party candidates for office can run credible campaigns. Modern party organizations have neither the power nor the inclination to designate all party nominees, as did local party leaders in the age of political bosses. Most nominees are still self-starters. But the party has a stake in encouraging experienced and qualified candidates to seek office under its label, a stake that might well become more important in those states that limit terms of office. Thus, party officials make it known that they are willing to provide campaign assistance, that they are committed to a race, and, at times, that they would prefer some candidacies over others (Herrnson, 1988:Ch.3).

A final, relatively new method that party officials can use to improve the quality of their nominees is to define the primary electorate that selects those nominees, as the Republican party did when its actions led to the *Tashjian* case. Since *Tashjian*, a number of state legislatures in closed primary states have passed laws permitting parties to open their primaries should they choose to do this (Epstein, 1989:260–270). The North Carolina Republicans did so choose. In West Virginia, the Republican primary was opened at the request of party leaders when the secretary of state informed each party that it would automatically have that option under the Supreme Court's ruling. But the reaction to the new option has generally been modest.

One can only speculate about other possible reactions to the *Tashjian* decision. [7] For instance, if the true impact of the decision is to free political parties from state domination in defining their membership, would it not be possible for majority parties in open primary states to close their primaries, if they perceived it to be to their political advantage? Could either party in Washington or Alaska void the blanket primary systems used in those states by defining their primary electorate in a more restrictive way? Taken to the logical extreme, could political parties in primary states decide, on their own and in opposition to state legislatures, that they preferred to nominate in convention? Party officials would have to examine the political consequences of any of these moves. Rules that appear to be undemocratic are difficult to justify in a media age, even if they do work to ensure better candidates for office. It is clear, however, that party officials have had options opened to them that were not on the horizon before the *Tashjian* decision.

A MODEL FOR DECISIONMAKING
BY POTENTIAL CANDIDATES

To this point the argument has been that one of the responsibilities of political parties is to guarantee that elections in the United States are competitive. This is a basic concern for a representative democracy, and American parties have been only partially successful in accomplishing the task. But the argument thus far is too simple. Whether an incumbent will face a credible challenger is dependent, in part, on decisions made by *potential candidates* for office, not simply by the parties (Fowler and McClure, 1989). Scholars of political parties and elections have gathered little empirical information to aid us in understanding how potential candidates for office weigh their options; yet we can isolate the variables that appear to be relevant and focus on the role that parties play in those decisionmaking calculi.

At this juncture it is important that we draw a distinction among the different paths to party nomination. At one extreme is the traditional group-based concept of candidate recruitment. In this case some external force, normally a political party, tries to influence a potential candidate to run for office. The party, or other external force, attempts to influence the potential candidate's decisionmaking. At the other extreme is candidate self-selection. In this case a potential candidate "emerges" on his or her own and then considers a run for office, assesses chances, and makes decisions independent of political party opinion or other external forces. In between are various "mixed" cases in which potential candidates might be encouraged to run or might "self-recruit," but in either case party and other external forces are part of the decisionmaking process. Our present concern is with the ways in which these decisions are made—and with the role of political party in the decisions.

FIGURE 7.3

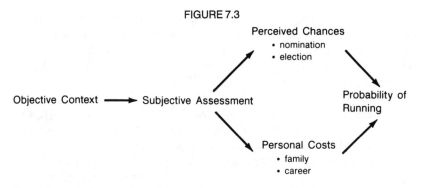

Model of potential candidate decisionmaking process.

Figure 7.3 depicts a model of *candidate* decisionmaking. The model asserts that an "objective" set of conditions determines the context of potential candidates' decisionmaking. These objective conditions must be perceived by the potential candidate (the "subjective assessment"), and these assessments in turn determine whether an individual will think it worthwhile to run.

While determining whether they have a chance of winning, potential candidates must also make judgments about other, more personal factors. Among other things, they must balance the costs associated with losing against the benefits—and quite different costs—of winning. The interplay of these personal factors and the perceived chances of success lead to the eventual decision of whether to run for office. Although this model is quite crude and remains untested, it does spell out many of the factors that enter into a candidate's decisions. In particular, it responds to the question "What causes a person to run for office?" by identifying at least four kinds of influence: the objective context, the subjective context, perceived chances of winning, and personal costs.

The Objective Context

The importance of the party organization as part of the objective context is difficult to overstate. Political parties have a continuing institutional interest in running strong candidates for office. If the party organization is reasonably strong, it controls important resources that are crucial to the success of a candidate. Can local party officials help a candidate gain the nomination? Are these officials strong enough to *prevent* candidates from running if they oppose them? What resources can the organization bring to bear on the general election race? What commitments can the organization make to the individual if he or she wins? What if the candidate loses? The key is whether the party organization is strong enough to be an independent actor in the process—whether, indeed, it has enough resources to alter the prospective candidate's calculations about career opportunities. A strong organization can increase the chances the candidate will win, and it can help cushion some of the costs associated with losing. A weak party organization leaves individuals to their own devices.

The partisan balance in the constituency, the nature of state and national forces and how they hurt or benefit the party, and the strength of the local party organization are also factors that help define what we mean by objective context. In a constituency where registration patterns strongly favor one party, winning the primary may be tantamount to winning the office. In more competitive areas winning the nomination is but a necessary step on the way to winning office.

Because running for office is a personal decision, the objective context also includes factors from prospective candidates' political backgrounds. Candidates with extensive experience in a related office or holding an office with an overlapping constituency are likely to be stronger than candidates with no experience in elective office. Even such factors as their ability to raise money and hire and direct a campaign staff are reasonably considered "objective."

The Subjective Context

Scholars can look at objective indicators and reach objective conclusions. But politicians must make subjective assessments of some of the same indicators (Maisel, 1986). For instance, would-be candidates must assess the strength of local party organizations and they must come to a perception of how well their personal goals fit with the interests of the party organization. Or a state legislator may know that his district overlaps with only 20 percent of the state senate district in which he is considering a race, but he must judge whether all of the people in that senatorial district are aware of his state legislative accomplishments.

Indeed, subjective assessments are critical to decisions about possible candidacies. They are essentially political judgments. What does the political environment look like for a candidacy for this position, against these likely opponents, at this time? The timing of these judgments varies from politician to politician, and politicians do not reach these judgments simultaneously but, rather, as they assess relevant information. Moreover, opinions change along with changes in the political environment. The local, state, or national economic context is one of the subjective variables that possible candidates tend to look at. Is this a good year for Democrats? For Republicans? For challengers or incumbents? But identifying that variable is not enough. It is also necessary to determine the point at which the assessment of that variable has an effect on candidate decisionmaking (Jacobson and Kernell, 1983; Bond, Covington, and Fleisher, 1985; Born,

1986). He or she must also ascertain whether local politicians view national factors as having an effect on their immediate political environment—or if it is possible that local interpretations have been applied to national economic indicators. The national economy might be on the rise, but if the local economy is suffering, the latter factor is the relevant one for a politician trying to assess whether economic trends will have an impact on his or her campaign.

Another subjective assessment concerns the strength of the local party organization. Can party officials help a candidate gain the nomination? Can party leaders discourage others from challenging for the nomination? Will they be helpful in a general election race? Will state or national party support be forthcoming? Will state or national leaders help raise money or run the campaign? Can the party be helpful in the post-election period if the campaign is not successful? Will running enhance one's political career within the party? Or will it help only if one wins? Clearly these and related issues can be important to the assessment of whether a candidate will run. Party leaders, at least those who themselves are sophisticated politicians, understand the significance of these factors and can use this understanding to influence potential candidates' decisions.

Perceived Chances of Winning

Our model posits that knowledge of the context of an election and assessments of the political environment affect an aspirant's perception of his or her chances of securing a party nomination and of winning an election. In some instances candidates are quite certain of the accuracy of their perceptions; in other instances they are much less certain. But in either case a potential candidate's perception of the chance of winning is an important variable that determines whether that candidate will in fact choose to run. A political party cannot force attractive, qualified candidates to run for office. Individuals, not parties, therefore control the first threshold in the sequence of activities that ultimately result in the presence or absence of strong competitive candidates.

Personal Costs

The final major variable intervening between perceptions of the political environment and the decision to run for office are the personal costs (and benefits) of seeking office. In this calculus potential candidates must consider a wide range of effects. One set of personal factors encompasses family considerations: additional loss of privacy, the commitment to a campaign, financial costs, the possibility of having to relocate, and so on. The other set of personal factors is career related: having to leave the position currently held, the effect of a campaign on alternative career paths, the impact of a potential loss of subsequent political plans, and the reaction of the party elite to a decision either to run or to forgo a race. Our model suggests that the relationship between these personal costs and the perceived chances of winning is nonrecursive. Indeed, personal costs and benefits may be very sensitive to the perceived chances of winning. For instance, a candidate would not have to worry much about the cost of relocating his or her family if the chances of winning (and of having to move) were remote. And, a candidate who perceived his or her chances of winning as good might well decide that the costs of relocating were too high to justify entering the race.

Summary of Model

The model we have proposed represents our best understanding of the decisionmaking process that any potential candidate must undoubtedly follow. But the model has not been tested. The importance of the various factors in this process, under what circumstances, is not yet clear. Nor do we know how perceptions are arrived at. These important research questions remain at the top of the agenda of those scholars examining the electoral process.

Nevertheless, our model does illuminate the role that political parties can in fact play in ensuring the existence of genuine competition in American elections. Genuine competition depends on the availability of quality candidates. When incumbents seek reelection to governorships or seats in the U.S. Senate, few have the luxury of running unopposed or of facing challengers who do not provide serious opposition. But those seeking reelection to the U.S. House of Representatives, or to many state legislatures and local positions, are generally not seriously challenged—if indeed they face any opposition at all. They do not face serious opposition because potential candidates for those seats often decide not to run. We do not know precisely how to define the population of potential candidates for any office. To a large extent that is the job of party organization. But once those candidates have been defined—or, as is frequently the case in American elections, once they define themselves—party leaders can have an impact on their decision either to run or not to run only in certain ways. No matter how hard party leaders try to increase their influence, their efforts, our model suggests, will meet with only limited success. A number of the factors important in candidates' determinations are simply beyond the control of political parties.

CONCLUSION

What, then, can one conclude about the role of political parties in the selection of nominees for offices below the presidential level? This essay ends as it began, by emphasizing the diversity of experiences within the American political system. The role that party leaders believe they should play, a role compatible with democratic theory, is to provide competition. At a minimum, this role involves finding a candidate to run for an office, such that one party's nominee does not attain office without facing an electoral test. But party leaders are not always successful in reaching this goal. Many offices go uncontested each election day. But more than competition is expected. Party leaders want to have candidates on the ballot who have a chance of winning or, at least, who can raise the level of debate in the election campaign and make the eventual winner pay attention. Hence party leaders must find good candidates for office. Yet defining a "good" candidate is an imprecise art. Party leaders must consider, among other qualities, previous electoral experience, visibility or stature within a district, personal wealth or the ability to raise money, articulateness, attractiveness, and intelligence. It must be conceded that many local party officials are amateur volunteers in the rankest sense of amateur and have neither time, inclination, nor ability to fulfill these tasks; but sophisticated local party leaders have a sense of who will be good candidates for the races in their area.

Identifying a potential quality candidate is only the first step, however. Party officials must convince that candidate to seek office—but even their encouragement plays only a small part in the decision calculus of many potential candidates. Their success is incomplete at best. Slates are most likely to be filled with quality candidates when the office is attractive and the chance of victory seems promising. In these cases one often observes candidate emergence, not candidate selection by party officials. The role of party officials is more pronounced, more significant, and more variable in the remaining situations, when they have to work within the existing institutional regulations to convince candidates to seek offices that are not so attractive, in races for which victory seems less likely. Parties were stronger as recruiting organizations before the Progressive reforms led to the near-total acceptance of primary elections as nominating tools. Few would suggest that the nation should return to the era of nominations decided in "smoke-filled" rooms. But various reforms have been suggested to enhance the role of party. The role of political parties in the recruitment process will remain nominal so long as valuable nominations go primarily to self-selected political entrepreneurs. But if those interested in nominations have incentives for seeking party support, because of changes in campaign finance laws or in nominating procedures that enhance the role of party, then party recruitment might well be as viable a route to nomination as the emergence of political self-starters. Such changes would certainly improve the ability of our party system to play the role it should be performing in our electoral process—that of guaranteeing meaningful contests for office at more levels of government in more areas of the country than has been the case in the recent past.

NOTES

1. Kentucky, Louisiana, Mississippi, New Jersey, and Virginia all hold statewide elections in odd-numbered years. In recent years the trend has been for states to move from statewide elections in presidential election years to nonpresidential election years (Maisel, 1987:140–141; Jewell and Olson, 1988:44–47).

2. This essay—and in fact the entire book—does not deal with nonpartisan elections. Although no one would deny the importance of local politics in the vast majority of localities that do not hold partisan elections, the task of examining such elections is clearly separable from the one at hand. (See, for example, Welch and Bledsoe, 1986; Hawley, 1973.)

3. The second column in Table 7.1 presents the percentages of primary winners who were successful in the general election. The data set does not include primary election results.

4. Certain states still permit party nominations to be determined by party conventions for some offices—or for some offices in one or the other party. Nominations by party officials are often made by minor parties. (See Maisel, 1987:Ch. 5; Sorauf and Beck, 1988:253–255.)

5. Jewell and Olson (1988:94–106) discuss the impact of party endorsement in some detail. (See also Jewell, 1984.)

6. *Legislature of the State of California et al. v. March Fong Eu, Secretary of State;* 54 Cal. 3d 492; 816 P.2d 1309, 1991.

7. This section draws heavily on Leon Epstein's (1989) thoughtful essay on state regulation of political parties.

8

The Rules Do Matter: Post-Reform Presidential Nominating Politics

ELAINE CIULLA KAMARCK
KENNETH M. GOLDSTEIN

Imagine for a moment that Franklin Delano Roosevelt, Dwight D. Eisenhower, and John F. Kennedy were to join us once again. Furthermore, imagine that they found themselves in the middle of a political strategy session for a presidential campaign. Strategy for the general election would be quite familiar to them. It would revolve around winning the majority of electoral votes. Each state would be categorized as safe for one party or the other, as a lost cause, or as a possible battleground. Candidates and their surrogates would move around the country giving speeches and holding rallies in an attempt to win the crucial battleground states. Much about the general election would be different, of course, but the underlying strategy for accumulating a majority of electoral votes would be very much the same as it had been in their day.

Suppose, however, that our three returned presidents were to find themselves in the midst of a strategy session for the Democratic or Republican nomination. The goal would be the same as it had been for them—to accumulate enough delegates to win the nod at their party's nominating convention. Beyond that, however, the similarities would end, for the strategy for achieving that goal is very different today from what is was in their time.

Imagine Franklin Roosevelt's bewilderment at the use of the term *momentum*. In his day this term was used to describe activity in the convention hall; now it refers to the boost in attention that a candidate gets from primaries and caucuses that take place months before the convention even opens. Imagine Eisenhower's surprise upon hearing that Senator Howard Baker (R-TN) had given up both his job as majority leader of the Senate and his Senate seat *four years* before the presidential election in order to run for president full time. Ike spent the years before the 1952 Republican Convention in Europe with NATO, arriving home in June to campaign for his nomination in July. Imagine Kennedy's puzzlement over the decision made by Walter Mondale, a former Democratic vice-president and favorite of the Democratic party establishment, to enter every single presidential primary. In his day a candidate avoided presidential primaries unless, like Kennedy, he was young, untested, and eager to prove himself to the party establishment.

What our three returned presidents would soon realize is that the strategies for winning the nomination have changed dramatically as the result of underlying changes in the structure of the nominating system. Until the early 1970s, winning the nomination of a major political party was essentially an inside game. Presidential candidates worked at winning the allegiances of the major party leaders, who controlled the minor party leaders, who in turn became delegates to the nominating convention. Presidential primaries were sometimes important, especially if a candidate had to demonstrate vote-getting ability; but to do that he had to keep favorite sons out and draw other national candidates in, a task that was often very difficult. More often than not, the public portion of the nomination campaign—presidential primaries—was not very important to the eventual outcome.

What was important was the semi-public search for delegates—a search that was difficult to observe and often downright mysterious even to careful observers of the process. The nomination system prior to 1972 was, to use Nelson Polsby's term, "a mixed system" (Polsby, 1983:185). The first stage was public and took place in a few contested presidential primaries. The second stage was semi-public at best and involved intense negotiations between serious national candidates and powerful party leaders. James Reston described this stage as follows: "This presidential election is being fought on several levels. The most important of these, so far as nominating candidates is concerned, is the least obvious ... the underground battle for delegates" (*New York Times,* June 24, 1968, p. 1). Usually the "underground" battle for delegates was fought in the proverbial smoke-filled rooms. Another political reporter, W. H. Lawrence, described the 1960 nomination race as follows: "With the end of the contested presidential primaries, the struggle for the nomination has moved from Main Street to the backrooms of individual party leaders and state conventions dense with the smoke of cheap cigars" (*New York Times,* June 8, 1960, p. 6E).

This process, of courting powerful and not so powerful party leaders in search of a convention majority, was hard to observe and impossible to quantify until the convention itself assembled and started to vote. Thus the race for the nomination used to be very visible during the weeks leading up to and including the convention. More recently, however, the race for the nomination is visible at least a year before the nominating convention and is usually over well before the convention itself ever convenes.

THE POST-REFORM NOMINATION SYSTEM

The presidential nomination system that exists today is the result of two reform movements that occurred at approximately the same time in American politics. Between 1968 and 1972 the Democratic party adopted a series of changes in the process by which delegates to its nominating conventions were chosen. This movement began as a reaction to the contentious 1968 Democratic convention; newcomers opposed to the Vietnam War felt that the party establishment had unfairly thwarted their attempts at participating in the nominating process (Polsby, 1983). At the time, few people (including party professionals) anticipated how profoundly these changes would affect the way that Democrats *and* Republicans elected delegates (Shafer, 1983). Even though the Republican party did not undergo anything even remotely like the reform movement in the Democratic party, so many Democratically dominated state legislatures had to change their laws to comply with the new dictates of the Democratic National Committee that the state Republican parties, more often than not, were inadvertently reformed as well.

The other reform movement began in 1971 with passage of the Federal Election Campaign Act. This law was amended in 1974 as part of the post-Watergate reforms designed to decrease the influence of money in politics, and again in 1979 when it became clear that the law was having unintended negative effects on party activity. The campaign finance reform laws affected both political parties and, like the reforms in delegate selection, had far-reaching implications for the conduct of presidential elections, particularly primary elections.

The effect of these two reform movements was to transform the nomination system into a totally public system where activity at every step of the process could be observed and quantified. In the post-reform system, the search for delegates was conducted in public primaries or caucuses (which became the "functional equivalent" of highly visible primaries), and the search for money took place under the new election law. By limiting the amount of money that any one individual could contribute to a candidate, the new law transformed the quest for money from a quiet search for a few "fat cats" to a public search for thousands of small- and medium-sized contributions. Changes of this magnitude in the underlying structure of the nomination process eventually affected the strategies of presidential hopefuls seeking their party's nomination, but before we can understand these strategies we must understand the structure of the new nominating system.

Primaries and Their "Functional Equivalents"

In the pre-reform era fewer than half of the convention delegates were elected in primaries contested by the major national candidates. In the post-reform era, however, nearly all delegates are elected as the result of contested primaries. A famous quote by former Vice-President Hubert Humphrey sums up the attitude of many presidential hopefuls in the pre-reform era: "[A]ny man who goes into a primary isn't fit to be President. You have to be crazy to go into a primary. A primary now is worse than torture of the rack" (quoted in Polsby, 1983:14, and originally in White, 1961:104).

No one who witnessed Bill Clinton's grueling campaign experiences in the New Hampshire and New York primaries would be surprised to hear the current president express similar feelings. But he had no choice. For modern candidates, ignoring the primaries is simply not possible—skipping primaries is akin to skipping the whole game.

The Democratic reformers who made up part of the famous McGovern-Fraser Commission did not set out to increase the number of presidential primaries, but just such an increase was the most immediate and dramatic result of the new rules they had proposed for delegate selection to the 1972 convention.[1] As Table 8.1 illustrates, the number of states holding primaries doubled after the reforms; from nine in 1968 to eighteen in 1972. By 1992, thirty-nine states had presidential primaries.

Most observers of the nomination process focus solely on the increase in the number of primaries that followed in the wake of the reform movement—but the increase in *number* is not nearly so important as the change in the *nature* of these primaries. The reform rules' requirement that delegates from a state "fairly reflect the division of preferences expressed by those who participate in the presidential nominating process in each state" greatly increased the importance of each primary by linking a presidential candidate's performance in the primary to the number of delegates that he could get from the state (Democratic National Committee, 1972:12).

Table 8.1 compares presidential primaries in the pre- and post-reform eras. During the former period, primaries did not always dictate which presidential candidate the delegates from that state should support; in other words, if presidential candidates decided to put their names on the ballot (and they more often did not), they could win the primary and not necessarily get any delegates from that state because the primaries were nonbinding (i.e., advisory). In 1952 Senator Estes Kefauver won the most primaries and yet Governor Adlai Stevenson, who did not enter even one,

TABLE 8.1
Presidential Preference Polls in Primary Elections: Binding Versus Advisory

	Total Number of Primaries with a Presidential Preference Poll on the Ballot	Preference Poll Is Binding	Preference Poll Is Advisory
1952	10	3	7
1956	10	3	7
1960	11	3	8
1964[a]	12	3	9
1968	9	3	6
Post-reform era			
1972	18	12	6
1976[b]	25	17	8
1980[c]	35	33	2
1984[d]	25	19	6
1988[e]	34	28	6
1992	39	36	3

[a]In 1964 the advisory presidential primary in Texas was held for Republicans only.

[b]From 1976 on, the Louisiana "firehouse" (i.e., party-run and party-financed) primary is included.

[c]In 1980 Michigan and South Carolina primaries were for Republicans only; Arkansas had a primary for the Democrats only.

[d]In 1984 the Michigan and Wisconsin primaries were for Republicans only.

[e]In 1988 the South Dakota primary was advisory for the Democrats and was binding for the Republicans, but the Democrats followed its choices when it came to delegate selection.

Sources: 1952 and 1956, David et al. (1960:528–534); 1960, *Congressional Quarterly Weekly Report*, January 17, 1964, p. 106; 1968 and 1972, Commission on Party Structure and Delegate Selection (1971); 1976, 1980, and 1984, Democratic National Convention, *Handbooks of the Democratic National Convention*, various dates; 1988, Democratic National Committee, Compliance Assistance Commission Memo, January 25, 1988; 1992, *Congressional Quarterly Weekly Report*, July 4, 1992.

got the nomination. In 1968, too, Vice-President Hubert Humphrey won the nomination without entering a single primary.

In the modern era, however, if a presidential candidate wants delegates who will vote for him at the convention, he must run all the primaries that are held. Not only did the number of presidential preference polls increase, but the vast majority became binding on the selection of delegates. For example, in 1992, the preference poll was binding in thirty-six out of the thirty-nine states that held primaries.

The reason there were so few presidential preference polls in the pre-reform era is that most presidential primaries were held for the sole purpose of electing delegates to the national convention and these delegates were often not identified as to their presidential preference. Ordinary voters who were not knowledgeable about the politics of the local party members running as delegates had no way of knowing how the people they were voting for were going to vote at the convention. But as the number of primaries with binding presidential preference polls increased, two things happened: The practice of electing delegates directly on the ballot became less popular (see Table 8.2), and the practice of allowing delegates to run unidentified by their presidential preference disappeared. By 1992 there were no Democratic primaries in which delegates were elected directly on the ballot. The Republicans had five primaries in which delegates were directly elected, but in all five, the delegates had to be identified by their presidential preference.

Thus the linkage between presidential primaries and delegate selection is far more important in shaping the structure of the post-reform nominating system than the simple increase in the number of primaries. The results of the presidential primary may or may not tell us who will be attending the nominating convention as a delegate (in many states the actual delegates are elected after the primary), but it *will* tell us exactly how many delegates each presidential candidate on the ballot will get. Hence presidential candidates must now either compete in every primary or risk having no delegates. Indeed, as the primaries have become more important to delegate selection, more and more presidential candidates have begun to compete in them. Not surprisingly, the number of contested primaries has risen dramatically in the post-reform era (see Table 8.3).

When delegates to national conventions are not elected in primaries, they are elected in caucus systems. In a caucus system, people meet at the local level and elect representatives to the next level—usually the county level. At the county level, the people elected locally meet and elect representatives to the state convention. The state convention then meets to select those who will attend the presidential nominating convention.

Traditionally, many state parties have held conventions to elect delegates to the presidential nominating convention. These conventions used to be closed; that is, only individuals who already held party office could participate in the selection of delegates. But the party reform movement turned these systems of delegate selection into smaller versions of presidential primaries.[2]

Three new requirements—that party meetings having to do with delegate selection be open to anyone who wished to be known as a Democrat; that every participant in the process as well as every candidate for delegate declare his or her presidential preference; and that all first-tier caucuses (i.e., those at the precinct level) be held on the same day—effectively abolished the party caucus and began the process of turning the caucus system itself into the "functional equivalent of a primary."[3]

In the pre-reform era, many party meetings were not open to the public; they were attended by previously elected party officials such as pre-

TABLE 8.2
Primaries in Which Delegates Are Elected Directly on the Ballot

	Total Number of Primaries in Which Delegates Are Elected Directly on the Ballot	Delegates Must Be Identified by Presidential Preference	Delegates May or May Not Run Identified by a Presidential Preference	Delegates May Not Run Pledged to or Identified with a Presidential Preference
1952	15	4	5	6
1956	15	4	5	6
1960	15	2	6	7
1964	15	2	6	7
1968	13	2	4	7
Post-reform era				
1972	10	2	5	3
1976[a]	13	2	10	1
1980[b]	3	0	3	0
1984	8	1	7	0
1988[c]	7	1	6	0
1992[d]	5	5	0	0

[a]In 1976 the New York Legislature decided, at the last minute, to make provisions on the ballot for the names of presidential candidates next to the names of the delegates.

[b]In 1980, in New York, only the Republicans held a delegate primary. They also chose to have all their delegate candidates listed as uncommitted, as did the Illinois and Pennsylvania Republicans.

[c]In 1988, in New York, the Democrats elected delegates on the ballot subject to the results of the binding primary, but the Republicans elected delegates directly.

[d]In 1992, there were *no* Democratic primaries in which delegates were elected directly on the ballot. The Republicans had five primaries in which delegates were directly elected, and in all, the delegates had to be identified by their presidential preference.

Sources: 1952 and 1956, David et al. (1960:528–534); 1960, *Congressional Quarterly Weekly Report,* January 17, 1964, p. 106; 1968 and 1972, Commission on Party Structure and Delegate Selection (1971); 1976, 1980, and 1984, Democratic National Convention, *Handbooks of the Democratic National Convention,* various dates; 1988, Democratic National Committee, Compliance Assistance Commission Memo, January 25, 1988; 1992, *Congressional Quarterly Weekly Report,* July 4, 1992.

cinct captains or county chairmen. Opening up local meetings to all who called themselves Democrats meant that the local party leaders could often be overruled by newcomers drawn into the party out of enthusiasm for a particular presidential candidate. That's what happened in caucus after caucus in 1972, when the old-time party regulars were beaten by supporters of George McGovern—that is, by young people who were drawn into the party by virtue of McGovern's opposition to the Vietnam War. In 1984 Walter Mondale spent more than $500,000 organizing the state of Maine and won the endorsement of every major Democratic politician in the state. But Senator Gary Hart, riding the momentum of his surprise victory over Mondale in New Hampshire, won the Maine caucuses handily

TABLE 8.3
Percentage of Delegates Elected in Primaries in Which There Were Contests (in percent)

	Democrats	Republicans
1960[a]	19	no nomination contest
1964[b]	no nomination contest	24
1968	47	18
Post-reform era		
1972[c]	78	no nomination contest
1976[d]	97	90
1980[e]	97	100
1984[f]	97	no nomination contest
1988	99	96
1992[g]	98	92

[a]In 1960, although Humphrey's name was on the ballot in Oregon and thus caused it to be counted as a contested primary, he was effectively out of the race ten days earlier due to the West Virginia primary results.

[b]In 1964, a slate of Goldwater delegates was run in Massachusetts, even though it was Lodge's home state.

[c]In 1972, Alabama and D.C. had favorite-son slates only, and no one contested McGovern in his home state of South Dakota. An insurgent slate was run in New York, but due to the absence of presidential preference on the ballot, it was difficult to contest and is not counted here.

[d]In 1976, Robert Byrd ran as a favorite son in West Virginia and was not contested on the Democratic side. On the Republican side, Reagan skipped New Jersey and Pennsylvania, and no Republicans entered the D.C. primary.

[e]In 1980, Kennedy and Carter did not contest the Michigan primary but competed in caucuses instead.

[f]In 1984, Mondale did not enter the North Dakota primary because it was only a "beauty contest"; he did enter the other three beauty contests in 1984.

[g]The June 9 North Dakota beauty contest was the only primary that was not contested by two or more candidates.

Sources: The 1960–1964 data were derived from the data presented in Scammon and McGillivrey (1985). The 1988 data were derived from Pomper (1989). The 1992 data were compiled by the authors.

as a brand new group of Democrats turned out to support him. In 1988 the Reverend Pat Robertson beat sitting Vice-President George Bush in the Iowa caucuses by organizing hundreds of evangelical Christians who had never before participated in the Republican party. And in 1992, Jerry Brown won a surprise victory in the Maine caucuses by mobilizing young voters and environmentalists.

In the pre-reform nominating system, the job of convention delegate was more often than not a reward for long and loyal service to the party. Convention delegates were elected first and expressed their presidential preferences later. In the new nominating system everyone, at every stage of the process, is required to state his or her presidential preference, and the selection of representatives to the next level must reflect the presidential preferences of the people who show up. This means that the most loyal party workers can be bypassed if they have chosen the wrong presidential candidate—which is just what happened in 1972 and 1976, when supporters of outsiders George McGovern and then Jimmy Carter surprised the party establishment in state after state.

Finally, the requirement that first-tier caucuses be held at the same time and on the same day meant that the delegate-selection system, the impact of which had heretofore been difficult to gauge, could now be treated like a primary. When precinct caucuses or county conventions were spread across several weeks or months, most reporters—especially those connected with the national news media—had to wait until the state convention met in order to see which presidential candidate would win the most delegates. Simultaneous precinct caucuses, the requirement that everyone present announce their presidential preference, and, of course, the use of computers and telephones to aggregate lots of data quickly meant that national reporters could descend upon a state such as Iowa and turn their hitherto-ignored precinct caucuses into a primary.

The Iowa precinct caucuses were "discovered" in 1976, when Jimmy Carter "won" them by coming in second to "uncommitted" and beating a field of much better known candidates. Four years earlier most of the press corps had overlooked the Iowa caucuses and in so doing had missed signs that George McGovern was a lot stronger and Senator Edmund Muskie (the reputed frontrunner) a lot weaker than most pundits had assumed. So the press was ready in 1976. As Jules Witcover explains: "For their romance with Muskie the press and television paid heavy alimony after 1972 in terms of their reputation for clairvoyance, let alone clear thinking and evidence at hand. ... [I]n 1976, if there were going to be early signals, the fourth estate was going to be on the scene en masse to catch them" (Witcover, 1977:200).

The popularity of this new, transformed Democratic caucus system became the envy of the Iowa Republican party. Since its delegate-selection rules were not governed by any state statutes when the Iowa Democratic party was "reformed," the Iowa Republican party wasn't reformed. The result was that, in 1976, the hard-fought battle between President Ford and Ronald Reagan began, as far as the public could see, in New Hampshire, not in Iowa—even though the Iowa Republican caucuses had been held on the same night as the Democratic caucuses that had attracted so much attention. No one paid attention to the Iowa Republican caucuses that year because they were traditional, old-fashioned caucuses that could not be easily counted and interpreted by the national press corps.

The lesson was not lost on the Iowa Republicans who, left out of the limelight in 1976 and eager to share in it in 1980, decided to hold a nonbinding straw poll at each precinct caucus in 1980 and to have the results reported to the Republican State Committee at a location in Des Moines convenient to the national press corps.

The Iowa caucuses were not a factor in 1992 because of the candidacy of favorite son Tom Harkin. There are, however, already early signs that Iowa will become a major battleground in the fight for the Republican presidential nomination in 1996. Potential challengers Jack Kemp, Phil Gramm, and Bob Dole have already been making the rounds of Iowa Republican party functions. Recounting his victory over George Bush in the 1988 caucuses, Senator Dole has quipped a number of times that he is still the president of Iowa.

Thus, in a relatively short period of time, the process of delegate selection in both political parties was transformed from a process understandable to only the most astute of political observers—and then only toward the end of the process—to a process that was easily quantifiable and therefore accessible to reporters from the earliest moments.

Money and the Need for an Early Start

Reform of the delegate-selection system shifted the focus of attention from the convention to the seven or eight months of primaries and caucuses before the convention; reform of the campaign finance laws shifted attention to the year before the primaries even began. Without going into detail on campaign finance reform, suffice it to say that, like delegate-selection reform, it transformed the search for money from a private (or at best a semi-public) undertaking to a highly public, easily quantifiable one.

The reasons are simple. In the pre-reform system a few very rich people could and did bankroll entire campaigns. Sometimes the public knew who these people were; often they did not. After campaign finance reform, the most that any one person could contribute to a presidential nomination campaign was $1,000. Thus candidates had to hold countless cocktail parties, dinners, luncheons, and other events in order to amass the millions of dollars needed to run in every caucus and primary in the country.

Furthermore, if a candidate raises at least $5,000 in individual contributions of $250 or less in twenty different states, another part of the campaign finance reform bill provides that any contribution up to $250 will be matched by the federal treasury. This means that large numbers of small contributions suddenly became very valuable. With money in lots of fairly small chunks doubling in value, presidential candidates therefore sought ways to become visible and to appear that they were doing well as early as possible—usually one full year prior to the beginning of the primaries and caucuses.

Direct-mail appeals were an obvious strategy to capture many small donations and gain both credibility and federal matching funds. Moreover, at first glance the matching funds would seem to help the less well known candidates. But in order to raise money and, specifically, in order to utilize direct mail, the candidate signing the letter has to be well known. As Nelson Polsby and Aaron Wildavsky have argued, the doubling of contributions because of the federal match may actually exacerbate the disparity in funds between candidates, since any differences are effectively doubled (Polsby and Wildavsky, 1988:55).

Another provision of the new campaign finance reform laws required that all presidential candidates make quarterly reports of the money they had raised and spent. These quarterly reports, which are made public, have occasioned news stories on how each presidential candidate is doing. A candidate who raises lots of money begins to be taken seriously, whereas a candidate who raises little money tends to get left out of television stories, newspaper columns, and all the other free press that is so important in campaigns. Media coverage then generates more money, and more money generates more media coverage, and so on and on in a self-fulfilling circle.

This is not to say that early money guarantees success. However, early money does make candidates look like winners and may allow them to withstand initial setbacks once the nomination season begins. Bill Clinton's financial resources enabled him to weather the various scandals that rocked his campaign before the New Hampshire primary. Obviously Clinton would have rather not faced such early troubles, but he did have plenty of resources to withstand early controversy and setbacks. Conversely, Paul Tsongas did not have enough resources to capitalize on some early successes. Knowing that he did not have the money to effectively campaign in the New York primary, Paul Tsongas withdrew from the race after the Michigan and Illinois primaries in mid-March.

STRATEGIES OF THE POST-REFORM ERA

Sequence as Strategy

The two reform movements and the changes they wrought in the structure of the nomination system created a set of new strategic imperatives for presidential candidates. The most important of these was understanding the role of sequence in winning the nomination. Once primaries and caucuses became binding, presidential candidates had to contest every single one or risk forfeiting delegates. But the new campaign finance laws limited both the amount of money that could be spent in any one state and the total amount of money that could be spent on the entire nomination race to a sum that was less than the total spending permitted in each state.[4] Thus, even if a presidential candidate could raise enough money to spend the maximum in each state, the campaign finance law forced him to pick and choose between states while the new rules for delegate selection were making it all the more important to contest every state.

The result was to make winning early the key to winning the nomination. If a candidate can win several early contests, he will possess "momentum"—and momentum buys things that money cannot buy, such as free media coverage and the perception that the candidate is a winner. Since 1976, when Jimmy Carter's surprise victories in Iowa and New Hampshire demonstrated the power of momentum in no uncertain terms, media coverage of the early contests (especially those in Iowa and New Hampshire) was vastly out of proportion to the size of those states and the number of delegates elected in each.[5] In recent years the major evening news programs have chosen to move their entire shows to Des Moines, Iowa, and to Manchester, New Hampshire, for the week leading up to the delegate-selection contests in those two states—but they paid nowhere near the same amount of attention to Pennsylvania and California, which (though much bigger states) hold primaries late in the season.[6] One reporter counted the number of journalists in Iowa during the 1984 caucuses and discovered that there was one journalist for every one hundred caucus goers (Klose, 1984:A3).

This kind of early media coverage tends to have a powerful effect on voters further down the line. As Larry Bartels has demonstrated, momentum itself, or the perception that the candidate is a winner, influences voters in subsequent primaries independent of other factors such as region and ideology. Unlike nomination contests in the pre-reform years, strategy in the post-reform era relies heavily on the sequence of victories. Bartels sums it up as follows: "The key to success, it appeared, was not to enter the nomination with a broad coalition of political support, but to rely on the dynamics of the campaign itself—particularly in its earliest public phases—to generate support" (Bartels, 1983:170,172).

Voters may be predisposed to support particular presidential aspirants but will cast their vote only for a candidate they believe to be viable. Perceptions are crucial as candidates and their strategists attempt to spin victories and losses in a way that makes it appear that the candidate is viable and the opponents are not. The work of the campaign is not over on primary night; strategists must not only prepare for the next primary but must spin the results of the just-completed one.

As winning early increased in importance, candidates paid more and more attention to the sequence of the early contests. If a candidate had the political power and opportunity to create a calendar to his liking, he did exactly that. Just as Jimmy Carter was the first presidential candidate to understand the significance of exceeding expectations in the Iowa caucuses, he was also the first to understand that the sequence of contests after Iowa would be important.

In 1975 Carter wanted to create the best possible calendar for his candidacy. An early southern contest was important to the overall Carter strategy. He needed to defeat George Wallace early, thereby removing any competition for southern delegates. The best opportunity was in Florida, but a bill in the legislature there threatened to move the primary from early March to late spring. So Carter, his campaign manager, and his lawyer got on a plane to Florida, where they made a successful appeal to the Speaker of the House and the governor to keep the Florida primary early.

In 1979 President Carter could count on a lot more than political friendship to help him create a favorable calendar for his renomination. With White House encouragement, Mississippi, South Carolina, Oklahoma, Georgia, and Alabama—all good states for the president—moved up to early March.

On the Republican side, the campaign of Ronald Reagan was not at all unhappy with the calendar that President Carter was creating—a calendar involving many early southern states. In 1976 Reagan had consistently beaten President Ford in the South, and with any luck Reagan expected to win there once again. But Reagan's campaigners knew that they had to beat Texan John Connally, the only other candidate in the race who had the potential to rival Reagan for southern delegates.

So, under the influence of a young Reagan operative, the late Lee Atwater (past chairman of the Republican National Committee), a special state convention was called in which the decision was made that South Carolina would hold its first and only (to that time) Republican presidential primary one week before the rest of the southern primaries. South Carolina was a state in which the Reagan people felt they could beat Connally. After a very heated and expensive primary, Reagan did win. Connally left the race, and Reagan went on to a series of important southern victories.

It is very difficult for presidential candidates to establish the most desirable sequence of contests: Deadlines for establishing the date of a primary or caucus are far in advance of the nomination year, and there are other complicated reasons for which a state chooses to hold a primary or caucus on a certain day. Furthermore, many presidential hopefuls lack the political clout necessary to accomplish such a huge task. But these and other efforts on the part of presidential hopefuls to create a favorable sequence only reinforce the main point—that in the post-reform era presidential candidates have to do well in the earliest contests or face having to drop out of the race altogether. Sequence has indeed become strategy.

The importance of winning early in the new nomination system was not lost on individual state parties. As they looked with envy at the attention and money spent on the early contests, more and more states moved their primaries early in the spring in order to get in on the media and candidate attention that went with being early. In order to gain more influence and not be forced to choose among an already winnowed field, the primary state with the richest delegate prize, California, seriously considered moving its presidential primary up to March in 1992 and has done so for 1996. Table 8.4 shows the number of contests and the percentage of delegates elected in them month by month for each of the post-reform years.

The percentage of delegates elected in March went up steadily throughout the post-reform years, but it rose sharply in 1988 due to the creation of the Southern Regional primary. In 1986 a group of southern Democratic legislative leaders, concerned that the Democratic party was nominating candidates (such as Walter Mondale) who were too liberal to carry the South, got together and decided to form a southern Super Tuesday. They did so by moving all the southern states' primaries to the second Tuesday in March, specifically in the hopes of giving these states a decisive role in the selection of the Democratic nominee.

The First Super Tuesday in 1988 was a dismal failure for the architects of a southern regional primary, concerned about the liberal candidates that their party was nominating. It not only failed to produce a southern, more conservative nominee but it gave a boost to two candidates who were arguably the most liberal of the seven in the Democratic field—Michael Dukakis and Jesse Jackson. In 1992, Super Tuesday did give Bill Clinton a huge boost after his early troubles and did help produce a more moderate nominee. But it remains to be seen whether such tinkerings with the primary schedule will always produce more moderate nominees.

Mobilizing the Ideological Extremes

Voters in presidential primaries have always been more liberal (in the case of the Democrats) or more conservative (in the case of the Republicans) than the rest of the electorate (Lengle, 1981). This factor was not very important in the days when the nomination was largely in the hands of party professionals. By and large, these people were in the business of winning elections and they judged potential candidates according to whether they could win, not on ideological grounds.

But in the post-reform era, primaries matter and party leaders do not. Presidential primaries attract a very small percentage of all voters—a percentage of people who tend to be more highly educated, more well to do, and more ideologically committed than most voters. Table 8.5 takes data from Voter Research and Surveys (VRS) exit polls in several states and compares the ideological preferences of Democratic and Republican primary voters with those of voters in the general election. In all instances the

TABLE 8.4
Determining Steps in the Delegate-Selection Process for
Selected Contested Primary Years

	Pre-March	March	April	May	June
1972 Democrats	7	9	11	18	7
	7%	14%	18%	33%	24%
1976 Democrats	9	8	11	20	8
	9%	17%	25%	29%	20%
1980 Democrats	4	18	9	14	11
	5%	35%	19%	20%	21%
1980 Republicans	12	11	7	15	9
	15%	25%	14%	24%	21%
1984 Democrats[a]	3	29	9	12	5
	6%	36%	17%	21%	13%
1988 Democrats[a]	2	36	7	6	4
	2%	50%	13%	9%	11%
1988 Republicans	3	33	5	6	4
	6%	55%	14%	11%	12%
1992 Democrats[b]	4	27	6	8	6
	2%	39%	14%	8%	15%
1992 Republicans[b]	5	24	5	10	7
	4%	47%	11%	14%	20%

Note: The first number for each entry is the number of primary or caucus contests in that month. The second number is the percentage of delegates to the nominating convention elected in that month.

[a]Percentages do not add up to 100 percent for the 1984, 1988, and 1992 Democrats because of the way in which unpledged party leader and elected official delegates were awarded.

[b]The House Super Delegates were included in March when they were chosen and the Senate Super Delegates in April when they were chosen, but the Democrats still add up to only 88% because of the remaining 509 Super Delegates who are governors, DNC members, and VIPs.

Sources: 1952 and 1956, David et al. (1960:528–534); 1960, *Congressional Quarterly Weekly Report,* January 17, 1964, p. 106; 1968 and 1972, Commission on Party Structure and Delegate Selection (1971); 1976, 1980, and 1984, Democratic National Convention, *Handbooks of the Democratic National Convention,* various dates; 1988, Democratic National Committee, Compliance Assistance Commission Memo, January 25, 1988; 1992, *Congressional Quarterly Weekly Report,* July 4, 1992.

pattern is the same: The primary electorate is further to the left or the right, depending on the political party, than is the general election electorate.

Because the primary electorates are so small, a candidate who can mobilize a faction of these loyal party voters has a leg up in seeking the nomination. Jesse Jackson's base in the Democratic party among black voters was very important to his successes in 1984 and 1988. Even though black

TABLE 8.5
A Comparison of Primary and General Election Voters in 1988,
by Ideology in Selected States (in percent)

Delegates or Voters Identifying Ideology	California	Florida	Illinois	New Jersey	Texas
Democratic Primaries					
Liberal	43	31	36	39	26
Moderate	42	45	46	48	44
Conservative	15	24	18	13	30
Republican primaries					
Liberal	11	11	13	12	8
Moderate	35	38	44	38	31
Conservative	53	51	43	50	60
General election					
Liberal	23	20	22	20	17
Moderate	50	47	52	54	43
Conservative	26	33	26	26	40

Source: Compiled by the authors on the basis of data provided by Voter Research and Surveys exit polls, 1989.

voters made up only 8 percent of the November electorate, they constituted an average of 17 percent of the electorate in the primary states. In some states black voters were a very substantial percentage of the primary electorate. In New York they constituted 27 percent of the Democratic primary, and in states with large black populations, such as Mississippi, they constituted nearly half of the Democratic primary electorate.

Being acceptable to the primary electorate is not, however, the same as being acceptable to the general electorate. The successful presidential candidate survives the marathon of primaries and caucuses ever mindful of two audiences: the small audience of party loyalists who participate in the primaries and who hold policy viewpoints far from the center, and the very large and more centrist audience that he will face in the general election.

Conventional wisdom has been that the Democrats have always suffered more from the ideological disparities in primary and general election electorates. The 1992 election, however, indicates that the Republicans suffer from similar problems. George Bush had to run a primary campaign and convention far to the right to fend off Pat Buchanan and appease fundamentalist conservatives. In the general election, Bush won the vast majority of self-identified conservatives, but he failed to garner enough moderate and independent votes to be reelected.

The Delegate Count

Once the initial contests are over, the field of candidates tends to narrow considerably—usually to one or two candidates by the end of March.

Presidential candidates continue to receive influxes of federal matching funds as the campaign season progresses; but the law stipulates that, once a candidate fails to win 10 percent of the vote in two consecutive primaries, he can be deemed ineligible for matching funds. Thus candidates who have won very small percentages of the vote have a powerful reason—lack of money—to get out of the race.

Beyond the early contests there are many simultaneous primaries and caucuses, and the delegate count becomes more and more important as a means of interpreting events and of judging who, among the remaining contenders, is closest to winning the nomination. Counting delegates used to be the exclusive domain of party insiders and political professionals who knew all there was to know about the party leaders (major and minor) and could predict how they would behave and whom they would vote for at the nominating convention. At the end of the 1960 primary season John Kennedy had only 134 delegates committed to him, or 18 percent of those he needed to get nominated, as a result of the primaries. Then, as Theodore White described it, the real work began: "Now the rest of the harvest proceeded, state by state, across the nation, fitting itself to the manners and morals of each state's politics like an exercise in the diversity of American life" (White, 1961:161).

In the post-reform era, the delegate count can be conducted even when actual delegates have not been elected. On April 3, 1984, for instance, United Press International reported that Mondale had 729 delegates, Hart had 440, and Jackson had 101. As of that same date, however, if someone had wanted to, he or she could have talked to real live delegates from only six states for a total of 434 delegates—or about one-third the number being reported in the delegate count. But in April no one was interested in talking to real live delegates, so absolute was the certainty that the delegates would simply represent the will of the primary voters.

The translation of the primary vote into a delegate count is accomplished by means of formal allocation rules. Because these rules dictate who wins how many delegates, they have been the source of endless controversy in the Democratic party. Because Republicans do not have centralized rules, and because these rules are often not part of state statutes, the Republican party has not been as affected by the Democratic allocation rules as by some of the Democrats' other rules. Thus there are real and significant differences between the two parties when it comes to the accumulation of a delegate majority.

Simply put, there are two basic ways to award delegates to a presidential candidate: winner take all, and proportional representation. The Republican party tends to use the former and the Democratic party, the latter. Winner-take-all rules award all of the delegates from a state or a congressional district to the candidate who wins the most votes in that state or district. Proportional rules divide the delegates from a state or district as nearly as possible in proportion to the vote that each presidential candidate won in that state or district. The Democratic party has come up with many variations on this theme, but these two rules are the most important for our purposes.[7]

The Democratic party's reform movement encouraged and eventually mandated the use of proportional representation to award delegates to presidential candidates. This development shows up in Figure 8.1, which compares the types of systems used in each party throughout the post-reform years. With the exception of 1972, during which the Democrats encouraged but did not require the use of proportional representation, the Democrats have tended to award delegates to presidential candidates in proportion to the primary vote whereas the Republicans have tended to award delegates to the winner of the state or district.

This difference has important consequences for the two parties. First, proportional representation increases the already-dangerous predisposition of the Democratic party to break down into factions; and, second, it reinforces the importance of a strong showing in the early part of the nomination season for Democratic candidates (Kamarck, 1987). Nelson Polsby argues that reform of the delegate-selection process has worked "disproportionately to the disadvantage of the majority party, the Democrats," who, according to Polsby, are disadvantaged in comparison to the Republicans because of their greater ideological diversity (Polsby, 1983:86).

Unlike losing Republican candidates, a losing Democratic candidate, especially a second-place finisher, can still win delegates. In 1992, Jerry Brown and Pat Buchanan both garnered around 20 percent of their respective party's total primary vote. This gave Brown 608 delegates under the Democrats' proportional rules; Buchanan earned only 78 delegates under GOP winner-take-all rules. Under Democratic rules, Buchanan would have won over 600 delegates. Ironically, even with these disparities in delegate allocation rules, which would seem to give extremists more power at the Democratic convention, Pat Buchanan ultimately had more influence on the convention and the general election than did Jerry Brown.

Nevertheless, in general, proportional representation increases the Democrats' predisposition toward internal disarray and discourages them from quickly unifying around their future nominee.

The losing candidate who is steadily accumulating delegates needs a rationale for staying in the race, for during the last few contests, the frontrunner and much of the party leadership are urging the loser to end the race as soon as possible. In the process of seeking such a rationale, minor differences between candidates tend to be enlarged and emphasized. Candidates who are not really very far apart become polarized on issues, and the divisions between factions in the party are accentuated at the very

FIGURE 8.1

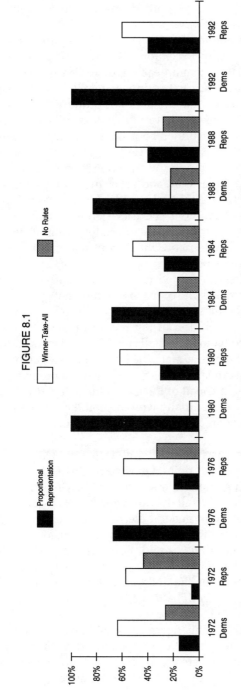

Percentage of convention delegates elected by allocation system (by election year and political party). *Note:* All Democratic primaries and caucuses were run using proportional representation in 1992. The Republicans used a variety of systems: seventeen states used winner-take-all systems (though Alabama was winner-take-all in congressional districts and proportional for at-large delegates; Connecticut and Texas were winner-take-all only if the winner garnered a majority [60 percent in Connecticut], otherwise proportional representation was used [in Connecticut, if the runner up had 20 percent]; and Louisiana used winner-take-all if the winner garnered a majority, otherwise the delegation was uncommitted); eleven states used proportional representation; eighteen states had no formal rules; and five states directly elected the delegates. *Source:* Compiled by the author on the basis of yearly convention summaries in *Congressional Quarterly Weekly Reports.*

point in time when they should be unified—usually to the detriment of Democrats in the general election.

The second effect of a nominating system dominated by proportional representation is, paradoxically, to reinforce the importance of the earliest contests. In a proportional system an early winner can withstand losses later on in the season because he can continue to win delegates even while losing primaries. There are no late bloomers in proportional systems: A candidate who suddenly starts to win or who enters late will find it very difficult to overtake the frontrunner because he can never win large chunks of delegates.

The best example can be found in the 1976 nomination season. Jimmy Carter was the early winner that year, and yet as the spring wore on more and more voters came to have doubts about him (doubts that crystallized in the formation of ABC—Anybody But Carter—groups), and he began to lose primaries. In May and June, Carter suffered a string of defeats, including a defeat in the delegate-rich California primary; but he was still able to accumulate delegates because proportional rules allowed him to claim a share. These delegates, added to those won earlier in the year, gave Carter the nomination in spite of his loss of momentum.

On the Republican side, President Gerald Ford, also an early winner, began (like Carter) to lose contests in the month of May to challenger Ronald Reagan. But due to winner-take-all rules, Ford's losses had serious consequences. In five of the twelve states he had lost to Reagan he won no delegates at all, and in the other states he won very small numbers of delegates. Ford went from being ahead of Reagan in the delegate count to being behind. Even though he eventually won the nomination, Ford was seriously threatened by Reagan all the way up to and including the convention.

In 1976 the controversy was on the Republican side, which lost. And thus we are brought to one final point. Divisive nomination contests in a political party in the spring—regardless of the underlying structure—do not help a party's chances in the fall. Incumbents who have faced internal challenges have done poorly in general elections. For example, the last three incumbent presidents who were seriously challenged for the nomination lost the general election: Gerald Ford, challenged by Ronald Reagan in the 1976 GOP primaries, lost to Jimmy Carter; Jimmy Carter, challenged by Ted Kennedy in the 1980 Democratic primaries, lost to Ronald Reagan; and George Bush, challenged by Pat Buchanan in the 1992 Republican primaries, lost to Bill Clinton.

This does not mean that challengers cause incumbent presidents to lose, and since weak presidents are more likely to draw strong internal challenges, it is difficult to measure the exact effect. Nevertheless, the fate of incumbents is certainly not helped when they are attacked from within.

Two lessons are implicit in this aspect of the nominating system. The first is that political parties should try to avoid systems that add to or generate divisiveness. (The Democrats have yet to learn this lesson.) The second is that presidential candidates should seek not only to avoid divisiveness in the primary season but also to reach the "magic number" of delegates as soon as possible. In 1984 Mondale successfully tied up the nomination on the day after he lost the California primary. He did this in a last-minute blitz of still-uncommitted delegates and managed to deflect attention from his California defeat onto the fact that he had enough pledged delegates to win the nomination on a first ballot.

The desire to go over the top as far in advance of the convention as possible requires that, when there are different allocation rules in effect, candidates must spend more time and attention in places where they can win more delegates by winning the primary. In other words, winner-take-all systems of delegate allocation are another way for a state to be important in the nomination system without having to select its delegates first.

The Dukakis Super Tuesday strategy was carefully crafted to win congressional districts in states where the delegate harvest would be greatest. For instance even though Dukakis lost more primaries than he won on Super Tuesday, his delegate count was slightly higher than anyone else's, thus giving him an important edge in the perceptions of those who were trying to interpret the race.

But the most dramatic use of the delegate count occurred during the Mondale campaign in 1984. Reeling from the unexpected victory by Gary Hart in New Hampshire, Mondale went south amid anticipation that his campaign was about to end and lost several important primaries, including the all-important Florida primary. But the vicissitudes of the delegate-selection process allowed Mondale to emerge from Super Tuesday 1984 with many more delegates than Gary Hart. This fact found its way into the hands of the press, which used it, to the dismay of the Hart campaign, to give new life to Mondale's candidacy (Orren, 1985).

The Four-Day Television Commercial

Why is it so important to wrap up the nomination before the convention? Because the post-reform convention has a new role. With rare exceptions, it is no longer the place were the nomination is won. As we have seen, the nomination is won in the primaries and in the caucuses, and the nominee is almost always know prior to the convention. In the pre-reform era, the weeks between the last primary and the opening of the convention were times of intense activity as the leading candidates sought to pin down the votes of delegates who were not already pledged to a presidential candidate. Table 8.6 shows the number of unaffiliated delegates at the end of the primary season in both the pre- and the post-reform years. During the

TABLE 8.6

"Unaffiliated" Delegates at the End of the Primary Season as a
Percentage of the Total Number of Convention Delegates

Year and Party	Percentage and Number of Unaffiliated Delegates	
1952 Republican	28%	336 delegates
1952 Democratic	72%	884 delegates
1956 Republican	39%	537 delegates
1960 Democratic	31%	469 delegates
1964 Republican	26%	335 delegates
1968 Democratic	29%	748 delegates

(Average pre-reform years = 38% unaffiliated)

1972 Democratic	23%	685.25 delegates
1976 Democratic	10%	295 delegates
1976 Republican	11%	244 delegates
1980 Democratic	3%	86 delegates
1980 Republican	5%	101 delegates
1984 Democratic	7%	272 delegates
1988 Democratic	11%	483 delegates
1988 Republican	9%	210 delegates
1992 Democratic	10%	527 delegates
1992 Republican	3%	27 delegates

(Average post-reform years = 9% unaffiliated)

Sources: Data compiled by the author from *Congressional Quarterly Weekly Report.* 1972 data from June 17, 1972, p. 1465; 1976 Republican data from July 12, 1978, p. 1473; 1976 Democratic data from June 12, 1976, p. 1473; 1980 Republican data from June 14, 1980, p. 1640; 1980 Democratic data from June 14, 1980, p. 1640; 1984 Democratic data from June 9, 1984, p. 1345; 1992 data from June 6, 1992.

former period, an average of 38 percent of the delegates remained to be wooed in the weeks prior to the convention; during the latter, that number generally dropped significantly.

Another way to look at the same phenomenon is to compare the delegate count for the eventual nominee at the end of the primary season with the first ballot vote for the nominee at the convention. In the pre-reform years, the nominee had barely 50 percent of what he needed to get nominated by the end of the primary season; in the post-reform years, the count at the end of the season tends to be a pretty good predictor of the vote on the first ballot (see Table 8.7).

In the modern nominating system, therefore, the actual nomination function is all but gone from the convention; suspense about the identity of the nominee is a thing of the past. It has been many years since either political party has had a convention that went past the first ballot, so effectively have the primaries and caucuses displaced the convention as the

TABLE 8.7

Relationship Between the Delegate Count at the End of the
Primary Season and the Nominee's Vote on the First Ballot at the Convention

	Needed to Nominate	Delegate Count at End of Primary Season for Nominee	First Ballot Vote (before shifts)	Ratio of Count to First Ballot Vote
1952 Republicans	604	393	595	.66
1952 Democrats	616	N/A	273	–
1956 Democrats	687	266	905.5	.29
1960 Democrats	761	339.5	806	.42
1964 Republicans	655	560	883	.63
1968 Democrats	1,312	662.5	1,759.25	.38

(Average ratio for pre-reform years = .48)

1972 Democrats	1,509	1,000.25	1,728.35	.58
1976 Democrats	1,505	1,091	2,283.5	.49
1976 Republicans	1,130	889	1,187	.75
1980 Democrats	1,666	1,783.1	2,129	.84
1980 Republicans	998	1,551	1,939	.80
1984 Democrats	1,967	1,974	2,191	.90
1988 Democrats	2,081	2,264	2,876	.79
1988 Republicans	1,139	1,669		
1992 Democrats	2,145	2,512	3,372	.75
1992 Republicans	1,105	1,846	2,166	.85

(Average ratio for post-reform years = .75)

Sources: Data compiled by the author from *Congressional Quarterly Weekly Report.* 1972 data from June 17, 1972, p. 1465; 1976 Republican data from July 12, 1978, p. 1473; 1976 Democratic data from June 12, 1976, p. 1473; 1980 Republican data from June 14, 1980, p.1640; 1980 Democratic data from June 14, 1980, p. 1640; 1984 Democratic data from June 9, 1984, p. 1345; 1992 data from June 6, 1992.

place where the most important decision is made. Other matters of importance still go on at conventions—the party platform and party rules are debated and adopted, for instance—but the big decision is generally made weeks if not months before the convention ever opens.

In the post-reform era, then, the convention has become the place where the general election campaign begins. Byron Shafer, whose book *Bifurcated Politics: Evolution and Reform in the National Party Convention* is an excellent treatment of the post-reform convention, sums up the changes as follows: "[T]he role of the convention in inaugurating the general election campaign grew enormously as the nomination receded. ... [N]ational news media, especially as embodied in full and national coverage, became the means by which public presentations at the convention could be turned explicitly to the task of advertising the candidate, his party, and their program" (Shafer, 1988:152–154).

Anything that detracts from the party's ability to put its best foot forward—platform fights, rule fights, and ongoing tensions such as those between Ford and Reagan in 1976, Kennedy and Carter in 1980, Hart and Mondale in 1984, Dukakis and Jackson in 1988, and Bush and Buchanan in 1992—is seen as a major impediment to the use of the convention to begin the general election.

Whereas political parties have become more and more adept at "managing" their conventions, network news executives, under pressure to cut the huge costs involved in covering a convention, have become increasingly reluctant to cover events that are little more than four-day-long advertisements for the party and its nominee. Conventions used to be covered "gavel to gavel," or from the time they opened until the time they closed. In the 1950s and 1960s, in fact, television coverage actually exceeded the amount of time that the convention was in session.

Beginning in 1980, however, coverage by all three networks declined dramatically (Shafer, 1988:276–280). When NBC News announced a plan to cut from its prime-time coverage of the Democratic convention to a "convention without walls" that it was producing itself, there was a predictable outcry from party officials. Joe Angotti, executive producer of the news, said that "[o]ur first and primary responsibility is to cover the news. I'd like nothing better than to throw all this out and cover a real breaking story" (Kamarck, 1988). In 1992 the major networks made good on their threats to scale back significantly their coverage of the conventions. On some nights only one hour of the proceedings was broadcast.

Thus the nominating convention, devoid of its old functions, may have a hard time hanging onto its new functions. The political parties and nominees want to stage the entire affair so as to put the best light on their party, whereas the networks want to cover real news. If some balance is not struck, the conventions could go the way of the electoral college and become a vestigial part of the body politic.

PROSPECTS FOR CHANGE

The basic characteristics of the post-reform nominating system are not likely to change. For the foreseeable future the nominating process will be dominated by highly visible public contests for money and delegates. Though flawed, this system does have one advantage: People perceive it to be fair and open. When polled on the subject, the public has continually favored more primaries (usually national primaries), not fewer primaries. Any attempt to go back in time and give significantly more power to party officials would most likely be perceived as illegitimate by large numbers of voters accustomed to open presidential primaries.

Aside from Congress, which has traditionally been reluctant to get involved in the nomination process, the only agent of change would be the Democratic party, given that the Republicans do not believe in dictating delegate-selection systems to state Republican parties. Having preached the virtues of openness and wide participation for nearly twenty years, the Democrats, no matter how unhappy they are with the results of their recent nominating contests, can ill afford to return the process to smoke-filled rooms.

But the Democrats have made changes that, at the least, will put some checks and balances into the nomination system. One recent change was to make all major party elected officials (especially governors, senators, and members of Congress) automatic voting delegates to the convention. This change was necessary because one of the consequences of party reform was that elected officials, reluctant to compete with constituents for delegate slots, had dropped out of the convention picture.

The "Super Delegates" have not exercised an independent voice in the nomination process thus far. In 1984 and 1988 they composed about 15 percent of the delegates at the Democratic convention, and many endorsed Mondale in 1984 and Gephardt in 1988. Although Dukakis forces attempted to appease Jackson at the 1988 convention by lowering the number of Super Delegates, the Democratic party quickly rescinded the decision and in 1992 Super Delegates composed 18 percent of the delegates. Most of them remained uncommitted until fairly late in the game when they overwhelmingly threw their support behind the eventual nominee, Bill Clinton.

The inclusion of the Super Delegates remains popular with the Democratic party for several reasons. Some see them as a centrist force that can serve as a counterbalance to the more ideologically extreme activists who tend to dominate the platform and other forums. Others want them there just in case the primaries fail to produce a winner one day and the nomination actually gets decided on the floor of the convention—an unlikely but still possible scenario. In that case the Super Delegates would be expected to exert a leadership role in bringing the convention to a decision, much as they did in the pre-reform era. And finally, the Super Delegates can provide an element of "peer review" that the primary voters and ordinary delegates cannot provide, inasmuch as many of them will have known and worked with potential presidential candidates.

Another set of changes that are talked about but have not been incorporated into the Democratic party thus far involve deregulating the party rules. Some students of the rules (these authors included) believe that the current system dictates too many details of the delegate-selection process and that in some instances the rules have become examples of regulation for the sake of regulation. Although we argue in this essay that rules matter and that changes in rules can have significant consequences, there has been too much tinkering and too many attempts to fine-tune results through changes in procedure. Indeed, there is no real reason to force every state to elect delegates in exactly the same way so long as the process in each state is clear, open, and easy to participate in. If the Democrats allowed for variations among states, one state could check and balance another, and they could all avoid the unanticipated consequences that have ensued every time they have attempted to "reform" the process by writing yet another rule.

Changes in the nomination process should not be tied to an attempt to recapture some prior moment in history, when nominations were decided in the smoke-filled rooms of party leaders. To the extent that changes do occur in the future, they should be made with the goal of building checks and balances into the current system so that it can work to produce the best nominees—of both parties.

NOTES

1. The first and most famous of the party reform commissions was the Commission on Party Structure and Delegate Selection, which met from 1969 to 1972 and was chaired initially by Senator George McGovern and then by Representative Donald Fraser; hence it is known as the McGovern-Fraser Commission. The work of delegate-selection reform was continued in 1972–1973 by the Commission on Delegate Selection and Party Structure, chaired by then Baltimore City Councilwoman Barbara Mikulski. The next commission, the Commission on Presidential Nomination and Party Structure (1975–1978), was chaired by Michigan Democratic Party Chairman Morley Winograd; it was followed by the Commission on Presidential Nomination, chaired by North Carolina Governor James Hunt from 1981 to 1982. The last of the delegate-selection commissions appears to be the Fairness Commission, chaired by former South Carolina party chairman Donald Fowler in 1985–1986.

2. In his book on the reform movement, Byron Shafer (1983:387) makes the following point: "Despite its status as the device by which the largest share of delegates to national party conventions in all of American history had been selected, the party caucus was abolished by rules which were not assembled in any one guideline, which were not presented in the order in which they had to be assembled, and which did not at any point claim to be making their actual, aggregate, institutional impact."

3. This phrase was coined by Senator Howard Baker (Germond and Witcover, 1985:96).

4. In 1988, for instance, the total amount that any presidential candidate was allowed to spend to get the nomination was $27,660,000, but the sum total of spending permitted in each state in the union was approximately $70,000,000—about two and a half times the first amount.

5. In a famous article, Michael Robinson and Karen McPherson (1977:2) noted that in 1976 New Hampshire received coverage in more than half of all television stories devoted to the nomination season and in more than one-third of all print stories. This pattern of coverage, whereby the two early contests get news attention out of proportion to their size, has persisted in subsequent years.

6. Consequently, for 1996 the California primary has been moved to March.

7. One of the most frequent fights among Democrats is waged over the issue of "threshold"—namely, the percentage of the vote that a presidential candidate must receive in order to be awarded a delegate. Traditionally, the threshold has been at around 15 percent, meaning that a candidate who fails to receive 15 percent of the vote in a district or a state cannot be awarded a delegate. But the threshold is known to have been as high as 25 percent and as low as 5 percent.

9

The 1992 Presidential Election: A Time for Change?

ANTHONY J. CORRADO

On February 27, 1991, in a nationally televised speech, President George Bush announced that after only 100 hours of ground warfare the Allied forces would cease military operations in Iraq. "Kuwait is liberated," he declared. "Iraq's army is defeated." The nation began to celebrate Operation Desert Storm, its first decisive military victory in a major war since the end of World War II. Bush, however, cautioned that "this is not a time for euphoria."

If not euphoric, the president's supporters and Republican party leaders were certainly elated a week later as Bush prepared to address a joint session of Congress. The victory in the Gulf served as the capstone to a series of dramatic foreign policy events, including the fall of the Berlin Wall, popular uprisings in Eastern Europe, and rapid changes in the Soviet Union, which were widely perceived as heralding the end of the Cold War. On the strength of his foreign policy success, the president's job-approval rating skyrocketed to close to 90 percent, the highest level ever recorded in public opinion polls. On the domestic front, the economy continued to experience sluggish growth, but the nation seemed to be emerging from a relatively short and mild recession. The uncertainty surrounding the outcome of the Gulf War and the president's popularity combined to discourage potential Democratic challengers from launching a bid for the presidency even though the New Hampshire primary was less than a year away. The conventional wisdom among party leaders and other political observers was that the president's reelection was a certainty, and the major topic in presidential politics was who would run for the office—in 1996.

One year later, in March 1992, Bush's reelection prospects had dramatically shifted. With the Gulf War fading in memory, the electorate focused on the nation's continuing economic problems and the uncertainties of the post–Cold War world. On these issues, the president appeared to be out of touch with the concerns of average Americans and lacking an agenda for addressing the needs of the future. As a result, dissatisfaction with his performance rose significantly and his approval rating dropped to 41 percent, with only about one in five voters expressing support of his handling of the economy. Reelection was no longer considered inevitable. Rather, Bush faced a serious intraparty challenge for the Republican nomination, and a CNN poll released on March 3 showed that for the first time he was trailing an "unnamed Democrat" in a hypothetical general election matchup.

Bush also found himself fighting against a popular mood that did not bode well for incumbents. The public optimism of the previous year had given way to a consensus about the need to move in a new direction. According to ABC News/*Washington Post* polls, 58 percent of the public felt that the nation was generally heading in the right direction in February 1991, and only 18 percent expressed this view in March 1992. The vast majority of Americans believed that the nation was "seriously off track" and agreed that it was time for "real change." More important, this desire for change was not directed only at the president. Most measures of public opinion revealed public frustration and a desire for an end to "politics as usual." The electorate was dissatisfied with the performance of all government institutions, tired of gridlock in Washington, and increasingly alienated from a government that was perceived to be out of touch with its concerns. This desire for a new direction gave new life to the Democrats and their candidate, Governor Bill Clinton of Arkansas, and gave rise to the most unlikely presidential candidate in recent history, multibillionaire Ross Perot, who without previous political experience or party backing mounted the most serious challenge to the major party candidates since 1912.

This essay examines the 1992 election in an effort to answer a number of questions. How do we explain the dramatic shifts in the voters' perceptions of the candidates? How did the major parties and their respective candidates attempt to respond to the changing political landscape and the challenge offered by the candidacy of Ross Perot? What were the factors that account for Bill Clinton's victory? Finally, what does the election tell us about the future of the major parties?

PRELUDE TO AN ELECTION

The Republicans: The Decline of Bush

Throughout the 1980s the Republican party was often said to be the majority party at the national level. In the decade's three presidential elections,

Ronald Reagan and George Bush led their party to three consecutive electoral landslides. The foundation of this presidential voting strength was the Reagan coalition, which consisted of traditional Republican voting blocs including self-identified conservatives, protestants, and upper-income voters, and crucial swing groups such as self-identified moderates, independents, and suburban and middle-income voters. This coalition was held together by a shared belief in the basic values that constituted the core of Reagan Republicanism: anticommunism and a strong national defense, opposition to taxes, a limited role for the federal government, and an emphasis on such "traditional values" as patriotism, family, and personal morality (Pomper, 1989b). In 1988, Bush was elected as Reagan's heir to maintain this coalition and its agenda, and early in 1991 it appeared that these values would once again be advanced as the core of the Republican campaign message. The Bush presidency, however, undermined this strategy.

After the Gulf War, Bush's accomplishments in foreign policy stood as "the natural centerpiece of a reelection bid" (Omestad, 1992:72). During his first term, Bush devoted most of his energies to foreign affairs, where he enjoyed considerable success. The Berlin Wall was torn down in November 1989, leading to the reunification of Germany; a few months later the United States successfully invaded Panama and captured dictator Manuel Noriega; the nations of Eastern Europe moved toward democratization; the Soviet Union formally dissolved in December 1991; and the forces led by the United States successfully opposed Iraq in the Gulf. These achievements seemed to confirm Bush's strength as a "foreign policy president" and helped to sustain his high levels of popularity throughout his first three years in office. The president's success as a leader in world affairs thus should have served as the cornerstone of the Republican campaign; but instead of strengthening Republican prospects, the changes in the international realm paradoxically served to weaken the president's chances for reelection.

Bush's foreign policy accomplishments failed to provide the long-term electoral benefits the administration expected. Bush claimed credit for "ending the Cold War" and argued that the role of the Reagan-Bush administrations in bringing about this achievement should be duly recognized, but "most people believed that Soviet communism had died mainly of natural causes" (Quirk and Dalager, 1993:60). Bush therefore received little credit from the American public for the apparent end of the communist threat. As for the defeat of Iraq, critics diminished the glow of victory by questioning the success of the administration's policy. Operation Desert Storm had failed to remove Saddam Hussein from power, which led some to question whether we had really "won" and gave rise to a popular bumper sticker that read: "Saddam Hussein Still Has His Job.

What About You?" (Omestad, 1992:72). Critics also charged that the administration had assisted in the military buildup in Iraq prior to the war and failed to warn Saddam convincingly about the American response to an invasion of Kuwait. In addition, the ongoing investigation of the Iran-Contra affair continued to raise questions about Bush's knowledge of the illegal arms-for-hostages deal. Instead of highlighting Bush's achievements and portraying the president as a world leader, the post–Cold War discussions of foreign policy raised issues that the administration hoped to avoid.

The primary electoral consequence of the collapse of the Soviet Union was to erode the "clarifying distinctions of the Cold War" (Omestad, 1992:74) and thus remove one of the pillars of the Republican party's successful electoral coalition. As Ceasar and Busch (1993:15) have noted, since 1968 the Republican party had been the party identified as stronger on defense, and its presidential candidates benefited from the security concerns generated by a bipolar world. With the end of the Cold War, Republicans could no longer rely on the theme of anticommunism and support of a strong national defense to mobilize their coalition. Moreover, the death of communism resurrected the internal tensions over foreign policy that had characterized the party in the years following World War II (Dionne, 1991:161–165). The old debate within the party between isolationists and internationalists was revived, with party conservatives, led by former Nixon speech writer and television commentator Patrick Buchanan, advocating an isolationist stance while the administration supported free trade and aid packages to bolster the democratic movements in Eastern Europe and the former Soviet Union.

The changes in the international realm also confronted the president with the task of developing a new paradigm for U.S. foreign policy. Although Bush had extensive experience in world affairs and often spoke of a "new world order," he was essentially a task-oriented pragmatist who maintained a Cold War perspective. In certain areas he continued to exert strong leadership; he promoted the reunification of Germany, initiated negotiations between Israel and Arab states, and agreed to a major reduction in nuclear arms with Moscow. Yet it appeared that he failed to grasp the new dimensions of international affairs. His administration's initial step toward a post–Cold War policy was to call for "the status quo plus." This cautious response to a brave new world, whether justified or not, evoked an old concern about Bush—the perception that he lacked an agenda for the future.

With the end of the communist threat abroad, the electorate became less concerned with foreign affairs and quickly focused its attention on problems at home, especially the nation's economic conditions. How quickly? According to Kathleen Frankovic, the director of surveys at CBS

News, "As early as three days after the war ended, foreign affairs had faded from the public's mind and was replaced again by economic issues" (1993:111). On these domestic concerns, Bush was in a vulnerable position. Unlike previous Republican administrations, Bush could not rely on the antitax and antigovernment messages of the past to shore up his support. Throughout the 1988 campaign, Bush constantly pledged that his administration would impose "no new taxes," but in assenting to the 1990 budget compromise he was widely seen as having broken this promise, especially by those within his own party who regarded opposition to taxes as one of the party's most fundamental issues. Despite this massive package of budget cuts and tax increases, federal spending continued to soar, surpassing the Reagan administration's record level of spending and annual budget deficits. Bush's budget policy thus weakened the Republican argument that it was better at managing federal spending and reducing the role of government.

Nor could Bush rely on a strong economy. Although the 1990 recession was not as deep as the 1982 downturn (the highest level of unemployment was 7.8 percent, which was well below the 10.8 percent of 1982), the anticipated recovery lagged well behind the rate experienced in previous downturns. As a result, the nation was mired in the worst period of economic growth since World War II. In contrast, 1984 and 1988 were, respectively, the first and second highest growth years of the 1980s. The public thus questioned Bush's performance in handling the economy. Indeed, even when Bush enjoyed record levels of approval, the public discriminated between his performance in foreign affairs and his performance with respect to the economy. An analysis of opinion polls reveals that Bush's high approval rating in 1991 was primarily a function of assessments of his foreign policy performance; ratings of his performance with respect to the domestic economy were approximately 30 points lower than his foreign policy ratings, with less than a majority approving of his economic performance throughout the year (see Figure 9.1). His failure to reverse these attitudes is one of the keys to understanding the 1992 election.

By objective standards, Bush's handling of the economy was not as bad as the public believed. Although growth was sluggish, unemployment and inflation, on average, were at levels below those of either Carter's or Reagan's first term (Samuelson, 1992:36). In the second half of 1991, unemployment began to creep downward slowly and was, for the most part, regionally concentrated: Over half of the increase in unemployment was a result of employment patterns in the nation's two largest states, California and New York (Ceasar and Busch, 1993:35). Inflation was minimal, home mortgage rates were at their lowest levels in two decades, business investment was on the rise, and the trade deficit had dropped significantly

202

FIGURE 9.1

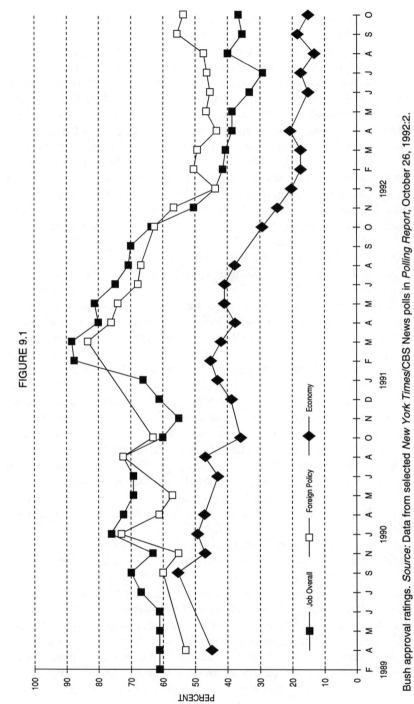

Bush approval ratings. *Source:* Data from selected *New York Times*/CBS News polls in *Polling Report*, October 26, 1992:2.

(Palmer, 1992:73). The economy appeared to be poised for recovery and most of the academic models designed to estimate electoral outcomes on the basis of economic performance and other variables predicted a Republican victory.[1] Bush consistently argued throughout the election that the economy was improving, and economists later supported his view, determining that the recession had ended in March 1991—but this judgment was not made public until seven weeks *after* the election (Berry, 1992:E1).

Bush's problem was that the majority of the electorate perceived the economy to be in a much worse condition than actual performance suggested. The public sensed that the economic problems plaguing the nation were qualitatively different from those of the past. One reason for this pessimism may have been the widespread job loss that accompanied the recession. In recent recessions about half of those who experienced unemployment were on temporary layoff. Many of those who have lost their jobs since 1990, however, permanently lost their positions; only about 15 percent were laid off (Samuelson, 1992:36). In 1992, 43.1 percent of unemployed workers—a record level—lost their jobs permanently because of corporate "downsizings" and business failures (Hage and Collins, 1993:42). Moreover, it was not just blue collar workers who entered the ranks of the unemployed. Professional and middle-class workers were also affected; for example, prestigious white collar jobs in such areas as computers, finance, and law "evaporated at a frightening clip," resulting in a loss of 200,000 positions (Barone, 1992:70). Middle- and upper-income voters also experienced a significant decline in the value of their assets, representing a loss of an estimated $842 billion in wealth (Barone, 1992:69–70).

A significant portion of the electorate thus became increasingly uncertain and insecure about the future. Voters began to wonder about their ability to meet their future financial needs, especially those millions of Americans who had no health insurance or existed one health crisis away from financial ruin. Voters increasingly feared that the long-term prospects for the nation's economy were worsening, and that a better quality of life might not be available to future generations. Consequently, the popular mood, as reflected in measures of consumer confidence, became increasingly pessimistic. As confidence fell, the percentage of the public disapproving of Bush's performance as president rose (see Figure 9.2).[2]

But even as public confidence began to level off during the election year, public disapproval of the president continued to rise. The vast majority of the public had lost confidence in Bush's ability to manage a return to prosperity. This perception was largely a result of his inaction with respect to the economic crisis. Many Democratic congressional leaders sounded the alarm and advocated some form of stimulus package, but Bush refused to acknowledge the seriousness of the nation's economic

204

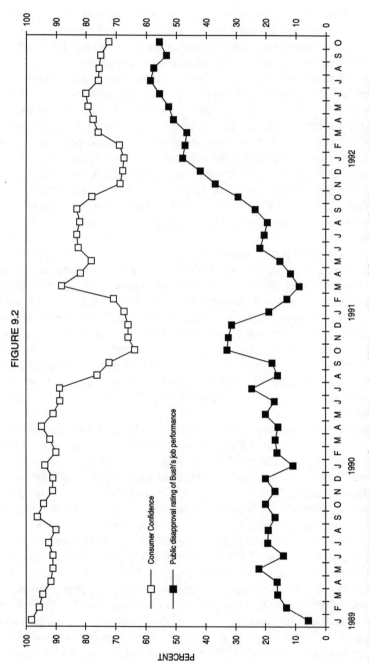

FIGURE 9.2

Public confidence and presidential disapproval. *Source:* University of Michigan Index of Consumer Sentiment and the Gallup Poll.

woes and accepted the view advanced by many economists that the economy would not benefit from a further increase in the budget deficit (Duffy and Goodgame, 1992:71–72). Not only did he not embrace the Democratic alternatives, he also failed to offer initiatives of his own. Despite numerous opportunities in 1991, Bush never set forth a detailed program for addressing the nation's domestic concerns. Even in his election year state of the union message, he offered no bold program. Instead, he outlined suggestions that "were largely incremental, or measures he had advanced unsuccessfully in the past, like a cut in the tax on capital gains, or measures he had only lightly defined, like his health care plan" (Toner, 1992b:E1). So in domestic affairs, as in foreign affairs, the administration pursued a policy of "status quo plus." This served to reinforce a popular image of Bush as being out of touch with the concerns of average Americans and lacking strong convictions or a vision for the future.

The public's image of Bush changed little during the course of the primaries. If anything, Patrick Buchanan's surprisingly strong bid for the nomination in New Hampshire reinforced negative perceptions of the president by emphasizing the broken tax pledge, cataloging the failures of the administration's economic and budget plans, and challenging the administration's free-trade policy. Although Bush easily captured the nomination, it was clear by the end of the primaries that Republican conservatives were dissatisfied with him as a candidate and that he had failed to change the consensus among the electorate that had formed before the primary season about his performance in the Oval Office.

The Democrats: A Party of Hope

In 1988 the Democratic party endured another disheartening loss in the presidential election. The party's nominee, Michael Dukakis, lost a 17-point post-convention lead in the opinion polls and suffered a solid electoral defeat. Once again, the party failed to attract the support of white southern moderates, independents, middle-income voters, and perhaps most important, the youngest voters (Pomper, 1989b:132–137). The Republicans' so-called lock on the electoral college continued, with the party winning twenty-one states, 191 votes, for the sixth consecutive election. This presumed advantage was reinforced by seventeen additional states, representing 217 votes, that consistently voted Republican in the 1980s. Yet the results of the 1988 election and Bush's declining fortunes offered the party new hope at the national level. The question was whether the Democrats would be able to take advantage of the opportunity that was available to them.

In the aftermath of the 1988 election, the Democrats took some solace in the fact that the party's performance in the electoral college voting was its best since Jimmy Carter's victory in 1976. Dukakis won ten states and the

District of Columbia for a total of 112 electoral college votes. In 1992, these states represented 108 electoral college votes. In an additional nine states, the Democrats were very competitive, with Bush taking 53 percent or less of the two-party vote (Pomper, 1989b:130–131).[3] Further, the Democrats had increased their share of the vote in these nine states by an average of 6.2 percent over their 1984 total. In 1992, these states represented 139 electoral college votes. The 1988 election therefore suggested the foundation of a Democratic general election strategy. To recapture the White House, the Democrats would have to concentrate on these nineteen states and the District of Columbia, together representing 247 electoral college votes, and target a number of southern states in an effort to expand their support in a region dominated by the Republicans in the 1980s.

The 1988 election thus rekindled the debate within the Democratic party concerning its strategy in national elections. Specifically, it raised the issue of how the party could best increase its share of the vote, which directly involved the question of whether the party should maintain its traditional message and ideology or modify its positions to promote a more moderate image. Some party leaders, most notably the Reverend Jesse Jackson, argued that the party did not need to alter its program or message dramatically. The party simply needed to maintain its liberal ideology and pursue a "politics of inclusion" to mobilize traditional partisans, especially minorities and the poor, to vote. By increasing turnout through the selective mobilization of these groups, the party could close the gap in competitive states and in the South and thus improve its ability to contest national elections (Galston and Kamarck, 1989:3–4). Others, especially the leaders of the Democratic Leadership Council (DLC), the organization of moderate and conservative Democrats formed after the 1984 election, argued that the Democrats could not rely on selective mobilization to win the presidency. Instead, they advocated the need to recast the party's themes and programs to attract the support of moderates, the middle class, and independents. This could be achieved, said DLC analysts, by advancing "a progressive economic message" based on the values of upward mobility, individual responsibility, and equal opportunity that would recognize the interests of the middle class as well as the traditional values and "moral sentiments of average Americans" (Galston and Kamarck, 1989:17).

Although the Democrats did not immediately resolve these questions of strategy, their potential appeal to key segments of the electorate grew as perceptions of Bush's performance declined. For just as voters' evaluations of government policy performance and economic conditions influence perceptions of the president's performance, so do they influence party identification and views of the performance of the major parties and their relative abilities to handle different tasks (Fiorina, 1979:84–130; Popkin,

1991:54–60). Accordingly, as voters' ratings on Bush's job performance and handling of the economy plummeted, the electorate's view of the Democratic party's ability to manage the economy improved substantially.

In March 1991, when public support for the president was at its peak, the Republican party enjoyed a significant advantage over the Democrats with respect to economic issues. Various polls revealed that the public viewed the Republicans as the party that would do a better job of ensuring a strong economy by a margin of 42 percent to 27 percent; do a better job dealing with taxes by a margin of 32 percent to 30 percent; and do a better job getting the country out of recession by 38 percent to 21 percent ("Public Opinion and Demographic Report" 1991:87–88). By spring 1992, however, public opinion had shifted against the Republicans.

Between October 1991 and April 1992, as public confidence in the economy and in Bush's ability to address the nation's problems fell, the electorate's confidence in the Democrats' relative ability to handle the economy rose. During this period, when the majority of voters felt that economic issues were the nation's biggest worry,[4] public opinion polls indicated a surge of support for the Democrats in comparative assessments of the major parties on the issues of overall management of the economy and taxes (see Table 9.1). In October 1991, the Republicans held a slight 1-point advantage over the Democrats on the question of which party would do a better job dealing with the economy; by July 1992, just days before the Democratic National Convention, the Democrats held an 8-point edge over the Republicans, a shift of nine percentage points. On the issue of taxes, the Democrats moved from a 5-point disadvantage to a 9-point advantage, a shift of 14 points in favor of the Democrats. On the issue of health care, which rose to prominence on the national agenda as a result of the special election for U.S. Senate in Pennsylvania in November 1991, the Democrats held a large advantage of more than 30 points. Conversely, the Republicans held their largest advantage in the area of foreign policy.

These shifts in public attitude toward the Democratic party are especially important because they reflect changing opinions among some of the key segments of the electorate that the Democrats hoped to attract to their presidential coalition. As noted in Table 9.2, the Democrats made significant gains among registered independents, white collar workers, and middle-income voters ($20,000 to $50,000 a year income). By April 1992, these groups favored the Democrats by substantial margins on the issue of handling the economy, with the largest gain among independents, who favored the Democrats by a margin of 18 points, a gain of 14 points over the percentage received in opinion polls in October 1991. Among middle-income and white collar voters, the Democrats realized a gain of 8 and 7 points, respectively. On the question of which party would

TABLE 9.1
Public Perceptions of the Major Parties

Which party do you think would do a better job dealing with ...	Dem	Rep	Both	Neither	Dem/Rep Margin
The economy					
October 1991	27	28	26	14	−1
January 1992	28	23	33	11	+5
March 1992	28	22	31	16	+6
April 1992	29	24	27	17	+5
July 1992	26	18	35	18	+8
Taxes					
October 1991	26	31	18	18	−5
January 1992	na	na	na	na	na
March 1992	35	26	17	17	+9
April 1992	30	24	18	23	+6
July 1992	29	20	20	25	+9
Health care					
October 1991	46	12	18	16	+34
April 1992	48	12	17	18	+36
July 1992	44	10	21	19	+34
Foreign policy					
October 1991	13	44	30	7	−21
April 1992	21	48	18	9	−27
July 1992	15	48	24	7	−33

Note: Figures do not total 100 percent because the percentage of respondents answering "Not Sure" or "Don't Know" are excluded. There is a variation in wording of the question in the October survey. This survey asked, "When it comes to keeping world peace, which party do you think would do a better job—the Democratic Party, the Republican Party, both about the same, or neither?" The April and July surveys asked, "When it comes to dealing with foreign policy...?"

Source: NBC News/Wall Street Journal polls. The dates and number of interviews were October 25–29 (N = 736, 762 on the economy); January 17–21 (N = 738); February 28–March 2 (N = 499); April 11–14 (N = 498); and July 5–7 (N = 550).

be best at dealing with taxes, the Democrats realized a gain of about 16 percent among all three groups. Preference for the Democrats on these crucial issues also increased substantially in the Northeast and Midwest, two regions crucial to the Democratic electoral college strategy.

Bill Clinton, a six-term governor of Arkansas and a founding member and former chair of the Democratic Leadership Council, was well-positioned ideologically to take advantage of the Democrats' improved political circumstances. Clinton framed his candidacy for the Oval Office largely around the strategy advocated by the DLC. He described himself as "a new kind of Democrat" who sought a new direction for the Democratic party, a "third way" between traditional Democratic liberalism

TABLE 9.2
Public Perceptions of Major Parties: Selected Readings and Demographic Groups

Margin of Preference for Democratic Party over Republican Party

	Overall	Men	Women	Northeast	Midwest	Middle Income	White Collar	Independents
The economy								
October 1991	−1	−10	+9	0	+2	+2	+1	+4
April 1992	+5	−4	+13	+18	+13	+10	+8	+18
Difference	(+6)	(+6)	(+4)	(+18)	(+11)	(+8)	(+7)	(+14)
Taxes								
October 1991	−5	−12	+1	−2	−5	−5	0	−5
April 1992	+6	+4	+7	+12	+11	+11	+15	+11
Difference	(+11)	(+16)	(+6)	(+14)	(+16)	(+16)	(+15)	(+16)

Source: NBC News/Wall Street Journal polls.

and Republican conservatism (Katz, 1992:2087). This "third way" was grounded on the concerns of middle-class and moderate voters. Clinton emphasized the need to relieve the tax burden on middle-class Americans, to encourage investment in the economy to create jobs and improve America's ability to compete in the international marketplace, and to provide universal access to affordable health care. He also supported the death penalty and promoted the values of individual responsibility and opportunity by seeking reform of the welfare system and a program of national service.

Clinton sought to win the presidential nomination by convincing victory-starved Democratic primary voters that he was an electable candidate who could win back moderate and independent voters who had left the party's fold in recent elections. This strategy was undermined by the series of scandalous disclosures that plagued him throughout the primaries. The issues associated with these allegations—marital infidelity, draft avoidance, and his "slick" image—raised questions about his character and trustworthiness. By the time of the April New York primary, 55 percent of those responding to exit polls believed that Clinton was not trustworthy, and two-thirds of those who voted *for* Clinton wanted a new candidate (Walsh et al., 1992:32; Ceasar and Busch, 1993:68). Throughout the final weeks of the primaries, exit polls documented deep concerns about Clinton's character. A May *Wall Street Journal*/NBC News poll found that only 22 percent of all voters felt Clinton "best represents traditional American values" (Harwood, 1992:A14). A June *New York Times*/CBS News survey showed that just as many voters, 40 percent, had an unfavorable view of the Democratic nominee as had a favorable view (Ifill, 1992:7). Consequently, by the end of the primaries, Clinton had won the largest share of the delegates to a Democratic convention since Lyndon Johnson in 1964, but he stood in third place in presidential trial heats, behind Bush and one of the most unlikely presidential contenders in American history, H. Ross Perot.

The Perot Phenomenon

Ross Perot was not the first independent candidate for the presidency in the modern era, but his candidacy differed significantly from other independent and minor party candidates in the twentieth century. First, Perot was not an established political leader who had previously held or sought political office. He was a successful businessman and entrepreneur, a former IBM salesman who had formed his own computer data company and turned it into a multibillion dollar empire. He achieved public recognition as a prominent citizen-volunteer on issues ranging from educational reform to POW-MIA investigations and was best known for the rescue of two of his executives from an Iranian jail in 1979, which served as the basis for a book and television movie. He had no party affiliation, no particular social or geographic constituency, no clear ideology. And no sharply defined policy views other than his constant call for a rapid reduction in the federal budget deficit. He even publicly disavowed his interest in serving as president but noted he would accept this responsibility if the people said "Ross, it's a dirty job but you've got to do it" (J. Broder, 1992:A17).

Second, Perot did not have to confront the resource limitations that have constricted the campaigns of recent independent candidates. With his immense personal wealth, Perot had the funds to finance "a world class campaign" and expressed his willingness to spend "whatever it takes" from his own pocket to match the major parties (Cook, 1992b: 1722). Further, he did not have to engage in costly legal battles to gain access to the ballot, as did John Anderson in 1980 (Anderson, 1992). For the most part, all Perot had to do was meet the ballot access requirements of the various states, which entailed the collection of a requisite number of signatures on ballot petitions. Although these procedures are a significant obstacle for most nonmajor party candidates (only one other nonmajor party candidate in 1992, Andre Marrou of the Libertarian party, successfully qualified for the ballot in all fifty states), Perot experienced such a large outpouring of support that he easily completed this task.

Third, Perot did not run a conventional campaign. He entered no primaries and eschewed most of the usual organizational and tactical strategies that have come to characterize modern presidential campaigns. He traveled very little, staged few media events, and refused to hire a large coterie of consultants and advisers, although he did eventually agree to hire some campaign professionals, including former Reagan adviser Ed Rollins and former Carter adviser Hamilton Jordan at one point. Instead he emphasized that his campaign was a volunteer effort and that he was running only because that was what the people wanted. His was a "grassroots campaign" consisting of state volunteer organizations (which were often subsidized by Perot with some leaders on his campaign payroll [Noah, 1992:A16]) loosely tied together by a sophisticated 800-number telephone network. His "campaigning" was primarily conducted through appearances on nationally broadcast "infotainment" talk shows and news programs. His quest began as a result of a comment on the "Larry King Show" in February, and throughout the campaign he continued to exploit the press corps' interest in his candidacy to deliver his views to the electorate. It was not until the last months of his campaign, after reentering the race, that he began to advertise on television, and then he again went beyond conventional approaches, broadcasting half-hour "infomercials" as well as conventional spot advertisements.

What propelled Perot's candidacy was the image he presented to an electorate dissatisfied with the direction of the nation, the government in

Washington, and the candidates being offered by the major parties. Perot cast himself as a nonpolitician, a modern-day Cincinnatus willing to make sacrifices for his fellow citizens, and as a success symbol, a modern version of the Horatio Alger myth with a can-do image. He was the ultimate outsider, espousing simple adages and folksy metaphors to explain the problems facing the nation. Like those who were frustrated with the status quo, Perot was opposed to "gridlock in Washington," the influence of "foreign lobbyists," and "the blame game." If sent to Washington, he would "get under the hood" and start to "get things done." These simple prescriptions were readily accepted by many voters who saw in Perot a candidate who both personified and advocated "real change" and "an end to politics as usual." In many ways, Perot served as an empty vessel into which alienated and angry voters could pour their frustrations and hopes. As they did, Perot's level of support in public opinion polls rose, and the press focused its attention on the "Perot phenomenon" and engaged in widespread speculation about his potential as a candidate and the effect he would have on the race. Perot thus rode a wave of voter discontent and favorable press coverage[5] to a point where some polls in June showed him leading the race even though he had not yet officially decided to run.

Yet even as Perot was rising in the polls, his campaign was beginning to unravel. Now that he was viewed as a major contender, the press corps began to subject his candidacy to the critical scrutiny generally imposed on presidential candidates. The tone of the coverage thus shifted from the novelty of Perot's endeavor to questions about his business practices, his past political activities, his seeming obsession with POW-MIA investigations, and his temperament. Thus, at the same time that he was enjoying the attention of the press, he was "also becoming a target—or so he thought—of the journalists' collective judgment that he was dangerous" (Ceasar and Busch, 1993:117).

This view was enhanced by the critical attacks of the Bush campaign, who decided in late spring to turn its attention to fighting off a potential challenge from Perot. Perot denied reports generated by the Republicans that he had a penchant for using private investigators and charged that the allegations were part of the "dirty tricks crowd" in the president's campaign (Specter, 1992:A16). But the stories raised additional questions about Perot's temperament and what he would do if given the power of the Oval Office.

Finally, Perot's management of his own campaign exposed his lack of preparedness for a presidential bid. In early June, he hired a number of campaign professionals to assist his insurgent candidacy, which tarnished his amateur status and led to internal divisions within the campaign and disputes over strategy and tactics. The perception of his "refreshing frankness" gave way to a recognition that he seemed ill-prepared to move beyond simplistic statements in discussing issues. In a rare public appearance, a speech before the NAACP on July 11, he offended many in the audience by referring to African Americans as "you people." Within a week, Rollins and a number of consultants had resigned. Suddenly, the campaign was "no fun" (Mintz and Von Drehle, 1992:A1). On the morning of July 16, the final day of the Democratic National Convention, Perot dropped out of a race he had never formally entered, announcing that "now that the Democratic Party has revitalized itself, I have concluded that we cannot win in November."

THE GENERAL ELECTION CAMPAIGN

The Conventions

Ross Perot's ascent diverted press attention away from Clinton's character problems and led the Bush campaign to reorient its strategy toward stopping Perot. Some observers speculated that this new dynamic would "marginalize" Clinton, but instead Clinton took advantage of this reprieve to modify his campaign strategy and hone his message. As a result, he was well-positioned to exploit the political reconfiguration that occurred when Perot unexpectedly left the race.

After the California primary, the Clinton campaign reassessed its strategic position and regrouped. First, the campaign was reorganized and James Carville, the Clinton adviser who had managed the successful campaign of Harris Wofford for U.S. Senate in Pennsylvania, was given authority to supervise the campaign's strategy. The campaign also established a "rapid response team" that was designed to monitor statements by the press and opponents in order to ensure a quick response to any misstatements or attacks. The campaign was thus prepared to avoid Dukakis's mistake of not responding immediately to charges made by the Bush campaign.

Second, Clinton responded to the new strategic environment. The campaign conducted extensive research on the character and trust issues. These surveys revealed that many voters knew little of substance about Clinton but were receptive to learning more. In particular, the campaign discovered that voters' opinions of Clinton became more favorable when they learned of his background and family (Ifill, 1992:7; Kolbert, 1992b:68; Kelly, 1992:9). The campaign therefore began to discuss Clinton's upbringing, his family, and his roots in a "place called Hope." In response to Perot, the campaign developed a more detailed economic plan to clarify how Clinton would encourage investment and job creation and approach the task of reducing the deficit. The campaign also followed Perot's lead and used television talk show, televised "town meetings," and popular magazines to reach voters directly without the screen of conventional, and more critical, news reporting.

Third, Clinton refined his message. The basic themes developed at the outset of the campaign continued to serve as the foundation of his candidacy. But Clinton focused the message in an attempt to concentrate on the issues of greatest concern to the electorate, sharpen his appeal to moderate and independent voters, and attract those leaning toward Perot who were dissatisfied with Bush and sought change. The core of this strategy was succinctly summarized in three brief statements that were posted in the Little Rock headquarters: "Change vs. more of the same. The economy, stupid. Don't forget health care."

Fourth, Clinton created a strong Democratic ticket with his selection of Senator Al Gore as his vice-presidential running mate. In choosing Gore, Clinton dispensed with traditional ideological and geographic considerations. He selected a fellow southerner, moderate, and baby boomer. Gore, however, complemented Clinton in a number of important ways: He was a Washington insider; he was a Vietnam veteran and an expert on defense issues; he had a strong environmental record; and he was a solid "family man." More important, his addition to the ticket signaled the Democrats' intention to contest the southern states seriously and generated enthusiasm for the ticket within the party.

Finally, Clinton was able to use the convention to highlight his message of change and establish his leadership with the party. With the assistance of party chair Ron Brown, Clinton enjoyed the support of a unified convention. Brown helped to persuade traditional Democratic constituencies to follow Clinton's lead in pursuing a more moderate course for the party and oversaw the framing of a platform designed "to separate the party from its reputation as a bedrock of support for old-style New Deal liberalism" (Maisel, 1994; Katz, 1992:2087). The platform reflected Clinton's call for a "new social covenant" based on the values of opportunity, individual responsibility, community, and national security. In his acceptance speech, Clinton presented himself as a "new kind of Democrat" and as a Washington outsider who cared about the middle class and sought to bring about change with new approaches to get the economy moving again, reform the health care system, and prepare the nation for the challenges it would face in the future.

The success of Clinton's strategy was reflected in the findings of public opinion surveys. Going into the convention, Clinton had improved his standing among the voters. A CBS News/*New York Times* poll showed that the race had tightened with Bush at 33 percent, Clinton in second place at 30 percent, and Perot falling to third at 25 percent. This shift was due in part to changes in opinion toward Clinton. In one month, he had reduced his unfavorable rating from 40 percent to 31 percent and increased his favorable rating from 16 percent to 20 percent (Toner, 1992c:A1). On the day after the convention, the CBS News/*New York Times* poll showed Clinton leading Bush by 55 percent to 31 percent, a 25-point increase. In addition, most voters now viewed Clinton as understanding the problems of the average voter, a plurality said he was different from previous Democratic nominees, and the image of the party had significantly improved (Frankovic, 1993:118).

This surge in Clinton's level of public support was also due in part to Perot's exit from the race. Former Perot supporters expressed a preference for Clinton over Bush by a margin of 45 percent to 25 percent (Apple, 1992:A1). This can be explained by the fact that Clinton was now the candidate of "change," although it was a different type of "change" than that advocated by Perot. Perot argued for a fundamental change in the political system, however ill-defined; Clinton represented change in the status quo. For those dissatisfied with the current administration, Clinton was now the alternative. And throughout the summer, Bush did little to dissuade voters from seeking out alternatives.

In sharp contrast to the Democrats, the Republicans failed to develop an effective convention strategy. Toward the end of the primaries, facing the likely prospect of a three-way race, Bush campaign officials framed a strategy designed to respond to this new political dynamic. This approach was based on the premise that, even in an electorate desirous of change, voters are essentially "risk-averse"; that is, they assumed that "voters seek first to protect the gains they have made and minimize the risks they may face in the future" (Duffy and Goodgame, 1992:272). Although this risk-averse constituency was dissatisfied with Bush's performance, they would support the president if he appeared to be the least of three evils. Further, by casting Clinton and Perot as more hazardous choices, Bush could secure the support of the Republican right wing, many of whom supported Buchanan in the primaries, and reach out to conservative Democrats. In a three-way race, this conservative coalition could produce the votes needed to win the election (Duffy and Goodgame, 1992:272).

To mobilize this constituency, Bush strategists returned to the theme of "cultural warfare" that had worked so well for the Republicans in previous elections (Dionne, 1991:109–115; Baer, 1992:34). By emphasizing "traditional family values," Bush strategists hoped to achieve a number of objectives. First, they could assuage right-wing conservatives, especially Buchanan and his supporters, whom they sought to appease as part of their convention strategy (Goldman and Mathews, 1992:68–69). Second, they could draw a clear distinction between Bush and Clinton and thereby elevate the concerns of the plurality of voters who did not trust Clinton and had an unfavorable view of his personal life (Kelly, 1992:9). Conversely, Bush could be cast as a candidate who shared the beliefs of these voters and could be trusted. Finally, an emphasis on "family values might shift the focus away from the economy, and [provide] Bush with a way to tap into voters' anxiety about the future at a time when many of those same Americans believed [he] was out of touch with the country" (Duffy and Goodgame, 1992:262–264).

The focus on family values fueled a debate within the party over the campaign's message. Some leaders, including Buchanan and Quayle, accepted this approach and believed that the party should position the Democrats as out of touch with average Americans due to their support of such issues as abortion and gay rights. Others, including Representative Vin Weber, argued that "values issues" had to be linked to an economic agenda (Baer, 1992:40). Bush appeared uncertain as to the direction the campaign should take. In the weeks leading up to the convention, he failed to set a clear course, and the theme of his acceptance speech was not determined until the final hours prior to his appearance before the convention. During this period the Republicans also displayed other signs of dissension, forcing Bush to reject the advice of party leaders "to drop Quayle from the ticket, to fire his economic team as a sign that he would now address the economy, and even to step aside and let another candidate carry the Republican banner" (Quirk and Dalager, 1993:69; see also, Goldman and Mathews, 1992:65–69).

Whether due to miscalculation or poor management, the Republican convention aggressively advanced the cultural agenda. The platform, reflecting the influence of the Christian right, was more conservative than those adopted by the previous three conventions (Oldfield, 1992:29–30). It opposed birth control counseling, advocated a constitutional amendment to ban abortion in all instances, gave prominent attention to tax cuts and voucher programs, and even called for the construction of a fence along the U.S.-Mexican border to thwart illegal aliens.[6] The featured speakers included Buchanan, who attacked Hillary Clinton as a "radical feminist" and declared that "there is a religious war going on in our country ... a cultural war, as critical to the kind of nation we will one day be—as was the Cold War itself"; Pat Robertson, who warned that Clinton supported "a radical plan to destroy the traditional family"; Marilyn Quayle, who told America that "most women do not want to be liberated from their essential nature as women"; and Dan Quayle, who proclaimed that "the gap between us and our opponents is a cultural divide."[7]

In his acceptance speech, Bush shied away from the family values issue, mentioning the subject only briefly. Instead he reviewed his foreign policy accomplishments, blamed Congress for the nation's economic problems, apologized for agreeing with the Democrats and raising taxes, and attacked Clinton as a tax-and-spend Democrat who had raised taxes 128 times as governor of Arkansas. He again failed to outline a plan for economic recovery and offered only one major innovation in his usual laundry list of economic proposals, a tax checkoff for directing funds to deficit reduction, which was widely perceived as a gimmick (Mashberg, 1992).

Opinion polls taken after the convention indicated that the public response to the proceedings was surprisingly negative. Perceptions of Bush's management of foreign policy improved, but voters felt that the president had spent more time attacking Clinton than discussing what he would do in a second term; and 76 percent of the public felt that the criticism of Hillary Clinton "was going to far" (Frankovic, 1993:119). More important, the emphasis on family values contributed to a widespread perception that the Republicans were not addressing voters' concerns. A CBS News/*New York Times* poll reported that approximately nine out of ten Americans, regardless of whom they were supporting, were most concerned with the health of the economy and the nation's health care system. Clinton was seen as the best candidate on these two crucial issues by a wide margin, with only 24 percent of voters believing that Bush had offered "specific ideas" to get the nation "out of recession" (as compared to 49 percent for Clinton). Ninety-five percent of the electorate said they wanted a "real change in the way things are going" and only 15 percent agreed that Bush would bring about "real change" (as compared to 61 percent for Clinton). The convention thus failed to give the Republicans the boost they were looking for. Although Bush narrowed Clinton's lead by the end of the convention, a week later the race returned to its pre-convention status, with Clinton leading the president by 15 points (Clymer, 1992:A19).

The Fall Campaign

The general election campaign was one of the most eventful presidential contests in recent history. Popular concern about the future of the nation, Perot's decision to enter the race, and a series of widely watched televised debates combined to produce a campaign that captivated the electorate.[8] Yet the race itself was relatively stable. Clinton maintained his lead in public opinion polls throughout the fall campaign, although his margin over the president narrowed in the final two weeks. His success was largely a result of the strategy he developed in advance of the convention. Clinton continued to frame the election as a referendum on Bush's handling of the economy and the need for change. He thus advanced a theme that conformed to the prevailing public mood, which placed him in a strong position to withstand the president's attacks and Ross Perot's entry as an alternative for those seeking a new direction.

Having failed to improve his position over the summer, Bush again altered his strategy. He jettisoned the unproductive family values message and focused on the economy and Clinton's character. Initially, he attempted to address the nation's concerns by providing further details of his economic plan in a September address before the Detroit Economic Club and by airing a series of campaign ads that described what he was "fighting for" for the future. But the majority of voters had already formed a consensus about the president's capacity to manage the economy that would not be altered by campaign tactics. He was therefore forced to adopt a defensive strategy, trying to frame the election around his experience and negative images of Clinton's character and proposals for change. This approach was designed to enhance the salience of such fundamental issues as trust and taxes to convince an electorate, assumed to be risk-averse, that in the context of a changing world Clinton was the more risky choice.

Bush criticized Clinton's economic plan and charged that his opponent was just another tax-and-spend Democrat. He repeated the claim made during the convention that Clinton had raised taxes 128 times while governor and argued that Clinton's plan, rather than providing relief to the middle class, would actually increase its tax burden. This claim was advanced in one of the most controversial ads of the campaign: a spot that depicted several middle-class taxpayers and presented estimates of the tax increases they would face under Clinton's plan. Although the Democrats refuted the estimates and attacked the ads, Bush strategists defended their allegations, explaining that they were based on calculations of the total projected cost of all of Clinton's proposals. Bush thus sought to cast Clinton's plan as the type of innovation that taxpayers should reject.

Bush also attacked Clinton's character and raised the issue of whether the Democrat could be trusted with the responsibility of the executive office. This approach was made possible by the lingering doubts about Clinton's trustworthiness[9] and renewed attention to his draft problems. In early September, the *Los Angeles Times* reported a new incident in the Clinton draft story, and two weeks later his former ROTC officer alleged that Clinton lied to him in 1969 (Rempel, 1992; Birnbaum, 1992:A6). Bush framed this issue as a question of trust, noting that "the fundamental difficulty is that he [Clinton] has not told the full truth, the whole truth, nothing but the truth" ("Campaign Time Line," September 21, 1992). In this way he hoped to remind voters indirectly of the allegations Clinton faced in the primaries and evoke the "slick" image of Clinton as a politician who refused to address questions straightforwardly and "flip-flopped" on the issues (Ceasar and Busch, 1993:166). Moreover, he hoped to induce voters to redirect their inquiry from the question "Who can best meet the challenges of a changing world?" to "Who can be trusted to lead the nation in a changing world?"

Clinton responded to Bush's attacks by refuting the particular charges leveled against him and by sticking to his message. He continued to present himself as a candidate of change and a "new kind of Democrat" who had a plan to address the nation's problems. On August 31, he began a series of campaign ads that promoted his economic plan (and urged viewers to write for a copy), and about a week later, he released a spot on his welfare reform plan, which was designed to reinforce the notion that he was not a tax-and-spend Democrat. In addition, Clinton used his economic message to undermine Bush's character attacks. First, he reversed the tax-and-spend argument by criticizing the administration's record level of federal spending and budget policies. Second, he recalled Bush's 1988 tax pledge and 1991 statements denying the recession to raise questions about the president's credibility on economic issues. One ad repeated these statements and juxtaposed them with facts about the nation's economic woes and then asked, "If George Bush doesn't understand the problem, how can he solve it?" Clinton thus questioned the president's capacity to lead the nation out of the recession and suggested that he was out of touch with the voters.

Clinton also pressed the "debate debate." The Commission on Presidential Debates, a bipartisan organization formed after the 1984 election and the sponsor of the 1988 debates, had proposed a series of three presidential debates and one vice-presidential debate to be held between September 22 and October 15. In response to criticism over the lack of interchange in previous debates and in order to provide better information to voters, the commission proposed a relatively free-flowing format that allowed a single moderator who would ask questions, an opportunity for follow-up questions, and direct exchanges between the candidates. Clinton accepted the proposal, but the Bush campaign rejected it and asked for direct negotiations between the two camps to determine dates and format (Berke, 1992:A1).

One reason for this refusal was the belief of Bush's strategists that the announcement of the debates would "freeze" the electorate; that is, it would encourage voters who might shift to Bush to wait until the debates to make their decision. Another may have been that acceptance would have elevated Clinton's status as challenger by placing him on the same stage with the president early in the race in a format in which he was expected to do well (Quirk and Dalager, 1993:72). Whatever the reason, the decision provided Clinton with another opportunity to criticize the president for his unwillingness to discuss the issues. Ultimately, the campaigns agreed to three presidential debates and one vice-presidential debate that would employ different formats and be held in a nine-day period from October 11 to October 19. And a third candidate would be invited to participate—Ross Perot.

On September 22, Perot announced that he "made a mistake" in deciding not to enter the race, because the major parties were not facing the issues (Lehigh, 1992:14). He thus began a series of unusual events that led to his formal entry in the race. These included appearances on television news programs, a telephone poll to solicit the views of supporters as to whether he should run (the poll was set up in such a way that every call was recorded as an endorsement of a decision to run), and highly publicized meetings between Perot's state coordinators and representatives of the Democratic and Republican tickets. On October 1, Perot declared that he would become an active candidate for the presidency.

Why Perot decided to enter the race and whether he always intended to run and thus was following a predetermined strategy are questions that generated significant speculation but were never clearly answered. What was known was that the Perot candidacy had been seriously damaged by his hasty withdrawal. Perot was no longer viewed in the favorable light that accompanied his earlier high poll standings. A CBS News/*New York Times* poll found that only 7 percent of registered voters held a favorable opinion of Perot, and 59 percent viewed him unfavorably; 69 percent felt he would not "bring about the kind of change the country needs"; and only 12 percent said he could "be trusted to deal with all the problems" a president has to face. Seventy-five percent were concerned that if elected president, he "might make serious mistakes" (Toner, 1992d:A8). A Gallup poll also found that one-third of his former supporters had switched to another candidate (Hugick, 1993:17).

Perot rehabilitated his image during the final weeks of the campaign, but "he never regained the advantage he enjoyed in the spring of being regarded more favorably than either of his two major-party opponents" (Hugick, 1993:17). Nor did he ever again reach as high as 20 percent in opinion polls. He did, however, resurrect the basic message with which he began the campaign. Perot railed against "gridlock in Washington" and cast himself as a "man of action" who was tired of "inaction." He focused on his economic plan and explained how his was the best solution for reducing the federal deficit. He also promoted his image as an unconventional candidate by avoiding most traditional campaigning techniques and instead relying on an extensive paid media campaign, which included a series of hour-long "infomercials" that reviewed the nation's economic problems, presented the details of Perot's plan, and traced his personal background. These ads were well received by their audience and played an important role in improving Perot's image. According to one survey, 72 percent of the viewers felt they "learned a lot" from Perot's programs and 40 percent said the ads "made them more likely to vote for him" (Times Mirror Center, 1992:3).

Perot also gained some support as a result of his performance in the debates. Indeed, of the three candidates, Perot did the most to raise his standing in the polls, increasing his showing to 15 percent after the final debate (Toner, 1992a:24). As with any challenger, the debate benefited Perot by offering him a forum before a national audience and allowing him to share a stage with both major party candidates, a distinction that had been denied all other independent candidates. Perot also benefited from the particular dynamics of the race. Neither Clinton nor Bush believed that Perot had a chance to win, and both hoped to attract the support of some of Perot's supporters. Accordingly, neither made him the object of their attacks; rather, they regularly noted their points of agreement with the feisty billionaire.

The clear winner of the debates, however, was Clinton, who was considered the winner or co-winner of each of the meetings and was considered the overall winner by 39 percent of registered voters, as compared to 31 percent for Perot and only 15 percent for Bush (Franovic, 1993:120; Toner, 1992a:24). Clinton entered the debates with a double-digit lead over the president. So, in general, he had to hold his own against the president and avoid any major mistakes that might raise public concerns about his capacity to serve as president. He achieved this end and more. Throughout the meetings, Clinton effectively discussed the need for change and his plans for the future by highlighting the failure of "twelve years of trickle-down economics" and his own proposals for encouraging investment to "grow the economy" and for reforming the health care system, which he presented as the keys to reducing the budget deficit. In response to Bush's character attacks, he implored voters to have the "courage to change," and in the first debate, he directly addressed Bush's criticism of his patriotism by recalling the efforts of Prescott Bush, the president's father, in speaking out against McCarthyism.

Bush also performed fairly well in the debates, but his performance was not sharp enough to overcome Clinton's lead. Bush continued his strategy of trying to raise doubts about Clinton's character and thus encourage voters to question whether the Democrat had the experience needed to lead the nation in a changing world. In the first debate, however, he did not press these issues very aggressively. In the second debate, which employed a format favored by Clinton that allowed an audience of undecided voters to question the candidates, he hardly had a chance to pursue this strategy because members of the audience insisted that the candidates avoid personal attacks and speak to the issues. The president also performed poorly in this debate. He appeared uncomfortable with the open format and looked to be out of touch with the concerns of the majority of voters when he stumbled in answering a vague question about how he had been personally affected by "the national deficit." He was also caught on camera looking at his watch, which was interpreted by the press as an indicator of Bush's disinterest (Dowd, 1992:A1). In contrast, Clinton appeared at ease and confident, occasionally walking toward the audience and making a point of directing his answers to the questioner as well as to the cameras.

In the final debate, Bush aggressively pushed his criticisms of Clinton's character. He warned voters to "watch your wallet" when Clinton said he would "tax the rich" because "he's coming right after you just like Jimmy Carter" ("Campaign '92," 1992:A24). He also deftly tied his challenger to the "spendthrift Democratic Congress" and noted his penchant for "waffling" on the issues (D. Broder, 1992:A1). Bush's attacks, however, were diminished by a challenge to his own credibility, initiated by Perot. Perot questioned the president's actions prior to the Gulf War, suggesting that the administration may have failed to produce all the facts about its activities leading to the invasion of Kuwait. He also asked Bush to release the instructions given to the American ambassador to Iraq so that the people could judge for themselves. Although saving his most heated rhetoric for the president, Perot also criticized Clinton, noting that his experience as governor of the small state of Arkansas did not necessarily provide him with the management experience needed to govern the nation.

Despite his uneven performance, Bush gained some momentum from the debates. Clinton's margin in opinion polls dropped to single digits, and the portion of the electorate that viewed him as the "least reliable" candidate rose from 21 to 32 percent (Pertman and Farrell, 1992:11). In the final weeks of the campaign, the president stepped up his attack on the Democrats, calling his opponents bozos and describing Gore as "ozone man" in an attempt to position him as an environmentalist extremist. But the final days of the campaign were dominated by charges leveled against Bush, not against his challenger. On October 25, Perot claimed that he quit the race in July because of reports he received that the Republicans planned to use a fake picture to "smear" his daughter and to "disrupt" her August wedding (Pianin and Mintz, 1992:A9). Republican officials vehemently denied the charges, which were never substantiated, and called Perot "a paranoid person who has delusions" (Isikoff and Mintz, 1992:A12). As this controversy was ebbing, Lawrence Walsh, the special prosecutor in the Iran-Contra affair, released a memorandum on the Friday before the election indicating that then-Vice-President Bush was more informed about the details of the secret arms deal with Iran than he had admitted. Clinton seized this opportunity to turn the character issue back on Bush and claim, once again, that it was the president who could not be trusted. Bush's role in Iran-Contra, a question that was raised in the aftermath of the Gulf War and sat beneath the surface of the debate throughout the election, thus finally came into prominence in the last days of the race.

So instead of concentrating on Clinton's credibility, Bush ended the race defending his own.[10]

EXPLAINING THE VOTE

On election day, the voters gave Bill Clinton a decisive victory. He received 43 percent of the vote, compared to 37.4 percent for Bush and 18.9 percent for Perot. On a two-party vote basis, he received 53.5 percent of the vote, or slightly less than the 53.9 percent Bush won in 1988. Clinton won thirty-two states and the District of Columbia for a total of 370 electoral votes; Bush carried eighteen states for a total of 168 electoral votes. Perot received the largest share of the vote of any nonmajor party candidate since Theodore Roosevelt, the Bull Moose party candidate in 1912, but failed to win a single state and finished second only in Maine and Utah.

The election was largely a referendum on Bush's handling of the economy and was determined by voters concerned about their personal economic situation and the future well-being of the national economy. Although Bush enjoyed a substantial advantage over Clinton in the areas of experience and foreign policy, these considerations were overshadowed by the predominant issues of the need for change and concern about the economy and health care. Clinton won because he convinced those voters seeking change and a new direction in government policy that he was the candidate most likely to address their concerns. But the results also suggest that the prevailing dynamic of the election was more the collapse of Bush's coalition than the creation of a new coalition by Clinton. This pattern, as well as the characteristics evidenced by the Perot voters, raises a number of important questions about the long-term implications of the election.

Clinton's share of the vote was the fourth lowest total of anyone elected president in U.S. history. Yet, given the dynamic of a three-way race, it allowed him to establish a broad electoral coalition. The Democrats won electoral votes in every region of the country (see Table 9.3). Clinton swept the northeastern states, a region where the image of the Democratic party had improved significantly and the economy was in especially poor condition. He also did well in the Midwest, another region with improved potential for the Democrats, winning all of the large states and losing only in Indiana, the Dakotas, Nebraska, and Kansas. He swept the West Coast and showed surprising strength in the Republican strongholds of the Rocky Mountain and southern states. Between 1980 and 1988, the Democrats only once managed to win one of the twenty-six states in the Rocky Mountains and the South: Jimmy Carter won his home state of Georgia in 1980. In 1992, the Democrats won nine of these states, including four in

TABLE 9.3
1992 Presidential Election Results

State	Bill Clinton Popular	%	Electoral	George Bush Popular	%	Electoral	H. Ross Perot Popular	%	Electoral	Other Popular	%	Total Vote
Alabama	690,080	40.9	—	804,283	47.6	9	183,109	10.8	—	10,588	0.6	1,688,060
Alaska	78,294	30.3	—	102,000	39.5	3	73,481	28.4	—	4,731	1.8	258,506
Arizona	543,050	36.5	—	572,086	38.5	8	353,741	23.8	—	18,098	1.2	1,486,975
Arkansas	505,823	53.2	6	337,324	35.5	—	99,132	10.4	—	8,374	0.9	950,653
California	5,121,325	46.0	54	3,630,575	32.6	—	2,296,006	20.6	—	83,816	0.8	11,131,722
Colorado	629,681	40.1	8	562,850	35.9	—	366,010	23.3	—	10,639	0.7	1,569,180
Connecticut	682,318	42.2	8	578,313	35.8	—	348,771	21.6	—	6,930	0.4	1,616,332
D.C.	192,619	84.6	3	20,698	9.1	—	9,681	4.3	—	4,574	2.0	227,572
Delaware	126,054	43.5	3	102,313	35.3	—	59,213	20.4	—	2,155	0.7	289,735
Florida	2,071,651	39.0	—	2,171,781	40.9	25	1,052,481	19.8	—	15,306	0.3	5,311,219
Georgia	1,008,966	43.5	13	995,252	42.9	—	309,657	13.3	—	7,250	0.3	2,321,125
Hawaii	179,310	48.1	4	136,822	36.7	—	53,003	14.2	—	3,707	1.0	372,842
Idaho	137,013	28.4	—	202,645	42.0	4	130,395	27.0	—	12,089	2.5	482,142
Illinois	2,453,350	48.6	22	1,734,096	34.3	—	840,515	16.6	—	22,196	0.4	5,050,157
Indiana	848,420	36.8	—	989,375	42.9	12	455,934	19.8	—	12,142	0.5	2,305,871
Iowa	586,353	43.3	7	504,891	37.3	—	253,468	18.7	—	9,895	0.7	1,354,607
Kansas	390,434	33.7	—	449,951	38.9	6	312,358	27.0	—	4,493	0.4	1,157,236
Kentucky	665,104	44.6	8	617,178	41.3	—	203,944	13.7	—	6,674	0.4	1,492,900
Louisiana	815,971	45.6	9	733,386	41.1	—	211,478	11.8	—	29,182	1.6	1,790,017
Maine	263,420	38.8	4	206,504	30.4	—	206,820	30.4	—	2,755	0.4	679,499
Maryland	988,571	49.8	10	707,094	35.6	—	281,414	14.2	—	7,799	0.4	1,984,878
Massachusetts	1,318,639	47.5	12	805,039	29.0	—	630,731	22.7	—	19,255	0.7	2,773,664
Michigan	1,871,182	43.8	18	1,554,940	36.4	—	824,813	19.3	—	23,738	0.6	4,274,673
Minnesota	1,020,997	43.5	10	747,841	31.9	—	562,506	24.0	—	16,603	0.7	2,347,947
Mississippi	400,258	40.8	—	487,793	49.7	7	85,626	8.7	—	8,116	0.8	981,793
Missouri	1,053,873	44.1	11	811,159	33.9	—	518,741	21.7	—	7,792	0.3	2,391,565
Montana	154,507	37.6	3	144,207	35.1	—	107,225	26.1	—	4,672	1.1	410,611
Nebraska	216,864	29.4	—	343,678	46.6	5	174,104	23.6	—	2,900	0.4	737,546
Nevada	189,148	37.4	4	175,828	34.7	—	132,580	26.2	—	8,762	1.7	506,318

TABLE 9.3 (continued)

State	Bill Clinton			George Bush			H. Ross Perot			Other		Total Vote
	Popular	%	Electoral	Popular	%	Electoral	Popular	%	Electoral	Popular	%	
New Hampshire	209,040	38.9	4	202,484	37.6	—	121,337	22.6	—	5,082	0.9	537,943
New Jersey	1,436,206	43.0	15	1,356,865	40.6	—	521,829	15.6	—	28,694	0.9	3,343,594
New Mexico	261,617	45.9	5	212,824	37.3	—	91,895	16.1	—	3,650	0.6	569,986
New York	3,444,450	49.7	33	2,346,649	33.9	—	1,090,721	15.7	—	44,740	0.6	6,926,560
North Carolina	1,114,042	42.7	—	1,134,661	43.4	14	357,864	13.7	—	5,283	0.2	2,611,850
North Dakota	99,168	32.2	—	136,244	44.2	3	71,084	23.1	—	1,637	0.5	308,133
Ohio	1,984,919	40.2	21	1,894,284	38.3	—	1,036,403	21.0	—	24,289	0.5	4,939,859
Oklahoma	473,066	34.0	—	592,929	42.6	8	319,878	23.0	—	4,486	0.3	1,390,359
Oregon	621,314	42.5	7	475,757	32.5	—	354,091	24.2	—	11,481	0.8	1,462,643
Pennsylvania	2,239,164	45.1	23	1,791,841	36.1	—	902,667	18.2	—	26,138	0.5	4,959,810
Rhode Island	213,299	47.0	4	131,601	29.0	—	105,045	23.2	—	3,420	0.8	453,365
South Carolina	479,514	39.9	—	577,507	48.0	8	138,872	11.5	—	6,634	0.6	1,202,527
South Dakota	124,888	37.1	—	136,718	40.7	3	73,295	21.8	—	1,353	0.4	336,254
Tennessee	933,521	47.1	11	841,300	42.4	—	199,968	10.1	—	7,849	0.4	1,982,638
Texas	2,281,815	37.1	—	2,496,071	40.6	32	1,354,781	22.0	—	21,351	0.3	6,154,018
Utah	183,429	24.7	—	322,632	43.4	5	203,400	27.3	—	34,538	4.6	743,999
Vermont	133,592	46.1	3	88,122	30.4	—	65,991	22.8	—	1,996	0.7	289,701
Virginia	1,038,650	40.6	—	1,150,517	45.0	13	348,639	13.6	—	20,859	0.8	2,558,665
Washington	993,037	43.4	11	731,234	32.0	—	541,780	23.7	—	22,179	1.0	2,288,230
West Virginia	331,001	48.4	5	241,974	35.4	—	108,829	15.9	—	1,873	0.3	683,677
Wisconsin	1,041,066	41.1	11	930,855	36.8	—	544,479	21.5	—	14,714	0.6	2,531,114
Wyoming	68,160	34.0	—	79,347	39.6	3	51,263	25.6	—	1,847	0.9	200,617
Total	44,908,233	43.0	370	39,102,282	37.4	168	19,741,048	18.9	0	669,324	0.6	104,420,887

Source: Data from Congressional Quarterly Weekly Report, January 30, 1993:233.

the Rockies (Nevada, Monatana, Colorado, and New Mexico) and five in the South (Arkansas, Tennessee, Kentucky, Louisiana, and Georgia).

Clinton won all but one of the states targeted by his campaign (North Carolina) and won one state that was not targeted (Nevada) (Carville, 1993). With respect to the "electoral lock," the Democrats won eight states for the first time since 1976; three for the first time since 1968; and nine for the first time since Johnson's landslide in 1964 (Cook, 1993:188). In only two states, however, did Clinton receive a majority—his home state of Arkansas and the heavily Democratic District of Columbia. In thirteen others, the Democrat received 45 percent of the vote or more; the remaining states were captured with less than 45 percent, including four states in which Clinton failed to reach 40 percent. Moreover, Clinton ran significantly better than Dukakis in only two states: his home state of Arkansas (an increase of 11 percent) and Gore's home state of Tennessee (an increase of 6 percent). In the South, even though the Democrats had two southerners on the ticket, Bush was surprisingly strong, winning eight states in the region and losing Louisiana, Georgia, and Kentucky by less than 5 percent. The Democrats thus managed to "pick the lock" on the electoral college and established a base upon which they can build for the future, but they did not necessarily find the key to a future winning coalition.

Clinton assembled his winning coalition by attracting broad support across the electorate. He maintained the core of the Democratic presidential constituency, the remnants of the New Deal Coalition, and added significant support from the crucial voting blocs that had been an essential component of recent Republican victories. Clinton won an absolute majority of the demographic and social groups that form the basis of the Democratic vote. These groups include blacks, Hispanics, Jews, union households, and the disadvantaged—those lacking a high school education, those with the lowest incomes, and the unemployed. There is, of course, substantial overlap among these categories, and the results suggest a class dimension to the vote: Democratic support declines as income increases, from 59 percent of those with family incomes of less than $15,000 supporting Clinton to 38 percent of those making $75,000 or more.[11]

Clinton also received the largest share of the vote from those groups that were a source of Republican strength in recent elections and were the specific focus of his campaign. Since 1976, independents had, on average, cast 57 percent of their votes for Republicans. Clinton won this bloc, which represented 27 percent of the electorate, taking 38 percent of the vote to 32 percent for Bush and 30 percent for Perot. His showing was even more impressive among self-described "moderate" voters (49 percent of the electorate), taking 48 percent of the vote to 31 for Bush and 21 for Perot. Clinton also gained substantial support from the middle class, which was the primary group his campaign hoped to attract to the Democratic column. Among those with incomes from $15,000 to about $30,000 (24 percent of the electorate), Clinton received 45 percent of the vote compared to 35 for Bush and 20 for Perot. Among those with incomes from $30,000 to about $50,000 (30 percent of the electorate), Clinton took 41 percent to 38 for Bush and 21 for Perot. Clinton also held a sizable advantage among first-time voters (11 percent of the electorate), winning this group with 48 percent; Bush received 30 percent of the vote, and 22 percent opted for Perot.

The key determinant of the election was the issue that was foremost in the minds of the voters throughout the campaign: the economy. In 1988, only 24 percent of the voters considered the economy to be the most important issue, and a majority of this group supported Bush (Schneider, 1992:2542). In 1992, the situation was dramatically different. Forty-three percent of the electorate told exit poll interviewers that the economy was the issue that mattered most in deciding their vote. Not since 1968, when 43 percent of the electorate listed the war in Vietnam as the most important issue, had there been such consensus among the voters as to the central issue of the election (Asher, 1988:159).

Of those who decided on the issue of the economy, 53 percent backed Clinton, compared to 24 percent for Bush and 23 percent for Perot. This outcome was a result of two different, yet related, concerns.[12] On one level, voters decided on the basis of their personal economic situations, displaying the sort of retrospective decisionmaking seen in previous elections and best summarized by the question, "Are you better off today than you were four years ago?" (Fiorina, 1979). About one-third of the electorate considered themselves worse off in 1992 than in 1988; 61 percent of this group supported Clinton, 14 percent, Bush. Those who considered themselves to be in about the same situation (41 percent of the electorate) split their vote evenly between Clinton and Bush. Those who felt better off (25 percent of the electorate) supported Bush by 62 percent, compared to 24 percent for Clinton.

It appears, however, that voters' decisions were also based on broader assessments of the nation's economic situation and that perceptions of the national economy were a more important determinant of the election than personal well-being. Numerous studies have shown that voters distinguish their personal economic performance from the performance of the national economy and that national economic conditions have a greater impact on voting than personal financial status (see, among others, Fiorina, 1981; Kinder and Kiewiet, 1981; Abramowitz, Lanoue, and Ramesh, 1988; Popkin, 1991:31–34). This was the case in 1992. Sixty-six percent of eligible voters judged their personal situations to be about the same or better than in 1988; 80 percent rated the overall condition of the economy as "not so good" (48 percent) or "poor" (32 percent). Of those who viewed the economy most negatively, 65 percent voted for Clinton and only 10 percent for Bush. Of those who said "not so good," 44 percent chose Clinton and 36 percent Bush. Indeed, a more detailed analysis of the survey data conducted by political scientist Gerald Pomper revealed that "whatever their subjective situation, those who saw the national economy as poor voted largely for Clinton, including *a majority of those doing well on their own*" (1993:147, emphasis added). Bush thus fell victim to public perceptions of the nation's economic performance and the fears shared by a majority of voters as to the future health of the economy.

The voters chose Clinton because he was perceived as the candidate most likely to address their major concerns. After the economy, the most important issues were the budget deficit and health care. Perot made the deficit the centerpiece of his campaign. Bush argued that he would be a better budget manager than his tax-and-spend opponent, but those who were concerned with the deficit preferred Clinton to the president, 37 percent to 26 percent. As for health care, Clinton dominated the issue, winning 67 percent of the vote compared to 19 percent for Bush. The president did do well among the voters who focused on the issues he stressed during the campaign. He won more than a majority of the votes cast by individuals who felt that taxes, family values, and foreign policy were most important. But these issues proved to be relatively minor concerns, with only about 15 percent of the electorate listing taxes or family values as the most important issue and only 8 percent citing foreign policy.

Clinton was also perceived as having the qualities that most voters preferred. In 1988, the leading characteristics that voters were looking for in a candidate were experience and competence, with half as many seeking change or a candidate with a "vision for the future" (Pomper, 1989b:143). In 1992, these preferences were reversed. More than any other quality, the voters wanted a candidate who "will bring about needed change." Thirty-eight percent of the electorate cited change as the factor most important to their voting decision, and this group chose Clinton 3 to 1 over Bush (59 percent to 19 percent). Another 25 percent of the electorate decided on the basis of which candidate had "the best plan for the future," and this group favored Clinton 2 to 1 over Bush (52 percent to 26 percent).

Clinton's message of change and his articulation of a plan for the future thus proved to be more important than Bush's experience and his emphasis on character. Although those who considered experience and judgment important qualities cast 63 percent of their votes for the president, smaller proportions of the electorate emphasized these characteristics (18 percent and 15 percent, respectively). Moreover, despite Bush's emphasis on character issues, only 14 percent thought trustworthiness the most important quality. Bush received 49 percent of the vote in this group, compared to 30 percent for Clinton. Thus, in 1992, the majority of voters were not "risk-averse." They opted for action over inaction, change over the status quo. They chose the candidate that shared their desire for change and had a plan for the future, even though that candidate was considered less experienced and less trustworthy.

Although Clinton received broad support, it is important to recognize that his percentage of the vote was equivalent to the average vote received by the Democratic candidate in the previous seven elections, albeit in a three-way contest. Indeed, Clinton significantly improved on Dukakis's performance among only two groups: he gained 14 points among Jewish voters, who represent only 4 percent of the electorate, and 5 points among white born-again Christians, who represent 17 percent of the electorate. Among other groups, his support essentially mirrored that of Dukakis, with an average difference of only 1 to 3 percent.

The major difference between 1988 and 1992 was the collapse of Republican support in 1992 as opposed to any gains by the Democrats. Bush experienced significant declines among all of the major groups that formed the core of the Republican coalition in the 1980s. He received only 73 percent of the votes cast by Republicans, a 19-point drop from 1988 and the lowest percentage received by a Republican candidate in the past five elections. Conservatives cast 65 percent of their votes for Bush, compared to 80 percent in 1988, which again was the lowest percentage received by a Republican in recent elections. Similarly, the support he received from moderate voters fell by 18 points, from college graduates by 21 points, from the wealthiest Americans by 14 points, from white protestants by 20 points, and from young voters by 18 points. As a result, Bush lost a sizable portion of his base, retaining the support of only 58 percent of those who cast their ballots for him four years earlier. Moreover, he did not compensate for his losses by attracting significant support from former Dukakis voters or from those who did not participate in 1988. By contrast, Clinton retained the support of 83 percent of those who voted for Dukakis and captured 22 percent of Bush's 1988 vote. He also received 50 percent of the vote from those who did not participate in 1988, as compared to 26 percent for Perot and 24 percent for Bush.

As for Perot, his support was widely distributed throughout the electorate, evidencing no particular ideological or demographic character. His strongest support came from independents, those voters with the least attachment to the major parties, who cast 30 percent of their ballots for him. His best regional showing was in the West, where he took 22 percent of the vote; here he fared slightly better than in the South, his worst region with 16 percent. He showed well among those voters most concerned with the budget deficit (37 percent), which was the central issue of his campaign, and with those who were concerned about the economy (23 percent). He also received the support of 25 percent of those voters who considered themselves worse off than in 1988.

Perot appears to have had little effect on the election's outcome. Exit polls suggest that his vote would have divided evenly in a two-way race, with 38 percent supporting each candidate, 6 percent choosing a minor candidate, and 14 percent deciding to abstain. His supporters also tended to split their ballots between Republican and Democratic congressional candidates. Although no state's electoral vote was obviously affected, Perot took more than 25 percent of the vote in eight states that were easily won by Bush in 1988.[13] Bush lost three of these states (Maine, Nevada, and Montana), and Clinton won with less than 40 percent of the vote. So Perot's candidacy may have influenced the outcome of these states, but they amounted to only 11 electoral college votes, a far cry from Clinton's margin of victory. In general, Perot took votes from Clinton in the Northeast, but the Democrat still won all of these states. He took votes from Bush in the South, but the president still won the region, which produced 116 of his 168 electoral college votes. In the other regions, Perot equally affected the two candidates (Pomper, 1993:142).

Yet, as Everett Carll Ladd (1993a:48–51; 1993b:21–25) had noted, Perot's supporters shared a philosophical view that resembled Bush voters more than Clinton voters. Like the Clinton voters, Perot supporters were seeking change and were most concerned about the economy and the budget deficit. Seventy-nine percent of the Perot supporters said that either the deficit or the economy was the issue that mattered most in their voting, as compared to 61 percent for Clinton supporters and just 40 percent of those who went with Bush. Yet this group did not necessarily embrace the type of change Clinton advocated. When given a choice between a government that would "provide more services but cost more in taxes" or a government that would "cost less in taxes but provide fewer services," Bush and Perot voters responded similarly, both choosing a smaller, less expensive government by margins of about 2 to 1. In contrast, a clear majority of Clinton voters (55 percent to 36 percent) opted for more government at greater cost (Ladd, 1993a:51). Similarly, approximately twice as many Clinton supporters (33 percent) as Bush (15 percent) or Perot voters (14 percent) felt that expanding domestic programs—as opposed to cutting taxes or reducing the deficit—should be the next president's highest priority.

The Perot voters also expressed "deep misgivings" about the Democratic nominee (Ladd, 1993a:51). When asked to describe their feelings about "what Clinton will do as president," the vast majority of Perot voters offered one of two negative assessments: Forty-three percent said they would be "concerned," 35 percent, "scared." Only 1 percent said they would be "excited" and 19 percent, "optimistic." Moreover, 56 percent of

Perot's backers had supported Bush in 1988, as opposed to only 17 percent who had sided with Dukakis. The Perot voters, concludes Ladd, "were, demographically and attitudinally, Republican voters who left Bush not for a Democrat but for a man they perceived as a no-nonsense billionaire interested only in restoring America's greatness" (Ladd, 1993a:51).

CONCLUSION

In 1992, the American people chose a new direction and gave the Democrats their first presidential victory since 1976. Yet this vote for change was without clear meaning. The image of the Democratic party improved significantly during the election year, especially among independent and middle-class voters, but party identification essentially remained constant (Ladd, 1993b:9). There were no major shifts in voting patterns of the sort that would suggest a possible shift in the partisan alignment of social groups. Nor was there a significant reconfiguration of policy preferences. The majority of voters still expressed a preference for fewer government services, lower taxes, and a reduction in the federal budget deficit. Such views were at the center of the successful Republican campaigns of the 1980s. Most of the electorate was responding to short-term forces such as the poor state of the economy and the extraordinarily high level of dissatisfaction with the political system, rather than to more durable factors that would signal significant change in the future.

The election results indicate the lingering strength of the two major parties. They also highlight the challenges they face in the future. Even with the test posed by the strongest independent candidacy since 1912, 80 percent of the electorate voted for one of the two major parties. But Perot's bid demonstrates that a substantial portion of the electorate is willing to consider alternatives to the major parties. Moreover, unlike every other independent candidate in this century, Perot actually gained strength as the election approached, and at least one-fifth of his voters supported him with considerable intensity (Galston and Kamarck, 1993:6).

The voters gave the Democrats a chance, not a mandate. They opted for action over inaction, change over the status quo. It is now up to Clinton to consolidate his gains among moderate, middle-class, and southern voters and expand his base of support in an effort to build a new majority coalition. In this regard, Clinton's position is reminiscent of Nixon's in 1968, when the Republican won the election with 43 percent of the vote in a three-way contest and then proceeded to assemble a new majority coalition at the national level.

In order to capitalize on this opportunity, the Democrat's performance in office will have to satisfy the majority's expectations of real change. Clinton must demonstrate substantial progress in improving the economy, reducing the budget deficit, and reforming the health care system. To achieve this, he will have to overcome the entrenched interests in Washington and maintain the support of congressional Democrats. This will not be an easy task, since even his fellow partisans are likely to have divergent political interests and policy goals. If he fails to accomplish these tasks, he risks losing some of the support he gained from independents and middle-class voters hungry for reform and will not be in a position to add Perot voters to his coalition. Moreover, he may face dissension from the liberal elements within the Democratic party. For the Democratic party did not transform its ideology in 1992; instead, liberals adopted a philosophy of pragmatism and agreed to follow Clinton's march toward moderation for the sake of victory. If their concerns are not addressed, the divisions that characterized the national party prior to 1992 may once again come to the fore.

Even if Clinton does succeed in setting a new direction for the nation, his ability to form a new coalition may depend on the nature of the changes advanced by his administration. In this respect, Clinton's situation is very different from that of Nixon in 1968. Nixon was able to convert Wallace voters with relative ease, since they were philosophically and attitudinally disposed toward his candidacy (Phillips, 1970:462–463; Asher, 1988:157). Perot's backers, however, do not share Clinton's ideology or agree with his solutions. Thus, if change comes in the form of expanded government services and higher taxes rather than spending cuts and political reform, Clinton may encounter difficulties in attempting to convert Perot supporters.

Of course, it may be that the core of Perot's voters are united less by particular policy preferences than by their anti-Washington, anti-government attitudes. In recent elections, Carter, Reagan, and Bush made opposition to Washington a central component of their campaign themes. In 1992, this attitude was especially pronounced, and Perot tapped into the electorate's feelings of frustration and dissatisfaction in a highly effective manner. If he can continue to maintain his visibility and prominence as the leading critic of government outside of Washington, both parties may find it difficult to attract his voters as permanent additions to their presidential coalitions.

The legacy of Perot's candidacy may thus be a new approach to campaigning rather than a new Democratic coalition. His success demonstrates that new campaign technologies, which facilitate direct communication with voters, present a challenge to the major parties that renews doubts about their efficacy and role in the political system. By the end of the campaign, all three candidates were relying on "infotainment" show appearances, call-in shows, paid advertisements, and other means of direct contact that circumvent party organizations to deliver their messages to voters. It is likely that future candidates will continue to use these vehicles for reaching out to voters, calling into question the purpose of the national party organizations in presidential campaigns other than their use as conduits for funneling money to state and local campaign organizations. The major change resulting from the 1992 race may thus prove to be more of the same: a continuation in the trend toward a diminished role for party organizations in national elections.

NOTES

The author thanks Beth Hermanson and Nicole Dannenberg for their assistance with research work and acknowledges the support of the Colby College Social Sciences Grant Committee.

1. Virtually all of these models predicted a Bush victory with the Republican share of the two-party vote ranging from 51 to 55–57 percent. For a general discussion of forecasting models, see Lewis-Beck and Rice (1992). On the performance of presidential election forecasting models in 1992, see, among others, Beck (1992), Campbell and Mann (1992), Greene (1993), and Kolbert (1992a). For an example of a forecasting model that correctly estimated the outcome of the 1992 election, see Abramowitz (1988).

2. Gary Jacobson, in an analysis of ten public opinion surveys, found that the correlation between assessments of the economy and Bush's handling of the economy is .96. The president's rating on the economy is also correlated with his overall performance rating at .96 (1993:181, n. 10).

3. The nine states were California, Connecticut, Illinois, Maryland, Missouri, Montana, New Mexico, Pennsylvania, and Vermont.

4. In a February 1992 *Washington Post*/ABC News poll, 57 percent of all respondents named an economic issue as the biggest problem facing the nation, up from 42 percent in an October survey. This was the first time since June 1983 that more than half of all Americans viewed economic issues as the nation's largest problem (Devroy and Morin, 1992:A1.)

5. According to the Center for Media and Public Affairs, 64 percent of the comments made about Perot on the network evening newscasts from April 7 to May 25 were positive, compared with 59 percent for Clinton and just 16 percent for Bush. (See Kurtz, 1992.)

6. For the text of the Republican party platform, see *Congressional Quarterly Weekly Report* 50 (August 22, 1992):2560–2581.

7. For the text of the major addresses delivered at the Republican National Convention, see *Congressional Quarterly Weekly Report* 50 (August 22, 1992):2543–2559.

8. According to the exit polls conducted by Voter Research and Surveys for the major networks, the voters took great interest in the election. Of those who responded to these surveys, 78 percent thought the election was interesting and only 17 percent described it as dull. In 1988, 42 percent of respondents thought the election interesting and 52 percent described it as dull.

9. An NBC News poll conducted September 3–5 and released in a special broadcast on September 6 asked registered voters whom they trusted more, Bush or Clinton. Bush was selected by 38 percent of the respondents, Clinton by 29 percent.

10. On election day, exit polls revealed that 49 percent of respondents felt Clinton had not told the truth with respect to the draft, and 45 percent felt he had told the truth. On Iran-Contra, 70 percent felt Bush had not told the truth; only 26 percent felt he had told the truth.

11. The data reported in this section, unless otherwise noted, are based on the results of exit poll surveys conducted by Voter Research and Surveys. Questionnaires were completed by 15,490 voters leaving 300 polling places, and the findings were reported in the *New York Times*, November 5, 1992:B9, and in the *National Journal* (November 7, 1992):2543–2544.

12. For a similar interpretation of the data, see Pomper (1993:144–150).

13. The eight states were Alaska, Idaho, Kansas, Maine, Montana, Nevada, Utah, and Wyoming.

10

Political Parties and Campaign Finance: Adaptation and Accommodation Toward a Changing Role

FRANK J. SORAUF
SCOTT A. WILSON

Depending on one's tolerance for repetition, the observation that the American parties are essentially electoral parties is either a commonplace or a fundamental truth. Whichever it is, the parties have historically been more involved in contesting elections than in governing, more concerned with electoral outcomes than with issues or ideology. In their heyday they were everywhere in the search for office—developing and recruiting candidates, engineering nominations, running the campaigns, and turning out the vote. Virtually nothing of importance in the quest for elective office was beyond their ken and influence.

Much of that has changed. The hordes of campaign experts, canvassers, and workers the parties once supplied have been replaced by new armies of professional consultants, pollsters, media experts, and data managers. The candidate who can raise the cash to rent their services is free to run his or her campaign—indeed, the candidate may be as unmarked by party loyalty or service as the campaign is unmarked by party participation. Especially in races for Congress and governorships, the candidate-centered campaign is the norm, and the party struggles to find not a dominant role but just a useful place in it.

The decline of the parties' campaign roles is only a symptom, though a major one, of their more general and widely heralded decline. Since the loss of their traditional roles in American politics is a part of party history, the parties now confront the necessity to adapt, to find a new and constructive role in a changing political environment. Central to that adaptation must be a new electoral role—a role that goes beyond merely lending their labels to candidates who use them without obligation. For what is an "electoral party" without a substantial role in election campaigns?

DIMENSIONS OF PARTY ACTIVITY IN CAMPAIGN FINANCE

In the cash economy of modern campaigning, the parties' adaptability has inevitably been tested by their ability to raise significant sums of money. To an increasing degree, it is cash that buys the implements and skills of campaign combat, for the parties as well as for the candidates.

Nowhere is the ability of the parties to raise new sums of money more evident than in their national party committees—the Democratic and Republican national committees, those committees formed by the delegates from the state parties, and the campaign committees of each party in each house of Congress, the so-called Hill committees.[1] These six national committees together increased their receipts from $149.6 million in 1980 to $296.2 million in 1992 (Table 10.1), an overall increase of 98 percent in little more than a decade. Although the overall trend is one of increase, there is also a subsidiary pattern to the growth: The advances are greater in the years of presidential elections. Nothing draws participants to American electoral politics—voters, newspaper readers, or financial contributors—as surely as does a presidential campaign.

Within the general pattern of growth, however, there still remain substantial disparities in the receipts of the two major parties (Table 10.1). Republican committees achieved an early advantage by the effective use of direct-mail solicitation, and they have never surrendered it. While Democratic leaders were struggling with a massive debt and the intricacies of party reform in the late 1970s, Republican National Committee chairman William Brock directed Republican resources to the development of computer-based lists of known contributors and direct-mail programs for soliciting them. These efforts yielded both an immediate surge in the receipts of Republican committees and the enrollment of some 2 million active contributors by the end of 1980 (Reichley, 1985). The Democratic committees started their own direct-mail operations in the early 1980s, and by the end of the decade they began to narrow the Republican advantage.

As to whether the Democrats can realistically expect to close the fund-raising gap, the data of Table 10.1 suggest they cannot. It is true that the Republicans have never again raised the sums they did in 1984 and 1986, but Democratic progress has been modest and irregular since then. The Democratic committees find it especially difficult to maintain fund-raising momentum in nonpresidential years; the Republicans raised more than four times the Democratic totals in both 1986 and 1990. Not even Democratic control of the Congress has helped the Democratic Congres-

TABLE 10.1
Receipts of the National Party Committees: 1980–1992 (in millions of dollars)

	1980	1982	1984	1986	1988	1990	1992
Democratic	19.9	28.6	65.9	43.0	83.1	41.1	104.1
Republican	129.7	191.1	246.1	208.1	191.5	167.0	192.1
Total	149.6	219.7	312.0	251.1	274.6	208.1	296.2

Source: Federal Election Commission.

sional Campaign Committee (DCCC) and the Democratic Senatorial Campaign Committee (DSCC) match the Republicans, and one simply must conclude that the Democratic constituencies cannot or will not match the generosity of Republican supporters.

The party receipts reported in Table 10.1 fund the full range of national Democratic and Republican party activities. The focus of this essay, however, is on their campaign role, and so it is necessary to look at direct party spending in campaigns. Since the data on spending in congressional campaigns are the most complete we have, we concentrate on them. Under the provisions of the Federal Election Campaign Act (FECA) of 1974 and its subsequent amendments, party committees are allowed to spend directly in their candidates' campaigns through two means: direct contributions and coordinated expenditures. Direct contributions are just what their name implies—contributions of cash, equipment, or services that go directly to a candidate's campaign committee for use at its discretion. Coordinated expenditures, also known as "on behalf of" expenditures, are spending by the party committee itself to help a candidate. When making a coordinated expenditure, the party committee is free to consult with the candidate, but the committee ultimately determines how and for what purposes the money will be spent.

Not surprisingly, the data on direct contributions and coordinated expenditures (Table 10.2) closely follow the contours of the data on party receipts—with one great exception: the increases of 1992. Both parties channeled irregularly increasing sums of money into congressional campaigns throughout the 1980s, followed by the significant dip of 1990. In 1992, however, they spent sums in congressional campaigns of a magnitude they had never before approached. Moreover, in 1992 the Democratic committees came closer to Republican spending than ever before; they did so by spending a higher percentage of their total receipts (27.5 percent) than did the Republicans (18.4 percent).

That exceptional spending total of $64 million in 1992 was well more than double any total of the 1980s and an indicator, surely, of one of campaign finance's "iron laws": Spending increases when elections are more competitive. Heightened competition in the 1992 elections was the result of greater numbers of primary candidates, greater numbers of general

TABLE 10.2
National Party Committee Spending in Congressional Elections:
1980–1992 (in millions of dollars)

	1980	1982	1984	1986	1988	1990	1992
Democrats							
Contributions	1.1	1.1	1.3	1.2	1.2	0.9	1.6
O.b.o. spending[a]	1.2	2.1	5.1	7.6	8.7	7.4	27.0
Total	2.3	3.2	6.4	8.8	9.9	8.3	28.6
Republicans							
Contributions	3.3	4.8	4.0	2.6	2.7	1.9	2.5
O.b.o. spending	7.1	13.9	13.0	14.1	14.4	10.6	32.9
Total	10.4	18.7	17.0	16.7	17.1	12.5	35.4
Grand total	12.7	21.9	23.4	25.5	27.0	20.8	64.0

[a]"On behalf of," or coordinated, expenditures.
Source: Federal Election Commission.

election candidates (i.e., fewer uncontested seats), greater numbers of open seats, and closer races even when incumbents were running. Some of the departures that created the open seats and some of the vulnerabilities of incumbents who chose to run again stemmed from the anti-incumbent, antipolitician animus of the time. But some also reflected the dislocations of the reapportionments following the 1990 census. We may well be on a ten-year cycle of competitiveness—one that renews itself each decade with the reapportionments and one that was obscured in 1982 by the steady and vigorous growth in expenditure levels following the reforms of 1974.

All of the data in Table 10.2 represent the combined spending of the four congressional committees and the two national committees. But the true national committees—the Democratic National Committee (DNC) and the Republican National Committee (RNC)—devote most of their time and resources to presidential campaigning and general party-building activities. The four Hill committees, therefore, dominate spending on House and Senate contests. In 1990 their share of the spending was at 98.3 percent, and in the massive spending of 1992 it was at 93.5 percent.

These data speak to the parties' progress in adjusting to modern electoral politics; one central trend makes this progress especially clear. The two-party increases in spending on congressional campaigns have come entirely in coordinated expenditures. Direct contributions totalled $4.4 million in 1980 and only $4.1 million in 1992 (Table 10.2). There are several reasons for this development. The FECA's limits on coordinated expenditures are higher than those on contributions. Some candidates also prefer these coordinated ("on behalf of") expenditures because they do not inflate their own receipt and spending totals. But the primary reason, and the one that connects the growth in coordinated expenditures to party adaptation, is the control that party committees have over coordinated expenditures. Controlling what an expenditure will pay for gives the party more leverage over a candidate's campaign than a simple cash contribution. Increasing their spending "on behalf of" candidates, that is, allows the parties greater influence over the campaigns per se.

Comparing the data in Tables 10.1 and 10.2, one can easily see that the combination of direct contributions and coordinated expenditures accounts for a relatively small share—about 22 percent in 1992—of Democratic and Republican income. Some of the other 78 percent goes toward a host of organizational expenses—office space, payroll, direct-mail fundraising costs, and assistance to state and local parties, to cite just a few examples. Another significant portion, however, is invested in what Stephen Frantzich (1989) has termed a "service-vendor" capacity. The parties (especially the Hill committees) now offer candidates a wide array of campaign services and expertise, including media production facilities, district polling, issue research, and fund-raising assistance (Herrnson, 1988). Part of the difference between receipts and campaign spending, therefore, goes to fund the professional services the national parties offer their candidates, often at surprisingly reasonable prices.

Despite the progress the parties have made in fund raising and campaign spending, their financial role remains small measured merely by dollar totals. In the 1992 congressional elections, for instance, all national Democratic and Republican committees made $63,963,462 in direct contributions and coordinated expenditures—a figure that constitutes 9 percent of the $737.9 million spent directly in the congressional campaigns by all candidates and parties. Nonetheless, that 9 percent total was a great jump over the 5 percent figure for 1990. Even though the party portion of the congressional spending total rises slowly, it is still far behind the 50, 60, and 70 percent totals that characterize party dominance of campaign finance in the European democracies. Indeed, it is the limited role of the parties that most clearly distinguishes American campaign finance from that of other industrial democracies.

Whatever the data say about the importance of parties in the campaigns, they underscore how important it is that parties make the best use of their limited resources. The provisions and amendments of the FECA do allow the party committees to spend respectable sums in individual campaigns. In House races, the party's national committee and its House campaign committee can each give $5,000 per candidate in direct contributions in both the primary and general elections (for a total of $20,000 per candidate). The statutory limit for coordinated expenditures, which is indexed to inflation, is $10,000 in 1974 dollars ($27,620 in 1992) for the primary and general elections combined.[2] Thus, each House candidate in the

1992 general election could legally receive $47,620 in assistance from his or her national-level party committees. For Senate candidates, the national and senatorial campaign committees are allowed a combined total of $17,500 in direct contributions per calendar year. The limit per committee for coordinated expenditures is the greater of either two cents (in 1974 pennies) times the voting age population of the state, or $20,000 in 1974 dollars. In 1992 the limits varied from a minimum of $55,240 to California's $1.23 million. Finally, the state party (which is subject to the same spending limits as the national committees) may designate the appropriate national committee as its "agent," thus allowing a national-level committee to spend the state's legal limit in addition to its own.

These are *limits*, of course, and the parties, especially the Democratic party, have often not had the resources to spend the legal maximum for all of their candidates. Given that scarcity, party committees must make strategic decisions about which candidates to fund and at what level. Central to their distribution strategy is the concentration of resources in close races. Individuals and PACs make contributions to help a particular candidate win and/or gain access to the winner; the parties pursue the broader electoral goal of maximizing the size of their contingent in the Congress. To reach such a goal, party committees must fund candidates in marginal contests rather than sure winners or losers. The sure winners (most often incumbents) need little party assistance; as strong and visible candidates they can raise all the money they need from other sources. Most of the certain losers are also poor investments. Although party spending may give them a boost, by itself it is unlikely to bring them victory. Quite simply, campaign spending is most influential in races that are otherwise close—races in which the party's strength in the district, national electoral forces, or the characteristics of an individual candidate make for a close election. For the parties, then, an electorally efficient distribution of resources is one that targets marginal candidates at the expense of those who are either safe or noncompetitive (Jacobson and Kernell, 1981; Jacobson, 1985–1986).

Both parties do a reasonably good job of distributing their resources in an electorally efficient manner (Table 10.3). The average size of a contribution or coordinated expenditure increases with the closeness of the candidate's race.[3] Nonetheless, a substantial amount of party money does find its way into the campaigns of certain winners and losers. In the House races of 1992, some 44 percent of the Democrats' direct contributions and 32 percent of their coordinated expenditures went to candidates in noncompetitive or safe elections; the comparable figures for the Republicans were 46 percent of direct contributions and 32 percent of coordinated expenditures.[4] In fact, as the party committees have increased the amounts of their spending since the early 1980s, they have actually increased the

TABLE 10.3
National Party Committee Support for House Candidates in
1992 General Elections, by Competitiveness of Outcome (in dollars)

General Election Vote (%)	Democrats		Republicans	
	Avg. Direct Contribution	Avg. o.b.o. Spending[a]	Avg. Direct Contribution	Avg. o.b.o. Spending
71–100	863	8,290	1,041	1,280
58–70	1,476	9,916	4,177	7,636
51–57	4,397	14,275	8,302	30,902
43–50	5,451	21,941	8,905	37,949
31–42	3,286	14,344	5,159	17,428
0–30	404	21,423	2,968	2,309

[a]"On behalf of," or coordinated, expenditures.
Source: Federal Election Commission.

percentage of their money going to safe and noncompetitive candidates (Wilson, 1989).

In part, that increase simply reflects practical obstacles. Since there is a limited number of candidates in close races and since statutory contribution limits prevent a party committee from spending large sums on these marginal candidates, the less competitive candidates are the beneficiaries. The relatively wealthy National Republican Senatorial Committee (NRSC), especially, has faced this problem repeatedly. In addition, the parties do not have perfect information on the competitiveness of their candidates' campaigns. As conditions change over the course of the campaign, races that once seemed competitive become one-sided. So, some of the party money going to safe or noncompetitive candidates goes because of legal and informational constraints.

More important, spending by party committees is subject to goals and demands other than seat maximization and electoral efficiency. Potential winners may need a number of attempts at office to gain campaign experience and name recognition, and financial support from the party can be critical in keeping such candidates interested. Support for a hopeless candidate may also help other party candidates on the ballot or support the party-building efforts of local leadership. Party committees can pursue some of these objectives only by investing in the campaigns of candidates who are presently noncompetitive.

At the other end of the spectrum of competitiveness, heavy demands for party resources may be made by what seem to be safely entrenched incumbents. Although they are reelected with surprising frequency (House incumbent reelection rates hover around the 95 percent mark), most incumbents do not think of themselves as safe candidates (Fenno, 1978; Jacobson, 1980). Moreover, incumbents generally believe in the deterrent value of a large campaign account; an impressive war chest, they think, will discourage would-be challengers. Numerous safe incumbents thus make demands for party money, and they are in a good position to do so. The congressional party committees, after all, are creatures of their respective House or Senate caucuses. So although the demands of safe incumbents conflict with the party's collective interest in an electorally efficient distribution of its resources, committee leaders cannot ignore all of their demands.

One sees the same mixture of strategy and pragmatism in the distribution of party spending on incumbent, challenger, and open-seat candidates. In 1990 the six national committees spent only 30.7 percent of their funding on their incumbent candidates. That percentage rose somewhat, to 36.5 percent in 1992, doubtless a reflection of the perceived threats to incumbents in the antipolitics, anti-incumbent mood of that year. Nonetheless, the important point is that the parties concentrate their money on challengers and open-seat candidates who have a chance of increasing the party's cohort in the Congress.

Overall, and despite the often conflicting goals and demands with which they are faced, the congressional party committees do concentrate their spending in the campaigns of marginal candidates. Indeed, they do so far more effectively than PACs, which in the 1992 House campaigns gave 78 percent of their contributions to incumbents in a year of exceptional opportunity for challengers and open-seat candidates. The party committees also time their spending for the greatest effectiveness, delaying coordinated expenditures until the latter part of the campaign—a time when the outcome of an election is more predictable (Sorauf, 1988). In the final analysis, however, strategy often comes down to the supply of money. Affluent party committees are better able to pursue a mix of objectives: funding marginal candidates while attending to the needs (real or perceived) of noncompetitive and safe candidates, and providing early "seed money" while saving enough for later, more strategic dispersal.

THE POLITICAL PARTY AS FINANCIAL BROKER

As important as the combination of contributions and coordinated spending may be, it by no means accounts for all of the party role in funding congressional campaigns. It is merely the most overt and identifiable part, the part about which the parties must make full reports and disclosures to the Federal Election Commission (FEC). Far less visible are the ways in which the parties function as brokers or intermediaries in raising campaign money—by cuing, channeling, and funneling the money of others to worthy candidates of the party. In these activities the party committee is neither the source nor the final spender of that money, but the mere mobilizing of money has become a major part of the parties' enhanced role in campaigns.

Much of the informal brokering involves simply giving cues and advice. The Hill committees, for example, routinely urge sympathetic PACs to give money to Candidate X or Candidate Y. Indeed, they have employees whose major duty is to oversee the mobilization of PAC money, even to stage the fabled "meat markets" at which the party's favored challengers make brief attempts to impress potential contributors. The mere fact of party support for a candidate is cue enough for some contributors looking for challengers and open-seat candidates with a chance of winning. None of this cue giving, of course, need be reported under either federal or state law, and thus there is no way to put a price on it. Many observers, however, argue that it is the most significant indirect party activity in congressional finance.

Of all the forms of financial brokering in which the parties engage, the most widely publicized and the least well understood unquestionably is the raising of "soft money." It is money raised beyond the restrictions of federal law, and thus it cannot be contributed to or spent on federal candidates. National party committees raise the greatest part of it and channel it to state parties for their spending on general party overhead expenditures, registration and get-out-the-vote campaigns, state and local campaigns—anything but the campaigns for Congress and the presidency. The largest share of the soft money the national committees raise comes from two sources that disqualify it under the FECA of 1974: individual and PAC contributions above the respective limits of $1,000 and $5,000, and contributions directly from the treasuries of corporations and labor unions, contributions forbidden by the FECA.

Soft money, in other words, is campaign money that moves in the American federal system to less regulated havens. Since federal law is more severely regulatory than the laws of virtually all the states, soft money flows in one direction: to the states, and usually to those with the most permissive statutes. Ironically, it is raised and channeled by party committees that cannot legally spend it in campaigns themselves.

Moreover, only since 1991 have the parties had to report their soft money transactions. Various experts estimated that the Democratic and Republican parties each raised between $20 and $25 million in soft money in 1988. According to the records of the Federal Election Commission for 1991–1992, the three national Democratic committees raised $36.9 million in soft money, and the three Republican committees raised $51.7 million. Of that two-party total of $88.6 million, $42.7 million went to pay for the state part of joint state-federal activities in the 1992 campaign, activities such as a media advertisement or a fund-raising event helping candidates for both state and federal offices. Another $19.5 million went in direct subsidies for state and local parties themselves, and $20.8 million went into party "building funds."[5]

The freedom to raise and allocate soft money greatly extends the power of the national party committees in electoral politics. At a time when state and local parties find it harder and harder to fund their activities, soft money sustains a great deal of local, grass-roots party activity. Furthermore, the organizational capacity it builds, the voters it gets to the polls, the campaigns it sustains, all indirectly increase local party capacity for affecting congressional and presidential campaigns. The local party's capacity for local campaigns, that is, is not easily separable from its capacity to influence the election of a U.S. senator. And that's the rub.

Critics of soft money charge the national committees plan their soft money allocations in order to have the greatest indirect impact on congressional and presidential elections. State and local parties may not legally spend those funds directly on federal elections (including presidential ones), but efforts on behalf of the whole party ticket or attempts to turn out the vote inevitably have some impact on all of the campaigns in a state. Critics—Common Cause most prominent among them—charge that the FEC's allocation formulas (under which those efforts that help federal candidates must be paid for with money raised under the FECA) are too lenient, that soft money is illegally spent by some state and local parties, and that soft money is raised in the first place with the intention of affecting presidential and congressional races.[6]

As with the raising of soft money, "bundling" can be practiced by both party and nonparty committees. A committee accepts and transmits the contributions of individuals to candidates specified by the contributors. The intermediary—the party committee or the PAC—need not count the sums bundled against its own contribution limits unless it "exercises direction or control over the choice of the intended recipient of the contribution." Virtually no intermediaries admit to such control. As for the reports of bundling or earmarking, they remain more or less buried amid the millions of pages of FEC reports. The FEC does not add them up, nor does it index them or bring them together in any accessible way.

In the world of PACs the practice of bundling is called "earmarking," and, indeed, that is what the regulations of the Federal Election Commission call it. PACs generally discourage it because it leaves the final decisions with the contributor rather than the PAC, but a few PACs employ bundling as their admitted modus operandi. EMILY's List, a feminist PAC, brought earmarking to popular attention with activities in the 1992 campaigns for Congress. Out of its regular PAC receipts EMILY's List made contributions to candidates totaling $365,318. But in addition, the contributors to EMILY's List ("members") agreed also to send individual contributions of at least $100 to at least two approved candidates on

EMILY's List. Those checks went to the list for bundling; sums well into six digits reportedly were gathered and transported to some Senate candidates.

Party committees engage in bundling very rarely these days. The major instance in the 1980s involved the National Republican Senatorial Committee, which reported approximately $3 million in earmarked money in both 1984 and 1986. After a lengthy review of the 1986 transactions, the Federal Election Commission split 3 to 3 along party lines over whether the $2.8 million raised for twelve candidates (eleven of whom lost) had entered "the direction or control" of the NRSC even though the funds had been deposited in NRSC bank accounts. The committee apparently has engaged in no bundling since.

Whatever the value of all these financial brokerings, one sees in them the effectiveness of the party, precisely because it *is* a political party. Because candidates bear its label on the ballot, voters look to it for guidance in election after election; and because candidates are identified as liberal or conservative by its very name, the party finds itself in a singular position to direct would-be contributors. The extensive national, state, and local structure of the party enables it to maneuver within the complexities of American federalism. And the superiority of its political knowledge and its strategic commitments permit it to make the political calculations essential to effective intermediating.

STATE AND LOCAL PARTY FINANCE

The ability of state and local committees to slip into the new financial role falls easily into two parts: their role in federal election campaigns (both congressional and presidential) and their role in state elections (from gubernatorial down to local). The first role must of course be reported to the FEC, and the latter only under variable state reporting requirements. Understandably, we know far more about the first than the second.

In the 1980s the two parties developed somewhat different roles for state and local parties in federal campaigns. The Republicans pioneered agency agreements by which state committees cede all or part of their authority to spend "on behalf of" candidates to a national committee. Democrats unsuccessfully fought the legality of agency agreements both before the FEC and in the federal courts, and then of necessity they capitulated to it. By the 1986 Senate elections the NRSC had spent sums well in excess of its limit—thus using a substantial part or all of a state committee's limit—in races in twenty-eight states; in 1990, the NRSC exceeded the limit in twenty-seven states. The DSCC, later and slower to negotiate the agreements, spent substantially into the state limit in seventeen states' Senate races in 1986 and in eighteen states in 1990. Moreover, the DSCC appears to have negotiated chiefly with less populous states with lower spending limits, perhaps recognizing that it is much cheaper to stage a winning campaign in some states than others—and that a senator is a senator regardless of the size of the state. In any event, no state party committee of either party spent to its full limit in any of the 1992 Senate races, and only one—the Connecticut Democrats—spent to even the 50 percent level.

Not surprisingly, then, state party committees—whose spending totals must also include those of local party committees—have spent a surprisingly constant sum on congressional campaigns since the early 1980s (Table 10.4). In 1984 their total spending, both in contributions and in coordinated spending, was $26.0 million. Spending then rose to $28.0 million in 1986 and $29.0 million in 1988 before slipping back to $23.8 million in 1990. Sums shift back and forth between House and Senate campaigns, largely as a reflection of differing degrees of competition in their races in a given year. Republicans maintain financial superiority, but here, too, the Democrats have narrowed the gap.

That is to say, the 100 state committees taken together spent only somewhat more than the four Hill committees did on House and Senate campaigns throughout the 1980s. All national committee spending on the 1990 races—98.3 percent of it by the four Hill committees—totaled $20.8 million; the state committees spent $23.8 million. Two years earlier the state committees outpaced the national committees by only $29.0 million to $26.9 million. The Hill committees are now full and equal partners in congressional campaign finance with the parties of the grass-roots and voting constituencies.

What of party spending in state and local elections? The best evidence is unquestionably found in campaigns for state legislatures—campaigns in which, for many years, party roles were substantial because of the limited visibility and political experience of the candidates. By the 1980s the party committees accounted for less than 10 percent of legislative candidate receipts in most of the larger states—for example, 9 percent in Pennsylvania in 1982 and 1.5 percent in California in 1986 (Sorauf, 1988). There is also evidence of declines in party funding. According to the data of the Minnesota Ethical Practices Board, for instance, party committees accounted for 12.4 percent of funds for lower house candidates in 1980; by 1990 the figure was 8.2 percent.

Inevitably, among the fifty states there are many political traditions and many forms of adaptation to the new politics of cash campaigns. By far the most common one, however, has been the development of a stronger role for state legislative parties, caucuses, and campaign committees in supporting state legislative candidates. In ways very similar to those of the Hill committees, they raise increasing sums and spend them strategically on close races and in support of the party's nonincumbent candi-

TABLE 10.4

State and Local Party Committee Support for Congressional Candidates by
House and by Party, 1980–1990 (in millions of dollars)

	Democratic Committee Spending		Republican Committee Spending	
	In House Elections	In Senate Elections	In House Elections	In Senate Elections
1980	1,400,108	1,762,002	6,117,513	6,154,676
1982	1,929,630	2,989,162	10,511,670	9,388,400
1984	3,141,603	4,881,076	10,516,436	7,430,288
1986	2,965,100	7,305,682	6,806,449	10,914,237
1988	4,150,104	7,094,041	6,819,276	10,979,606
1990	4,344,714	5,764,374	5,033,128	8,694,537

Source: Federal Election Commission.

dates. Moreover, they influence other contributors and increasingly provide campaign services at discount rates (Gierzynski, 1992).

Even with new data about state party finance, it is not easy to assess the ability of state and local parties to find a substantial place in financing campaigns. Clearly they have a role in congressional campaigns, although they appear to be losing it slowly to the party committees in the House and Senate. Their cash roles in state campaigns are often substantial in direct outlays, but there is no reason to think that their informal role—cue giving or bundling, for instance—matches that of the national committees. Perhaps the major reason for pessimism about their ability to adapt to cash politics rests in the increasing role of the Democratic National Committee and the Republican National Committee in funding the operation of state parties and the recruitment of state candidates.

Since the middle 1980s American campaign finance has in fact been increasingly nationalized. Most PACs by their very nature are national, and the national market (i.e., the "out-of-state" market) in individual contributions is increasingly important, especially for senatorial candidates (Sorauf, 1992). And the parties, too, have become a part of the centralizing. State parties cede their spending authority to national parties in agency agreements, and they in turn depend more and more on transfers, especially in soft money, from the national committees. Indeed, they sustain a role in congressional campaigns in part because the soft money transfers free other funds for supporting candidates.

THE IMPACT OF THE NEW FINANCIAL ROLE

What the new financial role has *not* done for the parties is clearer than what it has done. It has not brought them closer to the model of the programmatic, "responsible" political party. That is, party committees have not yet tied spending in campaigns to the candidate's position on party issues or programs or to the candidate's record of support for party positions. The goals of these committees have been the modest electoral goals of the classically electoral American parties: to win elections and to maximize the number of elective offices won. The hope that the parties would emerge as the central animating force in American government—that they would bring us "party government"—seems as remote as ever.

In pursuing their modest electoral goals, the parties have begun to recapture some of their lost role in electoral politics. Their ability to raise money and to direct the raising of money from others, as well as their ability to provide campaign technologies and services, has won the parties an active role in campaign politics that they did not have in the 1960s and 1970s. Thus they have adapted, even recouped a bit, in a campaign politics dominated by candidates and new technologies and technocrats. But how much have they recouped? If one employs the ultimate test—control of the content and strategy of the campaign—the parties are still some distance from the kind of party control they had in the first half of the twentieth century (Heard, 1960).

To some extent, the parties' recapture of a role in electoral campaigns was possible in the 1980s because they lost no further ground in the war of political organizations. The new era of American campaign finance, inaugurated by the passage of the FECA of 1974, coincided with a rise of interest group power (Scholzman and Tierney, 1986). The campaign instruments of the interest groups—political action committees—experienced a parallel growth under the fostering provisions of the FECA. There were 1,146 PACs registered with the FEC at the end of 1976 and 4,195 by the end of 1992; their contributions to congressional candidates jumped in the same years from $22.6 million to $180.5 million. By creating PACs interest groups entered electoral politics in an ever-expanding way for the first time. The traditional and informal division of labor—parties dominating electoral politics, groups dominating policymaking politics—had been irreparably broken.

Indeed, at the peak of PAC expansion in the early 1980s, it seemed possible that at least some PACs would expand their influence in electoral politics beyond the mere channeling of cash. Some PACs and their parent groups began to register new voters and encourage greater voter turnout; a few of the larger PACs began to make contributions not in cash but in campaign services (i.e., "in kind") that permitted them a more active role in the campaigns they supported. But most PACs never followed suit; very few, that is, followed the set traditions of labor PACS in endorsing candidates and mobilizing voters. Most never developed either the political will or the political knowledge and sophistication that once seemed likely to come with their experience and affluence. On the contrary, PACs became more "risk averse" as they grew and matured; the percentage of their contributions going to challengers and open-seat candidates in congressional campaigns declined steadily in the 1980s.

PACs, in other words, have demonstrated important limits on the capacity of interest groups to act in electoral politics. They do not easily reach the levels of political knowledge and sophistication, the intensity of political purpose, that the parties do even in their reduced condition. The symbolic and cue-giving value of interest groups, especially for voters, seems more limited in scope, perhaps even in intensity, than that of even weakened parties. Their members have been brought together for very specific and limited political purposes, and disunity threatens whenever the groups venture beyond them. Thus, they can limit the parties' hegemony in the electoral arena only to a point. It is increasingly clear that a party's chief rival is still the autonomous candidate who has the ability to raise substantial cash resources and thereby to rent the imposing new campaign technologies rather than seek them from the party.

The parties' competition with PACs aside, the parties' new role in campaign finance has had a second set of consequences: impacts on the parties themselves. The most obvious of these has been the emergence of a new financial elite. The "new fat cats," as they have been called, are no longer the big contributors but the organizers of the big contribution total. Under federal law they can no longer give $1 million, but they can mobilize 1,000 people to give $1,000 each. They can stage receptions or other fund-raising events, arranging not only the events themselves but also the presence of affluent guests. They come from all parts of American life; some are members of distinguished and/or wealthy families, many are captains of commerce and industry, and some are lobbyists, political lawyers, or individuals elsewhere employed in the influence industry.

Nowhere is the return of the money raisers more evident than in presidential and national committee politics. In the case of the party of the president, the fund raisers are in the presidential circle. Robert Mosbacher, the secretary of commerce in the Bush administration, was also its leading fund raiser. In 1988 the Dukakis campaign relied on the much-reported skills of Robert Farmer, a millionaire publisher from Boston; after the Dukakis defeat, Farmer became the treasurer of the DNC. In 1992 the Democrats relied less on a single dominant figure and more on regionally based fund raisers. The tapping of the New York wealth, for example, was led in substantial part by a number of Wall Streeters brought into centrist Democratic politics by the Democratic Leadership Council with which Bill Clinton had worked so long (Starobin, 1993).

Finally, the need to raise campaign money also readjusts the relationships between various parts of the party, simply because some parts are more successful in raising campaign funds than are others. It is increasingly clear, for example, that the national committees have been far more successful than those at the state and local levels. The agency agreements that permit national committees to use spending quotas testify to that. So, too, does the increasing practice by the RNC and the DNC of raising money and using it to subsidize state party operations. In the 1950s and before, the money flowed the other way; national committees lived off funds transferred to them by affluent state committees. The flow of money now leads a new centralizing, nationalizing trend within both parties.

Just as significant, the financial role has further empowered the legislative parties, both at the national level and in the states. By the early 1990s the four congressional party committees had taken over the funding of congressional elections from the two national party committees, leaving the RNC and the DNC to fund presidential campaigns and the state parties. Important political careers were made or nourished in the Hill committees. In the early 1980s Representative Tony Coelho turned successful leadership of the DCCC into election to a position in the House Democratic leadership. And in early 1989 the NRCC hired Ed Rollins, the campaign manager of the 1984 Reagan reelection committee, as its executive director at the unheard of salary of $250,000.

The legislative party, moreover, has triumphed in many states. Often the legislative caucus of the party directs the fund raising on behalf of the party's state legislative candidates, holding fund-raising events, marshaling big contributors, and even beginning direct-mail campaigns for money. In other states there are party committees, detached to some degree from the legislative caucus, that operate much the same way as the Hill committees do in congressional campaigns. And in still other states the major fund-raising responsibility is in the hands of the legislative leadership. The long-time speaker of the California Assembly, Willie Brown, repeatedly distributed more than a million dollars to fellow Democratic legislative candidates until a voter-passed initiative stopped him. His generosity had helped ensure both a Democratic majority and grateful support for Brown's speakership in the Assembly.

Whatever the mode, the effect is the same: an increase in the power of the legislative party to fund its own campaigns. That power results from the legislators' discovery of the fund-raising leverage of their incumbency, their electoral invincibility, and their making of public policy. That discovery, more than any other, may well mark the end of any hope for the creation of "responsible parties," for it marks the relative failure of the grass-roots parties of the constituencies to find a major new financial role in electoral politics. And so, the best fund raisers among the party committees, the legislative parties, are those most resistant to the development of programmatic parties that might try to make elected legislators carry out a party program.

MONEY AND THE FUTURE OF THE PARTIES

The sums spent in congressional campaigns leveled off in the late 1980s only to surge again in the hypercompetitive environments of 1992. Total party and candidate spending in all congressional campaigns in 1988 was $484.1 million, and it was only $466.8 million in 1990; the total for 1992 was $715.3 million, a jump of 53 percent. (Candidate receipts increased by only 40 percent; the additional spending was fed both by debt and by incumbents' use of their cash on hand from previous cycles.) The national party committees, which had contributed and spent $23.7 million in the 1990 congressional campaigns, met the challenge of 1992 with an outlay of $40.5 million. Like all other actors in the funding of the 1992 campaigns, they found sources of funds equal to the challenge of the year's heightened competition.

There is no way to calculate future party capacity to raise money, but there is certainly no reason to think it is infinite. Indeed, the party fundraising record since 1984 is mixed; it tailed off in the noncompetitive campaigns of the latter 1980s and in 1990. The reasons for the downturns in party receipts in the 1980s are still troubling. In the first place, direct-mail solicitations of campaign money have generally fared badly in recent years; a number of the PACs relying on direct mail have done poorly, and support for a few (e.g., the National Conservative Political Action Committee, or NCPAC) has completely collapsed. For whatever reasons—oversolicitation of lists, loss of novelty, the poor image and high overhead of some direct-mail operations—it seems clear that direct-mail fund raising is a volatile way to raise money, especially in a nonpresidential year. Second, the parties (and especially the Democrats) may be vulnerable at a time when a new, centrist politics replaces the ideological, confrontational politics of the Reagan years and robs politics of the emotional immediacy that underlies the most successful mass appeals for money.

In short, the financial role for the parties may be as perishable and time-rooted as all other party roles have been. Adaptation to earlier change does not protect a party against future change and the need to adapt once again. If electoral politics remains centrist and without searing issues or ideological conflict, and if the personas of candidates continue to dominate that sphere of politics, the parties may find it difficult to raise large sums of money. It is not easy to compete with personable candidates, for it is not easy to personify the abstract collectivity we call a political party. Nor is it easy to compete with PACs in setting out clear issue or ideological positions, especially at a time when many voters attend to highly specific, even single, issues.

Changes in the ground rules governing the getting and spending of money in elections might, however, ease the parties' problems in fund raising. Virtually all proposals for reforming the FECA since the mid-1980s have included some restriction on the ability of PACs to contribute funds to congressional candidates, either by cutting the PAC contribution limit of $5,000 per candidate per election or by imposing new limits on how much money a candidate may accept from PACs in general. Any new restrictions on PACs such as these might well provide a boon for party fund raising. So, too, might modest increases in the limits on contributions to them. But more substantial, direct legislative aid to the parties—public subsidies or major increases in their spending limits—seems unlikely, for political parties are not exempt from the popular attitudes that govern the regulation of campaign finance. The public is suspicious about the sources of money, especially "big money," and it will suspect the sources of party money just as surely as the sources of PAC money. It will also be suspicious of parties that spend large sums and will wonder what they want for their money.

Reform threatens the national parties' raising of soft money, however. If the flow of soft money were sharply reduced, the chief losers would be the DNC and the RNC and their roles in both presidential campaigns and in the shoring up of their state and local parties. The four Hill committees would scarcely be touched, and indeed their relative role in campaigns for the House and Senate might well be enhanced by the weakening of other party players in congressional campaigns.

So, whether by plan or inadvertence, the parties have begun to accommodate American candidate-centered campaigning. But the accommodation is not without its hazards, and, like all other things in party politics, it will certainly not last forever. Moreover, it is an accommodation that works better for some parts of the parties than for others. It has succeeded particularly well for the legislative parties. Greater powers of incumbency have joined with a greater ability to fund the electoral politics of the legislative party. The result, for now, is greater autonomy for legislative parties: freedom to frame their own campaign themes and strategies and to set policymaking agendas and positions without interference from the party organizations of the nation or the states. As always, it is not the whole political party, but only a part of it, that is strengthened by adaptation.

NOTES

We gratefully acknowledge the help of our research assistant, Peter Gronvall, and of Robert Biersack of the Federal Election Commission.

1. The four campaign committees in the Congress are the Democratic Congressional Campaign Committee, the Democratic Senatorial Campaign Committee,

the National Republican Congressional Committee, and the National Republican Senatorial Committee. Generally, they are better known by their acronyms: DCCC, DSCC, NRCC, and NRSC. Their colloquial designation as the Hill committees reflects their location on Capitol Hill.

2. The coordinated spending limit is doubled for states having only one congressional district.

3. The one anomaly in Table 10.3—the high average spending on behalf of Democrats who got 30 or less percent of the general election vote—results from the decision of the DCCC to spend $50,000 or more on behalf of six conspicuously unsuccessful challengers.

4. The safe candidates were those who won by 58 percent or more of the vote; the noncompetitive ones were those who received 42 percent or less of the vote.

5. "Building funds" are funds the national party committees are permitted to keep for their own facilities under a special amendment to the FECA passed in 1979.

6. The arguments against soft money also include others beyond the scope of an essay on the party role in campaign finance. In particular, those who are against soft money deplore the reentry of contributors of large sums of special-interest money into the funding of electoral politics.

11

Party Competition and Media Messages in U.S. Presidential Elections

ANDREW GELMAN
GARY KING

THE PARADOX

At one point during the 1988 campaign, Michael Dukakis was ahead in the public opinion polls by 17 percentage points, but he eventually lost the election by 8 percent. Walter Mondale was ahead in the polls by 4 percent during the 1984 campaign but lost the election in a landslide. During June and July of 1992, Clinton, Bush, and Perot each had turns in the public opinion poll lead.

What explains all this poll variation? Why do so many citizens change their minds so quickly about presidential choices?

But wait. The story gets more complicated.

It turns out that political scientists can actually predict the outcome of the election with information available at the start of the general election campaign. That may seem odd, and perhaps a well-kept secret from the general public, but predicting presidential elections is a relatively straightforward problem that has largely been solved. Predicting primaries and many other elections is a lot harder, but general elections for president have been successfully predicted four to five months ahead of time, to an accuracy of a few percentage points, for at least the past half-dozen elections.

So now we really have a paradox: Polls vary widely, academic political scientists can predict the election outcome before the campaign begins, and strategists on all sides spend hundreds of millions of dollars trying to influence an outcome that was predicted before they spent anything! What's a political analyst to make of all this? We provide some answers to these questions here.

By looking at day-to-day swings in the polls but ignoring systematic forecasting efforts, journalists and pundits are in part responsible for the relatively issue-free, or "horse race," aspect of presidential campaign media coverage, which at its most extreme finds journalists interpreting the race by deconstructing the claims of competing "spin doctors." If the early forecasts are at all accurate, the news organizations could save a lot of effort and money now devoted to tracking polls, and maybe they could spend some time doing what they claim they want—reporting substantive positions held by the candidates instead of the current array of scandals, gaffes, and strategic campaign maneuvers.

We focus on the 1988 election, in which the news media focused more than ever before on political advertising, sound bites, and trends in tracking polls.

Obviously, the news media report the details of campaign strategies because of their assumed relevance to the outcome of the election, with Bush's election credited in part to recent innovations such as professional spin doctors and focus group polls. Thoughtful news analysts such as Jack Germond and Jules Witcover decry the superficial "sound-bite" coverage of election campaigns, which they claim allowed Bush (and Dukakis too) to avoid serious discussion of the issues.

As citizens, we agree that the empty nature of recent TV election campaigns is undesirable, and perhaps even a threat to our democratic society. However, we do *not* think Bush won in 1988 because of his superior, media-savvy campaign, nor did he lose in 1992 because of campaign strategy.

As political scientists, we try to accept and reject theories based on empirical evidence. Three pieces of evidence justify the claim of many journalists that Bush outcampaigned Dukakis in 1988. First, Bush won, in a come-from-behind victory. Second, Bush advanced in the opinion polls following his campaign's attack strategy in late summer. Third, Bush's campaign was resourceful and unscrupulous, using the latest innovations in media manipulation.

In this essay, we question the logic of all three of these arguments. First, knowledgeable academic observers expected Bush to win all along—even before the campaign began—so his come-from-behind victory proves nothing; second, early polls move in response to just about any campaign event, so Bush's improvement in the polls was just evidence that early opinions were not well-formed; and third, had Bush lost in 1988, his campaign could easily have been seen as a desperate, floundering effort.

POLITICAL SCIENCE FORECASTS

Rosenstone's forecasting model is one of the most developed and successful of the recent contributions to political science, and it is the empirical results of this model on which we focus (Rosenstone, 1983). His model is based on measurable economic and political variables that were discovered and analyzed by numerous researchers over many decades, and not on trial heat polls. Even if one were to disagree with the particulars of Rosenstone's model, it would be hard to deny that past presidential elections have been forecast fairly accurately using these methods.[1]

Rosenstone summarizes his considerable success at forecasting presidential elections through 1980. Perhaps even stronger evidence is that his model has continued to forecast very well in the two elections since the publication of his book, as recounted by Rosenstone (1990).[2] In both 1984 and 1988, Rosenstone's forecasts fell within 1 percent of the nationwide popular vote and forecasted only a few states incorrectly, an excellent performance considering that the forecasts were performed months before the election. Table 11.1 summarizes the performance of Rosenstone's model, along with our forecasts for 1992 (see further on), by comparing forecasts made at the start of the general election campaign with those from the national polls, media prognoses, and judgments by political strategists taken at the same time.

Other forecasting models, also based on economic and political variables measured before the start of the campaign, have performed well, and often better, in recent years.[3] By contrast, public opinion polls at this time gave relatively useless forecasts of the election outcome. The predictions of media experts and political strategists were not much better.

To cover the 1992 election and poll results, we wanted to once again compare Rosenstone's forecasts to those of the pundits and pollsters. Unfortunately, as the November election approached, we could not track down any official Rosenstone forecasts, so we decided to make our own, even though several other forecasts were made.[4] Our purpose was not to perform the most accurate forecasts or to optimally select variables for prediction, but rather to combine the elements of existing forecasting methods in the political science literature and to accurately assess the uncertainty in our forecast. We started with what we viewed as the best currently available forecasting model, that of Campbell (1992), which predicts the Democratic share of the two-party vote for president in each state. We accounted for uncertainty in the model's forecasts in three ways: by including the forecasting error in the existing prediction model, by considering alternative sets of explanatory variables, and by modeling the variation in the nationwide vote from year to year, as distinct from the variation between states. According to our calculations, Clinton had a 0.85 probability of winning the election, with an expected total of 53.1 percent of the two-party popular vote and 368 (of 535) electoral votes.[5]

TABLE 11.1
Presidential Election Forecasting Errors

	Errors
1984 forecasts	
National popular vote	
Rosenstone	0.3%
National polls (average miss)	5.3%
National electoral vote	
Rosenstone	48 electoral votes
Media prognoses (average miss)	129 electoral votes
Political strategists (average miss)	115 electoral votes
1988 forecasts	
National popular vote	
Rosenstone	0.2%
National polls (average miss)	2.8%
National electoral vote	
Rosenstone	82 electoral votes
Media prognoses (average miss)	131 electoral votes
1992 forecasts	
National popular vote	
Gelman and King	0.3%
National polls, early September (average miss)	2.8%
National polls, mid-October (average miss)	5.4%
National electoral vote	
Gelman and King	5.6 electoral votes
State polls, September	59 electoral votes

Note: All popular-vote forecasts are expressed in terms of the Democratic candidate's share of the two-party vote. The 1984 forecasts were made in mid-July; the 1988 forecasts were made in early September; the 1992 forecasts were performed in early October but only used information available in early September. When the media declared states as toss-ups, the electoral votes were divided evenly between the two major parties, and states were counted as half a miss.

Source: For 1984 and 1988 forecasts, Rosenstone (1990:Tables 1 and 2); for 1992 forecasts, the authors.

NATIONWIDE PUBLIC OPINION POLLS

For comparison, we also provide a more detailed presentation of aggregate public opinion poll results over the previous eleven presidential election campaigns. Our data for this inquiry, and for the rest of this essay, include the Republican proportion of two-party support reported in surveys over these eleven elections. The data before 1988 are from Gallup; 1988 and 1992 also include all other polling organizations from which we could obtain data.[6] Our data include the aggregate information reported in Figure 11.1 and individual-level survey data from forty-nine cross-sectional polls during the 1988 campaign.[7] In total, the 1988 data include surveys of 67,492 people, 69 percent of whom were willing to state their candidate preference. The appendix describes these data in more detail.[8]

Figure 11.1 summarizes these data for each election since 1952. The triangle on the right side of each graph reports the actual election outcome, and the line traces out the changes in the Republican proportion of the two-party candidate support figures over the campaign.[9]

The graphs in Figure 11.1 show that, in most years, early public opinion polls give fairly miserable forecasts of the actual election outcome. The situation is somewhat better after the second party convention, but through almost the entire campaign it would not be wise to use polls to forecast the election outcome. Additionally, in virtually every presidential election in the past forty years, the polls converge to a point near the actual election outcome shortly before election day.

POLITICAL SCIENCE MODELS

Most existing political science forecasting models are based on state-level or national-level aggregates, derived from the same ideas and underlying variables as the models of individual-voter choice favored by political scientists. Being aggregate results, though, these election predictions cannot truly confirm the individual-level models. To understand individual-level behavior, political scientists have turned to numerous studies based on public opinion data.

Political scientists have developed numerous models of voter decisionmaking, mostly in the context of studies of presidential campaigns. In the broadest terms, we have the sociological models dominated by the Columbia School, the social-psychological models connected with the Michigan School, and the rational choice models developed by the Rochester School. These models, their descendants, and numerous others are derived from diverse perspectives of voter choice. For the purposes of this study, though, these models do not differ among each other as much as they differ as a whole from the models implied by journalists in their coverage of presidential campaigns.

Although much debate still exists over proper models of voter decisionmaking in political science, these models all seem to agree on some aspects of the same general picture: Voters take the decision about whom to vote for relatively seriously. They might not be able to recite the reasons for their vote for president to a survey researcher (indeed, they might not even know these reasons), but voters at least base their decisions on relatively known and measurable variables. These *fundamental variables* measure their (or their group's) interests and include economic conditions, party identification, proximity of the voter's ideology and issue preferences to those of the candidates, and so on. Political scientists' theoretical

FIGURE 11.1

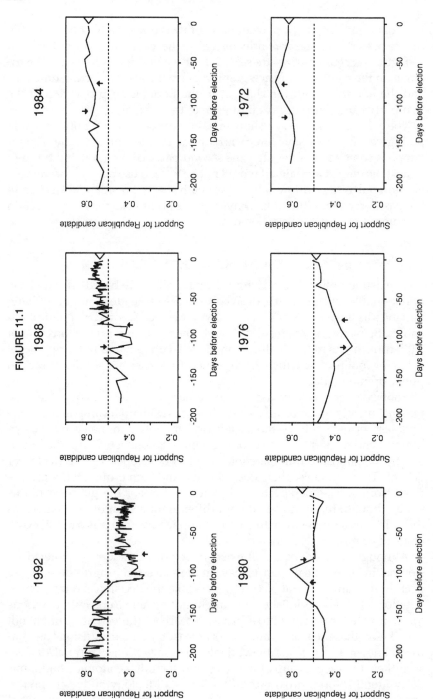

FIGURE 11.1 (*continued*)

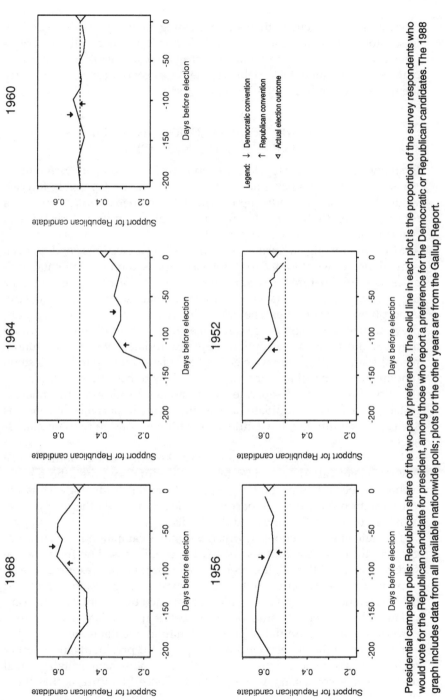

Presidential campaign polls: Republican share of the two-party preference. The solid line in each plot is the proportion of the survey respondents who would vote for the Republican candidate for president, among those who report a preference for the Democratic or Republican candidates. The 1988 graph includes data from all available nationwide polls; plots for the other years are from the Gallup Report.

models are consistent with their forecasting methods; as discussed by Rosenstone (1983; 1990) and Lewis-Beck and Rice (1992), all the serious forecasting methods try to predict the election result using some versions of the same fundamental variables to measure economic well-being, party identification, candidate quality, and so forth.

WHY ARE SOME ELECTIONS HARDER TO PREDICT THAN OTHERS?

First, and most obviously, close elections such as 1960 and 1976 will always be hard to predict, since in these cases the best possible forecast would be statistically indistinguishable from 50 percent. We consider a forecast successful if it closely predicts the vote, even if the forecast is 49 percent and the outcome is 51 percent.

More interesting, in primaries, low-visibility elections, and uneven campaigns, we would not expect forecasting based on fundamental variables measured before the campaign to work. The fast-paced events during a primary campaign (such as verbal slips, gaffes, debates, particularly good photo opportunities, rhetorical victories, specific policy proposals, previous primary results, etc.) can make an important difference because they can affect voters' perceptions of the candidates' positions on fundamental issues. Also, primary election candidates often stand so close on fundamental issues that voters are more likely to base their decisions on the minor issues that do separate the candidates. In addition, the inherent instability of a multicandidate race heightens the importance of concerns such as electability that have little to do with positions on fundamental issues.

In a low-visibility election, if all a voter knows about a candidate is a few statements about reducing defense spending, say, then these statements may be very important in gauging a candidate's ideology. Thus, the voter might not have the opportunity to learn later whether early statements accurately reflect the candidate's ideology.

The outcome of elections in which one side's campaign is much stronger than the other's would also be hard to predict based on fundamental variables alone. After all, it is well known that financial resources are an important influence on the outcomes of uneven congressional races and ballot referenda, an effect that could be explained by the ability of the candidate with greater media resources to better manipulate many voters' perceptions of the candidates' positions on fundamental issues.

However, in the general election campaign for president, and in other high-information campaigns in which the two sides have roughly equal resources, the consensus in the political science literature is that these events are largely ephemeral, having little effect on the eventual outcome. They can have important effects for short periods and on different localities (see Kessel, 1988), but the overall result is little affected. The length of the general election campaign and the ample resources on both sides allow early candidate mistakes and early voter misperceptions (perhaps based on these mistakes) to be corrected. By election day, voters are able to vote based largely on accurate measures of their fundamental variables. The argument here is that although presidential campaigns have an important effect, what is relevant is their *existence;* we expect the *details* of a competently run campaign to have a small effect on the election outcome. This is a similar argument to that of Markus.[10]

For example, among the first systematic studies of voting behavior was a six-wave panel survey of the 1940 presidential election designed to show what the authors thought were huge campaign effects (Lazarsfeld, Berleson, and Gaudet, 1944). In fact, they found very few campaign-specific effects of any kind. The considerable systematic research over the next half-century did little to change this basic conclusion (Bartels, in press). Even those scholars who focus on the endogenous effect of the campaign (or expected votes) on fundamental variables like party identification emphasize that these endogenous effects are minimal, especially in the short run.[11]

THE IMPLIED MODEL OF JOURNALISTS

Journalists have no similar tradition of detailing models of voter decision-making. However, we can discern their implicit model by looking at the focus of media attention during election campaigns and at some explicit statements from newspapers, magazines, and television. Of course, there are about as many opinions among journalists as among political scientists, but at least a "mainstream model" can be identified. According to this model, voters base their intended votes partly on fundamental variables, but considerably more on the day-to-day events of the presidential campaign. Voters are assumed to have very short memories, disproportionately relying for their decisions on the most recent campaign events and last piece of information they ran across. Candidates are thought to be able to easily "fool" voters by changing their policy stance during the campaign or causing the opposing candidate to say or do something foolish. For example, the *San Francisco Chronicle* reported (on September 13, 1988) that "the survey [of Bush leading 49 percent to 41 percent] is the latest evidence that the vice-president's tough attacks on Dukakis are working. ... The Pledge of Allegiance in public schools has been particularly effective, with voters expressing disapproval of the Democrat's action by a

2–1 ratio." Similarly, the *Dallas Times Herald* reported (on August 9, 1988) that "if the race is indeed narrowing, it is an indication that this strategy [of Bush actively attacking Dukakis] is working."

Also according to the journalists' model, voters do not take their role in the process very seriously, have very little information or knowledge of the campaign and the issues, and frequently do not vote on the basis of their own self-interest. For example, *Profiles* magazine (December 1991:21) approvingly quoted a top consultant who indicated that "people vote for character traits, not policies or issues." The typical advice of journalists to their colleagues is "Don't assume any voter knowledge. ... In other words, the press must occasionally bore itself in order to inform the public" (*Newsweek*, October 4, 1991:29).

Journalists justify their model (or stance) by interpreting public opinion polls. They do no formal studies, and so they cannot be very confident of these interpretations, but the causal inferences seem clear to them on the basis of their detailed knowledge of the campaign ant their close observations. For example, George Bush was gaining in the polls in 1988 just at the time when he was on the strong offensive against Dukakis, and Dukakis at the same time was avoiding getting into the fray. Dukakis lost a few point in the polls when he looked a bit foolish riding on a tank. Four days of the national media focusing on a candidate during a party convention certainly does seem to influence people to increase their support in the polls for that candidate. According to the journalists, Bush won because of these events, the Willie Horton TV ads (and especially the media coverage of these ads), his opposition to flag burning, and other campaign events. Campaign strategies and tricks play a central role in journalists' interpretation of poll results. For example: "It was beyond brilliance the way Michael Dukakis handled Jesse Jackson"; "Dukakis seemed to be stalled and passive"; "Dukakis is a sourpuss compared to this amazing new Bush person."[12]

A more-sophisticated news media analysis argues that character matters rather than campaign tricks: "The Democrats ... lost for a variety of reasons, but principal among them was that they presented a candidate whose virtues did not include plausibility as a president or, often, even an apparent feeling for the nature of the job" (Editorial, *Washington Post*, October 14–20, 1991). This explanation does not, however, specify where the independent judgments of the candidates' characters come from.

It is interesting that during the 1992 campaign, the messages of political science seemed to reach the journalists: There was more mention of the state of the economy and even of individual forecasters such as Lewis-Beck and Campbell amidst the usual saturation coverage of ephemeral campaign events.

FLAWED EXPLANATIONS

If political scientists can forecast the election outcome reasonably well on the basis of fundamental variables measured before the campaign, why do the polls vary so much? To put it another way, if the journalists' model is correct, then how can political scientists, or anyone else, accurately forecast the outcome? Alternatively, if the political science model is correct, why do polls vary at all, and why do they respond to specific campaign events such as conventions and advertising campaigns?

In this section, we raise several hypotheses that could explain this apparent paradox. Only some of these are competing hypotheses; many are complementary. We also provide, in most cases, sufficient evidence to discard each. We retain some features of some of the partially flawed explanations for later use. In most cases, we focus on the 1988 campaign, since our best data are from that contest.

We discuss flawed hypotheses for two reasons: First, they are plausible explanations, and many have been advanced by respected journalists and scholars. As such, they demand a hearing, and this work would be incomplete if it did not take them seriously. Second, exploring the implications of the various hypotheses gives us insight into the relation between political theories and electoral and poll data. By seeing how the data can refute certain ideas, we learn how to pose more sophisticated alternatives that are consistent with our observations.

We divide the flawed explanations into four classes: *measurement theories*, which explain the poll results as artifacts of flawed survey methods; *journalists' theories*, which dismiss the forecasts; *political science theories*, which are consistent with the forecasts but do not explain the poll variation; and *rational actor theories*, which are consistent with some parts of the evidence but not all.

Measurement Theories

It is possible to resolve the paradox presented in the opening of this essay by simply dismissing the pre-election poll results. We list three hypotheses, in order of increasing plausibility, under which we would not trust the opinion polls.

The Polls Are Meaningless. The simplest hypothesis holds that public opinion polls have nothing to do with real observable political behavior and are as meaningless as candidates behind in the polls make them out to be. Evidence for this hypothesis is the high rate of nonresponse, and the perception that respondents do not take the survey seriously, giving insincere or poorly thought-out answers to most questions.

There is obviously some truth to this hypothesis, since early polls in most election years appear to have very little to do with the eventual outcome of the general election. However, much evidence exists to conclude that survey responses are related to actual voting, notably the predictive accuracy of polls taken shortly before the election (see Figure 11.1). To some scholars, it was no great surprise that polls a few days before the election could forecast that election. However, this does confirm that the polls are connected in some important way to observable political behavior. These relationships hold even though as many as half of survey respondents refuse to state a presidential preference as late as the final week of pre-election polling.

In addition, relationships among variables within virtually all polls are quite predictable and consistent with our theoretical understanding. For example, those who identify themselves as Democrats support the Democratic presidential candidate more frequently, Republicans more frequently describe themselves as conservatives, those who have higher levels of education tend to have higher levels of income, and so forth. There are numerous observable consequences of the thesis that the polls are meaningful, and indeed most of the evidence seems quite consistent with this idea. This does not explain why early polls do not forecast well, but it does provide some reason to dismiss this hypothesis.

A closely related hypothesis is that variation in the polls is due to sampling error. However, this cannot be true, since the observed variation in the polls is often 10 or 20 percent or more, as compared to typical sampling errors of about 4 percentage points (Buchanan, 1986).

Wording of Questions and Survey Organization Methodology Affect Outcome. Several versions of this hypothesis can be posed. One simple version is that variation in the polls largely derives from variations in question wording. We know from considerable research in public opinion that minor changes in the wording of survey questions can have large effects on poll results.

In order to study this hypothesis, we compared surveys taken at about the same time but with different question wordings and found that support for Bush versus Dukakis was not strongly related to the questions that were asked. An example of the evidence for this point is the first graph in Figure 11.2. For eighteen groups of voters (Democrats, independents, Republicans, low education, high education, liberals, etc.), this figure plots the proportion of respondents in each group who supported Bush according to responses to the usual survey question posed in June and according to responses to another June survey that had an unusual question wording.[13] Most groups (represented by numbers in Figure 11.1) fall on or close to the 45-degree line, indicating that question wording did not have much effect on the measured level of support for Bush. There is a minor systematic pattern in the responses, since the nonwhites and the liberals fall above the line, whereas the Republicans and the conservatives

FIGURE 11.2

Bush support by question wording

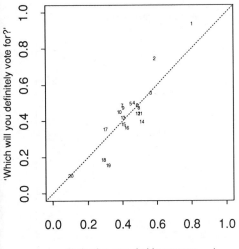

'If election were held tomorrow . . .'

Proportion undecided by question wording

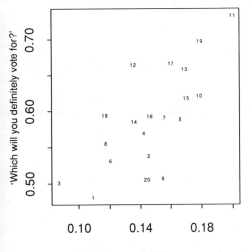

'If election were held tomorrow . . .'

Question-wording effects. This figure shows how the wording of survey questions affected the proportion of respondents who supported Bush, among those who expressed a preference, based on two surveys held at about the same time in July 1988. Along the horizontal axis is the standard question wording: "If the 1988 presidential election were being held today, would you vote for George Bush for president and Dan Quayle for vice president, the Republican candidates, or for Michael Dukakis for president and Lloyd Bentsen for vice president, the Democratic candidates?" The alternative question is represented along the vertical axis: "(George Bush is the Republican nominee for president and Michael Dukakis is the Democratic nominee.) Which (1988) presidential candidate will you definitely vote for in this year's election?" Each number in these figures represents a group of survey respondents, coded according to the legend at the right side of the graph. (The groups in the legend are ordered in decreasing support for Bush.) For example, at the top of the upper graph, the number "1" indicates that about 80 percent of Republican respondents supported Bush when asked the standard question as compared to about 90 percent under the alternative wording. Since most groups fall on or near the 45-degree line, we conclude that the differences in question wording are not very important to our analysis. However, the bottom figure indicates that question wording can greatly affect the proportion of undecided voters.

Legend: 1   Republicans
2   conservatives
3   over $50,000/year income
4   whites
5   $25,000–$50,000/year income
6   college education
7   non-South
8   men
9   over thirty years old
10   women
11   independents
12   under thirty years old
13   no college education
14   South
15   moderates
16   $15,000–$25,000/year income
17   under $15,000/year income
18   liberals
19   non-whites
20   Democrats

FIGURE 11.3

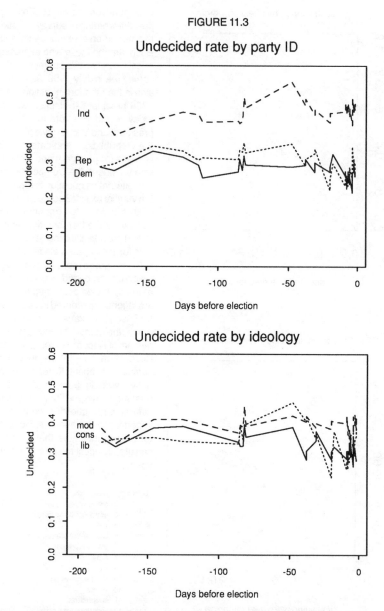

Trends in undecided respondents. This figure includes three time series plots of the proportion of survey respondents who reported being undecided as to their vote. Each line is a plot representing a different group of voters. The party identification graph tracks political independents ("Ind"), Republicans ("Rep"), and Democrats ("Dem"). The ideology graph tracks ideological moderates ("mod"), conservatives ("cons"), and liberals ("lib"). The final graph plots white and nonwhite respondents. In most cases, the lines representing different groups within each figure move in the same rather than opposite directions, which confirms that the proportion undecided did not vary by these groups.

FIGURE 11.3 (*continued*)

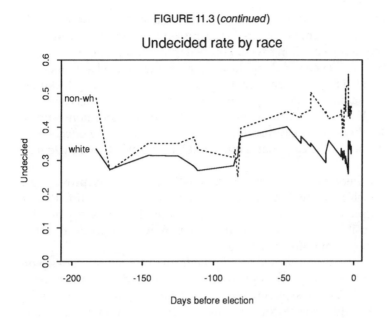

fall below it. This small effect appeared in a similar analysis, not shown here, of two September surveys. However, these patterns are much too small to account for significant parts of the main puzzle we seek to understand; moreover, they cancel out in the aggregate survey totals.

In similar analyses, we also rejected the related hypothesis that the different polling organizations produced systematically different results. We did extensive searches and explorations of this kind, finding only one systematic relationship: The proportion undecided or refusing to answer the survey question varied consistently and considerably with the question wording and polling organization. The bottom graph in Figure 11.2 demonstrates this by using the same two June polls. Groups of citizens in the two polls correlate moderately well; that is, since those groups more undecided on one question tend to be more undecided on the other, the groups fall roughly along a straight line. However, the average undecided rate differs substantially between the two surveys (about 15 percent undecided for the question on the horizontal axis and 60 percent for the question on the vertical axis), which, because of differing axes labels, can be seen in the figure by noting that 10 percent undecided on one poll does not predict 10 percent on the other. The unequal rate of undecided respondents is interesting but does not explain why support for the candidates varied so much over the course of the campaign.

Nonresponse Implies a Bias. Another hypothesis holds that survey respondents selectively refuse to answer, or say they will not vote, when their candidate is not doing as well as the other candidate. In other words, under this assumption, voters are embarrassed to support the candidate that appears not to be doing well. For example, during one party's convention, when an eventual Republican voter is interviewed at home after watching four days of a Democratic party convention, he may feel more comfortable saying he does not plan to vote or is unsure of his candidate preference. If true, this would produce a systematic item nonresponse bias. Under this scenario, campaign events would have a big effect on reported support for the candidates but could have no effect on the eventual outcome.

This is a theoretically satisfying explanation, essentially providing a completely self-consistent methodological answer to the question this essay addresses. Indeed, before we gathered our data, this explanation seemed plausible to us. Unfortunately, it is now clear to us that this nonresponse-bias hypothesis is false.

Figure 11.3 presents the evidence in the form of three time-series plots of the proportion undecided broken down by party identification, ideology, and race.[14] As can be plainly seen, the proportion undecided does not vary dramatically over the course of the campaign. But, more important for this hypothesis is that the groups vary *together*, whereas if the nonresponse-bias hypothesis were true, we would expect the opposite. Thus, it could not be that Republicans are more likely to report being undecided during the Democratic convention, and conversely. The same holds for race and for ideology.[15]

Journalists' Theories

An alternative way to resolve the paradox of volatile polls and accurate forecasts is to dismiss the forecasts, as in the first hypothesis, or to accommodate the forecasts to the journalists' interpretation of the polls, as in the second hypothesis.

The Forecasters Were Lucky Because Bush Ran a Good Campaign and Dukakis a Poor One. The simplest way to dismiss the pre-campaign forecasts of the political scientists and economists is to say they were just lucky and happened to coincide with Bush running a good campaign and Dukakis running poorly. Evidence for this hypothesis is that Bush's rapid gain in the polls coincided with what seemed to be his particularly adept campaigning.

The success of out-of-sample forecasts discussed earlier causes us to doubt this hypothesis. Moreover, as discussed by Lewis-Beck (1985), several other scholars have also produced relatively successful presidential election forecasts (for previous elections) based on different statistical models.[16] All these models do reasonably well in many election years, not only 1988. The success of all these forecasts is clearly due to more than chance, and we feel that, at this point, the burden of proof lies with the critics who still believe the forecasters are merely lucky.

In addition, what seemed to the journalists to be Bush's adept campaigning might just be a justification in hindsight of what "explained" the polls. How can we test this alternative explanation of the media's interpretation? In other words, what can be done to avoid rationalization after the fact? One possibility is to use what journalists identified as the keys to success in previous campaigns and see how the Bush and Dukakis campaigns should be judged according to those rules.

This is easily resolved: In all recent presidential election campaigns before 1988, the main rule, according to the media, was which candidate was better at "acting presidential." Bush was the first candidate in modern times to directly attack his opponent, which clearly violates the rule. In recent previous campaigns, this task was taken up by the vice-presidential candidate, campaign commercials, or prominent supporters, but never by the presidential candidate.

Thus, from this media perspective, Dukakis actually looked better than Bush during the campaign, since he was acting more presidential. If the polls continued to favor Dukakis, and he won the election, we doubt the media would have changed their criteria for evaluation. It may be that Bush's strategy was effective, but in this case the 1988 election provides only a hypothesis, not also confirmation of it. Although resolving these points without careful studies of the effect of campaign media events is probably impossible, it does seem (almost!) undeniable at times that events in the campaign are influencing the poll results.

Candidates' Fortunes Fluctuated but with Predictable Convergence. Another hypothesis holds that the polls were accurate indicators of the candidates' fortunes throughout, varying because Dukakis was legitimately ahead at the start of the campaign and Bush ran a better campaign and won the election. Rather than claiming that the forecasters were lucky, this model assumes that the election result was successfully forecast because the convergence of the poll results to the general election outcome was predictable. Thus, according to this hypothesis, support for the candidates really did change over the campaign, but this change was successfully predicted by the forecasts.

This hypothesis mixes journalists' and political science theories in that it accepts the forecast but still follows the story of the polls to understand why Bush won. It accords with the methods, but not the theories, of political science.

This hypothesis has a reasonable construction and is internally consistent. However, it does not explain why any forecasts should predict that Bush would run a better campaign—especially since the forecasting models include nothing that measures the two candidates' skills as campaign-ers. Certainly few journalists had any idea this was going to happen. Moreover, if Dukakis's advisers could have predicted that they were going to run a poor campaign, they certainly would have changed their strategy—thus making the forecast incorrect.

The Voters Were Uninformed. A final explanation posed by journalists is at the level of the voter. According to this idea, many people, or at least enough to swing elections, vote on the basis of factors that political scien-tists would not call "fundamental," such as the personality of the candi-dates, gaffes, speaking style, campaign events, and the like. According to this explanation, the voters who decide this way may truly care about these factors or may just not know enough about the fundamental vari-ables to make an informed decision. This model explains the swings in the pre-election polls but does not explain how pre-campaign forecasting methods predict so well given that the political science forecasts do not even try to account for personalities and campaign events.

Political Science Theories

In contrast, the political scientists' theories take as a starting point that the ability of economists and political scientists to accurately forecast election results months ahead of time is evidence that the election came out just as predicted. We present two flawed explanations here: The first is quite pos-sibly true, but incomplete, as it does not address the relation between the campaign and the opinion polls. The second hypothesis is plausible but can be refuted by our individual-level poll data.

The Campaigns Were Balanced. Under this hypothesis, forecasting mod-els worked in 1988 because the campaigns were balanced—that is, had roughly equal resources and expertise—and thus the election outcome oc-curred roughly as the forecaster and others had predicted on the basis of information available months before the election.

Although most journalists seem to deny this hypothesis, political scien-tists believe it to be almost certainly true. Unfortunately, even if true, it provides no solution to the key puzzle in the context of a model of voter de-cisionmaking. The 1988 presidential election, like all modern presidential elections in which no incumbent was running, pitted two major party cam-paigns that were roughly equal in strength, expertise, and resources. There are plenty of examples of astute political observers suggesting that a candi-date could have done something better; but with equal funding and the best advisers each party has to offer, it would be surprising to see cam-paigns as unbalanced as are many voter referenda and numerous local elections. We suspect that if a presidential election happened to be severely unbalanced (beyond the predictable unbalance associated with incumben-cy), political science forecasting models would probably not perform well. We happen not to have observed any such instances in modern times.

The fact that modern presidential campaigns seem to be balanced, which is consistent with the political science model of voter decisionmaking, does not solve the puzzle of why the polls varied so much. The media wisdom about the 1988 election is that the outcome is explained by Dukakis running a poor campaign. Of course, this denies the hypothesis that the campaigns are balanced.

Thus, under the political science model, balanced campaigns cause no theoretical problems, but they say nothing about why the polls vary so much. Under the journalists' implicit model, in which the polls accurately indicate the candidates' strengths, balanced campaigns are inconsistent with the observation that the polls vary a lot. In neither case does this hypothesis explain the paradox.[17]

Partisans Return to the Fold. According to another hypothesis, in January there is a large mass of undecided voters, and over the course of the campaign, the number of those who report being undecided drop as different groups move toward their natural home. This is observationally similar to the nonresponse-bias hypothesis but is theoretically very different. An elaboration of this hypothesis is that the strong partisans come home to their party first, then the weak partisans. Different events bring in different groups of voters, but under the hypothesis being discussed here, the strong ones come home first, then subsequent events bring in others later. In this model, the campaign ratchets in new groups of voters, who, once they migrate to the "decided" category, tend to stay with their preference (perhaps due to psychological justification mechanisms).

The key evidence against this thesis is that the proportion of undecided voters does not drop over the course of the campaign (refer to Figure 11.3). It is especially noteworthy that the proportion undecided does not drop during times of massive shifts in the polls (as recorded in Figure 11.1). The elaboration of this hypothesis also seems wrong, since strong Republicans supported Bush from the start and did not move much over the course of the campaign. This can be seen in the first time-series plot of Figure 11.4, Bush support by party identification.[18] Moreover, support for Bush among the Democrats actually increased during the campaign, exactly opposite to what would be expected according to this hypothesis. Short-term changes in overall support for Bush (conceivably in response to specific campaign events) actually appear to occur for Democrats, Republicans, and independents equally: The three series move together. Indeed, the same appears true for Bush support broken down by the other variables in Figure 11.4. It thus appears quite clear that support for this hypothesis in these data is largely nonexistent.

We do believe that voters are coming home to their natural preferences, but not that they are following the *particular* pattern of returning to the fold by party identification.

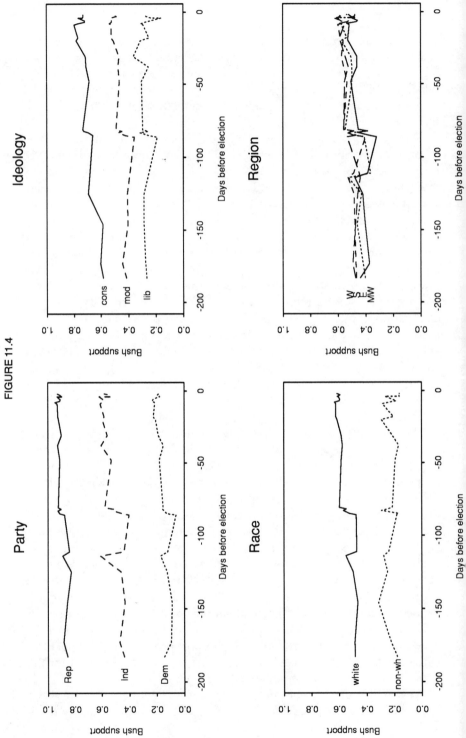

FIGURE 11.4

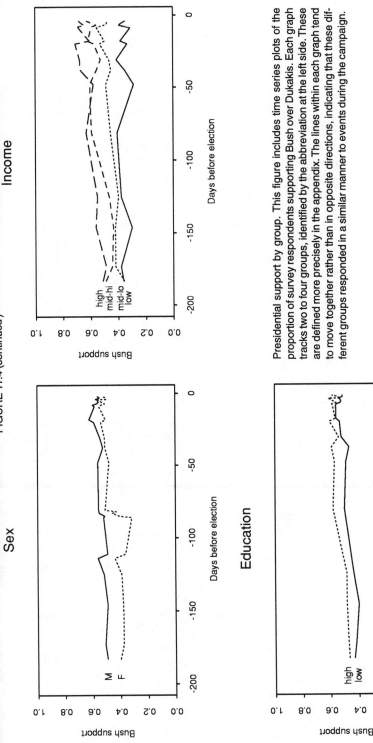

Presidential support by group. This figure includes time series plots of the proportion of survey respondents supporting Bush over Dukakis. Each graph tracks two to four groups, identified by the abbreviation at the left side. These are defined more precisely in the appendix. The lines within each graph tend to move together rather than in opposite directions, indicating that these different groups responded in a similar manner to events during the campaign.

Rational Actor Theories

These theories are also political science theories, but they differ from those in the other categories because they are based on specific assumptions about individual voters. Because of the lack of any contrary evidence, we assume for each of the theories that voters answer survey questions about candidate support sincerely. This is consistent with theoretical evidence from two-candidate, winner-take-all races, where there is not much point in strategic voting. Moreover, the assumptions of rational actor theories do not differ dramatically from the voting situation, which, although somewhat more behavioral, is not more costly.

Voters Are Fully Informed. Consider first the extreme version of the rational actor model. According to this model, people (1) have full information throughout the campaign about their fundamental variables, (2) are using all the information they have at any time to form their survey response or voting decision, and (3) are rationally accounting for their uncertainty, in the sense of maximizing some expected utility. If this model were accurate, political scientists would still forecast accurately, but the trial heat polls would not change at all over the campaign. Since the polls obviously do change, this model can be rejected, but it will nevertheless be useful in clarifying related models, as well as our preferred explanation presented earlier.

Voters Have Incomplete Information. An incomplete-information model assumes, from the full-information model, that 1 is incorrect but 2 and 3 hold. That is, voters gather information over the campaign, use this information in making their decisions, and rationally account for their uncertainty. If this model were correct, political science forecasts would work, as they do. On average over the whole campaign, we would expect changes in polls to occur in the direction of the forecasts; that is, as voters gathered more information, they would gradually move in the direction of their fundamental variables. This, too, is consistent with the evidence.

However, the model implies that changes at any one time during the campaign would be relatively small because voters would appropriately judge their uncertainty, at all times estimating the values of their fundamental variables and candidate positions. Sharp short-term changes in the polls—deviations from a trend toward the forecast poll positions—would occur only when campaign events were *unexpected,* such as if a candidate did much better than expected in a debate or made a surprise change in his or her stand on an important issue.

This model is partly right, but since we find (and show further on) that the polls do respond to information that almost certainly was anticipated by voters, we reject this explanation.[19]

TOWARD AN EXPLANATION FOR POLL VARIATION

The previous section provided sufficient evidence to dismiss several hypotheses that give plausible explanations for the great variance in trial heat polls, a variance that exists even though we are able to accurately predict presidential election outcomes. We now turn to our preferred, but quite tentative, explanation, for which we present evidence in the next section.

Our working hypothesis is that voters cast their ballots in general election contests for president on the basis of their "enlightened preferences." As with the concept of enlightened preferences in the political philosophy literature (Dahl, 1989), we do not require that people be able to discuss these preferences intelligently or even to know what they are; we only require that they know enough that their decisions are based on the true values of the fundamental variables. The function of the campaign, then, is to inform voters about the fundamental variables and their appropriate weights, notably, the candidates' ideologies and their positions on major issues.

According to this explanation, only the second of the three assumptions under the full-information rational model is correct. That is, voters do not have full information and do not rationally judge or incorporate their uncertainty, but they do gather and use increasing amounts of information over the course of the campaign, with the largest increase occurring just before election day (see Popkin, 1991). We also assume that voters answer surveys about candidate support sincerely. We elaborate this model here.

At the start of the campaign, voters do not have the information necessary to make enlightened voting decisions. Gathering this information is costly, and most citizens have no particularly good reason to gather it in time for the pollster's visit, so long as it can be gathered when needed on election day.

Most polls ask whether the respondent intends to vote, and the question appears to be answered sincerely and relatively accurately. Likely voters with insufficient information at the time of the poll still report that they will cast a ballot on election day. Unfortunately, those who consider themselves voters are willing to report to pollsters their "likely" voting decisions even if they have not gathered sufficient information to make this report accurate. The reason is the quite general point, as much psychological research has shown, that human beings are very poor at estimating uncertainty and at making fully rational decisions based on uncertain or incomplete information (Kahneman, Slovic, and Tversky, 1982). People also make decisions based on these incorrect uncertainty judgments, producing, in only this narrow sense, "irrational" decisions. Compounding the problem is the awkward situation of the survey interview: Imagine survey respondents who, when asked, indicate that they will vote; when later asked for the name of the candidate who will get their vote, they are embarrassed to reveal their ignorance or uncertainty, especially after already saying that they will vote.[20]

Thus, without sufficient knowledge of their fundamental variables, and when asked to give an opinion anyway, most respondents act as they will in the voting booth on election day: They use information at their disposal about their fundamental variables and report a "likely" vote to the pollster. We believe that this report to the pollster is sincere, but the survey response is still based on a different information set than will be available by the time of the election. It will therefore differ systematically from the eventual vote to the extent that the voter's information set improves over the course of the campaign. In relatively high-information, balanced campaigns, voters gradually improve their knowledge of their fundamental variables and generally have sufficient information by election day.

Thus, the campaign itself will confer no large unexpected advantages on one party or the other. This is why forecasting models, based on information available only at the start of the general election campaign, work well. However, this does not make the campaign irrelevant because without it election outcomes would be very different. Moreover, if one candidate were to slack off and not campaign as hard as usual, the campaigns would not be balanced and the election result would also be likely to change. Thus, presidential election campaigns play a central role making it possible for voters to become informed so that they can make decisions according to the equivalent of enlightened preferences when they get to the voting booth. This process then depends on the media to provide information, which they do throughout the campaign, and on the voters to pay attention, which they do disproportionately just before election day.

Note that we are *not* arguing that there exists an identifiable group of uninformed voters who gradually become more informed than other groups over the course of the campaign. Although it is undeniably true that knowledge varies considerably across citizens at any one time, we find that virtually *all* groups of eventual voters have their preferences gradually enlightened during the campaign by roughly the same amounts.

If this explanation for our central puzzle is correct, the only remaining question is not why the polls move in the direction they do; we already know that they move in the direction of the political scientists' forecasts. The relevant question is why they begin where they do. Our hypothesis is that the early position of the polls is a result of the information that is readily available at the start of the general election campaign. For example, Dukakis's race against only Jesse Jackson at the end of the Democratic nomination positioned him as quite conservative. In part as a result of this, Dukakis was seen at the start of the general election campaign as more conservative than he was (and at times even more conservative than Bush). As citizens learned more about the appropriate values of their fundamental variables, voter support for the candidates changed.

EVIDENCE FOR ENLIGHTENED PREFERENCES

As we indicated at the start of this essay, we have much more evidence proving many possible explanations wrong than proving one right. In particular, we are handicapped in our analysis here by having no direct measures of voter information over the campaign, or of some of the fundamental variables the forecasters use in their models.[21] Our strategy, then, is to extract whatever information is available in our data and leave it to future research to more firmly establish or refute this explanation.

We begin by providing evidence that preferences early in the campaign are relatively unenlightened. From one perspective, this should neither be difficult nor perhaps even necessary to show, since numerous scholarly studies have demonstrated the ignorance of Americans about most matters of policy and politics. However, we do not require citizens to be able to verbalize their motivations or detailed positions on their fundamental variables. The idea of making voting decisions on the basis of enlightened preferences only requires that voters cast their ballots in the same manner as if they had full information and time for complete consideration of all issues. Thus, survey questions about citizen knowledge would not directly deal with our concerns. For the same reasons, it would also not be a good strategy to ask survey respondents what their fundamental variables are. A measure of the "revealed preferences" of this group of citizens would be better, but one cannot observe individual-level political behavior in polling data.

Instead we look for systematic discrepancies between actual voter support and expected support, which we calculate on the basis of measured demographic and fundamental variables. We do this in four different ways in this section, each a different observable consequence of the same theory of poll variation described previously. We begin by demonstrating the "irrationality" of early poll movements. Next we show that the fundamental variables are of increasing importance over the campaign. We explore how voters weight the fundamental variables in decisionmaking in the next section and then demonstrate that changes in these weights, and not the values of the variables, are what account for poll fluctuations.

The "Irrationality" of Early Poll Movements

We first demonstrate that voters do not "rationally" account for uncertainty in using information to make decisions about supporting presidential candidates. We show this by focusing on predictable changes associated with totally expected campaign events, changes that should not occur if survey respondents are fully rational.

Figure 11.5 presents the proportion of supporters for each party over the course of the campaign, along with the times of the Democratic and Republican party conventions. In order to see more clearly the effects of these party conventions on support for the presidential candidates, we plot the proportion supporting the Republican candidate before and after each convention since 1964.[22] Republican conventions are marked "R" and Democratic conventions are marked "d." If a point appears above the 45-degree line, Republican support went up after the convention; if it is below the line, Republican support dropped. If these conventions had no effect on the level of support, the points would be scattered randomly on and about the 45-degree line. The results are unambiguous: Support for the Republican candidate increased after all Republican conventions and decreased after all but one Democratic convention. The 1988 conventions, which are circled, are fairly typical of the points on the graph, lending credence to our more detailed analysis of that election year.[23]

The clear results from Figure 11.5 are consistent with our earlier explanation, for if people were informed and reflective about their candidate preferences early on in the campaign, they would also be able to predict that their opinions would change after each party convention. In that case, they would realize that they should change these preferences immediately. Thus, if people were rationally incorporating their uncertainty about future events, we would not witness any *predictable* changes in support for the candidates. Recall that if the full- or incomplete-information rational models were correct, only *unexpected* information would change voter preferences. Yet, almost all aspects of modern political conventions have also been extremely predictable, from the nominee to most aspects of the platform, and even the "spontaneous demonstrations" on the convention floor for various candidates. We know that conventions produce, almost exclusively, expected information from merely watching the news on the days leading up to the conventions. Moreover, any voter who was aware during the convention four years earlier (or was reminded of this by the media) should not be surprised by anything that happened during any recent political convention.[24]

This logic also applies more generally if the political science forecasts can be believed. Since we can predict whom respondents will end up supporting on election day, if they were enlightened at the start or rationally incorporated their uncertainty all along, they would change their prefer-

FIGURE 11.5

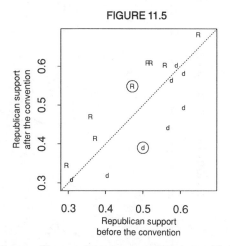

Effects of Republican and Democratic party conventions on presidential campaign polls, 1964–1992 (conventions in 1988 circled). This figure summarizes all the plots in Figure 11.1 before and after the party conventions. Each "R" refers to survey support for the Republicans before and after a Republican convention; each "d" indicates support before and after a Democratic convention. Symbols above the 45-degree line indicate that support for the Republican candidate increased during the convention, whereas symbols below the line indicate that support for Bush declined. Note that all R's appear above the line and almost all d's appear below the line. The 1988 conventions are circled and appear typical of public opinion swings during the conventions.

ences only minimally throughout the campaign. Since they do change their preferences, and since convention and other changes are largely predictable, we conclude that many people are unenlightened at the beginning of the campaign and are not rationally incorporating uncertain information in their decisions.

Another observable implication of the enlightenment hypothesis that we can evaluate is whether these changes are also predictable for subgroups of the electorate. Our data on groups include all two-way interactions among ideology, region, education, sex, income, party, and race—all the covariates on which we had information for a large number of our sample surveys (see the appendix). Two-way interactions include all combinations of groups such as nonwhite Democrats, highly educated southerners, lower-middle-income males, and conservative females.[25]

Figure 11.6 contains a particularly compact way of presenting a large subset of this group-level information. Consider first the party graph in Figure 11.6A. Each of the two-way groups that include party classification is plotted on this graph, with eventual Bush support on the horizontal axis and the trend in Bush support on the vertical axis. This trend in Bush support is calculated as the change from before to after the Democratic convention (11.6A), the Republican convention (11.6B), and the last forty days

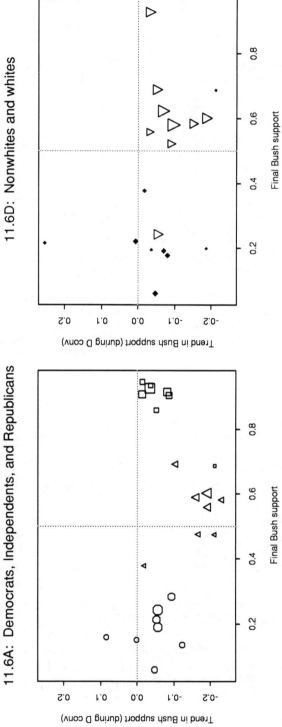

FIGURE 11.6

11.6A: Democrats, Independents, and Republicans

11.6D: Nonwhites and whites

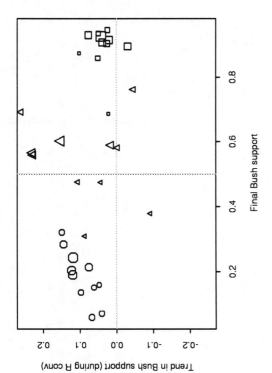

11.6E: Nonwhites and whites

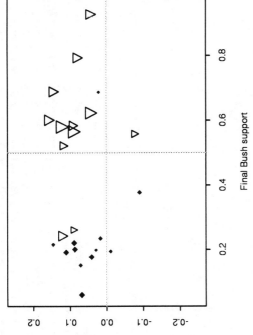

11.6B: Democrats, Independents, and Republicans

Legend: O Democrats
        △ Independents
        □ Republicans

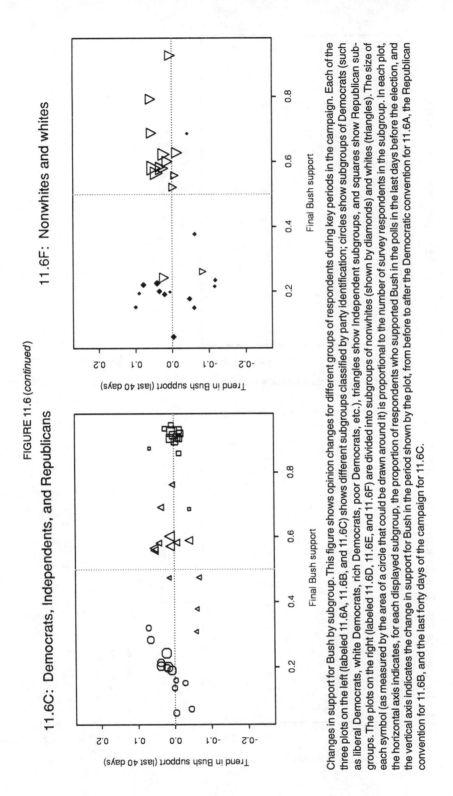

FIGURE 11.6 (continued)

11.6C: Democrats, Independents, and Republicans

11.6F: Nonwhites and whites

Changes in support for Bush by subgroup. This figure shows opinion changes for different groups of respondents during key periods in the campaign. Each of the three plots on the left (labeled 11.6A, 11.6B, and 11.6C) shows different subgroups classified by party identification; circles show subgroups of Democrats (such as liberal Democrats, white Democrats, rich Democrats, poor Democrats, etc.), triangles show Independent subgroups, and squares show Republican subgroups. The plots on the right (labeled 11.6D, 11.6E, and 11.6F) are divided into subgroups of nonwhites (shown by diamonds) and whites (triangles). The size of each symbol (as measured by the area of a circle that could be drawn around it) is proportional to the number of survey respondents in the subgroup. In each plot, the horizontal axis indicates, for each displayed subgroup, the proportion of respondents who supported Bush in the last days before the election, and the vertical axis indicates the change in support for Bush in the period shown by the plot, from before to after the Democratic convention for 11.6A, the Republican convention for 11.6B, and the last forty days of the campaign for 11.6C.

of the campaign (11.6C). We define only the party of each group by the type of symbol drawn—circles for Democrats, triangles for independents, and squares for Republicans. The size of each symbol (as measured by the area of a circle drawn around it) plotted for each group is proportional to the number of respondents it includes. Figure 11.6A shows that all Republican groups eventually supported Bush very strongly (all the squares are to the right on this graph), with only one small group (the nonwhite Republicans) containing less than 80 percent of Bush supporters. All Democratic groups also ended up being Dukakis supporters, although their support has a lower mean and a higher variance. Independent groups end up nearer to the middle, although most did wind up giving Bush majority support.

Figure 11.6A also demonstrates that almost all of the many groups during the Democratic convention predictably increased their support for Dukakis (as shown in 11.6A by almost all the symbols being below the horizontal line drawn at zero change). Independents moved the most in this direction, but change among Democrats and Republicans was about the same. Figure 11.6B shows the same relationship for the Republican convention; and the results are a mirror image, with almost all groups increasing their support for the Republican party's nominee. Democrats appeared to change somewhat more than Republicans, and independents still changed the most; but the pattern is about the same.

Figure 11.6.C portrays the trend in support for the candidates over the last forty days of the campaign. In this period, the action was among the Democratic and independent groups, most of which steadily moved toward Bush. Most Republican groups changed very little from their already high level of Bush support.

In total, the three party graphs (11.6A, 11.6B, and 11.6C) provide additional, more detailed group-level evidence. They show that even among the many groups of voters studied here, party conventions do not consolidate support among one's own partisans but rather affect partisans of both types in similar and predictable ways. These graphs also show that independents, and in general groups near the middle, respond most extremely to the conventions. This is consistent with our hypothesis, not because these citizens are the least enlightened, but because these voters tend to be on the margin; thus, changes in knowledge of fundamental variables produced by the conventions produce larger shifts in the fraction of respondents supporting one candidate or the other than in other groups not so near the margin. The same is true of other party groups near the middle of the graphs. Thus, this evidence is consistent with the idea that all voter groups become enlightened by roughly the same amount over the course of the campaign, even though such enlightenment has different effects on voter support for the various groups.[26]

Finally, Figures 11.6A, 11.6B, and 11.6C demonstrate that the picture was somewhat asymmetric with respect to the parties during the period after the last convention, and even partially during the Republican convention. Since Republican groups supported Bush much more uniformly than Democrats supported Dukakis (as is evidenced in the figures by the relative dispersion of the squares as compared to the circles), this too is consistent with the idea that voter groups more divided in support will respond more to changes in fundamental variables. But this result can also be explained in a more direct, substantive way: Bush supporters were more unified in part because Bush was the candidate more known by the public. Dukakis was a more unknown quantity; it should be no surprise that early Democratic voter support was more spread out between the parties. And because more of these voters were closer to indifference about the two candidates, changes in knowledge of their fundamental variables would have more of an effect.[27] Thus, roughly the same change in enlightenment that occurs to all citizens has different effects depending on their earlier support for the candidates.

Figure 11.6 also contains analogous figures for racial groups (11.6D, 11.6E, and 11.6F, with nonwhites represented by solid diamonds and whites by open triangles), and the conclusions are largely the same. The Democratic party convention increased support for Dukakis and the Republican convention increased support for Bush among almost all groups of white and nonwhite voters. Exceptions in these graphs include a group of white liberals and white Democrats, each of which appears to act more like the nonwhite groups. There is also a small group of nonwhite Republicans that appears among the white groups. During the three periods, the white groups were somewhat more cohesive and less variable.

The Fundamental Variables' Increasing Importance During the Campaign

If voters are becoming enlightened, then the fundamental variables should be increasing in importance over the campaign. Figure 11.6 is consistent with this hypothesis, since individual groups are becoming more homogeneous, thus increasing heterogeneity across groups, even within parties. More generally, if voters are basing their survey responses more on the fundamental variables over the course of the campaign, as we hypothesize, then groups of voters (categorized by these variables) should become increasingly distinctive—homogeneous within and heterogeneous across the groups. The observable implication of this process, which we now evaluate, is the extent to which voter groups are more heterogeneous as the campaign progresses.

One confirmation of increasing homogeneity within individual groups, and consequently increasing heterogeneity across groups, is shown in Figure 11.7. This figure plots a measure of the *true* heterogeneity across subgroups within parties by measuring the observed variance in support for Bush across subgroups and subtracting out the expected sampling variance of this measure.[28]

We consider each party separately in Figure 11.7 so as to see fine detail; if groups in different parties were included, the variances would be so large as to dwarf the changes over time.

Each circle in Figure 11.7 plots our measure of the heterogeneity across groups for a specific time during the general election campaign. For help in viewing trends in this graph, we plot a nonparametric regression line on each (called "lowess").[29] Consistent with the idea that enlightenment occurs throughout the campaign, heterogeneity across groups is clearly increasing for the Democrats and independents throughout the entire campaign (i.e., partisans are sorting themselves out more clearly by subgroup). As would be expected, this enlightenment mostly occurs just before election day, when voters must pay attention if they are to vote on the basis of their fundamental variables. However, heterogeneity is not changing noticeably among Republican groups. This is consistent with the idea that enlightenment, occurring to all citizens at roughly the same degree and speed, has the largest effect on the voter preferences of groups— such as independents and those who are the eventual supporters of the more unknown candidate—that were more indifferent about the candidates. Although we had guessed that the line for the Republican graph would be increasing too, it should be no surprise that many fewer Republicans were indifferent early on about both a Republican incumbent president and a considerably less well known Democratic challenger.

How Respondents Weight Fundamental Variables

We can now more directly address the issue of the role of the fundamental variables and the weights given to them by survey respondents throughout the election campaign. We do this by using all available covariates to predict support for Bush or Dukakis with a logistic regression in each survey. These explanatory variables—party, ideology, race, sex, income, education, and region—are not perfect measures for what political science research has taught are the fundamental variables on which most citizens base their voter preferences, but they are the best we have available given what questions happened to be asked in the surveys. They are also the most important individual-level variables, since scholars have found that incumbency and economic variables in the United States affect the vote

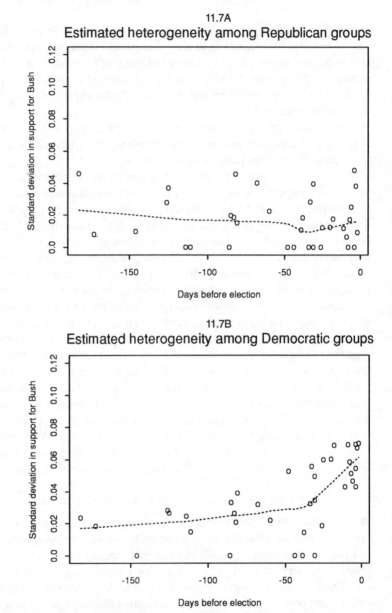

FIGURE 11.7

11.7A
Estimated heterogeneity among Republican groups

Days before election

11.7B
Estimated heterogeneity among Democratic groups

Days before election

Heterogeneity among party groups. Each circle in Figure 11.7A corresponds to a different national survey, with a measure of heterogeneity among subgroups of Republicans plotted versus the date of the survey. The heterogeneity measure is an estimate of the standard deviation in support for Bush across the subgroups, corrected for the sampling variability in the poll. The dotted line is a smooth curve designed to show the trend over time. Figures 11.7B and 11.7C similarly show heterogeneity across subgroups of Democrats and Independents, respectively. The increase in heterogeneity for two of these graphs indicate that survey respondents were sorting themselves out more clearly into their respective subgroups.

FIGURE 11.7 *(continued)*

11.7C
Estimated heterogeneity among Independent groups

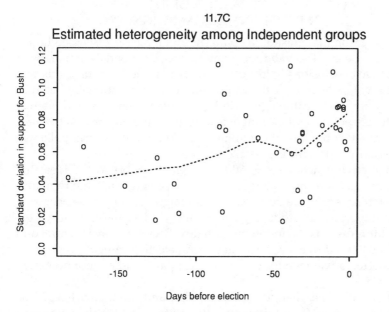

Days before election

decision primarily through their true, and not perceived, values. Certainly party, ideology, and race are among the fundamental variables, and all are expected to have a strong effect on voting (or support) decisions. Sex should have a small effect, with women supporting the Democrats slightly more; income and region should have a somewhat larger effect; but conditional on the other variables, education should have almost no effect. The fact that we do not have measures in these surveys of all the variables the forecasters use in their models is a real limitation of this logistic regression analysis, and this is an important area for the focus of future research.[30] These hypotheses from previous research only suggest the weights of the fundamental variables in the final analysis, as election day nears. Our enlightenment hypothesis suggests that early on in the campaign the importance of these variables may be different, although exactly what that difference is, we do not predict. Using a logistic regression analysis, we found that the movement in the polls in the five months before the election is consistent with the hypothesis that as survey respondents become more enlightened in the late stages of the campaign, their preferences align with their fundamental variables as predicted months earlier. For most of these variables, the effect estimates vary considerably over the entire campaign. In 1988, race and ideology mattered less at the start of the campaign than at the end, whereas the effect of region among nonwhites and the effect of gender were much higher early on.[31]

CONCLUSION: THE ROLE OF THE MEDIA
IN PRESIDENTIAL CAMPAIGNS

We see no reason that most of the patterns and forecasts discussed in this essay would be any less valid for many future presidential campaigns. If our tentative conclusions hold up to further empirical scrutiny, this will mean that voters learn over the campaign but do not rationally incorporate uncertainty. The campaigns will be relatively balanced, and we will be able to use political science models to forecast the outcome of the election accurately at the time the nominees are known. And early polls will not necessarily reflect the eventual outcome.

Our tentative conclusions would also lend support to the idea that presidential elections are one institution where voters use their enlightened preferences to make decisions.[32] Campaigns, as they have been run, are very important in producing this result. Underlying the puzzle explored in this essay is the following paradox: Because of their central and relatively balanced role, presidential general election campaigns produce no unexpected advantage for either political party and are not necessary for forecasting.

What specific role, then, do the campaign and the media have? The most important role, from this perspective, is to enlighten the voters—to give them sufficient information in a timely fashion so that they can make up their minds relatively easily. The media can continue to make the campaign relatively fair by giving both candidates a reasonable opportunity to express their views, thus continuing to help inform the voters. All this will help make voters aware of where the candidates stand and help them learn the values of their fundamental variables and their appropriate weights. Informing voters about candidates' positions on issues is therefore the most important role of the media, and it should hardly be controversial (or novel) to suggest that they spend more time on it. All of our forecasting models require that voters know where the candidates stand, so their being informed will also not change our ability to forecast. Moreover, even though more attention to informing voters by the media will probably not change the outcome of the election, it would not hurt to improve the level of "enlightened deliberation" during the campaign. Issues and proposed solutions do get raised and discussed, and increasing the level of explicit voter knowledge about these issues (which is presently quite low) could only improve the odds of reaching consensus among elected representatives.

Finally, journalists should realize that they can report the polls all they want and continue to make incorrect causal inferences about them, but they are not helping to predict or even influence the election.[33] Journalists play a critical role in enabling voters to make decisions based on the equivalent of explicitly enlightened preferences. Unfortunately, by focusing more on the polls and meaningless campaign events, the media are spending more and more time on "news" that has less and less of an effect.

The public opinion horse race of the early general election is of tremendous popular interest, so one can hardly blame the media for focusing on it so much. Perhaps the research presented here might help the media, and eventually citizens, to realize that winning this early "race" is worth nothing: It does not help win the election; and it does not even help the candidates raise money (since general elections for president are now publicly funded). Because being ahead in the early polls is worth almost nothing, perhaps journalists and then the public will understand that the polls are also not worthy of as much attention as they get. Do we really need to spend so much public attention on which horse first gets into the starting booth?

APPENDIX

The forty-nine national public opinion polls we used are listed in Table 11.2 with the polling organization, the number of days before the election on which the survey took place, and the sample size. We used all these surveys at different times in the analysis, but some analyses used only a subset of surveys (primarily CBS and ABC) due to the frequency with which various survey questions were asked. In all analyses, we weighted respondents by the survey weights supplied by the respective polling organizations.

For the figures in the essay, we used the following coding schemes for individual-level responses. For *Vote,* we used the respondent's preference for the Democratic or Republican ticket when available and otherwise for the Democratic or Republican presidential candidate. The most typical question wording can be found in Note 9. Those who reported leaning toward one party or another are not included. (Including or excluding "leaners" had little effect on our results.)

For *Education,* "low" refers to a respondent with no college, and "high" to one with some college experience (including those who fail to graduate). For *Race,* we used white versus nonwhite for the two-way graphs. *Party* is coded in three categories for the two-way graphs: Republican, Democratic, and a third category consisting of independents, no answer, and those who prefer minor parties.

Region of the country is coded as Northeast, Midwest, South, and West, and the logistic regression differences are South versus non-South. *Ideology* for graphs with two-way groups is coded in three categories: (1) very

TABLE 11.2
Individual-Level Presidential Campaign Polls in 1988

Days	Org.	n	Days	Org.	n	Days	Org.	n
183	CBS	1,382	81	CBS	1,689	19	Gallup	1,013
178	Roper	1,962	68	Harris	1,889	18	Gallup	1,009
173	ABC	1,508	63	AP	1,125	18	CBS	1,827
146	ABC	1,012	61	Roper	1,003	14	Yank	1,475
139	AP	1,223	60	LAT	1,418	11	Harris	1,899
126	CBS	1,177	48	CBS	1,195	10	Roper	1,976
126	LAT	2,277	44	ABC	1,307	9	CBS	1,650
125	ABC	1,539	39	Yank	1,008	8	CBS	1,690
122	Roper	1,968	38	CBS	1,530	7	CBS	1,862
114	ABC	603	34	ABC	1,392	6	CBS	1,977
111	ABC	622	33	Harris	1,999	4	CBS	704
110	Gallup	948	31	LAT	607	4	CBS	1,505
86	ABC	605	31	LAT	543	4	Yank	1,006
85	ABC	1,021	31	CBS	1,518	3	CBS	2,188
83	ABC	791	26	ABC	1,369	2	CBS	2,227
82	ABC	812	25	Harris	1,995			
82	Gallup	1,000	20	CBS	1,447			

Note: "Days" refers to the number of days before the 1988 Presidential election, "Org." is the polling organization (Harris, Yankelovich, CBS/New York Times, ABC/Washington Post, LA Times, Associated Press/Media General, Roper, or Gallup), and "n" is the sample size, including undecided voters. For reference, the Democratic convention began at 114 days and ended at 111 days, and the Republican convention ran from 86 days to 82 days.

conservative, conservative, moderate-conservative; (2) moderate, others, no answer; (3) moderate-liberal, liberal, very liberal.

Income for the graphs with two-way groups is broken into four categories: less than $15,000, $10,000–$25,000, $20,000–$50,000, and more than $50,000. The categories overlap slightly because of discrete reporting.

NOTES

We thank Eric Oliver and Maggie Trevor for research assistance; Larry Bartels, Neal Beck, Tom Belin, Mo Fiorina, John Kessel, Mik Laver, Eileen McDonaugh, Phil Paolino, Doug Price, Phillip Price, and Sid Verba for helpful comments; and the National Science Foundation for research grant SBR-9223637. This is a revised version of an essay that received the *Pi Sigma Alpha* award for the best paper at the annual meeting of the Midwest Political Science Association, Chicago, April 9–11, 1992. A longer, more technical version of this essay is forthcoming in the *British Journal of Political Science* under the title "Why Are U.S. Presidential Election Campaign Polls So Variable When Votes Are So Predictable?" Reprinted as adapted with permission from the *British Journal of Political Science*.

1. Lewis-Beck (1985) and Lewis-Beck and Rice (1992) review many other statistical forecasting models. Lichtman and DeCell (1990) and Forsythe, Nelson, Neumann, and Wright (1991) present some nonstatistical approaches to forecast-

ing presidential elections. Social scientists have been explaining and forecasting individual votes and aggregate election outcomes almost since the start of the discipline. The first quantitative article published in a political science journal (about political science) was on voting behavior (Ogburn and Goltra, 1919), and voting, particularly in presidential elections, has almost always remained a lively area of research.

2. In *Forecasting Presidential Elections* (1983:122), Rosenstone also reports sending letters on October 14, 1980, to twenty scholars with his forecasts of the November 1980 election.

3. See, for example, Budge and Farlie (1977); Tufte (1978); Fair (1978, 1982, 1988); Campbell (1992); Lewis-Beck and Rice (1992).

4. See Beck (1992, 1993); Greene (1993).

5. We presented these forecasts several weeks before the election in public lectures at Harvard University and the University of California, Berkeley, as well as in communications with several others.

6. Our extensive analyses, some of which are reported in this essay, indicate that one can safely merge the data from the different polling organizations in order to study trends in candidate support but not percent undecided or not responding.

7. We chose the 1988 election because it was the most recent when we began our analyses. We completed all but the final draft of this essay before the 1992 election.

8. These polls are a vast and relatively untapped data source for election studies. As the appendix describes, most of the surveys also include a number of useful explanatory variables. Although each poll does not always include the exact question we would prefer, these polls do contain a considerable amount of data—considerably more interviews from 1988 alone than the sum total of all the interviews from every presidential National Election Survey since 1952. See Asher (1988b) for a general review of polls and the public.

9. The survey question asked most often was, "If the 1988 Presidential election were being held today, would you vote for George Bush for President and Dan Quayle for Vice President, the Republican candidates, or for Michael Dukakis for President and Lloyd Bentsen for Vice-President, the Democratic candidates?" Analogous questions were asked in the other years. We confront potential problems of question wording further on in the essay.

10. For a similar argument, see Markus (1988).

11. See Franklin and Jackson (1983). We can distinguish between two kinds of fundamental variables: (1) characteristics of the voters and their situations, including their positions on issues, party identification, ideology, economic conditions, and so on; and (2) voter's perceived characteristics of the candidates, such as the candidates' ideology and positions on issues. There are also variables such as incumbency that modulate the effect of the second category of fundamental variable: If you run a stronger campaign, you are more likely to convey a positive message about yourself relative to the other candidate. Variables in the first category change very little over the campaign; variables in the second are directly influenced by the campaign.

12. Lesley Stahl, CBS News broadcast, July 22, 1988, during the Democratic convention; *Newsweek*, September 5, 1988; *Newsweek*, September 19, 1988.

13. The standard question wording is in Note 9 and the unusual question word-ing in this June poll is, "(George Bush is the Republican nominee for president and Michael Dukakis is the Democratic nominee.) Which (1988) presidential candidate will you definitely vote for in this year's election?"

14. These proportions are corrected for differences due to varying survey meth-odologies across the different survey organizations.

15. Other variables also give similar results. We show in the appendix that party identification and ideology are largely exogenous variables, not responding much to changes in voter preferences or anything else that changes during the campaign.

16. See, for example, Fair (1978) and updates.

17. The two models are also inconsistent with one another about the evidence they provide on who ran a better campaign in 1988. Contrary to the journalists' claims (and even Dukakis himself), most political science models showed Dukakis doing well or even better than expected, perhaps because Dukakis's vice-president selection was better (from an electoral perspective) than Bush's.

18. The appendix shows that party identification and ideology in the popula-tion are roughly constant during the campaign.

19. According to Condorcet's "jury theorem," if some voters have incomplete information, then, under certain conditions, a majority-rule electoral system will produce outcomes equivalent to the situation if all voters are informed. This is ob-viously relevant to our inquiry except that the assumptions required to prove this theorem are far too restrictive. Scholars have recently been quite successful at dropping some of these restrictive assumptions, so perhaps in the near future the two lines of research will converge. (See Miller, 1986; Ladha, 1992.)

20. Designing surveys so as to reduce this embarrassment, making it easy to re-port "no opinion," would not necessarily improve the forecasting ability of the polls, since those voters who express a "certain" opinion seem to mirror the sur-vey population as a whole; see the discussion of question wording in the essay and Figure 11.2. A very useful future research project would be to design a survey or experiment to encourage voters to account rationally for their uncertainty (per-haps by giving them more time or financial incentives to give the "right" answer) and see if it makes a difference in their answer.

21. Some of the most important variables forecasters use do not change over the course of the campaign, such as incumbency status and some other national vari-ables. That we have no information on these does not affect our inferences because they are effectively controlled by being held constant. The remaining variables that might have some effect include perceived economic well-being and perceived ideological distances between voters and candidates, both of which might change over the campaign.

22. We omit 1952–1960 from Figure 11.5 because Gallup did not list polls be-tween the two conventions for those years.

23. Campbell, Cherry, and Wink (in press) also discuss poll movements during conventions.

24. A small amount of uncertainty is reduced by the conventions, but this could not account for the systematically predictable shifts in voter support in Figures 11.1 and 11.5.

25. We also tried the following analyses with all three-way interactions and obtained similar results except that the many groups with small numbers of voters increased sampling error and thus made the results much more variable and more difficult to interpret.

26. We have conducted extensive analyses, not presented here, searching for identifiable groups of respondents who become relatively more "informed" or "enlightened" as the campaign progresses. Even using education and many other variables, we have found no clear evidence for differences across groups in the speed with which they learn during the campaign.

27. Indeed, this concept should be useful for predicting changes in group support over the campaign. In general, groups that are more divided at the start of the campaign will move the most as the campaign progresses.

28. For an explanation of how this was derived, see the discussion of Figure 7 in the longer version of this essay in the *British Journal of Political Science*.

29. Each point on the lowess curve is calculated by weighted least squares, with the points in closest proximity on the horizontal axis given the highest weights. See Cleveland (1979); Becker, Chambers, and Wilks (1988).

30. In fact, we do have many additional survey questions aside from those we analyze, but these were not asked in as many polls. Thus far, our auxiliary studies of these questions do not suggest any changes in the conclusions presented in this essay.

31. See the discussion of Figures 8 and 9 in the longer version of this article in the *British Journal of Political Science*.

32. Of course, we have shown only that voters base their decisions on the variables that political scientists call "fundamental." However, these are not trivial variables from a normative perspective, such as the candidates' personalities or good looks; they are at least a good portion of the variables on which voters "should" base their decisions in order to fulfill general notions of democratic citizenship.

33. Reporting the polls does not seem to influence the outcome, since there is no evidence of a "halo effect"—the winner in the early polls does not inevitably win the election—although it may work strongly in primaries.

PART FIVE

The Parties in Government

12

Parties in Congress:
New Roles and
Leadership Trends

BARBARA SINCLAIR

According to the theory of party government, the winning party is expected to organize the government, set the policy agenda, and enact that
agenda into law. In the United States, the congressional parties have traditionally played an important role in organizing the legislature, but the
governmental structure and the sort of parties it has fostered have often
made it difficult for Congress and its agent, the leadership, to perform the
policy functions. Because members of Congress do not and never have
owed their election to strong centralized parties, numerical majorities do
not translate directly into policy majorities. Although almost all members
of Congress are elected under the banner of one or the other of the two
major parties, individual members are not bound either to work with or to
vote with their party colleagues.

A constellation of changes in the Congress during the 1970s, most observers agreed, greatly exacerbated the already severe problems congressional party leaders faced. The dispersion of influence within the Congress and changes in the electoral arena that further reduced the influence
of parties on members' reelection chances, it was argued, made the congressional party increasingly irrelevant and policy-oriented party leadership impossible.

Yet by the mid- to late 1980s, a cohesive majority party led by an activist, policy-involved leadership had emerged in the House of Representatives. According to the usual voting measures, House Democrats are
more cohesive now than they have been at any time since the New Deal
era. When compared to its predecessors of the previous half-century, the
current majority party leadership is more involved in and more decisive
in organizing the party and the chamber, setting the policy agenda, shaping legislation, and determining legislative outcomes. Although stronger

in the sense of being more consequential, the contemporary congressional party and its leadership are not rigidly hierarchical or highly directive; they are, rather, inclusive and participatory. Members can pursue both their policy and their participation goals, now often most effectively, through the party and with the help of its leadership; as a result, the congressional party has become more central to members' congressional lives. The purpose of this essay is to describe the leadership's and the party's current expanded role and explain its emergence (see also Sinclair, 1992a, 1992b).

The essay begins with a brief sketch of the restricted role of party and party leadership in the 1950s and 1960s. Also discussed in that section are the changes in Congress in the 1970s that were widely interpreted as further constraining the exercise of party leadership. A description of the expanded role of the current majority party and its leadership in the House and an analysis of the leadership's emergence constitute the second section and the heart of the essay. The third section is devoted to Senate comparisons: Have the role of the party leadership and the importance of parties changed in the Senate as well? The final section represents an attempt to provide a systematic answer to a key question: Why has a stronger congressional party emerged in what is often regarded as a weak party era?

PARTIES AND PARTY LEADERSHIP DURING THE COMMITTEE GOVERNMENT AND EARLY POST-REFORM ERA

The period from approximately 1920 through 1970 can be characterized as an era of committee government in the House of Representatives (Fenno, 1965, 1973). Legislation was the product of a number of autonomous committees headed by powerful chairmen who derived their positions from their seniority on the committees. The chairmen's great organizational and procedural powers over their committees and mutual deference among committees protected most legislation from serious challenge on the floor of the House.

Within this system, the role of the majority party and its leadership was restricted. Both the Speaker's meager institutional resources and, especially for Democrats who were in the majority for most of the period after 1930 and continuously from 1955 on, party factionalism limited the scope of the party leadership's involvement and its influence. Committee assignments are made through the congressional party, and this potentially provides the leadership with its most significant role in organizing the party and the chamber. During the committee government era, the seniority rule for choosing committee chairmen and the norm guaranteeing members the right to stay on a committee once assigned to it limited the party's and the leadership's roles. The party leadership did exert considerable influence over the initial assignment of members to committees, but even here the leaders' role was restricted. The party leaders did not serve on the "committee on committees."

Since Franklin Roosevelt's time, whenever the president and the congressional majority are of the same party, the president sets the majority party's and the Congress's policy agendas. During the committee government era, when control of Congress and the White House was divided, the majority party's policy agenda consisted of whatever emerged from the autonomous committees. The House Democratic party lacked any mechanism either for developing a party agenda or for imposing one upon powerful committee chairmen. In the 1950s the ideological split between northern and southern Democrats would, in any case, have made agreement upon an agenda impossible.

The Democratic Caucus, the organization of all House Democrats, did not serve as a forum for policy discussion or for providing committees with party direction on matters of policy. It met only at the beginning of a Congress and then largely confined itself to ratifying decisions made elsewhere. The party leadership's role in the policy process was largely restricted to facilitating passage at the floor stage of legislation written by autonomous committees (Ripley, 1967). Party leaders seldom if ever interceded in committee to shape legislation; the chairmen's power and norms of deference to committee worked against such involvement.

Even the leadership's role at the floor stage was somewhat restricted. Although the Speaker as presiding officer had considerable control over the flow of legislation to and on the floor, the independence of the Rules Committee during this period meant that the party leadership's control over the scheduling of legislation for floor consideration was only partial. Intercommittee reciprocity meant that most committees could expect to pass most of their legislation on the floor without great difficulty; consequently, committees and their chairs did not often require help from the leadership. However, on highly controversial issues that were fought out on the floor, the leadership often confronted a deep North-South split and had great difficulty in successfully building winning coalitions.

Elections in the late 1950s and the 1960s brought into the House a large number of liberal northern Democrats who found this system ill-suited to advancing their goals. The powerful committee chairmen were largely conservative southerners; they, not the party leadership or the party as a whole, set the policy agenda and determined the substance of legislation. The chairmen thwarted the liberals' policy goals by blocking liberal legislation and frustrated the liberals' desire to participate meaningfully in the legislative process by the often autocratic way they ran their committees (see Bolling, 1965).

In the late 1960s and early 1970s reform-minded members succeeded in instituting a series of changes in chamber and party rules that transformed the House. Sunshine reforms opened up most committee markups and conference committee meetings to the media and the public. Resources (most important, staff) available to Congress and its members were increased and distributed much more broadly among members. A series of rules changes shifted influence from committee chairmen to subcommittee chairmen and rank-and-file members. The subcommittee bill of rights removed from committee chairmen the power to appoint subcommittee chairmen and gave it to the Democratic Caucus portion of the committee; it guaranteed subcommittees automatic referral of legislation and adequate budget and staff. Members were limited to chairing no more than one subcommittee each (Dodd and Oppenheimer, 1977).

Some of the rules changes of the 1970s were intended to enhance the policy role of the party and of the leadership as the party's agent. The requirement that committee chairmen and the chairmen of Appropriations subcommittees win majority approval in the Democratic Caucus was intended to make them responsive to a party majority. The Speaker was given the right to nominate Democratic members of the Rules Committee subject only to ratification by the caucus. The committee-assignment function was shifted to the new Steering and Policy Committee, which the Speaker chairs and a number of whose members he appoints. The new multiple referral rules gave the Speaker authority to set a deadline for reporting when legislation is referred to more than one committee. The budget process has centralizing potential (Ellwood and Thurber, 1981). These various rules changes either directly augmented the party leadership's resources or gave it new leverage.

Yet many scholars argued that, on balance, the reforms of the 1970s weakened the party leadership and reduced party influence (Cooper and Brady, 1981; Smith and Deering, 1984; Waldman, 1980; Oppenheimer, 1981b; and Rohde and Shepsle, 1987). Members' desires to participate fully in the legislative process in committee and on the floor, their greatly augmented staff resources, and the reduced power of committee chairmen led to a much less predictable legislative process. On the floor this manifested itself in a huge increase in amendments offered, making the leadership's task of building winning coalitions at the floor stage much more difficult. The reforms dispersed legislative decisionmaking power to 150-odd highly active subcommittees, it was argued, and the leadership lacked the resources to coordinate the resulting fractured process. With almost every majority party member possessing the resources to function as a free-lance policy entrepreneur, members' pursuits of their own individual agendas displaced collective action on behalf of a party agenda. As members increasingly perceived their reelection to be primarily dependent upon their own efforts and decreasingly dependent upon party success or even on the party's image, party became less relevant and the leaders' abilities to influence their members declined still further.

THE CONTEMPORARY HOUSE DEMOCRATIC PARTY AND ITS LEADERSHIP: EVOLVING ORGANIZATIONAL, AGENDA-SETTING, AND POLICY ROLES

By the mid- to late 1980s, the House had again transformed itself, but in a direction unexpected by those who had predicted the increased irrelevance of party. Democrats were voting with their party colleagues and in opposition to Republicans with a frequency unprecedented since Franklin Roosevelt's time. The party leadership's policy role had expanded in a major way: The leadership was regularly active on most major legislation and was increasingly representing its membership at policy "summits." House Republicans were bitterly complaining about majority party tyranny (Cheney, 1989). As we shall see in the following discussion, the leadership's expanded role can be linked to the altered political context of the 1980s combined with the reforms of the 1970s.

A significant increase in the ideological homogeneity of the Democratic House membership was, however, a prerequisite to this development. After the 1982 elections, the voting cohesion of House Democrats began to increase and in the late 1980s and early 1990s reached levels unprecedented in the post–World War II era. For the period 1951 through 1970, House Democrats' average party unity score was 78 percent; this fell to 74 percent for the period 1971–1982. After the 1982 election, the scores began rising and averaged 86 percent for the period 1983–1992. During this same period, the proportion of roll calls on which a majority of Democrats voted against a majority of Republicans also increased, averaging 56 percent compared with 37 percent during the 1971–1982 period.

Much of the increase in Democratic cohesion is the result of increased party support by southern Democrats. From 1985 through 1992, southern Democrats supported the party position on 78 percent of partisan roll calls; the average support of northern Democrats was 90 percent. Compare that modest 12-point difference with an average difference between the two groups of about 38 points for the period 1965–1976 and 24 points for 1977 through 1984 (Rohde, 1988; *Congressional Quarterly Almanac*, annual volumes).

Since the late 1960s, the constituencies of southern Democrats have become more like those of their northern colleagues (Rohde, 1988). In part, the convergence is the result of processes such as the urbanization of the South. More important, with the passage of the Voting Rights Act and growing Republican strength in the South, African Americans have become a critical element of many southern Democrats' election support. As a result, the policy views of the electoral coalitions supporting many southern Democrats are not drastically different from those of the average northern Democrat.

As southern electoral coalitions changed, incumbent southern Democrats began to modify their voting behavior, and newly elected southerners tended to be national Democrats (Sinclair, 1982:Ch. 7–8). Thus the House Democratic party became considerably less ideologically heterogeneous. The big budget deficits of the 1980s and 1990s, which constricted the feasible issue space by making expensive new social programs impossible, probably also made intraparty agreement easier to reach. As policy differences among Democrats declined, so did fears that the exercise of stronger leadership would pose a threat to individual members' policy or reelection goals.

Organizing the Party and the Chamber

The political parties have traditionally organized the House of Representatives. The Speaker, the chamber's presiding officer, is in reality chosen by the majority party, and the assignment of members to committees is carried out through the parties. All committees are chaired by majority party members, and the majority party holds a majority of the seats on all committees.

Every two years, after the elections and before the new Congress convenes, the members of each of the two parties meet. The Democratic Caucus, the organization of all House Democrats, nominates a candidate for Speaker and elects a floor leader, a whip, a caucus chair, and a caucus vice-chair. So long as the Democrats maintain their majority in the chamber, their candidate will be elected Speaker on the first day of the Congress, as the speakership vote is always a straight party-line vote. The Republican Conference, the organization of all House Republicans, chooses its candidate for Speaker, who will become the minority floor leader; it also elects a whip and a number of lesser party officials.

During the committee government era, rules and customs gave the Speaker a variety of opportunities to influence the organization of the party and the chamber. For example, the Speaker appointed all majority party members to select committees and special committees. The reforms of the 1970s, however, greatly augmented the leadership's role. In 1975, the committee-assignment function was shifted from the Democratic members of the Ways and Means Committee to the new Steering and Policy Committee, which the Speaker chairs. Currently, the thirty-one members of the committee include the Speaker; the majority leader; the whip and four chief deputy whips; the caucus chair, the vice-chair, and the chair of the Democratic Congressional Campaign Committee—all ex officio from the leadership—and ten appointees of the speaker.

Before 1975 the Speaker could influence the assignments made by a committee on committees, on which he did not serve. Now, although he cannot dictate, the Speaker is the dominant influence; he has, as a staffer explained, "operating control." Norms of fairness that dictate some attention to seniority and considerable attention to geographical balance constrain the leadership's discretion in making assignments to the most desirable committees. Nevertheless, the leaders can and do use their influence to ensure that loyalists are appointed to those committees most important to the party program. Before a Democrat receives an appointment to the key money committees—Ways and Means, Appropriations, and Budget—the Speaker usually has a talk with the candidate to make sure the candidate understands and can assume the obligation to support the party position in a crunch.

Leaders also use their influence over committee assignments to do favors for members, sometimes as a reward, and sometimes to amass chits useful in the future. When Jim Chapman received a coveted Appropriations assignment in late 1988, the leadership was rewarding him for casting a politically difficult vote that gave the leadership victory on a key element of its program (see Barry, 1989:452–457). It was also sending a clear message to the Democratic membership that a willingness to take risks for the party would be rewarded.

Members believe that their voting record makes a difference. Everyone knows that the leaders maintain their own party support scores. "[The leadership] was watching and so we who were interested in Appropriations did watch our votes at the end of the 101st, feeling that might make a difference, that we could screw things up if we didn't watch out," a member explained. Furthermore, members believe party support should make a difference. When, early in Tom Foley's speakership, two choice positions went to members who, though generally loyal, had defected on an important leadership vote, "there was a lot of grumbling by members" (interview with the author). In 1975 the Speaker was given the power to nominate at the beginning of each Congress the chairman and all the Democratic members of the Rules Committee, subject only to ratification by the caucus. The primary route by which major legislation reaches the floor is via rules from the Rules Committee that allow legislation to be taken up out of order and govern the amount of debate time and sometimes the amendments permitted. Consequently, the leadership controls floor scheduling only so long as the Rules Committee is a reliable ally. During much of the period of committee government, the Rules Committee was controlled by a bipartisan conservative coalition. To get legislation supported by a majority of Democrats to the floor, the Speaker was forced to bargain with the committee, and his resources for doing so were limited.

By the early 1970s changes in its membership had transformed the Rules Committee from an independent obstructionist force to a usually reliable ally (see Oppenheimer, 1981a). The 1975 rules change and the way in which speakers have used their appointive powers have made the committee an arm of the leadership. Reliability and political and institutional sagacity have been the criteria of choice. In addition to appointing members upon whom they can depend, speakers have guarded against the development of norms constricting the Speaker's discretion; for example, they have insisted on going through the formalities of reappointing Rules members in full at the beginning of a Congress so as to remind them that the Speaker has no obligation to reappoint.

During the committee government era, the party organization was skeletal by today's standards. When Sam Rayburn was Speaker (1940–1946, 1949–1952, 1955–1961), the caucus met only at the beginning of a congress and then only to ratify decisions made elsewhere. In Rayburn's view, meetings would only provide a forum for the factions in the party to confront each other directly and would thereby worsen the intraparty split. A Steering Committee existed on paper but never met. The whip system, which consisted of a whip, a deputy whip, and approximately eighteen regionally elected zone whips, was not very active. It seldom systematically gathered information on Democrats' voting intentions or engaged in organized persuasion efforts. Because the zone whips were chosen by the members of their regional zones, the leadership could not depend on their being loyal to the party position.

Since Rayburn's day, party organization has become much more elaborate, with many of the new positions being filled by leadership appointment (Dodd, 1979; Sinclair, 1983). The whip system underwent a major expansion in the 1970s and 1980s. To solve the problem of unreliable zone whips, the leadership appointed some at-large whips. As the House environment became increasingly unpredictable during the 1970s, more such whips were added to aid the leadership in information gathering and persuasion. Then, as more Democrats perceived a benefit to being a whip, the system expanded further. Such appointments became favors the leaders could dispense to their members. As of the 103rd Congress (1993–1994), the whip system consisted of the whip, four chief deputy whips, fifteen deputy or special whips, fifty-six at-large whips, and nineteen zone whips; all but the zone whips were leadership appointees.

Whip meetings, which take place every Thursday morning when the House is in session, are a key mechanism for the exchange of information between leaders and members. For leaders, the meetings provide information on the wishes and moods of their members and an opportunity to explain their decisions to a cross section of the membership. The whip meetings give members a regular opportunity to convey their concerns to their leaders on the whole spectrum of issues, to question them, to confront them and require them to justify their decisions; most whips report the weekly whip meeting to be the most valuable and the most enjoyable meeting they attend. The meetings give members a shot at influencing their leaders and shaping party strategy.

When an even more inclusive forum is considered necessary, the Democratic Caucus provides it. Rules specify that the caucus meet monthly or upon petition of fifty members. Meetings vary enormously; some are pro forma with no business whatsoever; others are gatherings of almost the entire Democratic membership for the exchange of information and debate on issues of deep concern to all. The Democratic Caucus, according to a recent chair, is "a forum for discussion and participation in debate over major issues facing Congress, a place where steam can be let off, differences aired, information disseminated."

Caucuses are called sometimes to discuss general party policy and sometimes to discuss specific legislation. Committee and party leaders can use the caucus to explain the politics and the substance of legislation, sometimes in blunter terms than they might use in a public forum, and members can state their positions and ask questions, more pointedly as well. In late 1990, after House Democrats and Republicans defeated a bipartisan budget summit agreement worked out by their leaders, the chairman of the Ways and Means Committee and the party leadership used a series of caucus meetings to guide them in working out a package that the great majority of Democrats could support. "There were eight caucus meetings in October and November, and going from a period when people were all over the map, we ended up united," a participant explained.

Caucus meetings provide members with a forum for sending messages, including policy messages, to their party and committee leaders. Although the caucus seldom passes policy resolutions and has not instructed committees in recent years, strongly held and strongly expressed member policy views do influence party and committee leaders. Those leaders know, as a top party leader said, "In the ultimate, the Caucus can establish party policy. It could be used to instruct the leadership to support a given position or instruct a committee."

Both the whip system and the caucus provide interested Democrats with a variety of opportunities to participate in the legislative process and in party affairs through working and discussion subgroups. Whip task forces (see further on), the Caucus Committee on Party Effectiveness, and caucus issue task forces are only some of these forums (see Price, 1992b:77–80).

The more elaborate party organization that has developed since the early 1970s serves members' participation and policy goals. Members have more access to their leaders and more opportunities to participate in and through the party. The leadership's expanded role in organizing party and chamber represents a major expansion of leadership resources. It provides the leaders with many opportunities to perform services and do favors for members. A major service function of the whip system, for example, is the dissemination of legislative information to Democrats. Since leaders do not control members' reelection chances, they must persuade, not command. Although explicit quid pro quos are seldom involved, the leaders' persuasion efforts are certainly facilitated by their having a supply of favors to dispense. In addition, the leadership's role in organizing party and chamber allows it to influence outcomes through the choice of personnel and provides it with some tools crucial to its expanded policy role.

Setting the Agenda

In December 1986, immediately after being chosen as the Democrats' nominee for Speaker, Jim Wright outlined a policy agenda for the majority party and the House. Deficit reduction achieved in part through a tax increase received the most press attention, but clean water legislation, a highway bill, trade legislation, welfare reform, and a farm bill were also included. In his acceptance speech on January 6, 1987, and in his televised reply to the president's state of the union address on January 31, Wright further specified and publicized the agenda, adding aid to education and insurance against catastrophic illness.

Over the course of the 100th Congress, the Speaker continued to call attention to and raise expectations of action on these items in a variety of public and in-House forums. He used his powers as Speaker to ensure that these bills were given preferential consideration in the chamber. As items were enacted, they were repeatedly cited as accomplishments, and some new issues were added to the agenda. By and large, though, the Speaker kept the focus upon the original agenda, and by the end of the 100th Congress, every item on that agenda had become law.

Special political conditions facilitated Speaker Wright's aggressive agenda setting. President Reagan had been weakened by the Iran-Contra scandal, the loss of a Senate majority, and his lame-duck status. House Democrats believed that they finally had the opportunity to pass legislation stymied during six years of the Reagan administration—if they were disciplined enough to exploit the opportunity. They very much wanted to establish a record of effective governance going into the 1988 elections. Thus House Democrats wanted policy leadership.

Agenda setting is a key aspect of policy leadership, one that Democrats have increasingly come to expect their congressional party leadership to perform during periods of divided control. House Democrats expect their leaders to consult extensively on the content of the agenda; They, of course, expect the political needs and policy goals of the Democratic membership to be the primary determinants of the agenda their leaders put together. But leaving the setting of priorities to the committees and subcommittees is no longer considered acceptable.

Despite much less favorable conditions and his own innate caution, Speaker Foley and his leadership team engaged in considerable agenda-setting activity in the 101st and 102nd Congresses. When Foley succeeded Wright in June 1989, he inherited an agenda consisting of minimum-wage, child care, clean air, ethics reform, and campaign finance reform legislation—an agenda that, as majority leader, he had participated in formulating. Foley pursued that agenda, he gave added emphasis to a combined pay raise–ethics package, and he added medical and family leave legislation to the list of top priorities. The Democratic agenda that emerged early in the 102nd Congress included energy policy, unemployment insurance extension, infrastructure renewal, and, again, campaign finance reform and family leave.

Yet despite a level of agenda setting far surpassing the speakers before Wright, Foley was subjected to considerable criticism. House Democrats called openly for a more clearly delineated agenda. During the 1989–1992 period of Foley's speakership, the process of agenda setting was more evolutionary than under his predecessor. Foley was also less aggressive and less single minded than Wright had been in keeping press attention on the agenda. As a result, the Democratic agenda was less clearly defined, and this produced criticism. Most Democrats believe that, under conditions of divided control, the congressional majority party does not get credit for the legislation it produces unless it has a clear, publicly enunciated agenda.

To prod their leadership to be more aggressive and to make their expectations of full cooperation clear to committee chairmen, Democrats in late 1992 established a new policy committee. Consisting of members chosen by the Speaker from Steering and Policy and from the rank and file, the Working Group on Policy Development is charged with helping the party set and implement a policy agenda (Donovan, 1992:3742).

With the election of Bill Clinton as president and the end of divided control, the primary responsibility for agenda setting has moved to the White House. In broad outlines at least, Clinton and most House Democrats ran on similar platforms. The inevitable differences in emphasis and detail will require Clinton to consult extensively, as he did on his economic program. In the days before the program's unveiling, the president met in small groups with most congressional Democrats, listening to their advice as well as persuading them to support him (Eaton, 1993:A18). House Democrats expect a party agenda and a central agenda setter, but they also expect to participate in the process that produces that agenda.

Shaping Legislation

Contemporary party leaders more frequently play a role in shaping the substance of legislation than did their predecessors of the committee government era. When party leaders do intervene in a process that used to be a committee monopoly, they do so as agents of the Democratic membership. That is, they do so primarily in order to advance legislation high on the Democratic agenda and to make sure it and other important legislation reflects the policy preferences of the Democratic membership.

The party leadership itself now sometimes directly negotiates over substance with other key actors such as Senate leaders and the president. During the budget summits of recent years, in negotiations over Contra aid and in the rewrite of the Gramm-Rudman budget-balancing legislation, for example, the key players for the House were not the committee chairmen but the party leadership.

In these cases, decisions highly consequential to the party and the membership as a whole were at stake; most involved broadly encompassing omnibus legislation and negotiations with cabinet-level administration officials. Under such circumstances, the party leadership perforce gets involved; it alone has the legitimacy that derives from being the elected agent of the majority party. As such, the leadership has a basis for speaking for and making agreements on behalf of the majority that other entities lack.

The leadership sometimes plays a direct role in within-House negotiations as well, particularly but not solely when legislation is referred to more than one committee. A great deal of the leaders' influence on legislative substance is the result of their behind-the-scenes efforts to get members at loggerheads to compromise and to persuade committee leaders to be responsive to majority sentiment in the party. For example, in recent years, the party leadership has played a central role on farm credit, catastrophic health insurance, minimum-wage, civil rights, and child care legislation.

Recent speakers have differed somewhat in how quick they are to intervene in the pre-floor legislative process. Speaker Jim Wright used the leverage his position gave him quite expansively. Tom Foley, as a former committee chairman, defers to chairmen more and tends to wait longer before he intervenes. These are, however, differences at the margin. House Democrats expect their leaders to produce legislative results; when this requires pressuring committees and their chairs, they expect their leaders to do so. Foley's reluctance to do so quickly has occasioned some criticism.

This expanded role of the party leadership in shaping legislation was made possible by the 1970s reforms that reduced the power and independence of committee chairmen. Weakened by the subcommittee bill of rights, which reduced their control over their committees' agenda, organization, and staffing, chairmen were made dependent upon a secret ballot majority vote in the Democratic Caucus for their position. Consequently, chairmen had to become responsive to the caucus majority and to the party leadership to the extent that it speaks for that majority.

Changes in the legislative process have made that expanded role necessary. In 1975, the House instituted a rule allowing the referral of legislation to more than one committee, and in the 1980s and 1990s an increasing proportion of major legislation has been multiply referred (Davidson, Oleszek, and Kephart, 1988; Young and Cooper, 1993; Sinclair, 1992a, 1992b). When several committees are involved in the drafting of legislation, a coordinating and integrating entity becomes essential. The huge budget deficit, which constrained legislative choices, and the deep ideological divisions between congressional Democrats and the White House during the Reagan and Bush years resulted in Congress doing much of its legislating through the passage of a small number of huge omnibus bills. Given the number of issues and the number of committees involved in these omnibus measures, as well as the stakes for the party, not only a coordinating entity but one that can speak for the party as a whole is needed to make such a process function.

As a consequence of the leadership's expanded role in shaping the substance of legislation, the policy preferences of party majorities undoubtedly have more influence on major legislation than they did during the committee government era. To be sure, most legislation is still written in committee without any party leadership involvement. Furthermore, when the leadership does bring the policy preferences of the Democratic membership to bear in the process, it is usually the leadership's reading of those preferences. Leaders do have many opportunities for learning what their members want, and the legitimacy of their involvement in the shaping of legislation depends upon their representing members' preferences with reasonable accuracy. Most of the time, leaders do act as faithful agents of the party majority.

Committees are much less insulated now than they were in the committee government era. In order to retain their positions, committee chairmen must be responsive to party majorities. As the next section will show, committees must also be responsive if they wish to receive the help they need to pass their legislation.

Influencing Outcomes

Superintending the House floor and shepherding legislation to passage at the floor stage are the core of the party leadership's responsibilities as traditionally defined. In recent years, the leadership has nevertheless become more active at their stage of the legislative process as well. As the members offered increasing numbers of amendments on the floor during the 1970s, committees faced a much greater challenge in passing their bills on the floor (Bach and Smith, 1988:28–29). If the bill at issue was a major controversial one, the committee majority often could not engineer passage on its own. Partly as a result of the 1970s reforms and partly in response to the problems they created, the party leadership obtained a command over resources it can use to give committee majorities the help they need. And as the adverse political climate of the 1980s and early 1990s made passing legislation satisfactory to Democrats even more difficult, House Democrats increasingly expected their leaders to use those resources aggressively.

Since the Rules Committee has become an arm of the leadership, party leaders truly control the scheduling of legislation for floor consideration. The capacity to decide when a bill will be considered is an important strategic resource, since it can affect outcomes. Thus the leadership can delay a bill until sufficient support for passage has developed or, more rarely, move legislation quickly before opposition has time to coalesce.

The special orders or rules reported by the Rules Committee govern the amending process on the legislation at issue; a rule may, for example, ban all amendments or make only certain specific amendments in order. In response to the expanded amending activity on the House floor, the party leadership in the 1980s increased its use of rules that restrict amendments in some way. From the 95th Congress (1977–1978) to the 102nd Congress (1991–1992), restrictive rules increased from 12 to 66 percent of all rules (Wolfensberg, 1992).

Restrictive rules save time and may protect members from having to cast politically perilous votes. Carefully crafted rules can reduce uncertainty and structure the choices members face on the floor, an advantage to the party position. Yet restrictive rules do restrict members' freedom, and every rule requires majority approval on the House floor. Since Republicans increasingly vote against most restrictive rules, approval depends upon a large proportion of Democrats voting in favor. The big increase in the use of such rules, thus, signifies most Democrats' approval of the leadership's aggressive use of this strategy. It also suggests that leaders use the strategy skillfully. Leaders frequently employ carefully crafted and often restrictive rules to enable their members to vote their policy preferences without paying too big a reelection price. Closed rules, for example, may provide "cover" for members by making the crucial vote a procedural one. Unpopular but necessary measures may be bundled with more popular provisions and voted on as a package under a restrictive rule. Thus members could justify a vote for a congressional pay raise by the inclusion in the package of a stringent ethics code. When a group of Democrats really needs to offer an amendment for policy or reelection reasons, it is given the opportunity to do so. On the civil rights bill, for example, the Black Caucus and a group of women members were given the chance to offer a liberal substitute to a more moderate version drafted to have broad appeal.

By adept use of its control over scheduling and over the character of rules, the party leadership can significantly increase a bill's chances of passing intact on the floor. The leadership's involvement in shaping the substance of legislation at the pre-floor stage is often aimed at producing legislation with support broad enough to pass the chamber. Nevertheless, on major controversial legislation, a floor-vote mobilization effort is often required.

On legislation of consequence, the party leadership conducts a whip count to ascertain the level of support among Democrats. Usually shortly before the leadership intends to bring the legislation to the floor, the regional whips are instructed to ask the members in their zones how they intend to vote. A whip task force will be formed by inviting all the whips and the Democratic members of the committee of origin who supported the bill to participate. The task force, working from the initial count, distributes the names of all Democrats not listed as supporting the party position among its members. The task is to talk to those Democrats, to ascertain their voting intention, and to persuade a number sufficient for victory to support the party position.

During the 100th, 101st, and 102nd Congresses, task forces functioned in about seventy instances per Congress. About 60 percent of the House Democrats served on one or more task forces during the 100th (the only one for which data are available). The task force device and the expanded whip system of which it is a part make it possible for the party leadership to mount much more frequent and extensive vote-mobilization efforts than was possible for earlier party leaderships. Task forces also provide members with opportunities to participate broadly in the legislative process, opportunities especially attractive to junior members who do not yet chair a subcommittee. They thus channel members' energies into efforts that help the party (see Price, 1992a:Ch. 6).

The party leadership, then, can very significantly help committees pass their legislation on the floor. The price for this aid is committee responsiveness to the party agenda and to party majority preferences on legislative substance. The party contingents on most committees are relatively representative of the party membership, and the need for caucus approval also works to keep committee chairmen responsive to party sentiment. Consequently, most committees can be expected to produce legislation reasonably satisfactory to most Democrats in any given case. Nevertheless, the committee majority's need for leadership to help pass its legislation does heighten its responsiveness to the leadership and the party majority. If the committee has put together legislation acceptable to a strong majority of Democrats, the leadership will work to protect that legislation from being picked apart on the floor and will use its command over rules and the vote mobilization apparatus to do so. The party majority's position is probably more determinative of the substance of legislation that passes the House than it used to be.

Parties and Party Leaders in the Senate

In the Senate, too, the parties organize the chamber. Each party elects a floor leader and a whip from among its membership. Senators receive their committee assignments from party committees.

The Senate majority leader is the leader of the majority party in the Senate but, unlike the Speaker, he is not the chamber's presiding officer. In any case, the presiding officer of the Senate has much less discretion than his House counterpart. The only important resource that the Senate rules give to the majority leader to aid him with his core tasks of scheduling legislation and floor leadership is the right to be recognized first when a number of senators are seeking recognition on the Senate floor.

Not only do institutional rules give the majority party leadership few special resources, they bestow great powers on rank-and-file senators. In most cases, any senator can offer an unlimited number of amendments to a piece of legislation on the Senate floor, and those amendments need not even be germane. A senator can hold the Senate floor indefinitely unless cloture is invoked, which requires an extraordinary majority of sixty votes.

During the late 1960s and the 1970s, the Senate increased the supply of staff and of desirable committee assignments and began to distribute those resources much more equally among its members. Norms dictating specialization and a highly restrained use of the great powers the Senate rules confer upon the individual lost their hold. As a consequence, senators now typically become involved in a broad range of issues, including some that do not fall into the jurisdiction of their committees. They are active both in the committee room and on the Senate floor (Sinclair, 1989).

In the Senate, unlike the House, rule and norm changes that increased rank-and-file members' opportunities to participate were not accompanied by leadership-strengthening changes. The Senate majority party leader, always institutionally weaker than the Speaker of the House, was given no significant new powers for coping with the more active, assertive, and hence less predictable membership.

A single senator can disrupt the work of the Senate by, for example, exercising his right of unlimited debate or objecting to the unanimous consent requests through which the Senate does most of its work. Clearly, a partisan minority of any size can bring legislative activity to a standstill. The Senate of necessity operates in a more bipartisan fashion than does the House. As he makes decisions on the floor scheduling of legislation the majority leader confers on an almost continuous basis with the minority leader and, in fact, touches base with all interested senators. In the negotiation of unanimous consent agreements, which the Senate often uses to set the ground rules for the consideration of legislation on the floor, the majority leader must obtain the assent not only of the minority leadership but also of all interested senators. An objection from any one senator kills such an agreement.

Like their House counterparts, Senate committees in the 1970s faced a more complex and unpredictable floor situation as the number of amendments rapidly increased. The 1980s and early 1990s political environment with its high-intensity ideological politics, the constraints of the big deficits, and, after 1986, divided control further complicated the situation the majority party and its committee contingents confront. Yet the majority party leadership's limited control over the floor agenda and its lack of a device such as House special orders (rules) for advantageously structuring choices severely limit the help the party leadership can give committees in passing their legislation on the floor.

Party cohesion has increased in the Senate, though not to the same levels as in the House. The percent of all roll calls evoking a partisan division increased modestly from 41.6 percent for the 1969–1980 period to 46.2 for 1981–1992, but important votes were much more frequently partisan (Hurley, 1989:131). On party votes during the 1980s and early 1990s, the Senate's majority party maintained high party cohesion. Republicans voted with their party 81.2 percent of the time on average from 1981 through 1986, the period they controlled the Senate, compared with 71.9 percent during the 1969–1980 period. From 1987 through 1992, Senate Democrats supported their party's position on 83 percent of the roll calls on average—compared with 74.3 percent for 1969–1980 and 76.2 percent for 1981–1986.

In the Senate, as in the House, the heterogeneity of Democrats' election constituencies has declined. Most of the southern Democrats whose election in 1986 returned control of the chamber to the Democratic party depend upon black votes. The alterations in partisan control that the Senate experienced during the 1980s enhanced the sense of shared fate among the party contingents.

Thus, by the late 1980s, Democrats' shared attitudes and interests provided a basis for greater intraparty policy cooperation and more policy-oriented leadership. The Senate majority leader faced the same problem the House leadership confronted, but in a much more intense form—how to provide the policy leadership members want without constraining too much members' full and free participation in the legislative process.

When George Mitchell of Maine became majority leader in 1989, his strategies for satisfying both aspects of members' expectations were, within the constraints imposed by the differences between the chambers, similar to those developed by House leaders. The party organization and party processes have been much elaborated to provide services to members and to include members in all aspects of party functioning (Baumer, 1992; Smith, 1993). The party policy committee and the whip system provide to members an enormous variety of information services and assistance with various aspects of their jobs, constituency communication, for example (see Smith, 1993:274–276). Mitchell has increased the number of members in party leadership positions; he created the posts of Policy Committee co-chair and of assistant majority leader and filled both with junior senators. He regularly shares floor management duties with these senators, his whip, and other colleagues. The whip system has become more active. Democratic senators' weekly lunch meeting provides an opportunity for policy discussion and for communication between leaders and members.

At the beginning of his tenure, Mitchell responded to his members' desires for Senate Democrats to have a greater impact on the congressional agenda by commissioning the Senate Democratic Policy Committee to draft a consensus agenda. This became a yearly exercise during the period of divided control. Enactment of that agenda was, however, frequently stymied by the majority leader's limited influence over floor outcomes.

The majority leader spends a great deal of his time attempting to work out differences among senators through direct negotiation or by facilitating negotiations. In negotiations with key actors outside the chamber on such major matters as the budget, a continuing resolution, Contra aid, or an omnibus drug bill, the Senate majority leader will play a role. He, like his House counterparts, commands the legitimacy derived from being the elected leader of the majority party. In this area, too, Mitchell has worked to include his colleagues. He frequently creates negotiating teams to work out differences among senators so that legislation can be brought to the floor under a unanimous consent agreement (Smith, 1993:273). He has used ad hoc policy task forces to work on issues of particular importance to the party (Smith, 1993:276).

In the Senate as in the House, party is more central to members' legislative lives than it was two decades ago. Democrats are more ideologically homogeneous, and the party provides a mechanism for furthering their collective policy goals. It also provides another forum for participation. The Senate majority party leadership is more policy-oriented than it used to be; this is a response to changing member expectations. Yet the Senate majority party leadership's meager resources for helping the Democratic membership, committee majorities, and committee leaders to protect their legislation from amendments and pass it on the floor do not provide the same leverage that the House leadership's much more potent resources do. Compared to his House counterparts, the majority leader must defer more to committee chairmen and to other interested senators. Since he can help them less than the House leadership can help its House counterparts, he also can influence them less.

A STRONG CONGRESSIONAL PARTY IN A WEAK PARTY ERA

The congressional majority party, especially the party in the House, plays a much more active policy role now than at any time in the post–World War II era; the membership is more cohesive and, particularly in the House, the leadership, its agent, is more central to the legislative process.

Why has the congressional party become stronger and more policy-relevant in what is often considered a weak party era? A constellation of changes over the past two decades has reduced the costs and increased the benefits to members of a stronger party and a more active leadership. The effective ideological homogeneity of the Democratic membership increased as the election constituencies of southern Democrats became more like those of their northern party colleagues and as the big deficits shrank the feasible issue space. Consequently, no appreciable segment of the Democratic membership need fear that the exercise of active, policy-oriented leadership will reduce its reelection chances. The reforms of the 1970s, especially when combined with the constraints of the 1980s and early 1990s political environment, greatly increased the difficulty of enacting legislation, particularly legislation that Democrats favor. The majority party leadership in the House possesses resources that, if Democratic members acquiesce in their use (by voting for restrictive rules, for example), can significantly increase the probability of legislative success. The Democratic membership, Democratic committee contingents, and Democratic committee leaders all benefit from a more active leadership using its resources aggressively to help them pass legislation that furthers their policy and reelection goals.

Bill Clinton became president at a time when his party in the Congress is, by twentieth-century standards, ideologically homogeneous. Members' sense that their electoral fate is closely linked to that of their party and its president is unusually strong by post–World War II standards. The party leadership in the House is well-equipped to give a president of its own party major assistance in passing his programs. Although he lacks the institutional powers of his House counterparts, even the Senate majority leader is more capable of providing the assistance a president needs than were his predecessors from the 1970s.

To be sure, Democrats' ideological homogeneity is far from perfect; party-splitting issues certainly exist. Furthermore, Clinton cannot expect congressional Democrats to follow his lead unquestioningly; members expect to be consulted and to participate in the formulation of policy. And, of course, congressional leaders are agents of the members who elect them; they can help the president only to the extent that members want them to. Still, the congressional party Clinton faces is much more amenable to skillful presidential leadership than was the party Carter confronted.

Yet because it is not based upon a strong party external to the Congress, the current congressional party's strength is potentially more fragile than that of strong congressional parties of the past. Internal party strength requires that the members of the congressional party see their individual interests as coinciding to a significant extent, and without strong parties in the electorate, the perception of coinciding interests is highly vulnerable to erosion by short-term forces in the political environment.

NOTES

This essay is based upon a fifteen-month period of participant observation in the office of the Speaker and in part upon interviews with members and staff. I would like to thank Jim Wright and his staff for giving me an unprecedented opportunity to see leadership in operation from the inside and all those people who took some of their precious time to talk with me. This research was supported in part by intramural grant funds from the Academic Senate, University of California, Riverside, and by a grant from the Dirken Congressional Leadership Research Center.

13

Coalitions and Policy in the U.S. Congress

DAVID W. BRADY
KARA M. BUCKLEY

In the United States, though not in most other Western democracies, analysis of political coalitions is complicated by variation in the nature of the groups that divide or come together to form temporary alliances. To talk of coalitions in the British party system is to refer to ideological factions within parties, whereas the Japanese party system has factions within parties that are not ideological but personal. In Germany one describes the two or more *parties* that must agree on policies and ministerial posts in order to form a coalition government. In the United States, however, factions within the two major parties sometimes form coalitions to set party policy; at other times cross-party coalitions are formed on the basis of common interests.

Contemporary commentators speak of the Roosevelt-Truman (New Deal) coalition of northeasterners and southerners that won five consecutive presidential elections between 1932 and 1948. By contrast, the Conservative Coalition in Congress refers to Republicans voting with southern Democrats against northern Democrats. The Urban-Rural Coalition is composed of rural and urban representatives, regardless of their party affiliation, who combine forces to pass legislation that favors price supports for farmers and food stamps for the urban poor (Ferejohn, 1986). In this essay, coalitions are viewed both as cooperating factions within the parties and as cross-party policy blocs.

The American electoral system is also relatively unusual in that the executive and legislative branches may be controlled by different parties. Although the United States is not the only country with this feature, few governments are designed to permit divided control of its branches as readily as ours does. There are exceptions, of course. During his first term, French President Mitterrand, a Socialist, had a National Assembly controlled by Chirac and the Conservatives. After a brief period of a Socialist majority, Conservative control of the Assembly returned in 1993 with the election of Prime Minister Balladur. The semi-presidential system has led to a relatively new phenomenon of "cohabitation," the French equivalent to divided government. In 1990, the Korean government had a president from the Democratic Justice party (DJP) as well as a legislature dominated by a coalition group that did not include the DJP. Clear unified control returned in 1993 with the election of President Kim Y. S. and the domination of his new Democratic Liberal party in the legislature. Nonexistent or sporadic in other countries, divided government remains the norm in the United States. The Carter and Clinton administrations diverge from a post-Kennedy pattern of Democratic domination of Congress and Republican occupation of the Oval Office. It is important to note the unique features of the U.S. system that permit this split control of government.

This essay begins with a discussion of some of the constitutional and institutional features that affect parties in America—features that in turn have led to the development of coalitions within and among parties. The argument here is that if we had a constitutional system that encouraged strong, responsible parties (each able to discipline members and to gain control of both executive and legislative branches), then a study of coalitions in Congress would describe the factions within the two major parties and discuss the ways in which these factions affected the parties' electoral and policy positions. However, since the American system does not encourage responsible parties, it is necessary to show that coalitions in the United States are both electoral and policy coalitions—and show how the operative electoral and legislative coalitions differ. For example, the electoral coalitions that make one party the majority in Congress do not ensure a majority position on issues such as tax rates, farm price supports, or affirmative action policy. Indeed, one can explain coalitions in American government by showing how electoral and policymaking activities in America are disjointed.

Constitutional constraints and institutional reforms have generated a weak party system in the United States. American parties no longer control the electoral fate of their members; the constituents, not the national party, hire and fire candidates. Any account of party voting in Congress devoid of these individual-member preferences may lead to either misspecification of causal factors or erroneous predictions on policy outputs. With some Democrats to the right of Republicans and some Republicans to the left of Democrats, cross-party coalitions are often the deciding factors in today's policy decisions. The question is whether these pivotal floor votes determine policy direction regardless of party control of the branches.

The press, the public, politicians, and even political scientists have all identified divided government as the culprit behind gridlock. The claim is that split control of the executive and legislative branches puts parties head-to-head, inevitably resulting in policy impasse and legislative paralysis. Unified government could reduce stalemates and yield significant policy shifts from the status quo; branches joined under one party label could bring efficiency and responsibility back to the policymaking machine. The underlying assumption in much of the work on divided and unified control is that party makes a difference in legislative outcomes. If party power over members of Congress is minimal, it is to coalitions and individual preferences we must turn for causes of gridlock.

The first unified government since 1980 provides fertile ground to test the power of party on the voting behavior of members of Congress. Can parties convince members, specifically those who fall between party positions on a given policy, to vote party over preference? Will moderate Democrats vote with the Democratic party or form coalitions with moderate Republicans on economic packages? Can the Democratic president and the Democratic Congress pass legislation without enlisting the aid of Republicans? Will interest and/or ideologically based coalitions pull Clinton away from the Democratic party mean toward the center? It would be a formidable task to tackle all of these questions in one essay. Certainly any attempt would be futile without an understanding of parties as either independent of or influencing legislators' preferences. By focusing on the formation of intraparty and cross-party coalitions in Congress during times of divided and unified control, we hope to come closer to a cohesive interpretation of party and consequently come closer to better conclusions.

CONSTITUTIONAL CONSTRAINTS ON AMERICAN PARTIES

The major features of the American Constitution that distinguish it from most other democratic countries' constitutions are federalism, separation of powers, and checks and balances. Federalism helped the founding generation to ensure that the Congress and the president would reflect and recognize the social, economic, and religious differences among states and regions. Federalism institutionalized the differences inherent in a growing, widespread, diverse population (recall *Federalist*, No. 51). The doctrines of separation of powers and checks and balances have resulted in an American system of government that is characterized by "separate powers sharing functions," which is in contradistinction to other Western democracies in which power is centralized and functions are specific.

Although many aspects of the doctrines of federalism, separation of powers, and checks and balances have changed so as to make the system more democratic and centralized, the American system of government remains fragmented and cumbersome. Shortly after the Constitution took effect, difficulties inherent in governing within its framework presented themselves. Alexander Hamilton, Washington's secretary of the treasury, could not implement the policies he considered necessary without appropriate legislation. Thus, he commenced work on building organized support in Congress for Washington's policies; in effect, he became the leader of the pro-national faction in the Congress. Over time, the factions that had opposing views regarding the direction the national government should take developed into political parties. The goal of these nascent parties was to elect others to Congress who shared their views in order to form a majority for the policies they favored. Yet, even though American parties were founded as a means to make governing less cumbersome, the same forces that produced them—federalism, separation of powers, checks and balances, and single-member districts with plurality winners—also worked to limit their strength.

The most basic effect of a federal form of government on the American party system is that, instead of one national two-party system, we have fifty state party systems. Each state's party system has demographic, ideological, structural, and electoral peculiarities. For instance, the Democratic party in the electorate and as an organization in New York is distinct from the Democratic party in the electorate and as an organization in Georgia. The same fact applies to the components of the Republican party in these states. The heterogeneity of the state party systems is such that, at the level of party in government, unlike-minded men and women bearing the same party label have come together in the U.S. Congress. Put another way, the federal system has brought built-in differences among states and regions to the Congress. Although this arrangement may be useful in maintaining system equilibrium, it has more often formed an extremely poor basis on which to build coherent congressional parties; in effect, it has encouraged cross-party coalitions. The New Deal coalition of rural southern agricultural interests and urban northern industrial interests is a case in point. Long after this coalition had passed its major policy changes and the reasons for its formation no longer obtained, it continued to serve as the basis of the electoral coalition for the Democratic party. Even with a successful electoral coalition, however, the party was often divided on major policy issues.[1] In fact, on a number of major policy issues such as civil rights and social welfare, the components of the New Deal coalition were poles apart. American political history abounds with examples of successful electoral coalitions that could not keep their members from forming cross-party legislative coalitions. Parties formed out of numerous and diverse state party systems tend to emphasize electoral success and to minimize policy cohesion.

The separation of powers and the system of checks and balances have contributed, as well, to the fragmentary, disjointed status of American parties. When sectional, coalitional parties are given the opportunity to seek numerous offices (both elective and appointive) in the various branches, they become further fractionalized. Thus, for example, one faction of the party may dominate presidential politics and another, congressional politics; and since both have powers over the courts, an equal division of court appointments may result. The Democratic party from 1876 to at least 1976 was characterized by just such an arrangement. The northern wing dominated presidential politics and elections, the southern wing dominated congressional leadership posts, and both wings influenced court appointments. Such a system may enhance representation of differences, but it does little to facilitate coherent party majorities capable of cohesive policymaking.

The constitutional arrangement of single-member-district plurality elections has also contributed to the fragmentation of the party system. House members elected on local issues by a localized party in the electorate generally build local party (or personal) organizations (Mann, 1978; Fenno, 1978; Mayhew, 1974a; Fiorina, 1989). Elected representatives—owing little loyalty to national party leaders—can behave in nonpartisan ways with few personal consequences. Indeed, throughout most of the Congress's history, party leaders have been able only to persuade, not to force, members to vote "correctly." Party leadership, without even the threat of sanctions, is likely to be unsuccessful in building consistent partisan majorities. It is thus not surprising that the highest levels of voting along party lines in the history of the Congress occurred at a time (1890–1910) when the Speaker's sanctions over members were greatest and the Senate was run by a hierarchy that also had powerful sanctions. In turn, representatives elected by local majorities can work and vote on behalf of those interests regardless of the national party position; congressional leaders do not "persuade" from a position of power.

Local and state diversity is institutionalized in the American system of government in such a way as to allow that diversity to work its way up, almost unchanged, from party in the electorate through party organizations to the congressional parties. Thus, at the top as at the bottom, the American party system reflects the cumbersome factionalism of the American system of government. It also facilitates cross-party coalitions. The fragmentation of the parties in the electorate and in government carries over into the organization of the legislature. In the following section the effect of this fragmentation on House organization is given as an example.

HOUSE ORGANIZATION

Like all such organizations, the House of Representatives has adapted to social change by creating internal structures designed both to meet the pressures or demands from its various constituencies and to perform its policymaking function.[2] To the enormous range of interests in the United States and the concomitant pressures they generate, the House has responded with a division of labor. The result is a highly complicated committee system. When the country was in its infancy and government was limited, the House formed ad hoc committees; however, by the Jacksonian era, a standing-committee system was in place. As the country grew more industrial and complicated, the House responded by expanding and enlarging the committee system. Early in this process, committees were established to deal with such policy domains as war, post offices, and roads, and the ways and means to raise revenues to support the government.

These committees—or "little legislatures," as George Goodwin (1970) described them—were organized around governmental policy functions; they were and still are decentralized decisionmaking structures. Both the making of Reconstruction policy after the Civil War and Woodrow Wilson's claim that "congressional government is committee government" attest to the power of committees at relatively early times (Wilson, 1885; see also Bogue, 1980; Benedict, 1974). Decentralizing power to committees was a necessary response to pressures for government action in certain policy areas; to the extent that the committees decided policy, however, party leaders were limited. The legislature has even further devolved with the proliferation of work groups, increasing the fragmentation of the institution (Cohen, 1992). As decentralized decisionmaking mechanisms, committees are dominated by members elected to represent local interests. The fact that members can choose (within limits) the committees they serve on determines to a large extent the direction that the committees' policy choices will take. This is essentially what William Riker (1983) means by "congealed preferences." The decentralized committee system, which allows members to represent local interests, has become a powerful force that encourages members from different parties to cross party lines in order to achieve policy results. Throughout the 1950s, for example, a coalition of conservative Democrats and Republicans on the House Rules Committee was able to block or weaken civil rights legislation favored by northern Democrats.

What the division of labor pulls apart in organizations, integrative mechanisms must pull together. In the House the major integrative mechanism is the majority congressional party. And as we have seen, congressional parties are limited by the governmental structure established by the Constitution as well as by the fact that members are elected by local parties (or groups) on the basis of local issues. Members responsible to and punishable only by local electorates tend to be responsive to constituents, not parties. Under such conditions, party strength tends to be low and coalitional strength high. Even when party voting was at its peak in the U.S. House of Representatives, it was low compared to that of other Western democracies. Even under ideal conditions the congressional parties in the House have limited integrative capacity. Under normal conditions policy decisions are thus likely to reflect localized committee interests, thereby limiting the national party leaders' attempts to build coherent congressional majorities. House voting patterns show that different coalitions are active on different policy issues (Clausen, 1973; Sinclair, 1982). Coalitions cut across regional party as well as social economic lines, making the party leaders' job a "ceaseless maneuvering to find coalitions capable of governing" in specific policy areas (Key, 1952).

Two other features of the American institutional arrangement should be emphasized as well. First, the Constitution provides for the separate election of a president and Congress; thus the electoral institution makes it possible to have divided government. The rules in most democracies make divided government highly unlikely. In the United Kingdom and Japan, for example, the prime ministers are members of Parliament, elected by their fellow legislators as chief executives. Divided control is possible in such cases only if enough Conservatives or Liberal Democrats vote with Labor or Liberals to elect the prime minister. The fact that divided government has become the norm in the United States since 1950 is important because it ensures a special role for coalitions in Congress. President Bush could not pass any of his policy proposals without some support from Democratic members of Congress, and the Democrats cannot pass their policies over the president's veto without some Republican support. In short, divided government both implies and necessitates cross-party policy coalitions. The question is whether cross-party coalitions will continue under unified control to capture those floor voters whose preferences are between both party positions on a given policy.

Second, the American Constitution ensured what Nelson Polsby (1975) has called "a transformative legislature." That is, the sharing of power between separate institutions (with the ability to check each other) helps ensure that what happens in Congress actually affects the direction of public policy. In most legislatures, committees (if they exist) do not significantly affect the direction of policy. In the U.S. Congress, however, committees do matter. Similarly, voting in most legislatures is party-responsible voting. The parliamentary party member, for instance, votes the government- or opposition-party position on crucial policy votes. But in Congress, party leaders have to exert themselves to get party members to support them, and often they fail. During the 101st Congress, the Democratic leadership pressed hard to get Democrats to vote against a capital gains tax reduction that President Bush preferred. In the final House vote, some seventy Democrats voted with the Republicans in favor of a capital gains reduction. This outcome would not have occurred on similar votes in most other democracies.

In sum, American institutional arrangements have constrained party responsibility, encouraged divided government, and made the legislature an important actor in the policy process. The combination of these features makes cross-party coalitions especially important in Congress; indeed, without analyzing such coalitions, we cannot account for the direction of public policy. But the institutional arrangements of the American system alone do not explain the importance of coalitions. One must also consider citizen preferences. If U.S. citizens wanted a strong party system, they could change the rules so as to strengthen parties; or, conversely, they could elect a Congress that would be of the same party as the president. But since they have not changed the rules and since they do not often elect presidents and Congresses of the same party, it must be the case that their preferences are consistent with weak parties and divided government. With the election of Clinton and the continued majority of Democrats in the Congress, unified government arrives as a potential solution to gridlock. Without incentives for cohesive policy direction in the form of strict party discipline, members of Congress will continue to face similar forms of gridlock that will require cross-party coalition building to challenge the majority party position. The number and complexity of explanations offered to account for the relationship between citizen preferences, institutions, and government action ranges from Marx's ideology of false consciousness to Friedman's invisible-hand solutions. We shall not try to resolve this broad issue; rather, we will focus on the electoral connection.

CROSS-PARTY COALITIONS

The prevalence in the U.S. Congress of cross-party policy coalitions is largely attributable to the electoral base of U.S. parties. The fact that liberals such as Senator Ted Kennedy (D-MA) and Representative Pat Schroeder (D-CO) share the same party label as conservatives such as Senator Sam Nunn (D-GA) and Representative Charles Stenholm (D-TX) helps to explain the existence of coalitions that feature Democrats and Republicans who vote alike. The intraparty heterogeneity of preferences leads directly to voting blocs that weaken party responsibility in the U.S. Congress. The coalitions are of two kinds: One is broadly ideological whereas the other is issue or policy specific. The Conservative Coalition is an example of a broad ideological coalition that has formed across a wide range of issues. The policy-specific coalitions are more diverse and numerous; the aforementioned urban-rural coalition is but one example. Policy-specific coalitions can be based on members' constituent interests or, as in the case of the pro-Israel coalition, on members' preferences or ideology.

Homogeneous and Cohesive Parties

The development of congressional coalitions is obvious when we compare the current arrangement with that which existed in 1890–1910, when parties were relatively cohesive and strong. During that earlier period the number of cross-party coalitions was low; by tracing their rise, we can determine the extent to which that rise was associated with electoral results.

Both the U.S. House of Representatives and the Senate at the end of the nineteenth century were partisan, centralized, and hierarchical. The congressional majority party for most of this period (i.e., the Republican party) was controlled by a small number of leaders who occupied both party and committee leadership positions, thus making power centralized and hierarchical in that members took their voting cues from these party leaders (Brady, 1973). Voting on the floor and in committees was highly partisan. For example, during the 55th and 56th Congresses (1897–1901), more than 90 percent of the roll-call votes were a majority of one party voting against a majority of the other party. In addition, more than half of all roll calls in these Congresses were 90 percent of one party versus 90 percent of the other. Thus it is fair to claim that, at the turn of the century, congressional parties more closely resembled European parties than contemporary American parties.

How did we evolve from a system in which congressional parties were strong and cross-party coalitions were nonexistent or weak to one in which cross-party coalitions are strong and parties are weak and/or unimportant (Broder, 1971)? The argument here is that, at the turn of the century, American parties were internally homogeneous and the two major parties had opposing views on appropriate governmental policy. The Republicans largely represented northern industrial districts, whereas the Democrats largely represented rural and southern districts. The Republicans, in calling for policies that favored continued industrial development, proposed tariffs to protect American industries, the gold standard (which favored Eastern moneyed interests and was the European standard), and the expansion of American interests abroad. The Democrats, who represented different constituencies, were opposed to the Republican ideas. They favored free trade, the coinage of silver at a 16-to-1 ratio with gold, and an isolationist foreign policy. In short, constituent preferences were in line with the parties (see Figure 13.1).

Heterogeneous Parties and Cross-Party Coalitions

As intraparty heterogeneity was introduced into the congressional parties, cross-party coalitions—both ideological and policy specific—re-

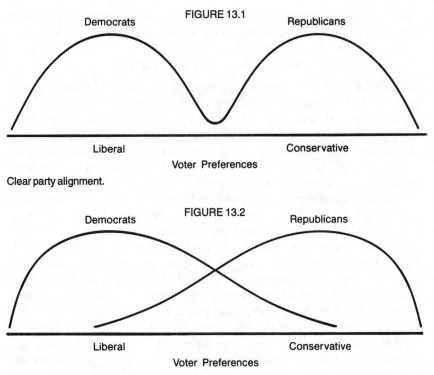

FIGURE 13.1

Democrats   Republicans

Liberal   Conservative

Voter Preferences

Clear party alignment.

FIGURE 13.2

Democrats   Republicans

Liberal   Conservative

Voter Preferences

Overlapping party alignment.

sulted. In other words, as the distribution of preferences and the party alignment changed (as shown in Figure 13.2), the probability of interparty coalitions increased. In contrast to the data in Figure 13.1, some Democrats were now closer to Republicans than to the Democratic median, and some Republicans were closer to the Democrats than to the Republican median. If we were to include more than one policy dimension in the model, we would see even more cross-party similarity. With the addition of a foreign policy factor, for instance, some Democrats might have shown up as economic liberals but foreign policy conservatives. In short, as the number of policy dimensions is expanded, the possibility of cross-party coalitions increases dramatically. The central point is clear: When intraparty heterogeneity exists, voting patterns and public policy change.

VOTER PREFERENCES

The rise of the Progressives in the early twentieth century introduced heterogeneity of preference into the majority Republican party. Progressives such as Robert Lafollette (R-WI), Albert Cummins (R-IA), and George

Norris (R-NE) disagreed with Republican stalwarts such as Speaker Joseph Cannon (IL) and Senator Nelson Aldrich (RI) over issues such as income tax, government regulation of industry and banking, tariff schedules, and electoral reform. There were similar splits between southern and northern Democrats over immigration and civil rights policies. The combined result of this intraparty heterogeneity was a cross-party coalition of Democrats and Progressive Republicans that effectively changed the leadership in the House and Senate and permitted the passage of policies associated with President Woodrow Wilson (Holt, 1967).

Under the alignment shown in Figure 13.1, the House and Senate were organized to accommodate a strong and unified majority party's policy agenda. In the House, for example, Boss Reed (the Speaker in 1889–1891 and 1895–1899) and Czar Cannon (the Speaker in 1901–1909) appointed committees, controlled the Rules Committee, and had the right to recognize anyone they chose to speak on the floor. In 1910–1911 a coalition of Progressive Republicans and Democrats stripped the Speaker of his appointive power, dropped him as chair of Rules, and restricted his floor powers. They did so largely because they believed that, with centralized Speaker control, they could not get their policies passed. In sum, after the Progressive reforms in the House and Senate, both bodies were organized to accommodate parties that had intraparty differences. This is not to say that party was irrelevant but simply that it was less important and had fewer sanctions over members' legislative careers.

In the 1920s the major cross-party coalition was the so-called farm bloc—a coalition of Republicans and Democrats representing agricultural interests. The American economy had developed rapidly after World War I, although agriculture continued to be depressed (because of overproduction and thus low prices) throughout the decade. Representatives and senators from farm districts and states proposed price supports and parity payments, among other policies, to alleviate the effects of the depressed agriculture sector. The most hotly debated proposal was the McNary-Haugen policy proposal. At various times either the House or the Senate passed versions of this proposal; but the president vetoed it, and it did not become public policy. Nevertheless, the farm bloc was a powerful force in the U.S. Congress, and it was cross-partisan.

The Great Depression brought Franklin Roosevelt and the Democrats to power, and from 1933 until 1938 they acted in a cohesive fashion. Levels of party unity and party voting increased during this era (Brady, 1988). Roosevelt and the Democrats achieved this unity and purpose by establishing what Theodore Lowi (1979) called "interest group liberalism." In each relevant policy area, that is, the affected parties were the relevant actors. The National Industrial Recovery Act tried to set quotas, prices, and wages by allowing each industry to define its equilibrium point. Agricultural policy was established by allowing the different commodities (corn, tobacco, sugar, rice, etc.) to work out their own arrangements regarding parity, price supports, and production levels; and much the same held for labor and other affected interests.

This arrangement was restricted by the rise of the Conservative Coalition in 1938. In 1937 Roosevelt had proposed the Fair Labor Standards Act to the Congress. Among its features was a set of provisions that would have reduced southern industry's ability to attract investment due to lower wage rates. Moveover, increasing union membership in the South would have equalized wages, thus stripping the South if its major economic advantage—cheap labor. Southern Democrats were opposed to the Fair Labor Standards Act because it adversely affected powerful interests in their states and districts. Many Republicans were opposed as well, on the grounds of both constituent interests and philosophy. The Republicans and southern Democrats combined to block passage of the act, and thus was born the Conservative Coalition. From 1938 to 1965 the Conservative Coalition was a dominant force in the Congress. It was able to stop or seriously water down the passage of Medicare, Civil Rights, and Fair Housing legislation; increases in government management of the economy; welfare policies such as Food Stamps and Aid to Families with Dependent Children; and other legislation.

All of the cross-party coalitions from 1920 to 1965 were broadly ideological and sought to enact policies consistent with broad interests. Parties still mattered on some important issues (Mayhew, 1966), and members of Congress were still elected primarily on the basis of their party affiliation. In the late 1950s and early 1960s, representatives and senators came to be elected less often according to party affiliation than on the basis of the personal vote. In the next section the development of the personal vote is traced and its rise is shown to be concomitant with an infusion of cross-party coalitions that are policy specific in a narrow sense.

The Personal Vote

Two prominent studies of the Congress have identified elections as determinative factors not only in the behavior of members but in the structure of Congress itself and, more broadly, in the nature of national politics and policy (Mayhew, 1974b; Fiorina, 1989). A connective thread in this literature is the subject of incumbency. Mayhew (1974a) and Erikson (1972) found that, as of the mid-1960s, incumbent members of Congress began winning by larger margins, thus reducing the number of competitive districts in congressional elections. Fiorina (1989) built on these earlier findings by arguing that increases in incumbents' domination of elections affected the policy choices made by the Congress. In essence, his point was that members of Congress supported big government and bureaucracy so as to provide their constituents with goods and services, for which they took credit.

But some scholars, most notably, Garand and Gross (1984), took exception to the incumbency theories. They argued that, beginning as early as the late 1980s, a three-point advantage was associated with incumbency. They also maintained that there was a greater incumbency advantage in the 1920s than in the 1970s. Thus their work showed that the apparent pro-incumbent shift in the 1960s was only an increase in incumbency advantage and not the source of the advantage. Garand and Gross failed, however, to distinguish between partisan incumbent advantage (which arose from the demographic or organizational strength of the incumbent's party in the district) and personal incumbency advantage (which was directly related to incumbency itself [Alford and Brady, 1989]). In other words, some districts are Republican or Democratic because they are populated by groups that are strongly Republican (e.g., whites within incomes over $75,000 per year) or strongly Democratic (e.g., blue collar union workers). We need to distinguish between the vote that is strictly partisan and the vote that belongs to the incumbent due to services the representative has performed or to the incumbent's name recognition or other personal factors.

The standard measures of the personal vote attributable to the incumbent are retirement slump and sophomore surge. In each measure the personal advantage of incumbency is taken to be the difference between a party's vote share in an open-seat contest and the vote margin of an incumbent of that party in an immediately adjacent election. For example, a Republican incumbent runs for reelection in 1948, wins 58 percent of the vote, and retires before the 1950 election, creating an open seat. In the 1950 election the Republican candidate wins with 56 percent of the vote, runs for reelection in 1952, and captures 59 percent of the vote. The 1948 and 1950 elections produce a 1950 retirement slump estimate of 2 percentage points (the 1950 open-seat margin of 56 percent minus the 1948 pre-retirement margin of 58 percent). The 1950 and 1952 elections produce a 1952 sophomore surge estimate of +3 percentage points (the 1952 first-incumbent reelection margin of 59 percent minus the 1950 open-seat margin of 56 percent).

This approach to measuring incumbency advantage provides two benefits. By focusing on a single district and a set of adjacent elections, it largely controls for district characteristics. Differentiating an incumbent performance from an open-seat performance removes from gross incumbency advantage that portion due to partisan advantage, as reflected by the party's performance in an open-seat contest. The remainder is the net personal advantage enjoyed by the incumbent, above and beyond that available by virtue of the partisan or party organizational strength of the district itself. It is this concept of personal incumbency advantage on which most of the incumbency literature, and the related work in the congressional literature, implicitly turns.

Figure 13.3 presents the data for sophomore surge and retirement slump over the period 1846–1990. In each case the value for a given election year was derived by computing the mean slump or surge value for each party separately and then averaging together the two party surges or slumps irrespective of their individual n's.

Any remaining doubt as to the historically unique nature of incumbency advantage in the post–World War II era should be put to rest by Figure 13.3. Prior to 1945 there was little evidence to indicate any, even short-term, personal advantage to incumbency. Had there been such an advantage, we would expect a sophomore surge to have been positive and retirement slump to have been negative. But at that time these trends occurred only nine times out of thirty-one elections (i.e., 28 percent of the total, compared to an expected 25 percent due purely to chance), whereas after 1945 they occurred in ten out of twelve elections. Moreover, slump and surge in the pre-1945 period never occurred in the expected direction for any adjacent pair of elections.

If we use a somewhat more rigorous test for the existence of personal incumbency advantage, such that both slump and surge occur in the expected direction and both equal or exceed their respective standard errors (though hardly a stringent test by the usual statistical standards), the pattern is even more distinct. This standard was not met even once until 1966, and in every election since then, both slump and surge have been more than twice their standard errors. Personal incumbency advantage, a fluctuation that figures so prominently in the congressional literature of the past twenty years, scarcely predates that literature.

The data presented thus far pertain to the House of Representatives. The data for the Senate are more difficult to interpret because there are only 33 or 34 elections per election year, compared to 435 House elections. If, however, the data on Senate elections are aggregated by decade, the number of elections rises to around 350. The results show that there is evidence for personal incumbency advantage in Senate elections.[3] The magnitude of both retirement slump and sophomore surge is lower in the Senate than in the House. The timing of the rise of the personal vote is similar to that found in the House. Thus the same conclusions drawn for the House results can be drawn for the Senate, albeit somewhat more weakly.

Since the rise in the personal vote during the mid-1960s, incumbents have been winning reelections by wider margins. In the current Congress, members are nominated in primaries during which they must raise their own funds, organize and staff the campaign machine, and distinguish themselves from opponents of their party. After winning the nomination,

FIGURE 13.3

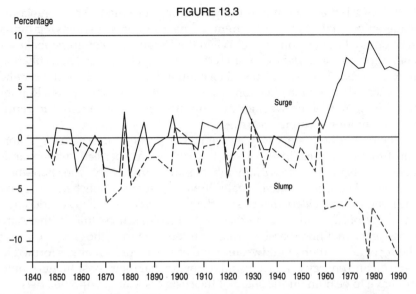

Sophomore surge and retirement slump, all House elections with major party opposition, 1846–1990. No data are shown for election years ending in 2 or 4. *Source:* Computed by authors from Alford and Brady (1989).

they rely on their personal organization and fund-raising abilities. Thus the role of the political parties has declined. In short, from the nomination through the election, members come to rely on personal resources at the expense of political parties. No other democratic political system has an electoral mechanism in which members are so independent of the party organization. Hence party is more effective and important in other countries.

Presidential coattails no longer ensure the electoral success of legislators. In the 1992 congressional elections, most Democratic candidates ran campaigns independent of the presidential race, and practically all received higher percentages of the vote than did President Clinton. Members of Congress elected on their own owe little to the party leaders on the Hill. At best, the leadership can coordinate the preferences of its party members; it has little or no ability to cajole or force members to vote with the party. As long as members can please their constituents, neither the national party nor the congressional party can affect members' electoral careers. Senator Phil Gramm (R-TX) is a classic example. Gramm was initially elected to the U.S. House of Representatives as a Democrat from College Station, the home of Texas A&M University. His voting record was very conservative. In 1981–1982 he voted with President Reagan more than 95 percent of the time. In fact, he jointly proposed with Delbert

Latta (R-OH) the now-famous budget-cutting resolution. The Democratic leadership sought to punish him in the next Congress by denying him a spot on the Budget Committee. When the Democratic congressional caucus supported its leaders, Gramm resigned his seat, changed his affiliation to Republican, and won a special election in his district to fill the seat he had vacated. In the 1984 election, he ran and won a Senate seat as a Republican. In sum, Gramm was not hurt by the Democrats' attempt to reprimand him for his voting record.

The point of this story is that given weak parties and strong legislator-constituent relationships, cross-party coalitions are perfectly understandable. Members can vote with members in the other party who share their ideology. The Conservative Coalition voting scores published yearly by the *Congressional Quarterly* attest to the pervasiveness of a major ideological coalition. In addition to cross-party ideological coalitions, there are cross-party coalitions based on district interest. During the energy crisis of the 1970s, a coalition of midwestern and eastern representatives formed to keep oil and energy prices low and to ensure that their constituents would not have to bear an undue share of the costs associated with the crisis. As John Ferejohn (1986) has shown, an urban and rural coalition has formed around price supports and food stamps. That is, rural representatives vote for food stamps to aid urban poor and, in exchange, urban representatives vote for price supports that aid rural communities.

Yet another type of coalition has formed around specific interests. Since the 1960s the number of special-interest caucuses in Congress has risen. Before 1970 there were 3 such caucuses, by 1980 there were 60, and in 1987 there were 120. The congressional Black Caucus, Women's Caucus, Hispanic Caucus, Irish Caucus, Coal Caucus, Copper Caucus, and many others have been formed. These caucuses meet on occasion, have staffs, present research papers, and in general try to influence relevant public policies. Although it is true that some of these caucuses are populated by members of only one party, their existence apart from the party system is a further indication of the importance of coalitions in the contemporary Congress.

Our listing of ideological, general, and special-interest coalitions is not meant to imply that representatives vote general (i.e., ideological) interests over their constituents' interests. Rather, our point is that representatives and senators can form coalitions with members of the other party if they can sell it to their constituents. Thus, in an important sense American public policy is less party-oriented than is public policy in other countries. In the American system, interest groups have a better chance to affect policy than do comparable special interests in other countries. The reason, in part, is that political parties can protect members from special interests by bundling policies and controlling nominations. In Britain, for example, a group like the National Rifle Association could not affect public policy as readily as it does in the United States. Within limits, British political parties control the nomination of members. Thus, they can ensure that the electorate never sees a candidate who favors gun control. Voters in Britain can choose between a party that favors policies A, B, C, D, and E and a party that favors V, W, X, Y, and Z. If the voters favor A, B, C, D, and Z, they will likely choose the first party. Because of the primaries in the United States, however, the parties cannot protect members from interests who favor Z. Thus the National Rifle Association is a powerful force in American politics, whereas it would not be so in other countries. In the United States, members of Congress must balance each interest in their district—in part because they are unprotected in primaries.

Party and Preferences

So far we have presented a portrait of a relatively weak party system in the United States, characterized by strong constituent-member ties, diminishing presidential coattails, the proliferation of cross-party coalitions, and an affinity toward divided control. Throughout the 1980s and on recent legislation in the Clinton administration, there is, however, a rise in members voting with their own party. Both the motor voter bill and campaign finance reform, passed in 1993, drew clear ideological lines between Democrats and Republicans with practically all members voting with their respective parties. Such a resurgence in partisanship, most notably in the House of Representatives, may indicate that the "party's *not* over" (Rohde, 1988, 1991). Those that document this apparent rise in party strength emphasize not only party voting but also the increasing role of the Speaker and the majority party in determining legislative procedures (Bach and Smith, 1988). Congressional parties may be weak in comparison to their European counterparts, but party still seems to be the primary and most pervasive influence on congressional behavior (Patterson and Caldeira, 1988). If roll-call votes are taken at face value, party matters.

The problem with this interpretation is the misleading measure of party strength. Roll-call votes that record a majority of Democrats against a majority of Republicans are vacuous without an understanding of *why* the individuals cast their ballots with their party. In order to assess the strength of party in the policymaking process, we must look at the distribution of legislators' preferences on any given issue.

For example, take two policies in the Senate. The roll-call vote is the same for each, 56 Democrats voting in favor and 44 Republicans voting against. In both cases, all members voted their party's position; two identical results occurred but a closer look at individual preferences tells two very different stories. The preferences are distributed as such in Figure 13.4. A vote of 56–44 is not surprising in Policy A, nor is it conclusive as to the power of party over members' votes. In this particular case, party hap-

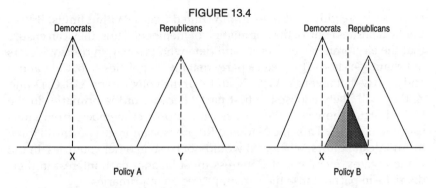

FIGURE 13.4

Alternative models of policy preferences and floor votes. *Source:* Krehbiel (1993).

pens to be a good measure of individual preferences. An example of such a distribution (though not as clean—a few crossed party lines) may be the partisan division on the vote for motor-voter legislation and campaign finance reform, with each side capturing an overwhelming majority of members. Was the vote, however, the result of strong party leadership or did the vote reflect the individual preferences of the members? The problem of determining whether party or preference accounts for the vote is illustrated by Policy B. To arrive at the same 56–44 result, some legislators had to vote against their own preferences (as established by the electoral connection) to support the party position. In these policy arenas with more heterogeneous preference distributions, votes cast with respective parties are indicative of strong party leadership.

Divided and Unified Control

With the extensive literature on the decline of party discipline in the government, in party organization, and in party identification among the electorate, it is ironic that party is commonly identified as the source of gridlock. Research on the repercussions of divided control have for the most part adopted the "party matters" interpretation, in which the president bargains with the median of the majority party (see Fiorina, 1992a; Jacobson, 1990; Mayhew, 1991; Kernell and Cox, 1991). A Republican president is presumably to the right of the Democratic party median; thus the Bush-Reagan years resulted in gridlock. The Clinton administration, with both branches under the same party label, should experience minimal problems in passing the budget resolution or the health care bill. Conservative Democrats will vote with the Clinton proposals rather than vote with the Republicans. If parties are the chief influence on behavior, then periods of unified governance will yield policy closer to the majority congressional party median. A "party matters" interpretation predicts major shifts in policy for the Clinton administration, unfathomable in times of divided control.

But perhaps gridlock is not a party-driven phenomenon. The heterogeneity of preferences among the electorate and complexity of policy areas may be the source of gridlock regardless of divided or unified control. In *Divided We Govern*, David Mayhew (1991) examines gridlock in terms of amount of legislation passed, successful and unsuccessful vetoes, congressional hearings, presidential treaties signed, and appointments approved. Excluding the number of vetoes, he concludes that there is no significant difference in these variables under divided versus unified control. In fact, "the number of laws per Congress varies more *within* universes of unified or divided times than it does between them" (Mayhew, 1991:76, emphasis added). Therefore, Mayhew's evidence, at a minimum, indicates that party is not the cause of gridlock and perhaps claims of paralysis are greatly overestimated. Still we are left in the dark as to the sources of gridlock, if not interparty conflict. Although Mayhew does not specify, his work is perfectly compatible with a median voter account of politics. Regardless of whether the president is a Democrat or a Republican, the policy output will be close to the preference of the median voter in Congress. The median voter need not be of the majority party; the position changes across issue areas. Some Republicans, such as Jeffords (UT) and Specter (PA) are to the right of some Democrats, such as Shelby (AL), and vice versa. This phenomenon is unlikely to change in a unified government.

When party preferences overlap, ideological and policy-specific coalitions encourage members to cross party lines when their preferences are not reflected in the party position. For example, conservative Democrats (such as Representative Charles Stenholm's Conservative Democratic Caucus) often vote with moderate Republicans on economic policy. A weak party view predicts Clinton policy will not move left toward the Democratic party median because bargains are made with the centrist voters in the House, not within the party itself. If party is the sum of constituent preferences and preferences are mixed, legislation will not assume a coherent direction even in times of unified control.

Given Mayhew's findings, coupled with the heterogeneity of preferences within the legislature, party may not be the source of gridlock. In fact, legislation that passes in both forms of government more than likely reflects constituent preferences. Thus our perception of the gridlock problem is that it may have less to do with party and more to do with preferences. The Carter administration, not remembered for sweeping change and swift legislation, proved that legislation cannot be expected to be pushed through merely because both the executive and legislative branches share the same party label. The heterogeneity of the Democratic party prevented unified control from promoting more agreement in the policy process. A president must bargain with the median voter position on the floor and, especially in the Democratic case, where the distribution of the party is more spread than in the Republican party, not get pulled too far left by the congressional party.

As a result, predictions on gridlock are contingent on interpretation of party. In both strong and weak party interpretations, the median voter on the floor pulls a Republican president to the right and a Democratic president to the left. But the two views of party lead to entirely different predictions on policy. The first unified government since 1980 provides an excellent opportunity for testing theories of divided government. With a theory based on congressional preferences instead of pure party, interests come to the forefront of policy assessment. Given the weakening of partisan ties in the electorate, a nonpartisan interpretation that reflects interest distribution seems the more logical and accurate predictor of policy. Table 13.1 shows how the two theories of party differ on divided government, gridlock, and the Clinton presidency.

CONCLUSION

We began by asserting that the major difference between congressional coalitions in the United States and coalitions in other countries is that U.S. elections and policy are disjointed. Beginning in the Progressive era, political parties came to be composed of members who held different views. From the 1920s through the 1950s a number of cross-party coalitions emerged, the farm bloc and the Conservative Coalition being the most important. With the rise of the personal vote, the hold of party over member was further diminished, and there was a concomitant rise in the number of general and special-interest coalitions. Understanding the contemporary Congress's legislative record is thus increasingly a task of understanding the cross-party coalitions that form and reform across a broad number of issues.

This scenario would seem to be somewhat contradicted by recent studies that show an increase in levels of party voting in the Congress, but that trend should not be overemphasized. Even with the rise in party voting, there is no doubt that legislative parties are weaker and cross-party coalitions are stronger in the United States than in other democracies. Furthermore, in order to claim that the rise in party voting is meaningful, one most know the extent to which policy content has been changed. In European party government, cabinets propose policies that regular members vote for in Parliament, and voters then choose between parties. If the increase in party voting in the U.S. Congress is attributable to the leaders' better coordination of members' preferences, then, in principle, there is a

TABLE 13.1
Two Theories of Party

	Strong Party ("party matters")	Weak Party ("aggregate of preferences")
Divided government	breaks gridlock	doesn't break gridlock
Primary actors	• party majority leaders • president	• median voter (both R and D according to policy) • president
Gridlock	divided government causes gridlock	no such thing as gridlock
Clinton presidency	breaks gridlock, shifts policy to the left	same as Carter

difference. That is, party positions are determined by calculating each member's preferences, and policy differences between parties are minimized by giving voters less to choose between. Thus party strength in Europe as well as Japan, and, more important, in the United States at the turn of the century, is clearly very different from party strength in the United States today.

It remains difficult to determine, policy to policy in both House and Senate, whether a vote is the result of constituent preferences or a response to party pressure. Electorally it is clear that the rise in the personal vote as calculated by sophomore surge and retirement slump is a reasonable measure of party influence on members' elections. It remains, however, difficult to determine party strength in Congress without an assessment of legislators' preferences. The key is to connect voters' preferences to election results to members' voting behavior. Until such a connection is made, any theory of unified and divided government will be incomplete.

We believe that coalitions will continue to be critical in policymaking even under unified control of government. Journalistic evaluations of Clinton's first 100 days used gridlock as a measuring stick of success or failure. We believe that a closer look at the variety of forces and avenues of opposition Clinton faced on the economic package will highlight the heterogeneity of preferences. Opposition comes in many forms, not just in the filibusters of the Republicans denouncing tax-and-spend legislation. Clinton faced opposition beyond Senate minority leader Robert Dole. Special interests from upper-class retirees to military to Western ranchers, miners, and loggers turned to senators and representatives from both parties to rally against Clinton's economic proposals. Most pertinent to our discussion is the opposition Clinton faced within his own party. Chair of the Ways and Means Committee Dan Rostenkowski and Finance Chair Daniel Patrick Moynihan opposed investment tax credit. But the strongest threat came from Senator David Boren, the swing vote in the Finance Committee, who led a cross-party "gang of four" up to the eleventh hour. Democratic energy interests and deficit hawks maintain the critical median vote position on economic policy. They hold the power to pull Clinton toward the center, to reduce a stimulus package of $16 billion to $4 billion. A lack of party discipline and no mechanisms for punishment have made coalitions essential. Members will continue to vote their constituent preferences, and under such conditions cross-party coalitions will continue to be present. As of this writing, the critical matter of the budget has narrowly passed both the House and Senate without a single Republican in support. With a Democrat majority of 56 to 44, Vice-President Gore had to cast the deciding vote. Now as the bill goes to conference committee, the question is whether Clinton and the Democrats can win without attracting the votes of some Republicans. Health care issues, the North American Free Trade Agreement, and environmental legislation all constitute areas where we believe that without Republican votes, President Clinton cannot win. Presidential proposals that veer too far from the median course, whether to the left or the right, will in fact fail unless changed and moved to the middle.

NOTES

1. This phenomenon is deeply rooted in the American federal system. The Republican party was divided on the gold-silver question prior to 1896 and on the question of welfare and government management of the economy in the post–Franklin D. Roosevelt period.

2. In this section, we rely on the work of Joseph Cooper (1975).

3. These data were taken from Alford and Hibbing (1983).

14

Partisan Leadership Through Presidential Appointments

G. CALVIN MACKENZIE

Politics is about control. Who controls the policymaking process, and to what end? In a democracy, the legitimate exercise of political power falls to those who win free elections. One of the benefits of victory is the authority to control appointments to those executive offices that are not filled by election but that contribute substantially to the determination of public policy.

Throughout much of American history, political parties have served as wholesalers in this democratic process. In choosing a president, the American people also choose a political party to run the executive branch. From 1800, when Thomas Jefferson's election signaled a transfer of power from the Federalists to the Democratic Republicans, until 1992, when Bill Clinton's election ended twelve years of Republican control, parties have been a primary conduit for the translation of electoral victories into public policies. As the election of Jefferson portended the appointment of Democratic Republicans with their policy preferences, so the election of Bill Clinton heralded the appointment of Democrats with their policy preferences.

To the casual observer, not much has changed. The tides that sweep into government after each election are party tides, carrying in the new president's co-partisans and carrying out the co-partisans of the old. But that surface appearance masks a set of important changes in the role that political parties now play in the staffing of presidential administrations and in appointments to the federal judiciary. Although party is the glue that seems to hold administrations together, its consistency is much thinner than ever before and its holding power is greatly reduced. What endures is the party label; what has changed is the meaning of the label and the influence of the party organizations in presidential personnel decisions. Elections are still about control, but now more than ever before, they are about policy control rather than party control.

This essay will examine the changes that have occurred in party impacts on federal executive staffing in this century.[1] It begins with a look at the pre–New Deal experience. The New Deal and post-war evolution are then explored. That is followed by an effort to illuminate the reasons for the change in party role and influence, and to explain the impact of that change on the governing process.

PARTIES IN GOVERNMENT: STAFFING THE EXECUTIVE BRANCH

The Birth of Parties

The Constitution, and the debates from which it sprang, anticipated no role for political parties in staffing the government. In fact, the framers of the Constitution did not very seriously contemplate the emergence of political parties, nor did they envision a government of such size that positions could not be filled by the president's personal acquaintances. There was little need for them to worry about the details of the appointment process, for they had not worried very much about the details of the executive or judicial branches.

The framers seemed to believe that a single person—the president— would make wiser personnel choices than any collective body sharing the appointment power. And, although they established the Senate's right of advice and consent as a check against defective appointments, they thought they had created a process that the president would dominate. As Alexander Hamilton pointed out in the 76th *Federalist*, that was their clear intent.

> [O]ne man of discernment is better fitted to analise and estimate the peculiar qualities adapted to particular offices, than a body of men of equal, or perhaps even of superior discernment.
>
> The sole and undivided responsibility of one man will naturally beget a livelier sense of duty and a more exact regard to reputation. He will on this account feel himself under stronger obligations, and more interested to investigate with care the qualities requisite to the stations to be filled, and to prefer with impartiality the persons who may have the fairest pretensions to them. ... [I]n every exercise of the power of appointing to offices by an assembly of men, we must expect to see a full display of all the private party likings and dislikes, partialities and antipathies, attachments and animosities, which are felt by those who compose the assembly. The choice which may at any time happen to be made under such circumstances will of course be the result either of a victory gained by one party over the other, or of a compromise between the parties. ... In the first, the qualifications best adapted to uniting the suffrages of the party will be more considered than

those which fit the person for the station. In the last the coalition will commonly turn upon some interested equivalent—"Give us the man we wish for this office, and you shall have the one you wish for that." This will be the usual condition of the bargain. And it will rarely happen that the advancement of the public service will be the primary object either of party victories or of party negotiations. (Cooke, 1961:510–511)

In filling appointive positions, George Washington relied—about as the framers had anticipated—on people of whom he had personal knowledge. Thomas Jefferson, Henry Knox, Edmund Randolph, and Alexander Hamilton filled the cabinet slots; Thomas Pinckney was appointed ambassador to Great Britain and Gouverneur Morris to France; and John Jay became the first chief justice. Washington's circle of acquaintances was large, and the number of positions he needed to fill was small.

When required to fill federal positions of primarily local importance, such as customs collectors or postmasters, Washington found it convenient to defer to the judgment of senators from the relevant states. This practice quickly acquired the veneer of custom when the first Senate rejected Washington's appointment of Benjamin Fishbourn to be naval officer for the port of Savannah, Georgia. Fishbourn was fully qualified for the post, but the two senators from Georgia preferred another candidate and succeeded in convincing their colleagues to reject the Fishbourn nomination (Mackenzie, 1981:93). Hence was born the concept of "senatorial courtesy," by which senators are granted significant influence over presidential appointments within their home states. (When parties later emerged, the courtesy was usually granted only to senators of the president's party.)

Although most of Washington's appointees shared his views on important issues, there was little sense of them and him as members of the same political party. Even as disagreements began to emerge on major issues of the day—the Jay treaty and the financing of state debts, for example— they produced cleavages that only slowly formed into lasting factions. Washington sought men of experience and judgment to aid him in running the government. Whatever political litmus test he might have applied was informal and primitive.

That changed rather rapidly, however, after Washington's retirement and the election of John Adams. With Washington gone, politics became more bare-knuckled and political factions hardened. Adams's appointees took on a clearly defined political coloration: Only Federalists need apply. On the eve of his departure from government and the transfer of power to the Jeffersonians, Adams sought to pack the government with Federalist appointments to many lower-level positions. Jefferson and his secretary of state, James Madison, tried to block these midnight appointments. The

Supreme Court, in the great case of *Marbury v. Madison*, permitted them to do so. The battle was joined, and appointments would forever after be a chief prize of partisan politics.

The Spoils System

Partisan control of presidential appointments reached its zenith with the election of Andrew Jackson in 1828. His approach to appointments came to be known as the "spoils system," following the old adage that "to the victor belong the spoils." In the case of victors in presidential elections, the primary "spoils" were federal jobs.

In truth, Jackson did not invent the spoils system, nor was he the first president to put it into practice. But he was so vigorous in using his appointment powers to place his own loyalists in government offices and so shameless about doing so that his presidency has usually been marked as a watershed in the development of federal personnel practices. Jackson's presidency was all the more noteworthy, perhaps, because it resulted in a significant change in the kinds of people who staffed the federal government. Earlier presidents, in seeking fit candidates for office, had often turned to members of the country's wealthier families, and through the first six presidencies there was a distinct upper-class cast to the executive branch. The turn toward popular democracy that Jackson's election signified found expression in his appointees, many of whom had little wealth or education.

To political observers of the time, this suggested not only that Jackson intended to sweep out all previous office holders in favor of his own supporters but also that political loyalty was to be the principal measure of fitness for office. Jobs in government began to be viewed as rewards for political services to the successful candidate.

Not coincidentally, this was a period of intense partisanship in American politics. Parties were becoming national political organizations and began to hold quadrennial national nominating conventions. Connections among partisans at the local, state, and national levels were becoming tighter. The trickle of immigration was also just beginning and would soon turn into one of the great floods in human history. As politicians sought the support of these new groups, increasing numbers of recent immigrants were finding work in government offices or party organizations. Before long, pressure began to build to expand the number of government jobs and to make as many of them as possible available for political appointment. The state and local political machines were growing, and they developed hearty appetites for government jobs (see White, 1954, 1958; Van Riper, 1958; Fish, 1904).

One consequence of these political developments was that government jobs were becoming an increasingly valuable currency. Political leaders and members of Congress began to contest with the president for control over the appointment process. Presidents came to realize that the well-timed appointment of a political supporter of a member of Congress or a party boss could often produce votes for legislation in Congress. Trading of this sort took place in earnest.

This was also a time when U.S. senators were chosen by their state legislatures, not by direct election. Since most of those senators were beholden for their offices to the leaders of their party, not to the people directly, they were eager to assist in whatever way they could to acquire federal government jobs for party members in their states. This situation only added to the pressure to treat the appointment process as a supplement to party politics rather than as a mechanism for attracting the country's most talented people into the public service. Political credentials were more usually valuable in seeking a federal job than talent or administrative experience.

Not surprisingly, the quality of the federal service during most of the nineteenth century was, at best, uneven. A great many positions were filled by appointees—sometimes called "spoilsmen"—who lacked any apparent substantive qualifications. The government survived this practice, in part, at least, because it was not engaged in many activities that required significant technical or management skills. In fact, most of the technical specialties that now exist in government agencies were unknown in the nineteenth century: astrophysics, econometrics, environmental analysis, and so on.[2] The principal preoccupations of government in the nineteenth century were the conduct of a small number of routine functions that required little skill or experience: delivering the mail, collecting customs duties and taxes, building roads and canals. In many cases, a political hack could do these jobs about as well as anyone else. What was good for the party, therefore, was not always terrible for the government.

Nevertheless, the spoils system began to produce the seeds of its own destruction. The principal failing, of course, was that many of the people employed by the government were not the most talented or the most qualified available. In many cases, in fact, they were totally without qualifications other than their political connections. The spoils system was also a hungry monster, a constant source of pressure for the creation of new government jobs to provide for more political appointments and to lighten the burden on office holders so that they could devote more of their time to political activities.

The spoils system also invited corruption of all sorts because appointees were not constrained by a sense of the honor of public service or confined by any ethical notions of holding a public trust. They had their jobs because their party won an election and attained political power. And so long as they held that power, there were few real limits on how they could exercise it. Knowing that their horizon extended only to the next election, appointees were also driven to take advantage of their offices as hastily as they could, for they might soon be out of a job. If the sun was to shine only briefly, they felt compelled to make hay all the more quickly.

Another troubling aspect of the spoils system was the pressure it put on the president to devote substantial amounts of time to filling low-level positions in the federal government. Presidents in the nineteenth century had none of the elaborate White House staff structure that exists today. There was no one to whom they could delegate responsibility for handling patronage matters. Thus many hours were consumed brokering conflicting demands for appointments to individual offices. A story about President Lincoln suggests the plague-like quality of these pressures. The White House was a public building for much of the nineteenth century, and there were few restrictions on access to the main lobby. Job seekers often came there hoping for a moment or two with the president to plead their case. Lincoln found it very uncomfortable to pass through the lobby on the way to his office because his very presence often set off a flurry of such pleading. Once, when he was suffering from a bad cold, he said to his secretary as he was about to enter the lobby, "Now, at last, I have something I can give them."

The Creation of the Civil Service

Efforts to reform the personnel staffing process of the federal government appeared as early as the 1850s and gathered steam after the Civil War. Rutherford B. Hayes was elected president in 1876, having campaigned for civil service reform. He made little headway against congressional resistance, however, during the next four years. His successor, James A. Garfield, had been a supporter of reform while serving in Congress. He was assassinated four months after his inauguration—in the legend of the time, by a "disappointed federal job seeker"—and reformers used his slaying as evidence of the rottenness of the spoils system and the acute need for reform. Two years later, in 1883, Congress passed the Pendleton Act, which created the federal civil service system.

This was hardly the death of the spoils system. Civil service protection spread slowly among government jobs. The majority remained subject to political appointment for years yet to come. Some categories continued to be filled through political appointment until well into the twentieth century. Local postmasters, for example, remained political appointees until 1970. And even the most vigorous of the reformers recognized that some positions would always be political in character and thus could never be blanketed under the coverage of a merit-based civil service. But a significant change had begun in 1883, and it would continue to spread in the century that followed, as Table 14.1 indicates.

TABLE 14.1
Growth of the Federal Civil Service System

Year	Total Civilian Employment	Percentage Under the Merit System
1821	6,914	
1831	11,491	
1841	18,038	
1851	26,274	
1861	36,672	
1871	51,020	
1881	100,020	
1891	157,442	21.5
1901	239,456	44.3
1911	395,905	57.5
1921	561,142	79.9
1931	609,746	76.8
1941	1,437,682	68.9
1951	2,482,666	86.4
1961	2,435,804	86.1
1970	2,921,909	81.9
1975	2,741,000	83.1
1980	2,772,000	78.5
1990	3,050,326	81.0

Sources: Data derived from Stanley and Niemi (1988:218); U.S. Department of Commerce (1987:309–311); Mace and Yoder (1992:307).

The Pendleton Act, including its subsequent refinements, accomplished several ends. First, it set the principle that government jobs should be open and available to all citizens and should be filled by those who successfully demonstrate that they are best qualified for the position. Second, it established the policy that examinations were the best and most objective way to determine those qualifications. Third, it provided civil servants with protections against political removal and established a pattern of continuity: Civil servants would continue in office even as the presidency changed hands. And, fourth, to supervise this system and protect its neutrality from politics, the act created a Civil Service Commission whose membership would have to reflect a degree of partisan balance.[3]

Growing out of the success of the reform movement was a new question, one that has continued to be debated into our own time. Once the principle was established that some positions in the government should be filled on the basis of merit, not politics, arguments ensued about where the line should be drawn. Which positions should be granted civil service protection and which should continue to be treated as political appointments? The spread of civil service protection indicated in Table 14.1 suggests that a steadily growing percentage of federal offices have been placed outside of the political stream. But what of those offices left unprotected by the merit system? How were they to be filled? And by whom? That is the topic of the rest of this essay.

PRESIDENTIAL APPOINTMENTS IN THE TWENTIETH CENTURY

1900–1932

Except that a slowly increasing number of government jobs were coming under the coverage of the civil service, the appointment process in the first third of the twentieth century varied little from what it had been in the second half of the nineteenth. The positions outside the civil service were still filled by means of a process in which political parties played an important role and appointments were still viewed as a reward for political services.

This is not to suggest that all presidential appointees lacked substantive qualifications for federal service. Many of those who had been party activists had also built impressive records of public service and would have merited high-level positions even without party sponsorship. Names like Charles Evans Hughes and William Jennings Bryan would have appeared on most lists of highly qualified eligibles for cabinet or other top positions in government. And presidents also retained the latitude to select appointees who had no significant record of party service, whose primary qualification was talent or experience. In this category were people like Josephus Daniels, Andrew Mellon, and Henry Stimson.

But partisan pressures in the appointment process were ever present. In putting together their cabinets, for example, presidents felt constrained to select people who represented different factions or regional elements in their party (Fenno, 1959:78–88). In this sense, Woodrow Wilson's cabinet was not very different from Abraham Lincoln's. Though strong-willed and independent leaders, both felt compelled to respect partisan concerns in staffing the top positions in their administrations.

Throughout this period, the national party organizations played an important role in identifying candidates for presidential appointments. It was quite common, in fact, for the head of the president's party to hold a position in the cabinet, usually as Postmaster General. This made sense, not only because the Post Office Department was the principal consumer of patronage appointments but also because a cabinet post provided a vantage point from which the party leader could work with the president and other cabinet secretaries to ensure a steady flow of partisan loyalists into federal posts throughout the government.

The party role was critical to the functioning of the government because there was at the time no alternative source of candidates for appointment. Each cabinet secretary had his own acquaintances and contacts, but few of them knew enough politicians to fill all the available positions in their departments with people who would be loyal to the administration, pass muster with appropriate members of Congress, and satisfy the political litmus tests of party leaders in the states and cities where they might serve. The party could help with all of that.

If some of those the parties brought forward to fill appointive positions were unqualified political hacks—and some surely were—the parties performed valuable functions well. Many of the appointees who came through the party channel were skilled and qualified. This was by no means merely a turkey trot. More important, partisan control of the appointment process usually guaranteed the construction of an administration that was broadly representative of the elements of the president's party and thus, in some important ways, in touch with the American people it was intended to serve. Equally important, the parties served as an employment agency upon which the government was heavily reliant. They provided a steady stream of politically approved candidates for federal offices. That was a function of no small significance in a government that lacked any other tested means of recruitment for positions outside the civil service.

1933–1952

Following the pattern of his predecessors, Franklin Roosevelt appointed James Farley, the leader of the Democratic party, to serve as Postmaster General and to superintend the selection of lower-level appointments in the first Roosevelt administration. Farley directed a patronage operation that bore a close resemblance to those of the previous half-century.

Despite the familiar look of FDR's patronage operation, however, changes were set in motion by the New Deal that would have lasting consequences for the staffing of presidential administrations. Three of those deserve some mention here.

The first was the very nature of the politics of the New Deal. The coalition that brought Franklin Roosevelt to office was composed of a broad divergence of groups and views. It provided FDR a sweeping victory by drawing support from Americans who disagreed with each other about important matters yet agreed on the need to elect a president of their own party. But the New Deal coalition soon proved as useless for running a government as it had been useful for winning elections. Even with the most delicate kind of balancing act, it was no small task to construct an administration of intellectuals and union members, northern liberals and southern conservatives, progressives and racists. The task was complicated all the more by the intensity of the new administration's efforts not merely to redirect but to *reconstruct* public policy in the United States. It simply could not be reliably assumed that Democratic appointees would fully support all the dimensions of the president's program.

Hence Roosevelt and his senior advisers increasingly began to end-run the Democratic party patronage system in filling key positions in the government. More and more, the people closest to the president—James Rowe, Louis Howe, Harry Hopkins, and others—began to run their own recruitment programs. Typically they would identify bright young men who were already serving in government or anxious to do so and cultivate them with the kind of ad hoc assignments that prepared them for more important managerial positions. These men were either lifelong or recently converted Democrats, but they tended not to be people with any history of party activism. It was the passions of the time and their commitment to the New Deal that inspired their interest in politics, not a pattern of service to local or state political machines.

The need for such people grew increasingly apparent as the consequence of a second change wrought by the New Deal. The government was growing. Total federal employment was 604,000 in 1933. It had nearly doubled by the end of the decade. The New Deal seemed to be spawning new agencies and programs almost daily. The result was a voracious need not merely for people to fill newly created slots but for skilled managers and creative program specialists to attend to problems at least as complicated as any the federal government had ever before tackled.

This complexity also had the effect of diminishing the importance of the party patronage system as a source of appointees. It became increasingly apparent that the party faithful did not always include the kinds of people required to operate technical agencies such as the Securities and Exchange Commission and the Agriculture Adjustment Administration. So Roosevelt turned to other sources, even occasionally risking the wrath of party leaders in so doing.

A third change in the New Deal years fed the momentum of the first two. That was the growing importance of the White House staff. As the energy of the federal government came to be centered in the president— and it was dramatically during the New Deal—the need for more support for the president became increasingly apparent. In 1936, Roosevelt appointed a committee headed by his friend Louis Brownlow to study the organization of the executive branch and to make recommendations. The report of the Brownlow Committee described the need for vigorous executive leadership to make a modern democracy work. But it also pointed out that "the President needs help" in this enterprise. It went on to recommend both the creation of an Executive Office of the President (EOP) and the creation of presidential authority to appoint a small personal staff that would assist in the management of the government (President's Committee on Administrative Management, 1936). In 1939, the Congress acted affirmatively on most of the recommendations of the Brownlow Committee.

In the past, presidents had little choice but to rely on their party's patronage operation because they lacked the staff necessary to run a personnel-recruitment operation of their own. With the creation of the EOP, that began to change. Embedded in the recommendations of the Brownlow Committee was a philosophy of public management that also threatened the importance of party patronage. Political control of the government, in the view of Brownlow and his many supporters in the schools of public administration, had come to mean policy control, not merely party control. It was no longer enough for a president to staff his administration with members of his own party and to let them work with co-partisans in Congress to superintend the routines of government. Instead, the president needed managerial support through broader control of the budget, government organization, and personnel selection to move public policy in the direction that he had set and for which he had earned the endorsement of the American electorate.

This gradual evolution in management philosophy clearly suggested the need for the president and his personal staff to play a larger role in recruiting appointees who supported his policy priorities and possessed the skills and creativity necessary to develop and implement them. In that scheme, government jobs could not be viewed primarily as rewards for party loyalty, and recruitment could not be left primarily to party patronage operations.

None of these changes took place overnight, but they slowly found their way into the operations of the presidency. Loyal Democrats continued to claim positions in the Roosevelt and, later, the Truman administrations. The pressure to fill vacancies with the party faithful did not abate. The Democratic National Committee continued to operate a full-service employment agency. But few of the appointments to important positions came via this route any longer.

The strains on the patronage operation grew more acute after Roosevelt's death. Truman found himself in an odd position. Though a Democrat like Roosevelt, he needed to forge his own identity as president. Members of his party often had difficulty in transferring their loyalties from the dead president to the new one, especially since many of them thought Truman was several cuts below Roosevelt in stature.

The 1948 election campaign widened the fissures in the Democratic party all the more. The southern wing of the party split off to support then Democratic Governor Strom Thurmond of South Carolina. The so-called Progressive wing had its own candidate in Henry Wallace. After winning reelection, Truman found that he had to temper his faith, slender as it already had become, in the ability of the Democratic party to provide candidates for appointment who were certain to be loyal to him and the important policies of his presidency.

Truman did what any reasonable leader would have done under the circumstances. He relied less heavily on candidates recommended by the party and built his own recruitment process. The latter never passed much beyond the primitive stage, and the former continued to play an important role. But change was under way, and its full impacts would emerge in the administrations that followed.

1952–1968

Dwight Eisenhower was the least partisan president of the twentieth century, and he came to office with fewer debts to his party than any of his predecessors. Though Republicans had not controlled the presidency for twenty years, Eisenhower's election did not signify the beginning of a flood of old-line Republican loyalists into federal offices. Eisenhower's chief of staff, Sherman Adams, reported that the president was often indignant at what he considered to be political interference in his appointments and that he "avoided giving the Republican National Committee any responsibility for the selection of government officials, a duty the committee would have been happy to assume" (Adams, 1961:125). Charles F. Willis, Jr., an Eisenhower aide who worked on personnel matters, said that the president "seemed to react against intense political pressure, more than anything else that I noticed, adversely, and I think that his appointments and the people he surrounded himself with at the top level reflected that he considered quality rather than political know-how" (Willis, 1968:28).

Eisenhower did intend to oust as many New Dealers and Fair Dealers as he could, but he sought to replace them with people who subscribed to his own brand of Republicanism. Being a Republican, even a lifelong member of the party faithful, was not enough to get a job in the Eisenhower administration—as soon became evident to Republicans across the country.

Although the new administration worked closely with Republican National Committee Chairman Leonard Hall and did in fact place a number of party loyalists, appointments to top-level positions were much more heavily influenced by a group of the president's close friends. During the 1952 transition, Lucius Clay, Herbert Brownell, and Harold Talbott commissioned the New York consulting firm of McKinsey and Company to do a study identifying the most important positions in the government. Then, in the years that followed, they were an important source of suggestion and advice to Eisenhower on matters of government staffing.

The composition of the Eisenhower administration quickly came to reflect the diminished role of the president's party as a source of senior-level personnel. A majority of Eisenhower's first cabinet had no significant history of Republican party activism. The subcabinet looked much the same, having drawn heavily on the practical talents of the business and legal communities, with only a scattering of officials whose primary credentials were partisan or political (Mann, 1965:293).

Eisenhower's second term marked an even more important turning point in the transition away from party dominance of the appointment process. The Twenty-Second Amendment, limiting presidents to two terms in office, had been ratified in 1951. Eisehnower was the first president to whom it applied, and his reelection in 1956 made him the first president ever to enter a term as a lame duck. Since he could not run again for reelection, there was less incentive for Eisenhower to be making appointments with an eye toward building partisan electoral support: He was freer than ever to distance himself from patronage pressures.

That freedom was reflected in the significant initiatives that developed during Eisenhower's second term for management of the personnel function in the presidency, not the party. The Eisenhower White House was the first to respond to a modern president's need for centralized control over executive branch personnel by seeking to construct procedures and organizational structures to serve that objective. The position of Special Assistant for Personnel Management was created, and the first elements of a systematic recruitment operation were put in place (Kaufman, 1965:66).

This momentum toward centralized presidential control of the appointment process and away from reliance on party patronage accelerated in the Kennedy and Johnson administrations. Kennedy, like Eisenhower, had won the presidential nomination by setting up his own organization and capturing the party. His was not a life of deeply committed partisanship nor did he grant the Democratic party organization much credit for his narrow victory in the 1960 election. So Kennedy felt little compulsion to staff his administration with party loyalists to whom he might have had any debt or obligation. From the very start, he and his staff operated their own personnel-recruitment operation.

After Kennedy's assassination, Lyndon Johnson continued the practice of operating a White House personnel office. He designated John Macy, then chairman of the Civil Service Commission, to handle presidential appointments as well. Macy expanded the personnel office and began to systematize its procedures, even employing computers to maintain records on thousands of potential appointees.

Under both Kennedy and Johnson, the White House personnel office worked with the Democratic National Committee, in varying degrees of cooperation. But the participation of the party was clearly subsidiary. Most of the time the National Committee's role was to determine that candidates for appointment selected by the White House would not incur the opposition of party leaders in their home states. The White House also conducted checks with home-state Democratic senators and members of Congress to avoid opposition from them. But as Dan H. Fenn, Jr., an assistant to Kennedy on personnel matters, said: "The kind of people we were looking for weren't the kind of people who were active in party activities" (Fenn, 1976).

These checks, which came to be known as clearances, emerged as a routine of the appointment process and provided a role for the party, albeit a limited one. Although party officials were a steady source of suggestions regarding potential nominees, genuine control over personnel selection had shifted to the White House. This process had begun in the early days of the New Deal; it accelerated as the size of the White House staff grew. The party ceased to have an initiative role in the appointment process and clearly no longer operated that process as it once had. The party had become a check point and, with but few exceptions, not much more. As Hugh Heclo has indicated, its influence was reduced to the exercise of "'negative clearance'; that is, nursing political referrals and clearing official appointments in order to placate those political leaders in Congress and in state, local, or other organizations who might otherwise take exception" (Heclo, 1977:71). The party no longer drove the appointment process, but its disapproval of an appointment could bring that process to a temporary halt.

1969 and Beyond

The movement to centralize control over presidential appointments reached new levels of sophistication and success in the administration of Richard Nixon and those that followed. Nixon himself never had much interest in personnel selection, but the people to whom he delegated that task tended to be experienced professional managers who saw personnel selection as a critical ingredient in efforts to establish control over the executive branch.

In the years after 1969, the White House Personnel Office (later called the Presidential Personnel Office) became an important component of the White House Office and grew in size. It now routinely employs more than thirty people, and often swells to more than fifty at particularly busy times. Appointment procedures have been systematized and routinized. Computers play an important role in tracking the progress of appointments. And clearances with leaders of the president's party, with relevant members of Congress, with officials in the agency to which an appointment is to be made, and with policy specialists in the administration are regular features of almost every appointment decision (Mackenzie, 1981; Bonafede, 1987).

But the most important characteristic of the modern appointment process, and the one that most critically affects the influence of political parties, has been the creation of a genuine and aggressive recruitment or outreach capability within the White House staff. Party influence in appointments remained significant as long as the White House lacked the ability to identify qualified candidates on its own. Then the president and his staff had little choice but to respond to recommendations and suggestions that came in, as the terminology of the time had it, "over the transom." It is an iron law of politics that "you can't beat someone with no one," and of football that "the best defense is a good offense." Both apply in the appointment process as well.

The thrust of most of the contemporary development of White House personnel operations has been to grasp the initiative, to relieve presidents from reliance on external sources for their appointees. Primary among those sources historically was the president's own political party organization, but the successful establishment of a recruiting capability in the White House has left the parties with little remaining control over a function they once dominated.

PARTIES AND PRESIDENTIAL LEADERSHIP: AN ACCELERATING EVOLUTION

The years after World War II have been a time of diminishing influence for the national party organizations in the operations of the presidency. This was a trend with pre-war antecedents, but its pace accelerated after the war. There is no simple explanation for the change. In fact, it resulted from a confluence of other changes occurring both inside and outside of the government in those years. The most important of those are summarized here.

The Game Changed

Party influence was always greatest with respect to appointments to positions outside of Washington. When an appointee was to serve as customs collector for the port of Philadelphia or as postmaster in Butte, local party officials generally had a determining influence in choosing the person to fill the slot. Even though this was technically a presidential appointment, presidents readily deferred to the leaders of their party in the local area. Until relatively recent times there were tens of thousands of such positions and they were a significant part of the political rewards system for party workers. A person who had spent years as party organizer, poll watcher, and minor office holder could reasonably expect to cap a political career with an appointment to a sinecure as a local official of the federal government.

But after World War II, largely at the behest of an increasingly vocal public service reform movement, many of these positions were taken out of the patronage stream and placed under some form of civil service coverage. What was good for the party was increasingly bad for the delivery of government services. And the reformers thought the solution was to take some of the politics out of appointments to these administrative offices.

The Number of Important Presidential Appointments Grew

From the beginning of the New Deal onward, the number of senior-level positions in the federal government grew. New cabinet departments and independent agencies were added. Old ones expanded as hordes of new programs were created. The bureaucracy thickened and new administrative layers were added to the federal government. Departments that might have had two or three presidential appointees before World War II now have a dozen or more. The Department of Defense, which came into being after World War II, has almost fifty senior positions filled by presidential appointment. And the Department of Education, created in 1979, has eighteen (U.S. House of Representatives, Committee on Post Office and Civil Service, 1988).[4]

Many of these new positions (e.g., under secretary of commerce for oceans and atmosphere, assistant secretary of defense for research and technology, and director of the Office of Energy Research) required appointees with a high level of technical or scientific competence because they bore responsibility for complex government programs. The kinds of people needed to fill these positions were unlikely to be found hanging out at party headquarters on election night.

As a consequence of the growth and increasing sophistication of the government's senior appointive positions, presidents needed to develop their own personnel-recruitment operations. It became apparent during the New Deal that party channels would simply not be adequate to provide the number and kinds of talented appointees that an increasingly active government required.

The inadequacy grew larger in the years that followed. And in response, successive administrations developed and then refined their own systems and procedures for staffing the senior levels of the executive branch. Parties had once played a central role in this process. By the end of the second decade after World War II, their role was essentially peripheral. Members of the president's party continued to fill most of the appointed positions, but their identification, selection, and recruitment were conducted at some distance from the formal organization of the president's party.

The Power Situation Changed

As the federal government came to play a larger role in American life, appointees who developed and implemented programs became more powerful. Consider the contrast between 1932 and the present. The federal government in 1932 did *not* provide aid to education, run a national pension system, provide health care for the elderly, fund the national highway system, regulate financial markets, shoot rockets into space, or serve as democracy's policeman around the world. It does all of those things and many more today, and it spends more than a trillion dollars each year doing them.

Management of those programs and of the distribution of the funds they involve affords a great deal of power to presidential appointees. Decisions on who fills those positions matter more than ever before. And the groups in American society affected by the choices made by these appointees have become increasingly unwilling to leave these choices to purely patronage appointees. They have sought instead to put pressure on presidents to select appointees with the necessary technical skills and experience and with particular policy views. Party loyalty and service have been largely irrelevant to these calculations.

As appointments became more important, parties became less important in filling them. Throughout much of American history, the principal contests for power were outside of government, in elections where the parties were strongest. With the beginning of the New Deal, the power struggle increasingly took place within government, in the modern bureaucratic state where the parties were weakest. When the terrain shifted, the locus of power shifted as well.

Changes Outside the Appointment Process

Nothing in government occurs in a vacuum. In fact, government is a great social mirror: What happens there usually reflects what is happening elsewhere in society. That is certainly true of the changes that took place in the appointment process during this century. The influence of political parties diminished in the appointment process because their influence was also diminishing elsewhere. Parties could claim a potent role in presidential appointment decisions only as long as they were able to exert influence elsewhere in American politics—to control the candidate-nominating process, to deliver votes, and to maintain their hegemony over critical political skills. But that too was changing during the middle decades of this century, as other essays in this book have amply demonstrated.

Parties lost their primacy as organizers of American political life. Direct primaries took control of the nominating process out of the hands of party leaders and gave it to voters. Candidates devised ways to raise their own money, build their own organizations, do their own advertising. They hired political consultants to provide the kinds of skills that parties had traditionally provided. As fewer Americans identified strongly with the two major parties, it became harder and harder for the parties to deliver votes.

The long-term impact of all this was that parties had fewer debts to call due in the appointment process. Presidents had less and less reason to feel obligated to their parties and party workers for their own elections, hence less incentive to appoint those workers to federal offices to meet such obligations. Once parties began to lose control of the electoral process, they lost control of the appointment process as well.

Simultaneous with the decline in party fortunes was an explosion in the number of national special-interest groups. Counting the number of national interest groups is no small task, but Ronald Hrebenar and Ruth Scott identified 20,643 national nonprofit organizations in 1988, more than double the number that existed in 1968 (Hrebenar and Scott, 1982:8; 1990 [2nd rev. ed.]:11). This figure, of course, omits profit-seeking corporations, which are themselves increasingly active political entities.

These groups were both much more substantive and much more focused than the major political parties. Typically, they were concerned with a relatively narrow set of policies and they represented the people most directly affected by the shape of those policies. This permitted them to concentrate their attention and political influence on the small number of presidential appointments that mattered most to them. It also allowed them to work closely with the congressional committee and subcommittee chairs who were most interested in those programs and who controlled their appropriations. These were often politically potent combinations that generated considerably more influence over presidential appointments than broad-based, coalition parties were able to generate. In the competition for influence over appointments, interest groups became increasingly successful, often at the expense of the political parties.

The decentralization of power in the Congress also worked against the interests of the parties in the appointment process. During the early decades of this century, real political power in Congress was concentrated in the hands of a relatively small number of institutional party leaders and committee chairs. Local political bosses and national party leaders regularly worked with them to influence the president's appointment decisions. If the leader of the Democratic National Committee or the mayor of Chicago called Sam Rayburn, the Speaker of the House, and asked him to try to get the president to appoint a particular Democrat to the Federal Communications Commission, it would have been hard for the president to deny the request. Sam Rayburn was a key factor in determining the fate of the president's legislative program. Keeping him happy was usually much more important than any particular appointment.

But increasingly after mid-century, the party leaders and committee chairs lost their grip on power in Congress. Younger members generated reforms that spread power around, to the subcommittee level in the House and to individual members in the Senate. The political calculus became much more complex, and it was much more difficult for local bosses or leaders of the national party organization to use the congressional lever to influence presidential appointment decisions. Individual members of Congress were less beholden and less connected to the national party in any case, having built their own personal political organizations and developed their own sources of campaign funds. Their interest in presidential appointments was much more ad hoc and personal in character: They sought appointments for their friends and supporters and staff members, not for traditional party workers. As parties became less important to the job security of members of Congress, incentives diminished for members to use their influence in the appointment process for purposes broader than their own personal objectives.

So the political landscape underwent broad transitions after World War II. Senior-level appointments grew more important as national political power moved to Washington. Lower-level appointments were transferred in large numbers to the civil service. The presidency was becoming a larger and increasingly sophisticated institution with management capabilities that had never before existed. The electoral process was no longer the sole realm of political party organizations. Interest groups were springing up everywhere and rapidly gained political potency. A decentralized Congress was less able and less willing to serve purely partisan interests in the appointment process. Individually and collectively, these changes eroded the influence that parties once exercised on the staffing of the executive branch of the federal government.

THE CONTINUING PROBLEM OF POLITICAL CONTROL

Two important trends have been the dominant themes of this essay. One is also the dominant theme of this book: that parties are not what they used to be. In virtually every aspect of American political life, organized political parties play a smaller role now than they did at the beginning of the century. That is certainly true, as we have sought to demonstrate, in presidential appointments to administrative positions.

The other trend, more directly relevant to the topic of this essay, has been the steady and successful effort to isolate public employment from political pressure, to create a federal work force that is "protected" from the tides of political passion in the country and among the electorate. At the beginning of this century, there were 240,000 federal civilian employees. Of these, more than half were political appointees of one form or another. In 1993, there are 3 million federal civilian employees. Of these positions, only a few thousand are actually filled by political appointment. This suggests a peculiar but familiar reality: that Americans are suspicious of politics and parties. For many of them, politics is a dirty business, and one that can easily mess up government. Hence there has been substantial public support for efforts to depoliticize the personnel-selection process in government, to eliminate all the pejoratives: cronyism and nepotism and the spoils system.

But Americans are also highly skeptical of bureaucrats, and so they respond positively to campaigning politicians who bash bureaucrats and promise to put government back into the hands of the people. The most popular American politician of recent times, Ronald Reagan, was a master of this strategy. "Government," he often said, "is the problem, not the solution."

Hence there exists a kind of public schizophrenia that deeply complicates the task of presidential leadership. Americans want a government that is isolated and protected from the worst aspects of partisan politics. But they also want a government that is controlled not by "faceless bureaucrats" but by elected leaders who will keep it responsive to popular concerns. Those are contradictory goals. How is it possible to have a government that is simultaneously free of politics and under political control? The answer, of course, is that it is not possible. And, as a consequence, conflict between these competing objectives constantly pervades the personnel process.

When parties were the dominant influence in presidential personnel selection, the notion reigned that getting control of the government meant establishing partisan control. The way to implement the will of the electorate was to fill as many positions as possible with members of the president's party. By filling all, or a large number, of the federal offices with the president's co-partisans, the government would move in the directions he had laid out.

It wasn't a bad theory, except that it didn't work in practice, especially after 1932. It didn't work for two reasons primarily. First, it couldn't work in the United States because of the nature of American political parties. The large national parties whose candidates won presidential elections were constructed of delicate coalitions. They rarely offered the electorate a very detailed or refined set of policy objectives. Their primary task was to win the elections, and to do that they clung to the center, trimming specifics to develop the broadest possible mass appeal. Even in the most intense periods of party conflict in the United States, it was difficult for most voters to perceive very broad *policy* differences between the parties. Parties provided few meaningful clues to what exactly the government would do if their candidate were elected.

There was thus little reliability in the notion that staffing the government with members of the same party would provide a unified sense of direction under presidential leadership. In fact, members of the same party often disagreed with one another, and with their own president, on a great many matters of policy. In many cases, all they shared was a party label. The spoils system and its successor constituted a very shaky foundation for getting control of the government through coherent policy leadership from the White House.

Even if American political parties had been more ideologically and substantively unified, the theory would have failed in implementation. Partisan domination of the appointments process was never viewed by party leaders as a system for aiding the president in establishing policy leadership. It was treated as a vehicle for party, not presidential, purposes. In suggesting party candidates for appointment, the party leaders seek mainly to sustain the vigor and the regional and ideological balance of the party, not to find loyal or effective supporters of the president's program. Many presidential appointments, as indicated earlier, were controlled by the local party organizations, which had little interest in national policy. They sought to get federal jobs to reward their own faithful servants and to prevent the federal government from upsetting their local control.

For both these reasons, party participation in presidential appointments failed to serve the purpose of aiding the incumbent administration in establishing policy leadership over the government. And, as we have seen in this century, American presidents began to reject that participation. Slowly but steadily they found ways to construct their own appointment processes, increasingly distanced from party influence. In the past few decades, party influence on appointments has faded almost to the vanishing point.

Presidents still struggle to "get control of the government." Few of them fully succeed. But no recent American president has sought party help in accomplishing this critical objective. And for good reason. American political parties were rarely very helpful in this respect when they were relevant and potent. They would be even less valuable today with their potency on the wane and their relevance to the task of governing very much in doubt.

NOTES

1. Partisanship in judicial appointments will not be discussed in this essay because of space constraints. Interested readers are referred to the excellent work that Prof. Sheldon Goldman has done on this topic.

2. It should be noted that a few technical specialties had begun to emerge in the nineteenth century. Many of those were in public health and agriculture. Even at the height of the spoils system, these positions were often treated as exceptions and were filled by the same people from one administration to the next, without regard to political loyalties.

3. In 1979 the Civil Service Commission was abolished and replaced by two new agencies: the Office of Personnel Management and the Merit Systems Protection Board.

4. The numbers in this paragraph refer to the so-called PAS appointments: presidential appointments that require Senate confirmation.

PART SIX

Toward the Future

15

Deconstructing
Bill Clinton's Victory

DAVID M. SHRIBMAN

American elections have a soundtrack; almost always the overture is performed by a big brass band full of ruffles and flourishes and shiny trombones. This time, of course, there were saxophones, too. There is also a visual element; increasingly elections are contested on television in the form of newscasts, advertisements, interview programs, and call-in shows. More than those of any other Western democracy, American elections have rhythms all their own.

They begin, almost always, far beyond Washington, in the meeting halls of the small towns, the courthouses of the county seats, the bleached white walls of the state capitol buildings. They start quietly, in small meeting rooms and tucked-away suites where the dreamers and the schemers and the technicians of American politics begin their journey with a simple roadmap: Establish your presence in the gritty streets and on the picturesque covered bridges of New Hampshire; make your breakthrough at the pig roasts, clogging performances, and gospel sings of southern politics; flex your muscles in the factory towns, union halls, and ethnic centers of the Midwest industrial heartland; and glide to victory on the carefree breezes of California and the West.

And so it was this time. In hindsight, where even political reporters have exceptional vision, it all began on a very humid morning in the unlikely venue of Little Rock, Arkansas, where the veteran governor of the state stood before the stone walls of the Old State House on the Arkansas River (*WSJ*, October 4, 1991).[1] The experts and the commentators, noting Bill Clinton's relentless ambition and drive, suggested that his speech was forty years in the making, but the truth of it was that Bill Clinton was still reworking it in the hours leading to midnight. When he delivered that speech half a day later one theme was clear: He was pitching this campaign to the middle class—a phrase he used a dozen times in a half-hour speech. "I refuse to be part of a generation of Americans that fails to compete in the global economy and so condemns hard-working, middle-class Americans to a life of struggle without reward of security" (*WSJ*, October 4, 1991).

That speech was important, not because it provides a convenient benchmark from which to measure the impact a little-known southern governor had on the world's most technologically sophisticated—and politically cynical—democracy, but because it was an early signal of the sort of campaign Clinton would run, and the sort of campaign he would win.

The 1992 presidential race turned out to be a complex affair, with a billionaire populist who had a taste for the paramilitary and for the demagogic entering the contest, withdrawing from it, returning to it, and then skewing it far beyond recognition. Ross Perot won more votes than did any other third-party presidential entrant since Theodore Roosevelt in 1912. The principal figure in the campaign, though neither the winner nor the most colorful character, was George Bush, president of the United States and successful commander of a huge alliance that only two years earlier had won a spectacular victory in the Gulf War. Though at center stage, he was outperformed—in votes by Clinton and in theatrics by Perot. But in the end, 57 percent of those who voted in the 1992 election didn't vote for the winner.

Yet the critical thing was that Perot and Clinton were complementary candidates. Clinton began his candidacy, as we have seen, with a blatant, almost obsequious appeal to the middle class. Perot entered the campaign with much the same idiom, and for a short while in late spring and early summer he even led nationwide polls. His drive forced Clinton, at the time a battered candidate fighting off charges of marital infidelity and moral turpitude, to reinforce his middle-class message. As a result, when Perot dropped out of the race the day Clinton delivered his acceptance speech in Madison Square Garden, the Arkansas governor was well-positioned to appeal to the Perot voters and consolidate his own base—all with the same speech. The presidential campaign might very well have ended that evening in July in New York City.

Indeed, the *Wall Street Journal* account of Clinton's convention speech carried the headline "Clinton Bids to Reclaim Middle Class." The language of the Clinton speech, moreover, underlined that notion. He argued that government "has been hijacked by privileged private interests" and "has forgotten who really pays the bills around here"—phrases redolent with appeal to the middle class and full of allusions to Perot's own appeals. The Democratic nominee talked of "the forgotten middle class" in ways that seemed, even then, to empower that group (*WSJ*, July 7, 1992).

Elections are also like novels. They have, to be sure, their story lines. They can also be deconstructed, and it is in the deconstruction that the movements during the election season that can be seen. In this case these movements illuminate much of the American political culture that provided the setting for Bill Clinton's triumph in November 1992.

For a better understanding of the plate tectonics of the 1992 election, then, let us look at several key groups in isolation.

THE CATHOLIC VOTER

White Catholics have been a major staple of Democratic coalitions since Andrew Jackson's victory in 1828 (Ladd, 1993a:48). The candidacy of Governor Alfred Smith of New York a full century later stands as the symbolic start of the identification between Democrats and Catholics—a trend that would help sweep Franklin Roosevelt into the White House four years after that, keep him there for four terms, and then propel Harry Truman to his own election in 1948. As post-war politics began to take form in 1952, Catholic voters—increasingly middle class in economic circumstance and political outlook—stayed with the Democrats, giving Governor Adlai Stevenson 56 percent of their support. But Dwight Eisenhower, who had commanded so many of them in World War II, chipped away at Catholic allegiances, and by 1956 this group was beginning to be mobile. Indeed, the Stevenson-Eisenhower rematch resulted in Catholics siding with the Democrats by a very slender 51 percent–49 percent margin (see Table 15.1).

John Kennedy, whose own Roman Catholic faith was such a factor in the 1960 election, retained more than three-quarters of the Catholic vote, as did Lyndon Johnson, whose 1964 election was so much a referendum on his commitment to, as he put it in his first speech after Kennedy's assassination, "let us continue." It wasn't until 1968 that the Republicans were able to wrest away Catholic voters. Richard Nixon's landslide against George McGovern four years later swept 52 percent of Catholic voters along with him—and this group was in play for the rest of the century.

Catholics had begun to lose their Democratic anchor when the GOP began speaking of conservative social values. "The Republicans were able to make people decide their votes on that bundle of issues rather than on what party was pro-union and who could help the little guy fight the economic royalists," said Tom Smith, director of the General Social Survey at the University of Chicago's National Opinion Research Center (interview with author). For that reason, Ronald Reagan took Catholic voters by a slender margin in 1980. These voters were Republicans—in outlook and vote if not in actual sentiment—for much of the remainder of the decade.

But it wasn't only domestic policy that turned this vote from its ancestral home. "We lost the urban Catholic blue-collar Democrats in the Reagan years because we weren't seen as being strong enough overseas,"

TABLE 15.1
The Catholic Vote

	GOP	Democrat
1952	44	56
1956	49	51
1960	22	78
1964	41	59
1968	47	41
1972	64	36
1976	41	57
1980	47	46
1984	61	39
1988	49	51
1992	37	42

Source: Gallup Organization and Voter Research and Surveys.

said William Hamilton, a Democratic political pollster. "A lot of them felt alienated as the party moved left and, because they were whites, felt left out as the party dealt with blacks" (interview with author). Moreover, Reagan courted these voters assiduously, appearing with John Cardinal Krol in Philadelphia in 1984 and then, pointedly, taking his campaign entourage to the Catholic stronghold of Waterbury, Connecticut, where John Kennedy had held a storied rally before 30,000 people gathered on the town green in front of the Roger Smith Hotel at 3:00 in the morning the Sunday before he was elected the first Catholic president of the United States (White, 1961:406).

Yet no Democratic victory strategy was plausible in 1992 without the Catholic vote. "Over the last 20 years these people are the swing vote," said John Kromkowski, president of the National Center for Urban Ethnic Affairs at Catholic University in Washington. "It's almost not too much to say that the candidate who attracts them wins the election" (interview with author). Clinton's middle-class-oriented campaign was, in principle, not incongruous with winning the Catholic vote. But both Clinton and his running mate, Senator Albert Gore of Tennessee, were Southern Baptists, and their silky-smooth political styles seemed out of place in the ethnic marketplaces and church rectories of the huge Catholic voting bloc. "A lot of these Catholic voters don't feel an affinity for Clinton or Gore," said Democratic Representative Marcy Kaptur, herself rooted politically and emotionally in the Catholic community of Toledo, Ohio. She worried that both Clinton and Gore seemed to her constituencies to be "white bread" (*WSJ*, September 14, 1992).

In the end, however, Clinton's personal-responsibility idiom and his emphasis on middle-class economic vitality appealed to Catholics. These voters, in the phrase that political strategists came to use by summer's end, "came home"; the governor eventually was able to move white Catholics into his column. He even scored well among voters of Eastern European heritage who had been part of the GOP constituency since the party aligned itself with the so-called captive nations in the early 1950s; Ukrainian Americans, for example, considered themselves devout Republicans but were alienated when President Bush was slow to recognize Ukraine and then were troubled that he didn't put on a state dinner for the Ukrainian president. On election day itself, Clinton took 42 percent of the Catholic vote—not a majority, to be sure, but enough to beat George Bush, who took 37 percent, and Ross Perot, who took 22 percent (*American Enterprise*, January-February 1993:92).

REGIONAL POLITICS

This election, like so many others in American history, was won in the middle-class heart of the country. From the start, Democratic strategists like the late Paul Tully argued that the Democrats had to lure back voters in the industrial Midwest; Tully assembled a chart for the Democratic National Committee showing where Democrats came closest in 1988 but still didn't win—and at the top of the list were Maryland, Pennsylvania, Illinois, and Missouri, industrial states all and, eventually, Clinton states.

Seven industrial states gave Clinton almost a third of his total. In 1988, Bush carried all but one of them, winning New Jersey, Pennsylvania, Illinois, Ohio, Missouri, and Michigan. (The one Bush lost was Wisconsin, which had given Dukakis only 51.5 percent of its vote.) If Bush had carried those states again in 1988, he would have won the election (*WSJ*, November 5, 1992).

The world into which Bill Clinton came of age had a definite geopolitical cast. His native South, in particular, had a political character all its own. It was, stated simply, Democratic: Two years before he was born, 71 percent of all voters in the region still considered themselves Democrats (Ladd, 1975:160). Though Eisenhower had carried the South in 1956, the region remained Democratic; as late as the mid-1980s there were still counties in the South where there hadn't been a single Republican office holder for a century. The West, by contrast, was Republican.

Though political commentators like to watch the big midwestern states, shifts in voting patterns in the South and the West are both illuminating and critical.

Though Jimmy Carter was a native southerner, Reagan won a healthy victory among southern voters in 1980, and Reagan and Bush both took the South in 1984 and 1988, respectively. In 1992, the Democrats played the southern card that so many Democratic moderate-to-conservative leaders had been pressing them to play for a decade, nominating a southern moderate who, in turn, selected another southern moderate as his running mate. And although pundits and experts expressed doubts about a ticket so heavily weighted toward Dixie, there was historical precedent; Harry Truman and Senate majority leader Alben Barkley prevailed in 1948 with a ticket that included two members whose states, Missouri and Kentucky, were contiguous, as are Clinton's Arkansas and Gore's Tennessee.

In the end, this strategy proved shrewd, giving the Democrats a go-get-'em, modernistic feel—this was, after all, the first baby boom ticket—and giving southern voters the sort of comfort that they never had when Walter Mondale and Michael Dukakis were party standard-bearers. No Democratic sheriff or county pol found reason to take ill the day Clinton and Gore came to town, as they did when Mondale and Dukakis rolled into the South. Even so, the Democrats failed to carry the South in 1992— Bush edged out Clinton 43 percent to 41 percent in the region—but the Clinton ticket played well enough to permit the Democrats to carry the country as a whole (*American Enterprise*, January-February 1993:91).

A look at the numbers is instructive. Dukakis and Clinton took an identical 41 percent of the vote in the region, but Dukakis ran against only one major competitor and Clinton ran against two. As a result, Bush lost 16 percentage points in four years—the precise amount that Ross Perot won in the region. Had Perot not run, Clinton could have counted upon much of that vote and perhaps even prevailed in the region. As it happened, the Democratic ticket was able to win in such places as Shelby County (Memphis), Tennessee, for the first time since 1980 and Dade County (Miami), Florida, for the first time since 1976 (Cook, 1992c:3811). The Democratic base in the South, which was nonexistent in the Mondale and Dukakis races, now included Clinton's native state of Arkansas and Gore's Tennessee along with Louisiana, Georgia, and Kentucky.

Similar progress was made in the West. Economic distress in California plus the lingering effects of the Los Angeles riots made that state—a bigger factor than ever now that the 1990 Census gave it 54 electoral votes, precisely one-fifth of the total needed to win the White House—a long shot for Bush. The president made noises about competing in the Golden State, but in the end he made only a token effort. That substantially changed the electoral map, for it gave the Democrats a head start of 54 electoral votes, permitted Clinton strategists to shift resources out of the biggest, most complex, and most expensive media market into other, more competitive areas and gave the Democrats a base from which to work other parts of the West.

The western strategy, as it was known, had long been pushed by West Coast Democrats, especially Oregon congressmen Ron Wyden and Les AuCoin, both of whom calculated that, with population shifts, the West would be the next big battleground of American politics. Dukakis and his strategists understood this and moved early in the 1988 cycle to consolidate their support in the region, moving high-powered operatives there and diverting funds from more traditional locales. In the end, it turned out to be a shrewd move, at least for western Democrats hoping to strut their stuff; Dukakis won both Washington and Oregon and came close in California. In 1992, Clinton swept the Pacific West, worth 72 electoral votes, and added Colorado and New Mexico for an additional 13. After election day, the Democrats controlled more western House seats (48) and more western state legislative chambers (15) than they had at any time in the 1980s.

But the traditional geopolitical cut of American politics doesn't show the entire picture. A *Congressional Quarterly* study of county votes shows where the Clinton victory came from, and it suggests that the Arkansan trailed previous Democratic candidates in blue-collar areas but made up for it elsewhere, especially in the South and in middle-class suburbs. This analysis shows that the Democratic vote didn't increase but that the Republican vote decreased—siphoned off by Perot. It is impossible to say with precision how the Perot vote would have split had the Texas billionaire not been a candidate, but it is safe to assume that the Democrats would have received at least some of that vote, especially since it was composed so heavily of people who felt alienation.

Some of the biggest defections from Bush came in the suburbs, increasingly an important power center in American politics. The Republican vote fell 20 percentage points or more in Orange County, California; Du Page County, Illinois; St. Louis County, Missouri; Montgomery County, Pennsylvania; and Collin County, Texas—Republican-oriented suburbs that all gave Bush 55 percent or more in 1988 (three of them gave him 68 percent or above). And six counties such as San Bernadino County, California, and Gwinnett County, Georgia, identified by *Congressional Quarterly* as "high-growth exurbs" all showed Republican defections of 19 percentage points or more, with the GOP ticket dropping 28 percent in Derry, New Hampshire, where the recession drove scores of voters out of the Republican column (Cook, 1992c:3811). Overall, Clinton took the suburbs by about 5 percentage points, giving the Democrats the edge in this category for the first time since the Johnson landslide of 1964 (Phillips, 1993:248).

GENDER POLITICS

Since 1980, female voters have been more likely than male voters to support Democratic candidates. Polls for the three television networks showed that women, by between 6 and 9 percentage points, were less likely to vote for Republican candidates than were men. In 1988, women split their votes about evenly between the two parties, but men showed what the Center for the American Woman and Politics at Rutgers described as "a clear and decisive preference" for George Bush (Center for the American Woman and Politics 1989:1).

Those Democratic leanings remained in force in the 1992 election. Overall, women are more Democratic than are men, with the gap largest among the young. Among voters aged eighteen to twenty-four, 52 percent of the females voted for Bill Clinton, as opposed to only 39 percent of the men. The sexes were more evenly split among older groups, and among voters sixty-five years and older, Clinton took 50 percent of the male vote and 50 percent of the female vote (*American Enterprise*, January-February 1993:98).

During this election cycle, however, there was increased attention to a newly emerging electoral bloc—bigger than the labor vote, the black vote, or the Catholic vote. This new block was the working-women bloc, and it included 57 million voters (see Table 15.2).

In the 1992 election, when the group first was identified as a voting bloc, working women focused on several key issues, bringing more attention to them and, in turn, winning more attention for them from the candidates themselves. These issues included abortion rights, child care issues, family leave, questions of economic opportunity, and broad questions of fairness. More than the Bush campaign, the Clinton campaign separated out these voters and courted them. Celinda Lake, a Democratic pollster who worked for the Clinton campaign, told the *Wall Street Journal:* "Working women are enough to take a Democrat over the top in a close race" (*WSJ*, October 15, 1992). Indeed, the Clinton campaign even fashioned advertisements especially aimed at this group. In Charlotte, North Carolina, for example, the campaign aired an advertisement built around a conversation of two women. At the conclusion, one of the women said that Clinton "is smart—and I believe he's a caring man" (*WSJ*, October 15, 1992).

This attention paid to working women didn't grow out of a philosophic awareness or a commitment to women's rights and opportunity. It was simply a pure, cold political calculation: This was an important voting group. But the group's emergence mirrored changes both in the electorate and in the broader society. The Bureau of Labor Statistics reported that only 37 percent of women worked outside the home in 1959, as compared with more than 57 percent at the time of the election.

This was not a homogeneous group, however; no bloc of voters that accounts for about a quarter of the electorate can be. But a *Wall Street Journal*/NBC News poll taken in early September illuminated the issues that move this group—and the direction the group was taking as the election neared. Overall, working women were more likely to see unemployment as the most important economic issue than were other voters. They were more alienated; 57 percent of them thought the country's political and

TABLE 15.2
Percentage of Women in the Work Force

1959	37.1	1976	47.3
1960	37.7	1977	48.4
1961	38.1	1978	50.0
1962	37.9	1979	50.9
1963	38.3	1980	51.5
1964	38.7	1981	52.1
1965	39.3	1982	52.6
1966	40.3	1983	52.9
1967	41.1	1984	53.6
1968	41.6	1985	54.5
1969	42.7	1986	55.3
1970	43.3	1987	56.0
1971	43.4	1988	56.6
1972	43.9	1989	57.4
1973	44.7	1990	57.5
1974	45.7	1991	57.3
1975	46.3		

Source: Bureau of Labor Statistics.

economic systems were stacked against them, as opposed to 50 percent of the voters overall (unpublished memo). "This is one of the explanations for the gender gap," says Linda DiVall, a Republican political pollster. "Working women tend to look at a government that is an activist force. On family leave and day care, they look to the government for solutions" (interview with author).

Moreover, these voters liked the Clinton economic plan more than did voters as a whole, and three out of five of them said that Clinton would do the best job of promoting equal rights for women. These voters were also more critical of Bush on character issues (Feld, 1992). In the end, men split their vote, with 41 percent going to Clinton and 38 percent to Bush, but women leaned heavily to Clinton, giving him 45 percent and giving Bush only 37 percent (*American Enterprise*, January-February 1993:91).

YOUNG VOTERS

For years after the election of John Kennedy in 1960, the Democrats prided themselves on being the party of young people, taking great satisfaction from their party's relatively strong position on issues of great concern to the young, including civil rights. So the irony was especially bitter for Democrats when the oldest man ever elected president, Ronald Reagan, made off with the youth vote in 1980. National Election Studies data show that Reagan took 50 percent of the vote of those aged eighteen to twenty-four in 1980, with Jimmy Carter taking only 35 percent in a three-way race with Representative John Anderson of Illinois. The margin was even greater four years later when Reagan made off with 58 percent of the vote. That prompted Walter Mondale, who had always regarded himself at the forefront of liberal causes, to say that the worst part of his forty-nine state defeat was the loss of young voters.

George Bush did almost as well as Reagan in 1988, taking 55 percent of the vote of those aged eighteen to twenty-four. But the Republicans' success with younger voters stopped right there. In the 1992 election, Clinton reclaimed the group for the Democrats.

Part of Clinton's success was stylistic and generational. The forty-six-year-old governor was vigorous and youthful, and he used the sort of generational idioms that John Kennedy had used in 1960, especially in his 1961 inaugural address. George Bush was, by contrast, the very model of the establishment generation—the last warrior, it turned out, of the World War II generation in presidential politics. All this was clear throughout the fall general election campaign.

But Clinton understood better the way the electorate had changed and, even more important, had to change. There were new kinds of power brokers now, people like Tabitha Soren, whose name was all but unknown in the newsrooms of the *New York Times* and the *Washington Post* but who, as chief political reporter for MTV, the music television network that reaches 57.2 million subscribers on 8,025 affiliates, was a force all her own. Her curriculum vitae distributed by MTV, a network that didn't even exist when Ronald Reagan won the White House, bespoke the difference; besides reporting on national politics, she also filled in as host of "The Day in Rock" and "The Week in Rock." The principal news anchor for the network was Kurt Loder, the author of *I, Tina*, a biography of Tina Turner, and a member of the nominating committee of the Rock & Roll Hall of Fame. The network targeted eighteen to twenty-four-year-olds for voter registration through its "Choose or Loose" campaign, and Clinton's media strategists seized on the possibilities MTV offered their campaign. An MTV poll after Clinton's first forum on MTV showed that 75 percent of the viewers said their impression of Clinton was better than it had been before the broadcast.

The reasons Clinton appealed to youth are clear. These voters are more likely to support abortion rights than is the electorate as a whole, more likely to choose environmental over economic considerations, and more liberal than voters overall. Young voters, according to the September *Wall Street Journal*/NBC News poll, were more likely than voters overall to say that Bush didn't spend enough time on domestic problems and to fault him for having violated his no-new-taxes pledge. They were, moreover, more likely to think the nation was on the wrong track than were voters overall. "The swing toward the Republican party among the young was disproportionate in 1988 and 1984," University of Rhode Island political scientist Maureen Moakley said during the final month of the campaign, "and in this election it's evaporated" (interview with author).

CONCLUSION

One way to deconstruct the 1992 election is to watch the destruction of the Republican coalition. The major elements of this coalition were, of course, Republicans, independents, southerners, white Protestants, Catholics, and the sort of Democrat who sided with Bush over Dukakis in 1988. We have seen the defections in some of these categories. But the most illuminating comes among independents, by definition a swing group in any election. In 1988, Bush won 55 percent of the independent vote; in 1992, he took but 32 percent (unpublished memo; *American Enterprise*, January-February 1993:91).

The reasons are impossible to quantify with precision, but an irresistible conclusion is that Bush relinquished his hold on the Republican coalition because, unlike Reagan and unlike during his own campaign in 1988, Bush in 1992 failed to speak to middle-class values and concerns. Clinton operatives hung a sign in their Little Rock headquarters that boomed the following message: "The economy, stupid." Soon that sign, and that sentiment, became known around the country because it encapsulated in three words, much like "Read my lips" had four years earlier, the key to the election. Nine out of ten Clinton voters disapproved of Bush's handling of the economy (*Washington Post*, November 12, 1992).

By midsummer it was clear that Bush had one major opportunity to change the dynamic of the election, the August Republican National Convention in Houston. But that, too, was mishandled. Before the convention opened, Republican theorist Kevin Phillips mused about the dangers the party was courting: "If this [convention] becomes a struggle between Pat Buchanan, Dan Quayle, and Phil Gramm over who read the latest Heritage Foundation briefing paper, they'll push too far. They could develop a fringe mentality. The danger for the Republican party is that it might move to right field and debate fine points of ideology" (interview with author). He wasn't alone with those concerns. Craig Berkman, the chairman of the Oregon Republican party, worried that the GOP was about to become marginalized. "If we've learned anything in this party since Goldwater, it's that we need to have broad principles in common," he said. "If we get pigeonholed and narrow, we're in trouble" (interview with author).

Both men were right—and the party suffered serious damage as Buchanan, Christian right leader Pat Robertson, and others spoke of cultural wars and litmus tests. They drove some middle-class voters from the Republican party and made it difficult for some voters who wanted to support Bush to remain in the Republican tent. In the end, many of them moved on—and out.

But other forces were at work. The public, as anyone who listened to talk radio and as any eavesdropper at the corner coffee shop knew, was impatient—with politics, with politicians, with business as usual. The president knew it, perhaps even feeling it himself. And he attempted to capitalize on it by talking of gridlock and by blaming it on divided government, the situation whereby one party, in this case the Republicans, controlled the White House and another, in this case the Democrats, controlled the Congress. This had become the architecture of American politics, prevailing for all but four years in the period between 1969, when President Nixon confronted a Democratic Congress, and the 1992 election (*WSJ*, September 9, 1992).

For years the public, which, after all, had sent these people to Washington, seemed comfortable with the situation. One branch, the public seemed to say, would watch the other, ensure that it couldn't get too far in front of the public. Public opinion polls, in fact, seemed to bear that out. In September 1986, for example, 64 percent of the public said that it was better to have different political parties controlling the Congress and the presidency, and only 28 percent thought it was better for the same political party to control both branches. But by August 1992, when the Republicans were gathering for their national convention, a stunning transformation had occurred; the public now was evenly divided on the question (*WSJ*/NBC News poll, August 10–12, 1992 [818 respondents]). The president pressed on with his rhetoric, and as it turned out the public listened: It ended divided government. It sent a Democratic president to Washington to work with the Democratic Congress.

The fault lines of the 1992 election were discernible long before the voters went to the polls in November. By August, 70 percent of the public thought the country was going in the wrong direction, about double the rate of people who held that view only twelve months earlier and a terribly ominous sign for Bush and his strategists. Forty-six percent of the public had positive views of the Democrats, as opposed to 34 percent who held positive views of the Republicans. Two voters in five thought Clinton was best-suited to deal with the economy, with only one in five naming Bush as best-suited for economic leadership (*WSJ*/NBC News poll, August 10–12, 1992).

By the time the voters actually filed into the courthouses, school gymnasiums, church basements, and firehalls that on election day are the real power centers of American life, Ross Perot had reentered the race, raising anew the question of the value and durability of the two-party system. And with good reason. Perot captured, rather than created, the public's angry mood, and his movement proved to be a powerful force in American politics and a sobering influence on both parties and on the political system at large.

Though never mentioned in the Constitution, political parties sprung out of the American soil naturally, thriving in our political culture and playing an indisputable and indispensable role in our national life. "Throughout American history," says Austin Ranney, a University of California at Berkeley political scientist, "political parties have been one of the most important social agencies working to moderate the conflicts among our diverse population and our multifarious interests and encouraging them to deal with issues in a positive and constructive way" (*Mandate Forum Proceedings*, 1993:12).

And yet Perot's candidacy highlighted the difficulties parties face at century's end. Voter Research and Surveys data, gleaned from interviews with more than 15,000 voters nationwide, show that Perot voters came from all parts of the political spectrum, with a quarter of the billionaire's support coming from Democrats and a third coming from Republicans. Their votes on House candidates underline the challenge Perot (or his successor, if any) could pose to both parties and to the two-party system itself; 49 percent of Perot supporters voted for Democratic House candidates, 51 percent for Republicans. His supporters were centrists, with 53 percent describing themselves as "moderates" (Dionne, 1992).

And so we conclude where we began—with the great middle in American life and politics. That is where elections are won and lost. "From the frontier vitality of Jacksonian Democracy in 1828 to the electoral revolution of 1992," Kevin Phillips (1993:258) writes in *Boiling Point*, "ordinary Americans—whether they be called yeomanry, the 'middling sort' or twentieth-century middle class—have made the U.S. system of politics and government one of the world's most effective." But the stakes from here on are even greater than a single election. The middle class is where the future of the two parties will be determined. And that may be where, even more ominously, the future of the two-party system may be determined.

NOTES

1. Much of the material for this chapter was gathered while the author was covering the 1992 presidential campaign for the *Wall Street Journal*. I want to acknowledge my debt to the *Journal* and my colleagues in that paper's Washington bureau. References "*WSJ*, date" refer to my articles in the *Journal* on those dates.

16

Political Parties
at the Century's End

L. SANDY MAISEL

The clock monitoring the House of Representatives roll-call vote on the budget reconciliation package read one minute and thirty-seven seconds to go when the vote was cast that put President Clinton's economic plan over the top. Immediately thereafter a number of Democrats cast nay votes, assured that their votes would not spell defeat for their party. It was June 1992, less than six months into the Clinton presidency, and this one vote spoke mountains about the role of party under unified government.

The House vote on the reconciliation package was important because President Clinton was perceived to be in trouble and incapable of providing effective leadership. It was important because it helped him regain momentum as he headed into a more difficult battle in the Senate. But, for our purposes, it was important because Democrats rallied to a Democratic president's side, signaling that they understood that they had a stake in his success or failure. And this vote is a symbol of the need to continuously rethink the role that parties play in the American political system.

Nearly fifty years ago, E. E. Schattschneider (1942:1) wrote that "[t]he rise of political parties is indubitably one of the principal distinguishing marks of modern government. The parties, in fact, have played a major role as makers of governments; more especially they have been the makers of democratic government. It should be flatly stated at the outset that ... the political parties created democracy and that modern democracy is unthinkable save in terms of the parties." A decade later the American Political Science Association (1950) issued a special report that was critical of the state of American political parties and called for a more responsible party system. As the 1970s began, the *Washington Post*'s award-winning columnist and reporter David Broder proclaimed in a widely circulated book that *The Party's Over* (1971). But, most recently, political scientist Larry Sabato discussed the reactions of political parties to the crisis they had faced in *The Party's Just Begun* (1988).

Political analysts have blamed parties for the evils of our society, decried the ways in which they perform their roles, and despaired over whether the nation could progress without them. They have sounded the death knell for parties (at times in mourning and at times in jubilation) and declared their resurrection. But scholars and journalists, activists and analysts, have not ignored political parties—and they have not been neutral toward them. The persistence of American political parties over nearly the entire history of the nation and the prominence given their role by all commentators on American democracy are vivid testimonies to their resilience.

Perhaps political parties can best be understood in terms of organizational theory. They arose to meet certain needs of the polity but, as time has passed, they have achieved a life of their own, responding to criticism, abandoning some roles and fulfilling new ones, changing with the system and the political environment in which they exist. Value-laden appraisals miss the point. Political parties per se are not inherently good or evil. Rather, they are functional. They are extra-constitutional institutions that bridge gaps in the constitutional structure of American democracy.

At times their roles are clear and at times cloudy. At times they perform their roles well and at times poorly. At times their roles have been central and at times peripheral. They persist and adapt to changing conditions because, like all such organizations, they are composed of individuals who have a stake in their survival. The key to understanding political parties, and to speculating about their future, is to view the parts as well as the sum of the parts. Who has a stake in the different roles that political parties fulfill? Who is involved in defining their role—from within the parties and from without?

Virtually all textbooks on political parties begin with a definition of what a party is (Sorauf, 1980:17; Maisel, 1993:9–10). But perhaps we should recall what V. O. Key (1964:200) concluded on the subject of definition: "Pat definitions may simplify discussion, but they do not necessarily promote understanding. A search for the fundamental nature of party is complicated by the fact that 'party' is a word of many meanings. ... The nature of parties must be sought through an appreciation of their role in the process of governance." It seems appropriate to keep that warning in mind as we speculate about the directions that political parties are going to take as the nation embarks on its third century.

THE CURRENT CONTEXT

The Leading Players

We begin our assessment by looking at those most involved in today's partisan politics. Certainly individuals are important in shaping institutions; in today's context the relationship of leading politicians to the political parties—because it is so different from that in the recent past—seems particularly worthy of note.

Students taking introductory courses are frequently told that one of the president's extra-constitutional roles is to serve as leader of his political party. But that role is as leader of his party in government; presidents have not typically been involved with their party's organization. The division of party roles into party organization, party in the electorate, and party in government has parallels in the individuals who perform each role. Only rarely in the last half-century has an elected government official played a key role in party organization. The exceptions that prove the rule have been in those communities that have retained the last vestiges of dominant party machines, in which the party boss has at times been a mayor or a county leader. Similarly, the vast majority of voters loyal to one party or another have little or no interest in working for the party, much less in serving in office.

Of course, a close connection between party organization and party in the government has always existed. Elected officials have run as candidates of organized political parties, whether the "organization" had any role in securing those nominations or not (see Chapters 7 and 8 of this volume). Once in office, elected officials become "celebrities" at party functions. But that is very different from playing an active role in working on the structure of the party.

More often the party has become a political tool of incumbents, helping them to gain reelection and serving as a way to enhance their political careers and those of their supporters. Presidents have nominated their allies to chair the national committee, and the party organization has become a political arm of the White House. The same has been true for governors and, to a lesser extent, legislators at the national, state, and local levels. It should also be recalled that few elected officials have come up through the party organization; the careers of elected politicians, particularly those of prominent national politicians, have typically been independent of party careers.

Against this background it is noteworthy that George Bush came to the White House with the perspective of one who had served as chairman of the Republican National Committee. But, as Warren Miller points out (in Chapter 5), Bush's tenure was not one marked by party gains. Bill Clinton's road to the White House included a stop as chair of the Democratic Leadership Council, an informal group of Democrats whose stated purpose is to move the party back toward the center. One test of his commitment to this goal will be the extent to which he uses the White House as a vehicle for ensuring the future direction of the party. Early indications, including explicit coordination between the White House and the DNC on Clinton's health care initiative, indicate that party will play a different role than it has for most recent presidents.

Of particular interest is the number of other contemporary leaders whose careers have bridged the various partisan roles. Senate Minority Leader Robert Dole (R-KS), like Bush, is a former chair of the Republican National Committee (RNC). Senator George Mitchell (D-ME), the majority leader, served as chair of the Maine State Democratic party and as a member of the Democratic National Committee and its Executive Committee; moreover, while the Republicans were in power during the Nixon administration, he was narrowly defeated by Robert Strauss in a bid to become the party's leader.

Furthermore, Mitchell's drive to Senate leadership was decisively aided by the role he played as head of the Democratic Senatorial Campaign Committee. The Hill committees of both parties are now viewed as important players in the political arena (recall Chapter 3). Mitchell's rise to Senate leadership and that of Tony Coelho (D-CA) in the House (before his resignation under the threat of an ethics investigation) have led aspiring congressional figures to see chairing the congressional campaign committees as a step on a career ladder in ways never before envisioned.

Two recent—and extremely influential—chairs of the two national committees also came to their roles with unique perspectives. Traditionally, party chairs have been supporters of the president who have worked within the party organization, either nationally or in their own state (e.g., John White for the Democrats and Richard Richards for the Republicans), or they have been political figures tied to their party's national leader (e.g., Democrat Kenneth Curtis, an early Carter supporter who had been governor of Maine, and George Bush, a former representative defeated in a race to become senator from Texas when appointed RNC chair), or they have been political fund raisers (e.g., Democrat Robert Strauss and Republican Frank Fahrenkopf).

Before assuming his position as Republican National Committee chairman, the late Lee Atwater was a political consultant—the very essence of an institutional rival to party organization as an influence in the electoral process. Democrat Ron Brown's career was as an establishment Washington lawyer and lobbyist and as an adviser first to Senator Ted Kennedy (D-MA) and then to Jesse Jackson, who in turn were quintessential examples of candidates whose rise toward power and celebrity status were aided more by the media than by party regulars. However, it is also noteworthy that their successors—Rich Bond and then Haley Barbour in the Republican party and David Wilhelm at the DNC—followed traditional routes, as nominees of presidential candidates and as long-time party activists.

To a greater extent than has ever before been the case in the era of modern campaigning, those in partisan leadership roles in the government and in formal organizations know politics and the roles of the political parties from a number of different perspectives. The leaders of the two parties in the government have experience in party organization as well as in more personalized campaigning. The four congressional campaign committees (the Hill committees) stand at the intersection of the worlds of party organization, modern campaigning, and governing. The leaders of the party organizations came to their current roles with backgrounds in other institutions that have competed with party for influence over electoral politics. All of these leaders have a commitment to political party— to partisan politics. One question, then, is how these commitments are played out in terms of the role that party plays in the political and governing processes. Another is whether the views of these leaders will be broader than those of individuals whose entire careers had been involved with only one aspect of what political parties have been called upon to do.

The Roles of Party Today

Party Organization. The earlier essays in this book have detailed various aspects of the roles performed by political parties in the 1980s. Consider first the formal party organizations. Perhaps they can best be described as institutions responding to changes and searching for roles. Although the national committees were never reputed to be powerful (recall that Cotter and Hennessy [1964] entitled their book on the national committees *Politics Without Power*), state and local party leaders were extremely influential in nominating politics at all levels of government. Because many areas were dominated by one or the other of the political parties, this control over the nomination process often meant control over elections. In those areas in which the two parties contested elections, party organization provided important tools for candidates' campaigns. Before the era of television and computers, before high-tech campaigning, electioneering was done largely on the street—and political parties provided the foot soldiers for their candidates' campaigns.

But many changes occurred quite quickly, and parties were somewhat slow to respond. Two changes stand out: the spread of the direct primary as the principal means of nominating candidates and the advent of new campaign techniques, emphasizing mass media approaches to the voters, candidate appeals through television and radio, computer-generated mailing, and targeted messages. Because of the first change, political parties lost control over the nominating process; party-designated candidates could be and were challenged by independent entrepreneurs who were seeking the party label and using the new techniques of campaigning. The new techniques carried over into the general election, with party organization playing a greatly reduced role.

The party organizations began to respond, although the two national parties responded differently. The Republicans, under the leadership of

National Chairman William Brock, decided that they would become important players in electoral politics. To do so, they needed to provide services that the candidates wanted. And to provide services, the national party needed money. The Republicans established a highly successful direct-mail operation, raising the vast sums that are necessary to mount a modern campaign operation. Then they systematically set about providing services that would help all Republican candidates. They established schools to train campaign staffs; they undertook negative research on incumbent Democrats to help Republican challengers; they developed media messages that could be adapted to various localities; and they helped their candidates with survey research as well as fund raising—essentially, with many of the services otherwise provided by consultants. The Republicans at the national level became active in recruiting candidates to run for the Senate and the Congress and even for seats in state legislatures. They used promises of needed services and financial assistance to recruit quality candidates, and they set national strategies and targets. In short, they proceeded as a modern campaign organization.

While the Republicans were building this impressive campaign apparatus, the Democrats were saddled with a large deficit and were divided by procedural quarrels. They spent much of the 1970s in troublesome debates over party rules, particularly those governing the presidential nomination. The changes in party rules that resulted (as discussed below) were important and contributed to the nationalizing of the Democratic party; but they also consumed time and energy and left the Democrats noticeably behind the Republicans in fund raising and the ability to provide services to their candidates. Under Chairman Charles Manatt, the Democrats began to emulate their Republican counterparts, but the effort was clearly one of catching up, not of matching performance.

At the local and state levels, parties have always looked for ways to influence elections. They began to provide services to candidates, achieving economies of scale by working for all of their candidates in a certain area. The Republican party has aided state and local organizations as they play this new role; again, the Democrats, because they lack a financial base, have not been able to match Republican efforts. Although state and local party organizations have not regained control of the nominating process, they do retain a role as players in the electoral game, because they developed resources that the candidates could use. This role, in turn, has established a connection between victorious candidates and party organization. Few candidates want to be dubbed "candidates of the organization," but as state and local parties gain in organizational and financial strength (see Chapter 2), candidates increasingly take them into account.

One aspect of the work of party organization that is often overlooked concerns the building of party platforms. These statements of how the party feels about the issues of the day theoretically link the organization (which has the responsibility for writing the platforms) to the electorate (which can look to the platforms to see how the party will address the issues of the day) and to elected party leaders (whose job it is to implement the platforms to see how the party will address the issues of the day) and to elected party leaders (whose job it is to implement the platforms). Some claim that platforms are meaningless documents, but Gerald Pomper (1972) has demonstrated that they distinguish the major parties in meaningful ways. Moreover, recent evidence (see Chapter 4) suggests that the differences among the party activists who write the platforms might well be widening—and that these differences could affect the electorate's view of the parties in the future. Certainly one could see this effect in 1992, when a Republican Committee on Resolutions produced an extremely conservative platform, one that contrasted dramatically with the Democratic counterpart (Maisel, 1994).

Parties and the Voters. But what about the voters? How do they relate to political parties? When Campbell, Converse, Miller, and Stokes wrote *The American Voter* (1960), the model of voting behavior they described sought to explain party identification, because party identification was the best predictor of vote. By the time Nie, Verba, and Petrocik wrote *The Changing American Voter* (1976), however, strength of party identification was on the decline and issues, as such, seemed more important to more voters. As Bob Dylan sang, "The times, they were a changin'." Vietnam and a series of social issues—as well as a long period of time since the cataclysmic events that shaped the New Deal coalition—strained voter allegiance. The candidates of the two parties did not necessarily reflect citizens' feelings about the salient issues of the day, and the citizens responded accordingly.

But more was happening than that. Candidates for different offices were campaigning in different ways. Presidential candidates were being associated with the party whose banner they carried—or, perhaps more correctly put, the parties began to be viewed in terms of the candidates who ran under their banner. The Democrats were the party of George McGovern (i.e., liberal) and then Jimmy Carter (i.e., weak); the Republicans were the party of Ronald Reagan (i.e., strong and conservative, fiscally and socially). Reagan might not have been involved with party organization, but he did work hard to rebuild the image of the Republican party in terms of his own policy agenda. As Warren Miller has demonstrated in Chapter 5, the voters read these signals and reacted to them.

But candidates for other offices, even when they used some of the resources of party organization, campaigned as individuals. They developed their own images, their own relationships with the voters. Many of them never revealed their party affiliation on any campaign advertising. The message was, "You know and like me! Vote for me! It doesn't matter what party you are in!" The high rate of return for incumbents seeking re-election, prevalent not only among members of Congress but also among candidates for local offices, is testimony to the success of this strategy. It further attests to the separation of party affiliation and the vote. As Fiorina notes in Chapter 6, the factor that most distinguishes today's elections from those of a half-century ago is ticket splitting. Whereas many states once provided party levers so that citizens could vote for all of one party's candidates with a minimum of effort, straight-party voting is now the exception, not the rule. Candidates encourage voters to vote for individuals rather than the party, except where majority party candidates in areas of strong one-party dominance are concerned. If voters feel an allegiance to one party or the other, that allegiance does not carry over as a cue for voting below the presidential level.

Parties in the Electoral Process. Political parties have always played many roles, but the primary role has been one involving the electoral process. In the 1980s their success in this role was mixed, and it remains so today. The party role in the nominating process is symptomatic of the problem faced by parties.

When a nomination is not highly valued (e.g., the nomination to run against an entrenched incumbent), the party role can be dominant. In that situation, in fact, the role of party is to recruit a candidate, to find someone to run, and to support that candidate. Where party organization is strongest, fewest seats go uncontested. Too often, however, party organization is weak in a particular area and many offices go uncontested. As competition is the key to democracy, this role for party is an important one and should not be dismissed. However, even in the case of attracting candidates for less sought-after nominations in areas with effective party organizations, the role of party is not decisive. Decisions regarding candidacy are essentially individual decisions. Strong party leaders can say to a sought-after candidate, "The nomination is yours, if you want it." But the same party leader often cannot convince a potential candidate that the benefits of running a campaign and of serving in office are worth the personal, political, and financial costs.

When a party's nomination is highly valued, the role that party can play is even less decisive because a number of candidates are likely to want to run under the party label. In many areas of the country, party organization must stay neutral in nominating contests. In others, the influence varies from considerable, to minimal, even to negative. But in all cases, individual candidates running their own campaigns can appeal directly to the voters. Until the recent Supreme Court decision in *Tashjian v. Republican Party of Connecticut*, 479 U.S. 208 (1986), parties were unable to define their own membership—that is, to determine the electorate in their primaries. Even with the Court ruling, most state parties are content to let state law specify party membership criteria; many choose to be inclusive, allowing anyone who wants to vote in their primary to do so, rather than exclusive, limiting primary participation to those who have allegiance to the party. Thus, the party role in determining these nominations, a decision critical to the electoral process, is limited by the decisions of potential candidates, the campaigns run by those candidates who decide to seek nomination, and the choice made by a primary electorate, which most frequently is not limited to those with strong allegiance to the party. It is difficult not to conclude that the party role in state and local nominations is a weak one (see Chapter 7).

Much the same can be said for presidential nominations. As noted earlier, the Democratic party has exerted a good deal of time and effort toward the goal of nationalizing the nominating process. Reform commission has followed reform commission in a continuing effort to increase participation, provide for fair representation, and guarantee procedural fairness. As Kamarck and Goldstein demonstrate in Chapter 8, national party rules in the Democratic party now structure the contest, with obvious implications for candidate strategy. To a certain extent, because many party reforms have resulted in changes in state law, the Republican party nominating contest has been affected as well.

But to say that party rules affect the nominating contest is not to say that party dominates the nominations. One of the clearest conclusions to be drawn from the recent spate of Democratic reform commissions is that the consequences of party reform are often difficult to predict. Party rules cannot keep candidates out of the process. They cannot determine who will adopt the most successful strategy or who will reach the voters with the most effective message. Campaign strategists, like losing generals, too often adopt strategies that have been successful in the past, but without realizing that the political climate has changed. Those interested in reforming party rules can fall prey to the same difficulties. Some rule changes—such as those calling for open and timely participation—have been adopted for philosophical reasons. And they have largely achieved their goals, though often with unintended and unpredicted consequences. Other reforms—such as those calling for a reduction in the time period during which convention delegates could be chosen (while allowing for some exceptions)—had political goals in mind. Again, as often as not, the results were neither predicted nor intended. For these reasons, party seemed to have as little control over presidential nominations in the 1980s as over decisions reached by primary voters at the state and local levels.

If party does not play the dominant role in determining nominations, has its role been enhanced in general election campaigns? Again the answer seems to be mixed. On the one hand, political campaigning is certainly no longer the "pound-the-pavement, glad-handing" enterprise it once was. The era of the ward boss and the precinct leader who delivered the votes of loyal party followers (and patronage recipients) is long gone. Incumbents build their own organizations and gain the loyalty of their constituents largely independent of party ties (Fenno, 1978; Cain, Ferejohn, and Fiorina, 1987).

On the other hand, party organizations seem to be adjusting to the cash economy of modern campaigns, as noted by Sorauf and Wilson in Chapter 10. One can see the role that party plays in a number of different ways. National party committees, including the two parties' Hill committees, are now collecting larger sums of money, donating them to campaigns to the extent possible and permissible, and passing them on to state and local committees when that is possible. Whereas the presidential campaigns have been federally funded for the last four elections, individuals who in 1992 had raised money for Bush and Clinton during the nominating battles had also raised money for the national committees during the general election, thus extending and seemingly legitimating a practice begun in 1980 and continued in 1984 and 1988. The money raised in this manner could be used for the general election so long as it was spent on activities that benefited the entire ticket. The money raised by fund raisers for the individual candidates was ultimately spent on party-building activities, because those activities were seen as aiding the presidential candidates. If the process seems circular, that's because it is. But the net result is increased "old-style" politics at the local level, run by political operatives who are frequently drawn in by the presidential candidates but who work for local organizations. And it seems clear that local candidates as well as those at the top of the ticket benefit from this increased activity. Campaign finance reform is again on the political agenda, however; and unfettered money going to party committees is an easy target for those seeking change.

What are the messages given out by these campaigns? For a time in the early 1980s, the Republicans experimented with a series of "Vote Republican" commercials, the most prominent of which featured an actor portraying Democratic House Speaker Thomas ("Tip") O'Neill (MA), who was driving a car and ran out of gas despite frequent warnings. Although the commercials were artistically successful, Democratic incumbents were reelected to Congress in record numbers. Apparently the ad campaign was a failure.

Much more frequently, party cooperation comes in the form of themes developed in one campaign that are picked up by co-partisans. In such cases, the transmitting agent is often the political consultant rather than a party official. Such was clearly the case in the 1992 election cycle with the extremely successful theme of health care reform that had been used by Senator Harris Wofford (D-PA) to win an upset victory in a 1991 special election. That same theme reappeared in campaign after campaign in 1992, including in the presidential campaign of Bill Clinton, whose principal strategist was the same James Carville who orchestrated Wofford's victory. These issues tend to be transmitted from campaign to campaign, but rarely are they the kind of issues that distinguish the two parties from each other. The parties have found a role as part of the cash economy of elections, but candidates still raise the vast majority of their money independent of party and run their campaigns based on issues that they feel will appeal to their political electorates.

Party in the Government. Those favoring a "responsible party model" feel that the party in power should be able to legislate its program—to govern. Though rare in the United States, the passage of such legislation has occurred in many constitutional democracies. In fact, between 1952, when Dwight Eisenhower was elected in the first campaign that made significant use of television advertising, and 1992, the party that has controlled the White House has also controlled both houses of the Congress for only fourteen out of forty years. Divided government was the norm, not the exception.

How did the parties respond to this situation? Even asking that question raises more questions. What is meant by "party" in that context? How can one have "party government," if that is taken to mean the victorious party has the ability to implement its program and the two branches of the government are controlled by opposing parties? "Party government" implies that the victorious party has demonstrated majority support and can then rule—but that concept is foreign to modern American democracy.

When President Clinton was elected in 1992, the era of divided government ended—at least for a short time; the Democrats won a sizable majority of the seats in the House and held a slim 56 to 44 margin in the senate (after the special election in Texas to fill the seat vacated by the appointment of Lloyd Bentsen [D-TX] as secretary of the treasury was won by Republican Kay Bailey Hutchinson). The American voting public seemed to favor unified government, giving one party a chance to put its plans into effect. According to exit polls conducted by Voter Research and Surveys, a consortium of ABC News, CBS News, CNN, and NBC News, on November 3, 1992, nearly two-thirds of those who voted for either Clinton or Bush felt that it was "better to have a president and Congress of the same party"; approximately one-quarter of the respondents felt that divided government was preferable, with the remainder answering that they did not know. It is interesting that Perot voters split nearly evenly on this question. These responses contrast markedly with those of a Louis Harris poll conducted just after the election in which Jimmy Carter was elected president in 1976; at that time only 40 percent favored unified government and 45 percent opposed it. In 1981, when President Reagan was battling a Democratic House (though his party controlled the Senate), an ABC News/*Washington Post* survey, conducted between November 17 and 22, found that 47 percent favored unified government and 34 percent thought divided government was a good thing. The public seems to be responding to the ways in which public officials work with each other. The challenge for the Democrats in the 103rd Congress is to demonstrate that they can govern when given control over both branches. The evidence at the time of this writing is inconclusive.

Local candidates are elected locally; they build local coalitions and represent local interests. For much of what they do, their horizons do not extend beyond the boundaries of the local district. Presidential candidates, by contrast, are elected nationally. Some claim that presidential elections reflect popular assessments of the job of the incumbent (Fiorina, 1981); others are less certain. But presidential candidates also campaign as individuals. And they campaign against their opponents as individuals. The 1988 campaign rhetoric was long on Pledge of Allegiance, Willie Horton, and Boston Harbor and short on differing views of the future of the nation. It was clear that Ronald Reagan's priorities and vision were different from those of Jimmy Carter in 1980—and that Walter Mondale in 1984 differed from Reagan on issue after issue. It might have been clear that George Bush was the heir to Reagan in 1988—and voters might well have supported him for that reason—but one had to look quite hard at the rhetoric of his campaign to see how he intended to govern. The 1992 presidential campaign featured this kind of individual campaigning, but it also featured a detailed program for change put forth by candidate Clinton. Again, the challenge he faces is whether he can lead his party and build coalitions with moderate Republicans to implement programmatic changes. How the public responds to him—and to unified party government—will depend on his success in this endeavor.

Thus the American national government features a Congress made up of representatives and senators elected as individuals, judged on the basis of their service to and relations with their constituents, and a president elected in a national campaign, based on image and short on ideas for future policies. How does party function in such a setting?

Recent party leaders in Congress have tried to regain the majority-building mechanisms that were lost among the decentralizing reforms of the 1970s. As the end of the 1970s neared, the House of Representatives was ruled by more than 200 subcommittees, each run by a chair who was protective of his or her own turf. The subcommittee reforms and efforts to break the grip of seniority leaders resulted in a wide dissemination of power but an inability to act. Beginning in 1977 Speaker O'Neill sought to regain some semblance of control. Recognizing that in order to move the legislative agenda forward the Speaker needed additional powers, the members assented to broadening the Speaker's appointive powers, allowing him to control the Rules Committee, permitting multiple referral of pieces of legislation and the establishment of task forces to handle certain key issues. O'Neill was a Speaker who knew the House and knew politics, but he was not very concerned about specific policies. He used his powers to aid others with their legislative proposals. In his short and doomed Speakership, as Barbara Sinclair notes in Chapter 12, Jim Wright (D-TX) gave evidence that he was going to use the newly expanded powers of his office to forward a Democratic policy agenda for which he was to be the chief spokesperson. However, although we caught glimpses of how this role might work, Wright's short tenure and forced resignation prevented it from reaching fruition.

Republican party leaders had the opportunity to work with a forceful ideological leader of their party throughout the decade of the 1980s. In the Senate, they did so with majority control throughout the first six years of the Reagan administration. The Republican experience demonstrated how a united party can come together behind a legislative program. Reagan lobbied hard with his co-partisans. He worked closely with Howard Baker (R-TN) and Bob Dole (R-KS), the Republican leaders in the Senate, and with Bob Michel (R-IL), the House minority leader. He achieved remarkable success in terms of the support that his programs received from Republicans in Congress.

But the Republican successes early in the Reagan years were not repeated at the end of Reagan's first term, nor during his second term. Again, the limits of party government—and of party as an organizing element within the government—are apparent. When Reagan was successful in implementing his legislative agenda, he was successful in the House because of a cross-party coalition (recall Chapter 13). Democrats supported his budget-cutting proposals because they felt that Reagan was in tune with their constituents. After the 1982 congressional election, during which Democrats who felt threatened were reelected, support for Reagan's program diminished. Legislative entrepreneurs created cross-party coalitions, legislators claimed that the elections gave no mandate for policy to the president, and the president struggled to translate his personal popularity into legislative achievements.

The Democrats face the challenge of governing under a unified government in 1993. President Clinton and the leaders of the 103rd Congress, Speaker Foley and majority leader Mitchell, have had great difficulty in the first year of the 103rd Congress. The House has tended to follow the president's lead on major policy initiatives, but more conservative senators, in a legislative body that is more closely divided on partisan grounds and in which the rules permit a minority to have greater influence, have defeated some proposals (e.g., the job stimulus plan) and caused major alterations in others (e.g., the energy tax). It is much too early for a definitive assessment of Democratic success at unified government, but the experiment merits careful attention.

How does a president govern in these circumstances? As Cal Mackenzie points out in Chapter 14, a president does so by staffing an administration with personal followers. But the political party is simply not very helpful in this task. A president does not want to reward hard work at political organizing. He wants to find individuals who believe as he does and who have the talent to implement his programs and to forward his ideas. If a president wants to change the way the government is functioning in a radical way, as Ronald Reagan sought to do, then he must extend his reach deep into the bureaucracy—again, as Reagan sought to do. The appointments constituted not "Republican patronage" but "Reagan patronage." Given the heterogeneity of the parties (and this is more true of the Democrats than of the Republicans), presidents want their personal followers in positions of power. Whereas parties once performed as giant personnel agencies for the government, they now serve as ad hoc organizations established in each new administration to guarantee implementation of the new leader's wishes. The experience of the Clinton administration as it took office in 1993 was frustrating to many. President Clinton was committed to making the government "look more like America." His search for minority and female candidates for top posts, combined with the increased scrutiny given all appointees' backgrounds, resulted in a situation in which many positions remained unfilled for long periods of time. This experience seems to have removed the parties even further from the "personnel agency" role. The Democratic National Committee was largely out of the loop as the new administration filled both top-level and more minor positions.

Some semblances of party in government still appear. The Hill committees provide a link between the party and incumbent legislators who are supported in reelection bids. But the link is not a strong one. It does not replace personal ties to constituents. Legislative leaders have asserted new authority, but the rank-and-file members look to their constituents' interests first. The president is the leader of his party in government, but the members owe their allegiance more to the president than to the party. And, most significantly, neither party can govern, in the sense of presenting a program to the electorate, gaining office, and implementing that program.

TOWARD THE TWENTY-FIRST CENTURY

The picture of political parties that emerges as the twentieth century draws to a close is thus a mixed one. Party—in all senses of the term—has attempted to adapt to changing situations. But these attempts have not been totally successful. Change has been an important part of the history of parties, in terms of the roles performed by parties, the centrality of that role for governing (recall Chapter 1), and the procedures followed by political parties.

The final report of the Democratic party's McGovern-Fraser Commission, the Commission on Party Structure and Delegate Selection appointed after the debacle at the 1968 presidential nominating convention, approvingly quoted Lord Thomas Babington Macaulay, the British poet and statesman who worked to revise the colonial penal system in the nineteenth century: "We reform that we may preserve." And so it has been with party leaders in recent decades.

As noted earlier, however, reform has been of two types. Political parties have proved remarkably successful at reforming party practices that have become passé: The machine is gone; smoke-filled rooms are gone; male domination is gone. The existence of party as an organization has been preserved by such reforms. Indeed, party leaders have responded to the dissatisfaction that has threatened their existence, and the threat has abated.

The other, more basic sense of reform pertains to party renewal. In this enterprise, parties have been less successful. Renewal involves building parties into better-structured, more active, more effective, and more policy-oriented organizations. This effort has begun, but only just begun. Parties have adopted an electoral role and have built an organization to perform it. (The Republicans have been more successful than the Democrats in this regard.) The effort was started in Washington and is only slowly spreading to the states and local units. But as the essays in this book make clear, building an electoral role is only one part of renewing a party structure. What has been missing is a sense of the role of political party in the governing process. And that involves a systematic division of the two parties on the issues that affect the electorate.

Is such a renewal possible? In the early 1970s those people looking to renew the Democratic party called for party conferences to discuss policy matters in between presidential nominating conventions. These so-called midterm conferences were designed to invigorate the national party—and, through the delegate-selection process, state and local parties, too—as a forum for discussing the critical issues of the day. In 1985, after only two such conferences, the Democratic National Committee moved quickly (but quietly) to end the practice, fearing that the appearance of divisiveness, the inevitable result of discussing critical issues, would hurt the party's chances to present a unified front and regain the Senate in 1986 and the White House in 1988. So discussion of issues was removed from the Democratic party agenda in favor of winning elections. The Democrats did regain the Senate in 1986, but they lost the presidency once again in 1988, during a campaign in which the electorate did not know what the party stood for.

Meaningful party renewal depends on the willingness of partisan leaders to distinguish their party from the other one. In responding to criticism that he had not been sufficiently partisan in his first year as Senate majority leader, George Mitchell stated, "I reject the view that I should oppose for the sake of opposition and confront for the sake of confrontation" (Harkavy, 1989). Yet the Democratic leadership in both houses of Congress, unsuccessfully in the House but successfully in the Senate, opposed President Bush's effort to reduce the capital gains tax on the specifically partisan grounds that this proposal would aid the affluent and not those more in need.

The 103rd Congress opened with a Democrat in the White House and Democrats controlling both houses of Congress; the Republicans, particularly those in the Senate, have relished the role of opposing—and delaying or defeating—Democratic initiatives. Minority leader Robert Dole has taken on the role of the great naysayer and has been most forceful in discussing in forum after forum how the Republican view of effective government differs from that of the Democrats.

The question of the role of party in the twenty-first century is thus one of issues. If party is to be meaningful, if the two-party system is to play a more central role than it has for decades, then the voters must come to understand that a candidate's party affiliation will have an impact on the performance of that candidate in office. They must also understand that Republican and Democratic leaders differ on the issues important to the public—and that elected officials will stand by these differences.

The return to unified government after the 1992 election presents the country with what has become an unusual opportunity to watch the parties play out against each other. President Clinton is intent on presenting a new image for the Democratic party. He rejects the claim that Democrats are a party of "tax and spend" and asserts that his proposals represent a third way, requiring the government and the private sector to work to solve the nation's problems.

The Republican party has tried to paint Democratic programs with an old brush; for example, they opposed President Clinton's economic package as more of the same: increased taxes to pay for an expanding government. The alternative they presented in the Senate stressed spending cuts and rejected tax and user-fee increases.

On the sideline stands Ross Perot, with his billions of dollars and constant criticism of the government. He presents a true challenge to the two parties. Perot's criticism is a criticism of outcome. He does not have to produce in order to make his point—that government does not work—because he is not in power. But he attracts followers who agree with him that what we have has not been successful.

The last decade of the twentieth century is the first in fifty years in which the citizens of the United States have not been overly concerned with foreign affairs, with wars in Europe, with the threat of communism, with Vietnam and its aftermath. Although those in government still must face difficult decisions regarding the nation's role in the world, citizens will evaluate the government, those holding office, and the major political parties on how they respond to domestic concerns, to the precarious state of the nation's economy, to the increasingly troublesome federal debt, to the calls for improved health care.

The Democrats will be evaluated on their ability to use their control over the executive and legislative branches to produce substantive policy change—and on the effectiveness of those policies in addressing the issues of concern to the citizenry. The Republicans will be evaluated on their ability to present alternatives and even to implement them. And both the party system and our government as a whole will be evaluated on their ability to avoid stalemate and name-calling and to get on with the business of government. For if the public is not satisfied with the results, the results of continuing failure to govern could well be a turn toward the antiparty and antigovernment politics of Ross Perot.

Acronyms

ACIR	Advisory Commission on Intergovernmental Relations
ANES	American National Election Study
DCCC	Democratic Congressional Campaign Committee
DJP	Democratic Justice party
DLC	Democratic Leadership Council
DNC	Democratic National Committee
DSCC	Democratic Senatorial Campaign Committee
EOP	Executive Office of the President
ERA	Equal Rights Amendment
FCC	Federal Communications Commission
FEC	Federal Election Commission
FECA	Federal Election Campaign Act
IMF	International Monetary Fund
NCPAC	National Conservative Political Action Committee
NRCC	National Republican Congressional Committee
NRSC	National Republican Senatorial Committee
PACs	political action committees
RNC	Republican National Committee
VRS	Voter Research and Surveys, a consortium of ABC News, CBS News, CNN, and NBC News

397

References

ABC News. 1989. *The 88 Vote*. New York: ABC News.

Abramowitz, Alan I. 1988. "An Improved Model for Predicting Presidential Election Outcomes." 21 *PS* 843.

Abramowitz, Alan I., David J. Lanoue, and Subha Ramesh. 1988. "Economic Conditions, Causal Attributions, and Political Evaluations in the 1984 Presidential Election." 50 *Journal of Politics* 848.

Abramson, Jeffrey B., F. Christopher Arterton, and Gary R. Orren. 1988. *The Electronic Commonwealth: The Impact of New Media Technologies on Democratic Politics*. New York: Basic Books.

Achen, Christopher. 1975. "Mass Political Attitudes and the Survey Response." 69 *American Political Science Review* 1218.

Adamanay, David. 1984. "Political Parties in the 1980s." In Michael J. Malbin, ed., *Money and Politics in the United States*. Chatham, NJ: Chatham House.

Adams, Sherman. 1961. *Firsthand Report*. New York: Harper and Brothers.

Advisory Commission on Intergovernmental Relations. 1986. *The Transformation in American Politics: Implications for Federalism*. Washington, DC: Advisory Committee on Intergovernmental Relations.

Agranoff, Robert. 1972. "Introduction: The New Style Campaigning." In Robert Agranoff, ed., *The New Style in Election Campaigns*. Boston: Holbrook.

Albany Argus. 1846. November 3.

Alexander, Herbert E. 1992. *Financing Politics: Money, Elections and Political Reform*, 4th edition. Washington, DC: Congressional Quarterly Press.

_____ . 1984. *Financing Politics*. Washington, DC: Congressional Quarterly Press.

Alford, John, and David Brady. 1989. "Personal and Partisan Advantage in U.S. Congressional Elections, 1846–1986." In Lawrence C. Dodd and Bruce I. Oppenheimer, eds., *Congress Reconsidered*, 4th edition. Washington, DC: Congressional Quarterly Press.

Alford, John, and John Hibbing. 1983. "Incumbency Advantage in Senate Elections." Paper presented at the Annual Meeting of the Midwest Political Science Association, Chicago.

Allwright, Smith v. 1944. 321 U.S. 649.

American Political Science Association, Committee on Political Parties. 1950. *Toward a More Responsible Two-Party System*. New York: Rinehart.

Anderson, John. 1992. "Can Any Independent Win the Presidency?" *USA Today*, July 20.

Andersen, Kristi. 1979. *Creation of a Democratic Majority: 1928–1936*. Chicago: University of Chicago Press.

Ansolabehere, Steven, David Brady, and Morris Fiorina. 1992. "The Vanishing Marginals and Electoral Responsiveness." 22 *British Journal of Political Science* 21.

Apple, R. W., Jr. 1992. "Poll Gives Clinton a Post-Perot, Post-Convention Boost." *New York Times*, July 18:A1.

Asher, Herbert B. 1988a. *Presidential Elections and American Politics*, 4th edition. Chicago: Dorsey Press.

Asher, Herbert. 1988b. *Polling and the Public: What Every Citizen Should Know*. Washington, DC: Congressional Quarterly Press.

Babcock, Charles R. 1992. "Parties Rack Up 6-Figure Gifts of 'Soft Money'." *Washington Post*, September 28.

———. 1988. "Being There Unnecessary for Republican Victories." *Washington Post*, November 25.

Bach, Stanley, and Steven S. Smith. 1988. *Managing Uncertainty in the House of Representatives*. Washington, DC: Brookings Institution.

Baer, Denise L., and David A. Bositis. 1988. *Elite Cadres and Party Coalitions*. New York: Greenwood Press.

Baer, Donald, et al. 1992. "The Race." *U.S. News & World Report*, August 31-September 7:34.

Balz, Dan. 1990a. "Democrats Split over Plans to Close Donation Loophole." *Washington Post*, March 2.

———. 1990b. "When Party Cash Crosses State Lines." *Washington Post*, February 7.

Banner, James. 1970. *To the Hartford Convention: The Federalists and the Origins of Party Politics in Massachusetts, 1789–1815*. New York: Alfred A. Knopf.

Banning, Lance. 1978. *The Jeffersonian Persuasion: Evolution of a Party Ideology*. Ithaca: Cornell University Press.

Barber, James David. 1986. Private communication.

Barnes, James. 1989. "Reinventing the RNC." *National Journal*, January 14.

Barnes, James, and Carol Matlack. 1989. "Running in the Red." *National Journal*, July 8.

Barnes, James, and Richard E. Cohen. 1988. "Unity—Will It Last?" *National Journal*, September 30.

Barone, Michael. 1992. "The Cry for More Direction." *U.S. News & World Report*. November 16:68.

Barrett, Lawrence I. 1990. "Can the Right Survive Success?" *Time*, March 19.

Barry, John. 1989. *The Ambition and the Power*. New York: Viking.

Bartels, Larry. Forthcoming. "Stability and Change in American Electoral Politics." In David Butler and Austin Ranney, eds., *Electioneering*. New York: Oxford University Press.

———. 1983. *Presidential Primaries and the Dynamics of Public Choice*. Ph.D. dissertation submitted to the University of California, Berkeley.

Bates, Richard, Executive Director, DCCC. 1989. Personal interview, January 9.

Baumer, Donald. 1992. "Senate Democratic Leadership in the 100th Congress." In Ronald Peters and Allen Herzke, eds., *The Atomistic Congress*. Armonk, NY: M. E. Sharpe.

Beck, Nathaniel. 1992. "Forecasting the 1992 Presidential Election: The Message Is in the Confidence Level." 6 *Public Perspective* 32.

Beck, Paul Allen. 1984. "The Electoral Cycle and Patterns of American Politics." In Richard G. Niemi and Herbert F. Weisberg, eds., *Controversies in American Voting Behavior.* Washington, DC: Congressional Quarterly Press.

_____. 1979. "The Electoral Cycle and Patterns of American Politics." 9 *British Journal of Political Science* 129.

_____. 1977. "Partisan Dealignment in the Postwar South." 71 *American Political Science Review* 477.

Beck, Paul Allen, and Frank J. Sorauf. 1992. *Party Politics in America,* 7th edition. New York: HarperCollins.

Becker, Richard A., John M. Chambers, and Allan R. Wilks. 1988. *The New S Language: A Programming Environment for Data Analysis and Graphics.* Pacific Grove, CA: Wadsworth.

Benedict, Michael. 1974. *A Compromise of Principle: Congressional Republicans and Reconstruction, 1863–1896.* New York: Norton.

Benjamin, Gerald, and Michael J. Malbin, eds. 1992. *Limiting Legislative Terms.* Washington, DC: Congressional Quarterly Press.

Benson, Lee. 1981. "Discussion." In Patricia Bonomi, ed., *The American Constitutional System Under Strong and Weak Parties.* New York: Praeger.

_____. 1961. *The Concept of Jacksonian Democracy: New York as a Test Case.* Princeton: Princeton University Press.

_____. 1955. *Merchants, Farmers, and Railroads: Railroad Regulation and New York Politics, 1850–1887.* Cambridge: Harvard University Press.

Benson, Lee, Joel H. Silbey, and Phyllis F. Field. 1978. "Toward a Theory of Stability and Change in American Voting Behavior: New York State, 1792–1970 as a Test Case." In Joel H. Silbey, Allan G. Bogue, and William H. Flanigan, eds., *The History of American Electoral Behavior.* Princeton: Princeton University Press.

Berke, Richard. 1988. "True Tales of Spending in the Presidential Race." *New York Times,* December 11.

_____. 1992. "First TV Debate Canceled as Bush Sticks to Objections over Format." *New York Times,* September 17:A1.

Berry, John M. 1992. "1990–91 Recession Is Officially Over, Panel Declares." *Washington Post,* December 23:E1.

Beth, Richard S. 1984. "Recent Research on 'Incumbency Advantage' in House Elections: Part II." 11 *Congress and the Presidency* 211.

_____. 1981–1982. "'Incumbency Advantage' and Incumbency Resources: Recent Articles." 9 *Congress and the Presidency* 119.

Bibby, John F. 1986. "Political Party Trends in 1985: The Continuing but Constrained Advance of the National Party." 16 *Publius* 90.

_____. 1983. "State House Elections at Midterm." In Thomas E. Mann and Norman J. Ornstein, eds., *The American Elections of 1982.* Washington, DC: American Enterprise Institute.

_____. 1981. "Party Renewal in the National Republican Party." In Gerald M. Pomper, ed., *Party Renewal in America: Theory in Practice.* New York: Praeger.

_____. 1979. "Political Parties and Federalism: The Republican National Committee Involvement in Gubernatorial and Legislative Elections." 9 *Publius* 22.

Birnbaum, Jeffrey. 1992. "Ex-ROTC Leader Escalates His Attack on Clinton Deferral." *Wall Street Journal,* September 17:A6.

Black, Earl, and Merle Black. 1987. *Politics and Society in the South.* Cambridge: Harvard University Press.

Black, Gordon S., and Benjamin D. Black. 1992. "Americans Want and Need a New Political Party." 4 *The Public Perspective* 3.

Blasi, Vince. 1977. "The Checking Value in First Amendment Theory." *American Bar Foundation Research Journal* 521–649.

Blumenthal, Sidney. 1980. *The Permanent Campaign: Inside the World of Elite Political Operatives.* Boston: Beacon Press.

Bogue, Allan. 1980. *The Earnest Men.* Ithaca: Cornell University Press.

Bohmer, David. 1978. "The Maryland Electorate and the Concept of a Party System in the Early National Period." In Joel H. Silbey, Allan G. Bogue, and William H. Flanigan, *The History of American Electoral Behavior.* Princeton: Princeton University Press.

Bolling, Richard. 1965. *House Out of Order.* New York: Dutton.

Bonafede, Dom. 1987. "The White House Personnel Office from Roosevelt to Reagan." In G. Calvin Mackenzie, ed., *The In and Outers.* Baltimore: Johns Hopkins University Press.

Bond, Jon R., Cary Covington, and Richard Fleisher. 1985. "Explaining Challenger Quality in Congressional Elections." 47 *Journal of Politics* 510.

Born, Richard. 1986. "Strategic Politicians and Unresponsive Voters." 80 *American Political Science Review* 599.

Brady, David W. 1988. *Critical Elections and Congressional Policy Making.* Stanford: Stanford University Press.

――――. 1973. *Congressional Voting in a Partisan Era.* Lawrence: University Press of Kansas.

Brady, David W., and Douglas Rivers. 1991. "Term Limits Make Sense." *New York Times,* October 5:21.

Brief of James MacGregor Burns, Barbara Burrell, William Crotty, James S. Fay, Roman B. Hedges, John S. Jackson III, Everett C. Ladd, Kay Lawson, and Gerald M. Pomper. 1986. *Tashjian v. Republican Party of Connecticut,* 479 U.S. 208.

Brief of William J. Cibes, Jr., Clyde McKee, Sarah McCally Morehouse, and Wayne R. Swanson. 1986. *Tashjian v. Republican Party of Connecticut,* 479 U.S. 208.

Brinkley, Alan. 1990. "The New Deal and the Idea of the State." In Steve Fraser and Gary Gerstle, eds., *The Rise and Fall of the New Deal Order, 1930–1980.* Princeton: Princeton University Press.

Broder, David S. 1992. "Strong Show By Bush May Change Little." *Washington Post,* October 20:A1.

――――. 1990. "Five Ways to Put Some Sanity Back in Elections." *Washington Post,* January 14.

――――. 1986. "The Force." *Washington Post,* April 2.

――――. 1971. *The Party's Over: The Failure of American Politics.* New York: Harper and Row.

Broder, John. 1992. "Perot's Ambiguity Generates Hope, Confusion, Disgust." *Los Angeles Times,* September 19:A17.

Bruce, Harold R. 1927. *American Parties and Politics*. New York: Henry Holt.

Buchanan, William. 1986. "Election Predictions: An Empirical Assessment." 50 *Public Opinion Quarterly* 227.

Budge, Ian, and Dennis Farlie. 1977. *Voting and Party Competition*. New York: Wiley.

Bullitt, Stimson. 1977. *To Be a Politician*. Rev. ed. New Haven: Yale University Press.

Burnham, Walter Dean. 1982. *The Current Crisis in American Politics*. New York: Oxford University Press.

_____. 1975. "American Politics in the 1970s: Beyond Party?" In Louis Maisel and Paul M. Sacks, eds., *The Future of Political Parties*. Beverly Hills: Sage.

_____. 1973. *Politics/America: The Cutting Edge of Change*. New York: D. Van Nostrand.

_____. 1970. *Critical Elections and the Mainsprings of American Politics*. New York: Norton.

_____. 1965. "The Changing Shape of the American Political Universe." 59 *American Political Science Review* 7.

Burns, James MacGregor. 1956. *Roosevelt: The Lion and the Fox*. New York: Harcourt, Brace.

Cain, Bruce, John Ferejohn, and Morris Fiorina. 1987. *The Personal Vote: Constituency Service and Electoral Independence*. Cambridge: Harvard University Press.

"Campaign '92: Transcript of the 3rd Presidential Debate." 1992. *Washington Post,* October 20:A24.

"Campaign Time Line: March 1990–November 1992." 1992. Manuscript prepared by the Kennedy School of Government, Harvard University.

Campbell, Angus, Philip E. Converse, Warren E. Miller, and Donald E. Stokes. 1960. *The American Voter*. New York: John Wiley and Sons.

Campbell, James E. 1992. "Forecasting the Presidential Vote in the States." 36 *American Journal of Political Science* 386.

_____. 1986. "Presidential Coattails and Midterm Losses in State Legislative Elections." 80 *American Political Science Review* 45.

Campbell, James E., and Thomas E. Mann. 1992. "Forecasting the 1992 Presidential Election: A User's Guide to the Models." 10 *Brookings Review* 22.

Campbell, James E., Lynna L. Cherry, and Kenneth A. Wink. Forthcoming. "The Convention Bump." *American Politics Quarterly*.

Cannon, Lou. 1982. *Reagan*. New York: Putnam.

Carmines, Edward G. 1986. "The Logic of Partisan Transformations." Paper presented at the Annual Meeting of the American Political Science Association, New Orleans.

Carmines, Edward G., Steven H. Renten, and James A. Stimson. 1984. "Events and Alignments: The Party Image Link." In Richard G. Niemi and Herbert F. Weisberg, eds., *Controversies in American Voting Behavior*. Washington, DC: Congressional Quarterly Press.

Carmines, Edward G., and James A. Stimson. 1989. *Race and the Transformation of American Politics*. Princeton, N.J.: Princeton University Press.

Carr, Craig L., and Gary L. Scott. 1984. "The Logic of State Primary Classification Schemes." 12 *American Politics Quarterly* 465.

Carville, James. 1993. Remarks delivered before the National Press Club, January 19.

Ceasar, James, and Andrew Busch. 1993. *Upside Down and Inside Out: The 1992 Elections and American Politics*. Lanham, MD: Rowman and Littlefield.

Center for American Women in Politics. 1989. "The Gender Gap in Presidential Voting." New Brunswick, NJ: Eagleton Institute, Rutgers University.

Chalmers, Wally, Executive Director, DNC. 1989. Personal interview, January 12.

Chambers, William N. 1963. *Political Parties in a New Nation: The American Experience, 1776–1809*. New York: Oxford University Press.

Chambers, William N., and Walter Dean Burnham. 1975. *The American Party System: Stages of Political Development*. New York: Oxford University Press.

Cheney, Richard B. 1989. "An Unruly House." 11 *Public Opinion* 41.

Chlopak, Robert, Executive Director, DSCC. 1989. Personal interview, January 12.

Chubb, John E. 1988. "Institutions, the Economy and the Dynamics of State Elections." 82 *American Political Science Review* 118.

Clausen, Aage. 1973. *How Congressmen Decide*. New York: St. Martin's Press.

Cleveland, William S. 1979. "Robust Locally Weighted Regression and Smoothing Scatterplots." 74 *Journal of the American Statistical Association* 829.

Clubb, Jerome M., William H. Flanigan, and Nancy H. Zingale. 1980. *Partisan Realignment: Voters, Parties, and Government in American History*. Beverly Hills: Sage.

Clymer, Adam. 1992. "Bush's Gains from Convention Nearly Evaporate in Latest Poll." *New York Times*, August 26:A1.

Clymer, Adam, and Kathleen A. Frankovic. 1981. "The Realities of Realignment." 4 *Public Opinion* 42.

Cohen, Richard E. 1992. *Washington at Work: Back Rooms and Clean Air*. New York: Macmillan.

———. 1987. "Quick-Starting Speaker." *National Journal*, May 30.

Collie, Melissa P., and Joseph Cooper. 1989. "Multiple Referral and the New Committee System in the House of Representatives." In Lawrence C. Dodd and Bruce I. Oppenheimer, eds., *Congress Reconsidered*, 4th edition. Washington, DC: Congressional Quarterly Press.

Commission on Party Structure and Delegate Selection. 1971. *Mandate for Change*. Washington, DC: Democratic National Committee.

Converse, Philip E. 1976. *The Dynamics of Party Support*. Beverly Hills: Sage.

Converse, Philip E., and Gregory B. Markus. 1979. "Plus Ca Change ... the New CPS Election Study Panel." 73 *American Political Science Review* 32.

Converse, Philip E., Aage R. Clausen, and Warren E. Miller. 1965. "Electoral Myth and Reality: The 1964 Election." 59 *American Political Science Review* 321.

Conway, M. Margaret. 1983. "Republican Party Nationalization, Campaign Activities, and Their Implications for the Political System." 13 *Publius* 1.

Cook, Rhodes. 1993. "Clinton Climbs to Power on Broad, Shaky Base." 51 *Congressional Quarterly Weekly Report* 188.

———. 1992a. "Clinton Win Would Redraw Electoral College Map." 50 *Congressional Quarterly Weekly Report* 3333.

———. 1992b. "Perot Positioned to Defy a Past Seemingly Carved in Stone." 50 *Congressional Quarterly Weekly Report* 1721.

_____.1992c. "Republicans Suffer a Knockout That Leaves Clinton Standing." 50 *Congressional Quarterly Weekly Report* 3811.

_____. 1988. " '88 Vote: Stress Persuasion over Registration." *Congressional Quarterly Weekly Report*, October 1.

_____. 1981. "Chorus of Democratic Voices Urges New Policies, Methods." *Congressional Quarterly Weekly Report*, January 17.

Cooke, Jacob E. 1961. *The Federalist*. New York: Meridian.

Cooper, Joseph. 1975. "Strengthening the Congress: An Organizational Analysis." 12 *Harvard Journal on Legislation* 307.

Cooper, Joseph, and David W. Brady. 1981. "Institutional Context and Leadership Style: The House from Cannon to Rayburn." 75 *American Political Science Review* 411.

Cotter, Cornelius P., James L. Gibson, John F. Bibby, and Robert J. Huckshorn. 1984. *Party Organizations in American Politics*. New York: Praeger.

Cotter, Cornelius, and Bernard C. Hennessy. 1964. *Politics Without Power: The National Party Committees*. New York: Atherton Press.

Crotty, William. 1985. *The Party Game*. New York: W. H. Freeman.

_____. 1984. *American Parties in Decline*. Boston: Little, Brown.

_____. 1983. *Party Reform*. New York: Longman.

Cutright, Phillips, and Peter Rossi. 1958a. "Grass Roots Politicians and the Vote." 23 *American Sociological Review* 177.

_____. 1958b. "Party Organization in Primary Elections." 64 *American Journal of Sociology* 262.

Dahl, Robert. 1989. *Democracy and Its Critics*. New Haven: Yale University Press.

_____. 1956. *A Preface to Democratic Theory*. Chicago: University of Chicago Press.

David, Paul T., Ralph M. Goldman, and Richard C. Bain. 1960. *The Politics of National Party Conventions*. Washington, DC: Brookings Institution.

Davidson, Roger H., Walter J. Oleszek, and Thomas Kephart. 1988. "One Bill, Many Committees: Multiple Referrals in the U.S. House of Representatives." 13 *Legislative Studies Quarterly* 3.

Dean, John, Director of the Office of Voter Participation, DNC. 1989. Personal interview, January 12.

Deckard, Barbara Sinclair. 1976. "Political Upheaval and Congressional Voting." 38 *Journal of Politics* 326.

Democratic National Committee. 1972. *Report of the Committee on Rules for the 1972 Democratic National Committee*. Washington, DC: Democratic National Committee.

Devroy, Ann, and Richard Morin. 1992. "Democratic Governors, Bush Tangle on Budget." *Washington Post*, February 4:A1.

Dionne, E. J., Jr. 1991. *Why Americans Hate Politics*. New York: Simon and Schuster.

_____. 1989. "Attack Shows G.O.P. Strategy Shift." *New York Times*, June 11.

_____. 1988. "Dukakis Campaign Battling in Last Democratic Trench." *New York Times*, October 20.

Dodd, Lawrence C. 1979. "The Expanded Roles of the House Democratic Whip System: The 93rd and 94th Congresses." 7 *Congressional Studies* 27.

Dodd, Lawrence C., and Bruce I. Oppenheimer. 1977. *Congress Reconsidered*. New York: Praeger.

Donovan, Beth. 1992. "Democrats Expect a Tuneup, Not a Complete Overhaul." *Congressional Weekly Report*, December 5.

Dowd, Maureen. 1992. "A No-Nonsense Sort of Talk Show." *New York Times*, October 16:A1.

Downs, Anthony. 1957. *An Economic Theory of Democracy*. New York: Harper and Row.

Drew, Elizabeth. 1983. *Politics and Money: The New Road to Corruption*. New York: Macmillan.

Duffy, Michael, and Dan Goodgame. 1992. *Marching in Place: The Status Quo Presidency of George Bush*. New York: Simon and Schuster.

Eaton, William. 1993. "Key Democrats Back Retiree Tax Hikes." *Los Angeles Times*, February 13.

Edsall, Thomas B. 1989. "Branching out with Burgeoning Influence." *Washington Post*, January 17.

———. 1988. "The Reagan Legacy." In Sidney Blumenthal and Thomas Byrne Edsall, eds., *The Reagan Legacy*. New York: Pantheon Books.

Edwards, George C. III. 1983. *The Public Presidency*. New York: St. Martin's Press.

Ehrenhalt, Alan. 1987. "Changing South Perils Conservative Coalition." *Congressional Quarterly Weekly Report*, August 1.

Eldersveld, Samuel J. 1964. *Political Parties: A Behavioral Analysis*. Chicago: Rand McNally.

Ellwood, John W., and James A. Thurber. 1981. "The Politics of the Congressional Budget Process Re-examined." In Lawrence C. Dodd and Bruce I. Oppenheimer, eds., *Congress Reconsidered*, 2nd edition. Washington, DC: Congressional Quarterly Press.

Emerson, Thomas I. 1970. *The System of Freedom of Expression*. New York: Random House.

Epstein, Leon D. 1989. "Will American Political Parties Be Privatized?" 5 *Journal of Law and Politics* 239.

———. 1986. *Political Parties in the American Mold*. Madison: University of Wisconsin Press.

Erikson, Robert. 1972. "The Advantage of Incumbency." 3 *Polity* 395.

Fair, Ray C. 1988. "The Effect of Economic Events on Votes for President: 1984 Update." 60 *Review of Economics and Statistics* 159.

———. 1982. "The Effect of Economic Events on Votes for President: 1980 Update." 64 *Review of Economics and Statistics* 322.

Federal Election Commission. 1993. FEC Press Release, March 11.

———. 1989. FEC Press Release, March 27.

———. 1988a. FEC Press Release, February 5.

———. 1988b. FEC Press Release, November 8.

———. 1984. FEC Record, March 10.

Feldman, Stanley. 1991. "What Do Survey Questions Really Measure?" 4 *Political Methodologist* 8.

Fenn, Dan H., Jr. 1976. Interview with the author. Waltham, MA, March 26.

Fenno, Richard F., Jr. 1978. *Home Style: House Members in Their Own Districts*. Boston: Little, Brown.

———. 1973. *Congressmen in Committees*. Boston: Little, Brown.

———. 1965. "The Internal Distribution of Influence: The House." In David B. Truman, ed., *The Congress and America's Future*. Englewood Cliffs, NJ: Prentice-Hall.

———. 1959. *The President's Cabinet*. New York: Vintage.

Ferejohn, John A. 1986. "Logrolling in an Institutional Context: A Case Study of Food Stamp Regulation." In Gerald Wright, Leroy Reiselbach, and Lawrence Dodd, eds., *Congress and Policy Change*. New York: Agathon.

Ferejohn, John A., and Randall Calvert. 1984. "Presidential Coattails in Historical Perspective." 28 *American Journal of Political Science* 127.

Ferejohn, John A., and Morris P. Fiorina. 1985. "Incumbency and Realignment in Congressional Elections." In John E. Chubb and Paul E. Peterson, eds., *The New Directions in American Politics*. Washington, DC: Brookings Institution.

Ferguson, Thomas, and Joel Rogers. 1986. *Right Turn*. New York: Hill and Wang.

Fiorina, Morris P. 1992a. *Divided Government*. New York: Macmillan.

———. 1992b. "An Era of Divided Government." In Bruce Cain and Gillian Peel, eds., *Developments in American Politics*. London: Macmillan.

———. 1990. "An Era of Divided Government." In Bruce Cain and Gillian Peele, eds., *Developments in American Politics*. London: Macmillan.

———. 1989. *Congress: Keystone of the Washington Establishment*. New Haven: Yale University Press.

———. 1981a. "Short- and Long-Term Effects of Economic Conditions on Individual Voting Decisions." In Douglas A. Hibbs, Jr., and H. Fassbender, eds., *Contemporary Political Economy*. Amsterdam: North-Holland.

———. 1981b. *Retrospective Voting in American National Elections*. New Haven: Yale University Press.

———. 1979. *Retrospective Voting in American National Elections*. New Haven, CT: Yale University Press.

———. 1977. *Congress, Keystone of the Washington Establishment*. New Haven: Yale University Press.

Fischer, David Hackett. 1965. *The Revolution of American Conservatism: The Federalist Party in the Era of Jeffersonian Democracy*. New York: Oxford University Press.

Fish, Carl R. 1904. *The Civil Service and the Patronage*. Cambridge: Harvard University Press.

Fleming, Thomas, and Paul Gottfried. 1988. *The Conservative Movement*. Boston: Twayne Publishers.

Formisano, Ronald P. 1983. *The Transformation of Political Culture: Massachusetts Parties, 1790s–1840s*. New York: Oxford University Press.

———. 1981. "Federalists and Republicans: Parties, Yes—System, No." In Paul Kleppner et al., eds., *The Evolution of American Electoral Systems*. Westport, CT: Greenwood Press.

———. 1974. "Deferential-Participant Politics: The Early Republic's Political Culture, 1789–1890." 68 *American Political Science Review* 473.

———. 1971. *The Birth of Mass Political Parties: Michigan, 1827–1861*. Princeton: Princeton University Press.

Forsythe, Robert, Forrest Nelson, George Neumann, and Jack Wright. 1991. "The Iowa Presidential Stock Market: A Field Experiment." 4 *Research in Experimental Economics* 1.

Fowler, Linda L., and Robert D. McClure. 1989. *Political Ambition: Who Decides to Run for Congress.* New Haven: Yale University Press.

Fowler, Linda L., and L. Sandy Maisel. 1990. "The Changing Supply of Competitive Candidates in House Elections, 1982–1988." In Glenn R. Parker, ed., *Changing Perspectives on Congress.* Knoxville: University of Tennessee Press.

Franklin, Charles H., and John E. Jackson. 1983. "The Dynamics of Party Identification." 77 *American Political Science Review* 457.

Frankovic, Kathleen A. 1993. "Public Opinion in the 1992 Campaign." In Gerald M. Pomper, ed., *The Election of 1992.* Chatham, NJ: Chatham House.

Frantzich, Stephen E. 1989. *Political Parties in the Technological Age.* New York: Longman.

Frendeis, John P., James L. Gibson, and Laura L. Vertz. 1990. "The Electoral Relevance of Local Party Organizations." 84 *American Political Science Review* 225.

Galston, William, and Elaine Kamarck. 1993. "Converting the Perotistas." 5 *New Democrat* 5.

———. 1989. *The Politics of Evasion: Democrats and the Presidency.* Washington, DC: Progressive Policy Institute.

Gans, Herbert C. 1982. *The Urban Villagers: Group and Class in the Life of Italian-Americans.* New York: Free Press.

Garand, James C., and Donald A. Gross. 1984. "Changes in the Vote Margins of Congressional Candidates: A Specification of Historical Trends." 78 *American Political Science Review* 17.

Gelman, Andrew, and Gary King. 1993. "Forecasting the 1992 U.S. Presidential Election." Unpublished manuscript.

Germond, Jack W., and Jules Witcover. 1985. *Wake Us When It's Over: Presidential Politics of 1984.* New York: Macmillan.

Gibson, James L., Cornelius P. Cotter, John F. Bibby, and Robert J. Huckshorn. 1985. "Whither the Local Parties? A Cross-Sectional and Longitudinal Analysis of the Strength of Party Organizations." 29 *American Journal of Political Science* 139.

Gibson, James L., John P. Frendeis, and Laura L. Vertz. 1989. "Party Dynamics in the 1980s: Changes in County Party Organizational Strength 1980–1984." 32 *American Journal of Political Science* 67.

Gienapp, William. 1987. *The Origins of the Republican Party, 1852–1856.* New York: Oxford University Press.

———. 1982. "'Politics Seem to Enter into Everything': Political Culture in the North, 1840–1860." In Stephen Maizlish and John Kushma, eds., *Essays on American Antebellum Politics, 1840–1860.* College Station: Texas A&M University Press.

Gierzynski, Anthony. 1992. *Legislative Party Campaign Committees in the American States.* Lexington: University of Kentucky Press.

Gierzynski, Anthony, and Malcolm Jewell. 1989. "Legislative Campaign Committee Activity: A Comparative State Analysis." Paper presented at the Annual Meeting of the Midwest Political Science Association, Chicago.

Godwin, R. Kenneth. 1988. *One Billion Dollars of Influence: The Direct Marketing of Politics.* Chatham, NJ: Chatham House.

Goldman, Peter, and Tom Mathews, et al. 1992. "How He Won." *Newsweek Special Election Issue,* November/December:20.

Goodman, Paul. 1964. *The Democratic-Republicans of Massachusetts.* Cambridge: Harvard University Press.

Goodwin, George. 1970. *The Little Legislature: Committees in Congress.* Amherst: University of Massachusetts Press.

Gotffried, Paul, and Thomas Fleming. 1988. *The Conservative Movement.* Boston: Twayne.

Graber, Doris A. 1984. *The Mass Media and American Politics.* Washington, DC: Congressional Quarterly Press.

Greene, Jay P. 1993. "Forewarned Before Forecast: Presidential Election Forecasting Models and the 1992 Election." 26 *PS* 17.

Grove, Lloyd. 1988. "Putting the Spin on the Party Line." *Washington Post,* July 18.

Hage, David, and Sara Collins. 1993. "Betting on Wall Street." *U.S. News & World Report,* February 22:42.

Hager, George. 1992. "Platform Ignores Dissenters, Holds to Core Values." 50 *Congressional Quarterly Weekly Report* 2466.

Hallin, Daniel. 1990. "Sound Bite News." In Gary R. Orren, ed., *Blurring the Lines: Elections and the Media in America.* New York: Free Press.

Handlin, Oscar. 1952. *The Uprooted.* Boston: Little, Brown.

Harkavy, Jerry. 1989. "Mitchell Reflects on Anniversary as Senate Leader." *Central Maine Morning Sentinel,* November 29.

Harwood, John. 1992. "Clinton Struggles to Get His Message Across As the Media Seem to Be Looking Elsewhere." *Wall Street Journal,* May 21:A14.

Hawley, Willis D. 1973. *Nonpartisan Elections and the Case for Party Politics.* New York: Wiley.

Hays, Samuel P. 1959. *Conservation and the Gospel of Efficiency: The Progressive Conservation Movement.* Cambridge: Harvard University Press.

_____. 1957. *The Response to Industrializationism, 1877–1914.* Chicago: University of Chicago Press.

Heard, Alexander. 1960. *The Costs of Democracy.* Chapel Hill: University of North Carolina Press.

Heclo, Hugh. 1977. *A Government of Strangers.* Washington, DC: Brookings Institution.

Herrnson, Paul S. 1990. "Resurgent National Party Organizations." In L. Sandy Maisel, ed., *The Parties Respond: Changes in the American Party System.* Boulder, CO: Westview Press.

_____. 1989. "National Party Decision-Making, Strategies, and Resource Distribution in Congressional Elections." 42 *Western Political Quarterly* 301.

_____. 1988. *Party Campaigning in the 1980s.* Cambridge: Harvard University Press.

Herrnson, Paul S., and David Menefee-Libey. 1988. "The Transformation of American Political Parties." Paper presented at the Annual Meeting of the Midwest Political Science Association, Chicago.

Hoffman, David. 1989. "Bush Makes Rare Bow to GOP's Conservatives." *Washington Post,* October 18.

Hofstadter, Richard. 1969. *The Idea of the Party System: The Rise of Legitimate Opposition in the United States, 1780–1840*. Berkeley: University of California Press.

Holloway, Harry, and John George. 1979. *Public Opinion: Coalitions, Elites, and Masses*. New York: St. Martin's.

Holt, James. 1967. *Congressional Insurgents and the Party System, 1909–1916*. Cambridge: Harvard University Press.

Holt, Michael. 1978. *The Political Crisis of the 1850s*. New York: John Wiley and Sons.

————. 1973. "The Antimasonic and Know Nothing Parties." In Arthur M. Schlesinger, Jr., ed., *History of U.S. Political Parties*. New York: Chelsea House.

Hook, Janet. 1987. "Speaker Jim Wright Takes Charge in the House." *Congressional Quarterly Weekly Report*, July 11.

Howe, Daniel Walker. 1979. *The Political Culture of the American Whigs*. Chicago: University of Chicago Press.

Hrebenar, Ronald J., and Ruth K. Scott. 1982 [1988, 2nd rev. ed.]. *Interest Group Politics in America*. Englewood Cliffs, NJ: Prentice-Hall.

Huckhorn, Robert J. 1976. *Party Leadership in the States*. Amherst: University of Massachusetts Press.

Hugik, Larry. 1993. "Perot's Own Actions Determined His Fate." 4 *Public Perspective* 17.

Huntington, Samuel. 1965. "Political Development and Political Decay." 17 *World Politics* 386.

Hurley, Patricia A. 1989. "Parties and Coalitions in Congress." In Christopher J. Derring, ed., *Congressional Politics*. Chicago: Dorsey Press.

Ifill, Gwen. 1992. "Discipline, Message and Good Luck: How Clinton's Campaign Came Back." *New York Times*, September 5:7.

Isikoff, Michael, and John Mintz. 1992. "Charges Revisited Bitterly by Perot." *Washington Post*, October 27:A12.

Jackson, Brooks. 1988. *Honest Graft: Big Money and the American Political Process*. New York: Knopf.

Jackson, John E. 1975. "Issues, Party Choices, and Presidential Votes." 19 *American Journal of Political Science* 161.

Jacobson, Gary C. 1993. "Congress: Unusual Year, Unusual Election." In Michael Nelson, ed., *The Elections of 1992*. Washington, DC: Congressional Quarterly Press.

————. 1990. *The Electoral Origins of Divided Government*. Boulder, CO: Westview Press.

————. 1987a. "The Marginals Never Vanished: Incumbency and Competition in Elections to the U.S. House of Representatives, 1952–82." 31 *American Journal of Political Science* 126.

————. 1987b. *The Politics of Congressional Elections*, 2nd edition. Boston: Little, Brown.

————. 1985–1986. "Party Organization and Distribution of Campaign Resources: Republicans and Democrats in 1982." 100 *Political Science Quarterly* 603.

————. 1985. "Parties and PACs in Congressional Elections." In Lawrence C. Dodd and Bruce I. Oppenheimer, eds., *Congress Reconsidered*. Washington, DC: Congressional Quarterly Press.

_____ . 1980. *Money in Congressional Elections*. New Haven: Yale University Press.

Jacobson, Gary, and Samuel Kernell. 1981 (2nd edition, 1983). *Strategy and Choice in Congressional Elections*. New Haven: Yale University Press.

Jennings, M. Kent, and Gregory B. Markus. 1984. "Partisan Orientations over the Long Haul: Results from the Three-Wave Political Socialization Panel Study." 78 *American Political Science Review* 1000.

Jennings, M. Kent, and Richard Niemi. 1981. *Generations and Politics*. Princeton: Princeton University Press.

Jensen, Richard. 1981. "The Last Party System: Decay of Consensus, 1932–1980." In Paul Kleppner, ed., *Evolution of Electoral Systems*. Westport, CT: Greenwood Press.

_____ . 1978. "Party Coalitions and the Search for Modern Values, 1820–1970." In Seymour Martin Lipset, ed., *Emerging Coalitions in American Politics*. San Francisco: Institute for Contemporary Studies.

_____ . 1971. *The Winning of the Midwest: Social and Political Conflict, 1888–1896*. Chicago: University of Chicago Press.

Jewell, Malcolm E. 1984. *Parties and Primaries*. New York: Praeger.

Jewell, Malcolm E., and David Breaux. 1988. "The Effect of Incumbency on State Legislative Elections." 13 *Legislative Studies Quarterly* 495.

Jewell, Malcom E., and David M. Olson. 1988. *Political Parties and Elections in American States*, 3rd edition. Chicago: Dorsey Press.

Jones, Ruth S. 1984. "Financing State Elections." In Michael J. Malbin, ed., *Money and Politics in the United States: Financing Elections in the 1980s*. Chatham, NJ: Chatham House.

Jones, Ruth S., and Thomas J. Borris. 1985. "Strategic Contributing in Legislative Campaigns: The Case of Minnesota." 10 *Legislative Studies Quarterly* 89.

Kahneman, Daniel, Paul Slovic, and Amos Tversky, eds. 1982. *Judgement Under Uncertainty: Heuristics and Biases*. New York: Cambridge University Press.

Kamarck, Elaine Ciulla. 1988. "Who Will Control Coverage of the Conventions?" *Newsday*, July 11.

_____ . 1987. "Delegate Allocation Rules in Presidential Nominating Systems: A Comparison Between the Democrats and the Republicans." 4 *Journal of Law and Politics* 275.

Katz, Jeffrey L. 1992. "Party Reaches for 'Third Way' in Reshaping Its Policy." 50 *Congressional Quarterly Weekly Report* 2087.

Kaufman, Herbert. 1965. "The Growth of the Federal Personnel System." In Wallace S. Sayre, ed., *The Federal Government Service*. Englewood Cliffs, NJ: Prentice-Hall.

Kayden, Xandra, and Eddie Mahe, Jr. 1985. *The Party Goes On*. New York: Basic Books.

Keefe, William J. 1976. *Parties, Politics, and Public Policy in America*. Hinsdale, IL: Dryden Press.

Keith, Bruce E., David B. Magleby, Candice J. Nelson, et al. 1992. *The Myth of the Independent Voter*. Berkeley: University of California Press.

Keith, Bruce E., et al. 1987. "The Myth of the Independent Voter." Unpublished manuscript, University of California, Berkeley.

Kelly, Michael. 1992. "The Making of a First Family: A Blueprint." *New York Times*, November 14:1.

Kent, Frank R. 1923. *The Great Game of Politics*. New York: Doubleday.

Kernell, Samuel. 1986. *Going Public: New Strategies of Presidential Leadership*. Washington, DC: Congressional Quarterly Press.

Kernell, Samuel, and Gary Cox. 1991. *The Politics of Divided Government*. Boulder, CO: Westview Press.

Kerr, Peter. 1988. "Campaign Donations Overwhelm Monitoring Agencies in the States." *New York Times*, December 27.

Kessel, John. 1988. *Presidential Campaign Politics*. Chicago: Dorsey Press.

Key, V. O., Jr. 1966. *The Responsible Electorate*. Cambridge: Harvard University Press.

———. 1961. *Public Opinion and American Democracy*. New York: Alfred A. Knopf.

———. 1956. *American State Politics: An Introduction*. New York: Knopf.

———. 1955. "A Theory of Critical Elections." 17 *Journal of Politics* 3.

———. 1952 (3rd edition; 1958, 4th edition; 1964, 5th edition). *Politics, Parties, and Pressure Groups*. New York: Crowell.

Kilday, Anne Marie, and Mark Edgar. 1988. "Bentsen Forces on the Move." *Dallas Morning News*, October 16.

Kinder, Donald R., and D. Roderick Kiewiet. 1981. "Sociotropic Politics: The American Case." 11 *British Journal of Political Science* 129.

King, Anthony. 1978. *The New American Political System*. Washington, DC: American Enterprise Institute.

King, Gary. 1989. *Unifying Political Methodology: The Likelihood Theory of Statistical Inference*. New York: Cambridge University Press.

Kleppner, Paul. 1979. *The Third Electoral System, 1853–1892: Parties, Voters and Political Cultures*. Chapel Hill: University of North Carolina Press.

Kleppner, Paul, et al. 1981. *The Evolution of American Electoral Systems*. Westport, CT: Greenwood Press.

Klinge, Kenneth, Political Director, DSCC. 1989. Personal interview, January 12.

Klose, Kevin. 1984. "Up from Obscurity: Ratio of Journalists to Iowa Caucus Goers Hits One to One Hundred." *Washington Post*, February 20.

Kolbert, Elizabeth. 1992a. "As for All That Lore About Sure-Thing Election Prophecies, Forget About It." *New York Times*, November 5:B1.

———. 1992b. "Test-Marketing a President." *New York Times Magazine*, August 30:18.

Kontnik, Ginnie, Director, Harriman Communcations Center. 1989. Personal interview, January 6.

Kousser, J. Morgan. 1974. *The Shaping of Southern Politics: Suffrage Restriction and the Establishment of the One-Party South, 1880–1910*. New Haven: Yale University Press.

Kramer, Gerald H. 1970–1971. "The Effects of Precinct-Level Canvassing on Voter Behavior." 34 *Public Opinion Quarterly* 561.

Krehbiel, Keith. "Where's the Party?" 23 *British Journal of Political Science* 235.

Kurtz, Howard. 1992. "Media's Arrows Don't Seem to Wound Perot." *Washington Post*, June 11:A16.

Ladd, Everett Carll. 1993a. "The 1992 Election's Complex Message." 4 *American Enterprise* 45.

———. 1993b. "The 1992 Vote for President Clinton: Another Brittle Mandate?" 108 *Political Science Quarterly* 1.

———. 1985. "As the Realignment Turns: A Drama in Many Acts." 7 *Public Opinion* 2.

Ladd, Everett C., with Charles E. Hadley. 1975. *Transformations of the American Party System*. New York: W. W. Norton.

Ladha, Krishna. 1992. "Condorcet's Jury Theorem, Free Speech and Correlated Votes." 36 *American Journal of Political Science* 617.

Lazarsfeld, Paul F., Bernard Berleson, and Hazel Gaudet. 1944. *The People's Choice: How the Voter Makes Up His Mind in a Presidential Campaign*. New York: Duell, Sloan and Pearce.

Lehigh, Scot. 1992. "Perot Says Decision on Run Is up to Supporters." *Boston Globe*, September 23:14.

Lengle, James. 1981. *Representation and Presidential Primaries: The Democratic Party in the Post Reform Era*. Westport, CT: Greenwood Press.

———. 1980. "Divisive Presidential Primaries and Party Electoral Prospects: 1932–1980." 8 *American Politics Quarterly* 261.

Lewis–Beck, Michael S. 1985. "Election Forecasts in 1984: How Accurate Were They?" 18 *PS* 53.

Lewis–Beck, Michael S., and Tom W. Rice. 1992. *Forecasting Elections*. Washington, DC: Congressional Quarterly Press.

Lichtman, Allan J., and Ken DeCell. 1990. *The Thirteen Keys to the Presidency*. Lanham: Madison Books.

Loftus, Tom. 1985. "The New 'Political Parties' in State Legislatures." 58 *State Government* 108.

Longley, Lawrence. 1992. "The Gradual Institutionalization of the National Democratic Party in the 1980s and 1990s." 2 *Vox Pop Newsletter of Political Organizations and Parties* 4.

Louisville Journal. 1852. September 8.

Lowi, Theodore J. 1979. *The End of Liberalism: The Second Republic in the United States*. New York: Norton.

Lundberg, Kirsten, 1989. "General Electric and the National Broadcasting Co.: A Clash of Cultures." Kennedy School Case Program. Cambridge: Kennedy School of Government, Harvard University.

Lynn, Frank. 1987. "Part-Time Legislature Finds Little Time to Ponder Ethics." *New York Times*, March 1.

Mace, Don, and Eric Yoder. 1992. *Federal Employees' Almanac, 1992*. Fall Church, VA: Federal Employee's News Digest.

Mackenzie, G. Calvin. 1981. *The Politics of Presidential Appointments*. New York: Free Press.

Mackenzie, G. Calvin, L. Sandy Maisel, and Lisa B. Prenaveau. 1992. "Congressional Term Limits: A Solution Inappropriate for the Problem." Paper presented at the Annual Meeting of the New England Political Science Association, Providence, RI.

Maddox, John, Deputy Director of the Executive Division, NRCC. 1989. Personal interview, January 5.

Maisel, L. Sandy. 1994. "The Platform-Writing Process: Candidate-Centered Platforms in 1992." 109 *Political Science Quarterly*.

——. 1993. *Parties and Elections in America: The Electoral Process*. 2nd ed. New York: McGraw-Hill.

——. 1987. *Parties and Elections in America: The Electoral Process*. New York: Random House.

——. 1986. *From Obscurity to Oblivion: Running in the Congressional Primary*. Knoxville: University of Tennessee Press.

Maisel, L. Sandy, G. Calvin Mackenzie, and Lisa B. Prenaveau. 1992. "Congressional Term Limits: A Solution Inappropriate for the Problem." Paper presented at the Annual Meeting of the American Political Science Association, Chicago.

Malbin, Michael J. 1975. "Republicans Prepare Plan to Rebuild Party for 1976." *National Journal*, March 1.

Mann, Dean E. 1965. *The Assistant Secretaries: Problems and Processes of Appointment*. Washington, DC: Brookings Institution.

Mann, Thomas E. 1978. *Unsafe at Any Margin*. Washington, DC: American Enterprise Institute.

Markus, Gregory B. 1988. "The Impact of Personal and National Economic Conditions on the Presidential Vote: A Pooled Cross-Sectional Analysis." 32 *American Journal of Political Science* 137.

Mashberg, Tom. 1992. "Analysts Question Bush's Tax Checkoff for Deficit." *Boston Globe*, August 22:7.

Mayer, William G., and Nelson W. Polsby. 1993. "Ideological Cohesion in the American Two-Party System." Paper presented at the Annual Meeting of the New England Political Science Association, Northhampton, MA.

Mayhew, David R. 1991. *Divided We Govern: Party Control, Lawmaking, and Investigations, 1946–1990*. New Haven: Yale University Press.

——. 1986. *Placing Parties in American Politics*. Princeton: Princeton University Press.

——. 1974a. "Congressional Elections: The Case of the Vanishing Marginals." 6 *Polity* 295.

——. 1974b. *Congress: The Electoral Connection*. New Haven: Yale University Press.

——. 1966. *Party Loyalty Among Congressmen*. New Haven: Yale University Press.

McClosky, Herbert, Paul J. Hoffman, and Rosemary O'Hara. 1960. "Issue Conflict and Consensus Among Party Leaders and Followers." 54 *American Political Science Review* 406.

McCormick, Richard L. 1986. *The Party Period and Public Policy: American Politics from the Age of Jackson to the Progressives Era*. New York: Oxford University Press.

——. 1981. *From Realignment to Reform: Political Change in New York State, 1893–1910*. Ithaca: Cornell University Press.

——. 1979. "The Party Period and Public Policy: An Exploratory Hypothesis." 66 *Journal of American History* 279.

McCormick, Richard P. 1982. *The Presidential Game: The Origins of American Presidential Politics.* New York: Oxford University Press.

_____ . 1967. *The Second American Party System: Party Formation in the Jacksonian Era.* Chapel Hill: University of North Carolina Press.

McCurry, Michael, Communications Director, DNC. 1989. Personal interview, January 11.

McGerr, Michael. 1986. *The Decline of Popular Politics.* New York: Oxford University Press.

McSeveney, Samuel T. 1971. *The Politics of Depression: Voting Behavior in the Northeast, 1893–1896.* New York: Oxford University Press.

McWilliams, Wilson Carey. 1981. "Parties as Civic Associations." In Gerald M. Pomper, ed., *Party Renewal in America.* New York: Praeger.

Meiklejohn, Alexander. 1948. *Free Speech and Its Relation to Self-Government.* New York: Harper & Brothers.

Merriam, Charles E. 1923. *The American Party System.* New York: Macmillan.

Messick, Deborah, Deputy Director of Communications, RNC. 1989. Personal interview, January 13.

Miller, Nichals R. 1986. "Information, Electorates, and Democracy: Some Extensions and Interpretations of the Condorcet Jury Theorem." In Bernard Grofman and Guillermo Owens, eds., *Information Pooling and Group Decision Making.* Greenwich, CT: Jai Press.

Miller, Warren E. 1986. "Party Identification and Political Belief Systems: Changes in Partisanship in the United States, 1980–84." 5 *Electoral Studies* 101.

Miller, Warren E., and M. Kent Jennings. 1986. *Parties in Transition.* New York: Russell Sage.

Miller, Warren E., and J. Merrill Shanks. 1982. "Policy Directions and Presidential Leadership: Alternative Interpretations of the 1980 Presidential Election." 12 *British Journal of Political Science* 299.

Mintz, John, and David Von Drehle. 1992. "Why Perot Walked Away." *Washington Post,* July 19:A1.

Morlan, Robert L. 1949. "City Politics: Free Style." 37 *National Municipal Review* 485.

Nelson, Michael. 1993. *The Elections of 1992.* Washington, DC: Congressional Quarterly Press.

New Republic. 1984. "The Electronic Plebiscite." Editorial, October 29, p. 8.

Nichols, Roy F. 1967. *The Invention of the American Political Parties.* New York: Macmillan.

Nie, Norman H., Sidney Verba, and John R. Petrocik. 1976 (enlarged edition, 1979). *The Changing American Voter.* Cambridge: Harvard University Press.

Noah, Timothy. 1992. "Perot Waters His Grass Roots Heavily, Paying 'Volunteers' and Orchestrating Poll of Supporters." *Wall Street Journal,* September 30:A16.

O'Donnell, Thomas, Political Director, DCCC. 1989. Personal interview, January 11.

Ogburn, William, and Inez Goltra. 1919. "How Women Vote: A Study of an Election in Portland, Oregon," 34 *Political Science Quarterly* 413.

Oldfield, Duane M. 1992. "The Christian Right in the 1992 Campaign." Paper delivered at the Northeastern Political Science Association Annual Meeting.

Omestad, Thomas. 1992. "Why Bush Lost." 89 *Foreign Policy* 70.

Oppenheimer, Bruce I. 1981a. "The Changing Relationship Between House Leadership and the Committee on Rules." In Frank H. Mackaman, ed., *Understanding Congressional Leadership*. Washington, DC: Congressional Quarterly Press.

_____. 1981b. "Congress and the New Obstructionism: Developing an Energy Program." In Lawrence C. Dodd and Bruce I. Oppenheimer, eds., *Congress Reconsidered*, 2nd edition. Washington, DC: Congressional Quarterly Press.

Oreskes, Michael. 1989. "Cold War No Longer Wins Votes." *New York Times* News Service, December 3.

Ornstein, Norman J., Thomas E. Mann, and Michael J. Malbin. 1987. *Vital Statistics on Congress, 1987–1988*. Washington, DC: Congressional Quarterly Press.

Orren, Gary R. 1987. "The Linkage of Policy to Participation." In Alexander Heard and Michael Nelson, eds., *Presidential Selection*. Durham: Duke University Press.

_____. 1985. "The Nomination Process: Vicissitudes of Candidate Selection." In Michael Nelson, ed., *The Elections of 1984*. Washington, DC: American Enterprise Institute.

_____. 1982. "The Changing Styles of American Party Politics." In Joel L. Fleishman, ed., *The Future of American Political Parties*. Englewood Cliffs, NJ: Prentice-Hall.

_____. 1981. "Presidential Campaign Finance: Its Impact and Future." 4 *Common Sense* 50.

_____. 1978. "Candidate Style and Voter Alignment in 1976." In Seymour Martin Lipset, ed., *Emerging Coalitions in American Politics*. San Francisco: Institute for Contemporary Studies.

Orren, Gary, and Nelson Polsby, eds. 1987. *Media and Momentum: The New Hampshire Primary and Nomination Politics*. Chatham, NJ: Chatham House.

Ostrogorski, M. 1964. *Democracy and the Organization of Political Parties*, Volume 2: *The United States*. Garden City, NY: Anchor Books.

Palazzolo, Dan. 1989. "The Speaker's Relationship with the House Budget Committee." Paper presented at the Annual Meeting of the Midwest Political Science Association, Chicago.

Palmer, Thomas C. 1992. "Too Heavy a Helping of Economic Gloom." *Boston Globe*, October 18:73.

Patterson, Samuel C., and Gregory A. Caldeira. 1988. "Party Voting in the United States Congress." 18 *British Journal of Political Science* 111.

_____. 1984. "The Etiology of Partisan Competition." 78 *American Political Science Review* 691.

Patterson, Thomas E. 1989. "The Press and Its Missed Assignment." In Michael Nelson, ed., *The Elections of 1988*. Washington, DC: Congressional Quarterly Press.

Pertman, Adam, and John Aloysius Farrell. 1992. "Clinton Fires Salvo at Bush, Borrows from Perot." *Boston Globe*, October 26:1.

Pessel, Peter, Producer, NRCC. 1989. Personal interview, January 13.

Phillips, Kevin P. 1993. *Boiling Point*. New York: Random House.

_____. 1970. *The Emerging Republican Majority*. Garden City, NY: Anchor Books.

Pianin, Eric, and John Mintz. 1992. "Dirty Tricks Charged by Perot." *Washington Post,* October 26:A9.

Piazza, T., Paul Sniderman, and Phillip Tetlock. 1989. "Analysis of the Dynamics of Political Reasoning: A General-Purpose Computer Assisted Methodology." In James A. Stimson, ed., *Political Analysis.* Belmont, CA: Wadsworth Publishing Co.

Pines, Burton Yale. 1990. "Go Ahead, Slash the Military." *New York Times,* March 14.

Plott, Charles R. 1989. "An Updated Review of Industrial Organization: Applications of Experimental Methods." In R. Schmalensee and R. D. Willig, eds., *Handbook of Industrial Organization,* Volume 2. New York: Elsevier Science Publishers.

_____. 1982. "Industrial Organization Theory and Experimental Economics." 20 *Journal of Economic Literature* 1485.

Polsby, Nelson W. 1983. *Consequences of Party Reform.* New York: Oxford University Press.

_____. 1975. "Legilsaures." In Fred I. Greenstein and Nelson W. Polsby, eds., *Handbook of Political Science.* Reading: Addison-Wesley.

Polsby, Nelson W., and Aaron Wildavsky. 1984, 1988. *Presidential Elections.* New York: Charles Scribner's Sons.

Pomper, Gerald M. 1993. *The Election of 1992.* Chatham, NJ: Chatham House.

_____. 1989a. "The Presidential Nominations." In Gerald M. Pomper, ed., *The Election of 1988: Reports and Interpretations.* Chatham, NJ: Chatham House.

_____. 1989b. "The Presidential Election." In Gerald M. Pomper, ed., *The Election of 1988.* Chatham, NJ: Chatham House.

_____. 1972. "From Confusion to Clarity: Issues and American Voters, 1956–1968." 66 *American Political Science Review* 415.

Poole, Keith T., and Howard Rosenthal. 1984. "The Polarization of American Politics." 46 *Journal of Politics* 1061.

Popkin, Samuel L. 1991. *The Reasoning Voter: Communication and Persuasion in Presidential Campaigns.* Chicago: University of Chicago Press.

_____. 1988. "Optimism, Pessimism, and Policy." 11 *Public Opinion* 51.

Price, David E. 1992a. *The Congressional Experience.* Boulder, CO: Westview Press.

_____. 1992b. "The Party Connection." In John Kenneth White and Jerome M. Mileur, eds., *Challenges to Party Government.* Carbondale: Southern Illinois University Press.

_____. 1984. *Bringing Back the Parties.* Washington, DC: Congressional Quarterly Press.

"Public Opinion and Demographic Report." 1991. 2 *American Enterprise* (May-June):87.

Quirk, Paul J., and Jon K. Dalager. 1993. "The Election: A 'New Democrat.'" In Michael Nelson, ed., *The Elections of 1992.* Washington, DC: Congressional Quarterly Press.

Ranney, Austin. 1983. *Channels of Power.* New York: Basic Books.

_____. 1978a. *The Federalization of Presidential Primaries.* Washington, DC: American Enterprise Institute.

_____ . 1978b. "The Political Parties: Reform and Decline." In Anthony King, ed., *The New American Political System*. Washington, DC: American Enterprise Institute.

_____ . 1975. *Curing the Mischiefs of Faction*. Berkeley: University of California Press.

Rapoport, Ronald B., Alan I. Abramowitz, and John McGlennon. 1986. *The Life of the Parties*. Lexington: University Press of Kentucky.

Register of Debates. 1826. United States Congress, Nineteenth Congress, 1st Session.

Reichley, A. James. 1992. *The Life of the Parties: A History of American Political Parties*. New York: Free Press.

_____ . 1985. "The Rise of National Parties." In John E. Chubb and Paul Peterson, eds., *The New Direction in American Politics*. Washington, DC: Brookings Institution.

Remini, Robert. 1951. *Martin Van Buren and the Making of the Democratic Party*. New York: Columbia University Press.

Rempel, William C. 1992. "Induction of Clinton Seen Delayed by Lobbying Effort." *Los Angeles Times*, September 2:A1.

Republican National Committee. 1989. *1988 Chairman's Report*. Washington, DC: Republican National Committee.

_____ . 1980. *1986 Chairman's Report*. Washington, DC: Republican National Committee.

Riker, William. 1983. *Liberalism Against Populism*. San Francisco: W. H. Freeman.

Rintye, Peter, PAC Director, NRCC. 1989. Personal interview, January 5.

Ripley, Randall. 1967. *Party Leaders in the House of Representatives*. Washington, DC: Brookings Institution.

Robinson, Michael J. 1981. "The Media in 1980: Was the Message the Message?" In Austin Ranney, ed., *The American Elections of 1980*. Washington, DC: American Enterprise Institute.

Robinson, Michael J., and Karen McPherson. 1977. "Television News Coverage Before the 1976 New Hampshire Primary: The Focus of Network Journalism." 21 *Journal of Broadcasting* 2.

Rodgers, Daniel T. 1982. "In Search of Progressivism." 10 *Reviews in American History* 113.

Rohde, David W. 1991. *Parties and Leaders in the U.S. House of Representatives*. Chicago: University of Chicago Press.

_____ . 1989. "'Something's Happening Here; What It Is Ain't Exactly Clear': Southern Democrats in the House of Representatives." In Morris P. Fiorina and David W. Rohde, eds., *Home Style and Washington Work*. Ann Arbor: University of Michigan Press.

_____ . 1988. "Variations in Partisanship in the House of Representatives: Southern Democrats, Realignment and Agenda Change." Paper presented at the Annual Meeting of the American Political Science Association, Washington, DC.

Rohde, David W., and Kenneth A. Shepsle. 1987. "Leaders and Followers in the House of Representatives: Reflections on Woodrow Wilson's *Congressional Government*." 14 *Congress and the Presidency* 111.

Roseboom, Eugene H. 1970. *A History of Presidential Elections.* New York: Macmillan.

Rosenstone, Steven J. 1990. "Predicting Elections." University of Michigan, unpublished manuscript.

_____. 1983. *Forecasting Presidential Elections.* New Haven: Yale University Press.

Rusk, Jerrold G. 1970. "The Effects of the Australian Ballot Reform on Split Ticket Voting, 1876–1908." 64 *American Political Science Review* 1220.

Russert, Timothy. 1990. "For '92, the Networks Have to Do Better." *The New York Times,* March 4.

Sabato, Larry J. 1988. *The Party's Just Begun: Shaping Political Parties for America's Future.* Glenview, IL: Scott, Foresman.

_____. 1984. *PAC Power.* New York: Norton.

_____. 1981. *The Rise of the Political Consultants: New Ways of Winning Elections.* New York: Basic Books.

Sait, Edward M. 1927. *American Political Parties and Elections.* New York: Century Company.

Salmore, Barbara G., and Stephen A. Salmore. 1989. *Candidates, Parties, and Campaigns: Electoral Politics in America.* Washington, DC: Congressional Quarterly Press.

Samuelson, Robert J. 1992. "Bush's Unlucky Economy." *Boston Globe,* September 1:36.

Scammon, Richard C., and Alice V. McGillivrey, eds. 1985. *American Votes: A Handbook of Contemporary Election Statistics.* Washington, DC: Congressional Quarterly Press.

Schattschneider, E. E. 1942. *Party Government.* New York: Holt, Rinehart, and Winston.

Schlesinger, Joseph A. 1985. "The New American Party System." 79 *American Political Science Review* 1151.

Schlozman, Kay L., and John T. Tierney. 1986. *Organized Interests and American Democracy.* New York: Harper and Row.

Schneider, William. 1992. "A Loud Vote for Change." *National Journal,* November 7:2542.

_____. 1988. "The Political Legacy of the Reagan Years." In Sidney Blumenthal and Thomas Byrne Edsall, eds., *The Reagan Legacy.* New York: Pantheon Books.

Schwartz, Mildred A. 1990. *The Party Network: The Robust Organization of the Illinois Republicans.* Madison: University of Wisconsin Press.

Shade, William G. 1981. "Political Pluralism and Party Development: The Creation of a Modern Party System, 1815–1852." In Paul Kleppner et al., *Evolution of American Electoral Systems.* Westport, CT: Greenwood Press.

Shafer, Byron E. 1988. *Bifurcated Politics: Evolution and Reform in the National Party Convention.* Cambridge: Harvard University Press.

_____. 1983. *Quiet Revolution: The Struggle for the Democratic Party and the Shaping of Post Reform Politics.* New York: Russell Sage Foundation.

Shalope, Robert. 1972. "Toward a Republican Synthesis: The Emergence of an Understanding of Republicanism in American Historiography." 29 *William and Mary Quarterly* 49.

Shanks, J. Merrill, and Warren E. Miller. 1989. "Alternative Interpretations of the 1988 Election: Policy Direction, Current Conditions, Presidential Performance, and Candidate Traits." Paper presented at the Annual Meeting of the American Political Science Association, Atlanta.

Shively, W. Phillips. 1979. "The Development of Party Identification Among Adults: Explorations of a Functional Model." 73 *American Political Science Review* 1039.

Silbey, Joel H. 1991. *The American Political Nation, 1838–1893*. Stanford: Stanford University Press.

_____. 1985. *The Partisan Imperative: The Dynamics of American Politics Before the Civil War*. New York: Oxford University Press.

_____. 1977. *A Respectable Minority: The Democratic Party in the Civil War Era, 1860–1868*. New York: W. W. Norton.

_____. 1967. *The Shrine of Party: Congressional Voting Behavior, 1841–1852*. Pittsburgh: University of Pittsburgh Press.

Sinclair, Barbara. 1992a. "The Emergence of Strong Leadership in the 1980's House of Representatives." 54 *Journal of Politics* 658.

_____. 1992b. "Strong Party Leadership in a Weak Party Era—The Evolution of Party Leadership in the Modern House." In Ronald Peters and Allen Herzke, eds., *The Atomistic Congress*. Armonk, NY: M. E. Sharpe.

_____. 1989. *The Transformation of the U.S. Senate*. Baltimore: Johns Hopkins University Press.

_____. 1983. *Majority Leadership in the U.S. House*. Baltimore: Johns Hopkins University Press.

_____. 1982. *Congressional Realignment, 1925–1978*. Austin: University of Texas Press.

Smith v. Allwright. 1944. 321 U.S. 649.

Smith, Steven S. 1993. "Forces of Change in Senate Party Leadership and Organization." In Lawrence C. Dodd and Bruce I. Oppenheimer, eds., *Congress Reconsidered*, 5th edition. Washington, DC: Congressional Quarterly Press.

Smith, Steven S., and Christopher J. Deering. 1984. *Committees in Congress*. Washington, DC: Congressional Quarterly Press.

Sorauf, Frank J. 1992. *Inside Campaign Finance: Myths and Realities*. New Haven: Yale University Press.

_____. 1988. *Money in American Elections*. Glenview, IL: Scott, Foresman.

_____. 1980. "Political Parties and Political Action Committees: Two Life Cycles." 22 *Arizona Law Review* 445.

_____. 1964 (1980, 4th edition; 1988 [with Paul Allen Beck], 6th edition). *Political Parties in the American System*. Glenview and Boston: Scott, Foresman/Little, Brown.

Specter, Michael. 1992. "Running Against His Ambivalence: Five Months of a Not-Quite Campaign." *New York Times*, July 17:A16.

Squire, Peverill. 1989. "Competition and Uncontested Seats in U.S. House Elections." 14 *Legislative Studies Quarterly* 281.

Stanley, Harold W., and Richard G. Niemi. Forthcoming, 4th edition. *Vital Statistics on American Politics*. Washington, DC: Congressional Quarterly Press.

_____. 1988. *Vital Statistics on American Politics*. Washington, DC: Congressional Quarterly Press.

Starobin, Paul. 1993. "An Affair to Remember?" *National Journal*, January 16.

Stewart, Potter. 1975. "Or of the Press." 26 *Hastings Law Journal* 631.

Stokes, Donald E., and Warren E. Miller. 1962. "Party Government and the Saliency of Congress." 26 *Public Opinion Quarterly* 531.

Stone, Walter J., and Alan I. Abramowitz. 1983. "Winning May Not Be Everything, But It's More than We Thought." 77 *American Political Science Review* 945.

Stone, Walter J., Alan I. Abramowitz, and Ronald B. Rapoport. 1989a. "How Representative Are the Iowa Caucuses?" In Peverill Squire, ed., *The Iowa Caucuses and the Presidential Nominating Process*. Boulder, CO: Westview Press.

_____. 1989b. "Candidate Support in Presidential Nomination Campaigns: The Case of Iowa 1984." 54 *Journal of Politics* 1074.

Stonecash, Jeffrey M. 1988. "Working at the Margins: Campaign Finance and Strategy in New York Assembly Elections." 13 *Legislative Studies Quarterly* 477.

Sundquist, James L. 1988. "Needed: A Political Theory for the New Era of Coalition Government in the United States." 103 *Political Science Quarterly* 613.

Taylor, Paul. 1988a. "Testing the Electoral College 'Lock.'" *Washington Post*, September 18.

_____. 1988b. "GOP Strategist 'Carpet Bombs' Buckeye State." *Washington Post*, November 4.

Thompson, Pamela S. 1988. "The Selling of the Candidate." *The Political Report*, July 22.

Thornton, J. Mills. 1978. *Politics and Power in a Slave Society, Alabama, 1800–1860*. Baton Rouge: Louisiana State University Press.

Times Mirror Center for the People and the Press. 1992. "Campaign '92: Voters Say Thumbs Up." *Survey* 13 (November 15).

Toner, Robin. 1992a. "Contest Tightens as Perot Surges and Clinton Slips." *New York Times*, October 25:1.

_____. 1992b. "Critical Moments: How Bush Lost Five Chances to Seize the Day." *New York Times*, October 11:E1.

_____. 1992c. "Democrats Display a New Optimism, Reflected in Poll." *New York Times*, July 13:A1.

_____. 1992d. "Poll Finds Hostility to Perot and No Basic Shift in Race." *New York Times*, October 6:A1.

Tufte, Edward R. 1978. *Political Control of the Economy*. Princeton: Princeton University Press.

U.S. Department of Commerce. 1987. *Statistical Abstract of the United States, 1987*. Washington, DC: Government Printing Office.

U.S. House of Representatives, Committee on Post Office and Civil Service. 1988. *Policy and Supporting Positions*. Washington, DC: Government Printing Office.

U.S. President's Committee on Administrative Management. 1937. *Report of the Committee, with Studies of Administrative Management in the Federal Government*. Washington, DC: Government Printing Office.

Van Riper, Paul P. 1958. *History of the United States Civil Service*. New York: Harper and Row.

Victor, Jayne, Deputy Director of the Local Elections Division, RNC. 1989. Presentation to the Committee for Party Renewal, January 10.

Visclosky, Annamarie. 1989. Business Manager, Harriman Communications Center. Personal interview, January 6.

Waldman, Sidney. 1980. "Majority Leadership in the House of Representatives." 95 *Political Science Quarterly* 373.

Wallace, Michael. 1973. "Ideologies of Party in the Early Republic." Unpublished Ph.D. dissertation, Columbia University.

———. 1968. "Changing Concepts of Party in the United States: New York, 1815–1828." 74 *American Historial Review* 453.

Walsh, Kenneth T., et al. 1992. "Thinking About Tomorrow: The Clinton Era Begins." *U.S. News & World Report,* November 16:31.

Ward, Stephen, PAC Director, DCCC. 1989. Personal interview, January 6.

Watson, Harry L. 1981. *Jacksonian Politics and Community Conflict.* Baton Rouge: Louisiana State University Press.

Wattenberg, Martin. 1991. *The Rise of Candidate-Centered Politics: Presidential Elections of the 1980s.* Cambridge: Harvard University Press.

———. 1990. *The Decline of American Political Parties, 1952–1988.* Cambridge: Harvard University Press.

———. 1986. *The Decline of American Political Parties, 1952–1984.* Cambridge: Harvard University Press.

———. 1984. *The Decline of American Political Parties, 1952–1980.* Cambridge: Harvard University Press.

Watts, Steven. 1987. *The Republic Reborn: War and the Making of Liberal America, 1790–1820.* Baltimore: Johns Hopkins University Press.

"Week in Review." 1980. *New York Times,* August 3.

Weisbrot, Robert. 1990. *Freedom Bound: A History of America's Civil Rights Movement.* New York: Norton.

Wekkin, Gary D. 1985. "Political Parties and Intergovernmental Relations in 1984." 15 *Publius* 19.

Welch, Susan, and Timothy Bledsoe. 1986. "The Partisan Consequences of Nonpartisan Elections and the Changing Nature of Urban Politics." 30 *American Journal of Political Science* 128.

Westlye, Mark C. 1991. *Senate Elections and Campaign Intensity.* Baltimore: Johns Hopkins University Press.

White, Leonard D. 1958. *The Republican Era.* New York: Macmillan.

———. 1954. *The Jacksonians.* New York: Macmillan.

White, Theodore H. 1961. *The Making of the President, 1960.* New York: New American Library.

Whitehead, Ralph. 1978. "Mayor Daley's Personal Media." *Illinois Issues,* March.

Wicker, Tom. "Victims of War." *New York Times,* March 2:A23.

Wiebe, Robert. 1967. *The Search for Order, 1877–1920.* New York: Hill and Wang.

Williamson, Chilton. 1960. *American Suffrage: From Property to Democracy, 1760–1860.* Princeton: Princeton University Press.

Willis, Charles F., Jr. 1968. Oral history interview with John T. Mason, Jr., March 15, Columbia University.

Wilson, James Q. 1962. *The Amateur Democrat.* Chicago: University of Chicago Press.

Wilson, Scott A. 1989. *Congressional Party Committees and the Distribution of Campaign Resources.* Summa Cum Laude thesis, University of Minnesota.

Wilson, Woodrow. 1885. *Congressional Government.* Baltimore.

Witcover, Jules. 1977. *Marathon: The Pursuit of the Presidency 1972–1976.* New York: Viking Press.

Wolfensberg, Don. 1992. "Comparative Data on the U.S. House of Representatives." Compiled by the Republican staff of the House Rules Committee, November 10.

Wolfinger, Raymond E. 1963. "The Influence of Precinct Work on Voting Behavior." 27 *Public Opinion Quarterly* 387.

Young, Gary, and Joseph Cooper. 1993. "Multiple Referral and the Transformation of House of Decision Making." In Lawrence C. Dodd and Bruce I. Oppenheimer, eds. *Congress Reconsidered,* 5th edition. Washington, DC: Congressional Quarterly Press.

Young, Joseph, and Don Mace. 1989. *Federal Employees' Almanac, 1989.* Falls Church, VA: Federal Employees' News Digest.

About the Book and Editor

The elections of 1992 demonstrated once again how Americans love to hate political parties, and, in a new way, the American party system responded to the challenge by flexing to accommodate the essentially anti-party candidacy of Ross Perot.

The second edition of *The Parties Respond* updates trends in party organization, campaign roles played by parties, voter identification, and governing in by now well-established essays from the first edition. All-new chapters have been added on the 1992 presidential election, party competition and the media, and the Clinton victory. Throughout, the connections between parties, campaigns, and elections have been drawn and heightened in the aftermath of a spectacular year for party politics.

Looking ahead to 1996, this new edition begins to anticipate the parties' responses to continuing change and challenge: Republican factionalism, Democratic cohesiveness, continued gridlock despite unified government, and vulnerability to third party challengers. Original essays by leading scholars show novice and serious students alike where American political parties have been and where they're headed, from the grass roots to the national level.

L. Sandy Maisel is William R. Kenan, Jr., Professor of Government at Colby College, chair of the Political Organizations and Parties Section of the American Political Science Association, and president of the New England Political Science Association. He has studied American politics as a participant and a scholar. His own unsuccessful campaign for Congress is documented in his important study of primary elections, *From Obscurity to Oblivion: Running in the Congressional Primary*. In addition to being the author of numerous articles, Maisel is also the author of one of the leading texts on parties and the general editor of *Political Parties and Elections in the United States: An Encyclopedia*. He is still hard at work, however, on his true passion, a cookbook for those who love to eat but hate spending hours in the kitchen.

About the Contributors

Alan I. Abramowitz is professor of political science at Emory University. A student of congressional as well as presidential elections, he is the author of a large number of articles, coauthor and coeditor of *Life of the Parties: Activists in Presidential Politics*, and coauthor of *Nomination Politics: Party Activists and Presidential Choice*

John F. Bibby is professor of political science at the University of Wisconsin, Milwaukee. A former staff member of the Republican National Committee, he is coauthor of *Vital Statistics on Congress* and *Party Organizations in American Politics* and author of *Politics, Parties, and Elections in America*. His only complaint about the first edition was that it did not include his golf handicap, reputed to be under 5.

David W. Brady is the Bowen H. and Janice Arthur McCoy Professor of Political Science, Business, and the Environment in the Graduate School of Business as well as professor in the Department of Political Science at Stanford University. He is more widely known, however, for his jump shot from the top of the key, his aggressive play at the net, and his deft flycasting. His book *Critical Elections and Congressional Policy Making* won the 1989 Richard F. Fenno, Jr., Prize as the best book published in the area of legislative studies.

Kara M. Buckley is a Ph.D. student in political science at Stanford University. Her research interests include public policy under unified and divided control and careerism in Congress.

Anthony J. Corrado is assistant professor of government at Colby College. A longtime activist in Democratic party politics, he served on the campaign staffs of Jimmy Carter, Walter Mondale, and Michael Dukakis as well as in the Carter White House. An expert on campaign finance, he is the author or coauthor of a number of articles and author of the recently published *Creative Campaigning: PACs and the Presidential Selection Process*.

Morris P. Fiorina is professor of government at Harvard University. Among his works in the area of electoral behavior are *Retrospective Voting in American National Elections* and *The Personal Vote: Constituency Service and Electoral Independence*. The latter won the 1988 Richard F. Fenno, Jr., Prize for the best book on legislative studies.

Linda L. Fowler is professor of political science in the Maxwell School at Syracuse University. A former chair of the Legislative Studies Section of the American Political Science Association, she is coauthor of *Political Ambition: Who Decides to Run for Congress.*

Andrew Gelman is assistant professor of statistics at the University of California at Berkeley. His research interests include elections and voting behavior, survey sampling, Bayesian statistical methods, spatial statistics, and statistical graphics; he has coauthored several journal articles in the fields of political science and statistics.

Kenneth M. Goldstein is a Ph.D. candidate in political science at the University of Michigan. He previously worked three years for CBS News and currently consults for Voter Research and Surveys (VRS).

Paul S. Herrnson is associate professor in the Department of Government and Politics at the University of Maryland and executive director of the Committee on Party Renewal. His book *Party Campaigning in the 1980s* builds on his continuing research into the campaign activities of the national party organizations.

Ruth S. Jones is professor of political science at Arizona State University; in 1989–1990 she served as the executive on loan to the Arizona State Board of Regents. She is an acknowledged expert in and author of a number of articles on state campaign financing and on sources of campaign funds.

Elaine Ciulla Kamarck currently serves on the staff of Vice-President Gore. Previously she was senior fellow of the Progressive Policy Institute in Washington, D.C., and worked on the staffs of the Winograd Commission, the 1980 Platform Committee for the Democratic party, and the 1984 Mondale for President and 1988 Babbitt for President campaigns.

Gary King is professor of government and director of the Government Data Center at Harvard University. A student of political methodology, American politics, and other fields, he is the author or coauthor of numerous journal articles and books, including *Scientific Inference in Qualitative Research, Unifying Political Methodology: The Likelihood Theory of Statistical Inference,* and *The Elusive Executive: Discovering Statistical Patterns in the Presidency.*

G. Calvin Mackenzie is the Distinguished Presidential Professor of American Government at Colby College and the director of the Presidential Appointee Project of the National Academy of Public Administration. Among his many publications in the area of presidential staffing are *The Politics of Presidential Appointments* and *The In and Outers.*

L. Sandy Maisel is William R. Kenan, Jr., Professor of Government and director of the Washington Program at Colby College. A former candidate for Congress and Democratic party activist, he is the author of *From Obscurity to Oblivion: Running in* *the Congressional Primary* and *Parties and Elections in America: The Electoral Process* as well as general editor of *Political Parties and Elections in the United States: An Encyclopedia.*

Warren E. Miller is Regents Professor of Political Science at Arizona State University and senior research scientist at the Center for Political Studies and adjunct professor of political science at the University of Michigan. Among his widely cited works are *Without Consent: Mass-Elite Linkages in Presidential Politics* and the seminal study of voting behavior, *The American Voter: Parties in Transition.*

Ronald B. Rapoport is professor of government at the College of William and Mary. His long-term study of party activists at state nominating conventions has resulted in a number of articles as well as two books including *Life of the Parties: Activists in Presidential Politics.* He is the Houston Astros' most prominent fan.

David M. Shribman is assistant managing editor and Washington bureau chief of the *Boston Globe.* A graduate of Dartmouth College and a James Reynolds Scholar at Cambridge University, England, where he did graduate work in history, he joined the *Globe* after covering presidential elections and national politics for the *Wall Street Journal,* the *New York Times,* and the *Washington Star.*

Joel H. Silbey is the President White Professor of History at Cornell University. He is the author or editor of numerous articles and books on American political history, including *The Partisan Imperative: The Dynamics of American Political History Before the Civil War.*

Barbara Sinclair is professor of political science at the University of California, Riverside. A former American Political Science Association Congressional Fellow and frequent participant-observer of the Congress, she is the author of *Congressional Realignment, 1925–1978, Majority Party Leadership in the U.S. House, The Transformation of the U.S. Senate,* and many other works in this area.

Frank J. Sorauf is Regents Professor of Political Science and former dean of the College of Liberal Arts at the University of Minnesota. A leading scholar of campaign finance in an age of reform and regulation, he is the author of *Inside Campaign Finance: Myths and Realities* (the winner of the 1993 Richard F. Fenno, Jr., Prize for the best book in legislative studies), *What Price PACs?, Money in American Elections,* and *Party Politics in America.*

Walter J. Stone is professor of political science and research associate of the Institute of Behavioral Sciences at the University of Colorado. Editor of *Political Research Quarterly* and a frequent contributor to professional journals, he is also the author of *Nomination Politics: Party Activists and Presidential Choice* and *Republic At Risk: Self-Interest in American Politics.*

Scott A. Wilson graduated summa cum laude from the University of Minnesota and is currently a graduate student in political science at Stanford University.

Index

WHITMAN COLLEGE LIBRARY

DATE DUE

JAN 03 1996

DEC 16 1996

BRODART